e frontispiece of the Acta Sanctorum, *volume 1, Januarii. Antwerp: J. van*
643.

MEDIEVAL SCHOLARSHIP

From t
Meurs,

GARLAND REFERENCE LIBRARY OF THE HUMANITIES
VOLUME 1350

MEDIEVAL SCHOLARSHIP
BIOGRAPHICAL STUDIES
ON THE FORMATION
OF A DISCIPLINE

VOLUME 1: HISTORY

EDITED BY

HELEN DAMICO
†JOSEPH B. ZAVADIL

GARLAND PUBLISHING, INC.
NEW YORK AND LONDON
1995

Library of Congress Cataloging-in-Publication Data

Medieval scholarship : biographical studies on the formation of a discipline /
   edited by Helen Damico, Joseph B. Zavadil.
       p.   cm. — (Garland reference library of the humanities ; vol. 1350)
     Includes bibliographical references and index.
     Contents: v. 1. History —
     ISBN 0-8240-6894-7 (v. 1)
     1. Medievalists—Biography.   I. Damico, Helen. II. Zavadil, Joseph B.,
   d. 1992. III. Series.
   D116.5.M43   1995
   909.07'07202'2—dc20
   [B]   95-6189
                                   CIP

Cover illustration: Frederic William Maitland. Photograph courtesy of
Robert Brentano.

Printed on acid-free, 250-year-life paper
Manufactured in the United States of America

Contents

PREFACE

Medieval Scholarship: Biographical Studies on the Formation of a Discipline: Volume 1: History is the first volume of three that present biographies of scholars whose work impacted the study of the Middle Ages and transformed it into the discipline known as Medieval Studies. Volume 1 contains accounts of twenty-three men and women from the seventeenth century to the twentieth who shaped medieval history into a profession. Their subject was Europe and the Middle East from about the fifth century through the fifteenth, and they labored to define those protean and multinational cultures. Forthcoming volumes will deal with preeminent figures in the study of medieval literatures (Volume 2) and philosophy, art history, and music (Volume 3).

The biographies, which are limited to scholars no longer living, attempt to represent character, convey an impression of the subject's temperament and milieu, and note facts of personal experience and activity. They likewise aim to set forth a relationship—if you will, a continuum—between scholars, sometimes successfully, sometimes not. The subjects' lives in some measure reflect developing selves, but they do so in the context of their emergence as pioneers and shapers of medieval history over some 300 years.

Medieval Studies is international, multidisciplinary, and chronologically vast: we wanted the biographies to reflect that complexity and variousness. Hence we aimed to include biographies from the major disciplines—history, literature, philosophy, music, and art history—and their representative fields. Our objective was representation and balance. In general our criteria for selection included:

1) *Individuals of uncontested merit who pioneered or revolutionized particular fields.* Jean Mabillon, who established the principles for determining the authenticity and historical contexts of medieval manuscripts, is an example. Henri Pirenne, whose economic theories changed permanently the

way we characterize the Middle Ages, is another.

2)   *Multinational representation.* Subjects hail from Austria, Belgium, England, France, Germany, Italy, Russia, Spain, and the United States. We attempted to show crossnational influence. An example is Georg Waitz, who, as the guiding light and leading historian of the massive Monumenta Germaniae Historica project, did for constitutional history what William Stubbs would later do for England.

3)   *Gender representation.* In those cases where a female scholar had unquestionable standing in a field often represented by a male, we chose the female. Dorothy Whitelock over Frank Stenton was a case in point: in the same field, they also were related as mentor and student. In addition, Whitelock's approach was markedly interdisciplinary; she worked in literature and history.

4)   *Disciplinary representation.* We wished to exemplify the vastness of the discipline. Hence there are representative essays from economic, social, and constitutional history (Power, Pirenne, Bloch, Stubbs, Waitz, Whitelock, Maitland); manuscript and archival studies (Mabillon, Delisle, Muratori); symbology and intellectual history (Kantorowicz, Schramm, Smalley); general and cultural history (Gibbon, Adams, Haskins, Sánchez-Albornoz); ecclesiastical history (Bolland, Lea), and the history of magic and medieval science (Thorndike). Some scholars pioneered comparative and interdisciplinary studies; all published work that is still essential to our understanding of the past and, more important, the present. When faced with the choice between subjects of equal standing, the choice was determined by:

a)   the subject's exemplifying a professional energy and charisma that was self-reflective yet dedicated to the building of a discipline and

b)   the appropriateness and professional standing of the biographer.

Where unavoidable omissions have occurred, we have attempted to touch upon the work of the omitted scholars in the essays included.

The essays are not meant to be full biographical and critical accounts. Nonetheless some are moving records of individual lives, such as Bloch's, who apparently told a young man standing beside him as they both faced the firing squad that the bullets would not hurt; or Delisle's, who a few days before he died confessed to a friend, "J'ai manqué ma vocation"; or Henry Adams's, who prophesied, "The woman who is known only through a man is known wrong. . . . The American woman of the nineteenth century will live only as the man saw her. . . ."

Each essay is accompanied by a selected primary and secondary bibliography that reflects the subject's work in the medieval period. In some instances we have had to condense the bibliography even further to keep within reasonable page limitations. Our aim was to offer as much information as possible for future work on the subject in the space available. In some cases we have not provided information on Letters and Papers either because there were none (as in the case of Beryl Smalley, who gave strict instructions that all papers and letters be burned) or because information was unavailable.

The project began as a collaboration between me and Joseph B. Zavadil, who died in late spring of 1992. A valued colleague, he participated in the conception of the project and the arrangement of this first volume, although after his death I continued as editor alone. Yet any venture of this size is a type of collaboration, and I am grateful to the many scholars, in addition to those who contributed to this volume, who took part in the selection process: Bernard Bachrach, John Baldwin, Caroline Barron, Christopher Brooke, Robert I. Burns, Marshall Clagett, Janet Coleman, William Courtenay, Richard Dales, Natalie Zemon Davis, Katherine Drew, John Elliott, Sir Geoffrey Elton, John V.F. Fine, Jr., Edward Grant, Barbara Hanawalt, C. Warren Hollister, Alexander Kazhdan, Simon Keynes, Peter Linehan, Lester K. Little, George P. Majeska, George Makdisi, Sir Dimitri Obolensky, James Powell, Richard Rouse, Kenneth Setton, I.B. Ševčenko, Nancy Siraisi, Sir Richard Southern, Pauline Stafford, Luke Wenger, and Grover Zinn.

Others whose contributions made this volume possible and who have my unreserved thanks are Susan Tarcov, for her assistance in editing; at the University of New Mexico, my colleague in history Donald Sullivan, whose balanced good humor lightened difficult moments; David G. Null (now Director of Reference at Memorial Library, University of Wisconsin, Madison), Felicia J. Steele (now at the University of Texas, Austin), Donald Fennema, and Karmen Lenz for their help in checking bibliographical references and proofing; Jonatha Jones for preparation of the manuscript; and Jason Seth Kottler for placing it in its final electronic form. I am indebted also for the support I received from the Research Allocations Committee, Michael R. Fischer, Chair of the Department of English, and Ellen H. Goldberg, Associate Provost for Research.

At Garland Publishing I am grateful for the care and attention expended on this volume by Phyllis Korper, Eunice Petrini, and Jason Goldfarb, and I owe much to my editor, Gary Kuris, for his generous and enthusiastic support.

Finally special thanks must go to Giles Constable, whose guidance and support on all three volumes have been invaluable, and to the authors of these essays for contributing their time and talents and thus serving as notable witnesses to the greatness of these human lives.

Helen Damico
University of New Mexico

INTRODUCTION

Giles Constable

The period of European history known as the Middle Ages was created in the fifteenth and sixteenth centuries by humanists who saw a gap, a *medium aevum*, between classical antiquity and their own time. The people who lived between about 500 and 1500 were not conscious of living in a distinctive period, but the humanists regarded themselves as living in a new age, which was marked by a revival or renaissance of classical learning and values. They reacted against the ignorance and superstition of the immediate past, as they saw it, and felt an identity between their times and antiquity. "Medieval" therefore started as a term of opprobrium, like "Gothic," which was later used for the barbaric architecture of the twelfth to fifteenth centuries. The humanists defined themselves in reference to the past, and some of them took an interest in recent history. Such men as Pierre Pithou and Etienne Pasquier in France, and John Bale, John Leland, and Matthew Parker in England laid the basis of the subsequent study of medieval history. Later attitudes toward the Middle Ages varied from period to period, and the history of medieval history is to some extent a history of how people in different countries and different times have seen themselves and their past.

Unlike some of the sciences, which seem to show a steady progress toward agreed goals, the study of history tends to circle around its subject, shedding light here and there, and what passes for progress is often only a different, and not necessarily truer, view of the past. The changing views of medieval scholars toward themselves and their sources were analyzed by Lars Mortenson in a talk at the First European Congress of Medieval Studies at Spoleto in May 1993. He distinguished three periods in the study of medieval Latin historiography since 1500. The first period, down to 1820, was antiquarian and accumulative, when scholars saw themselves as in direct continuity with their medieval predecessors and regarded their own works as supplementing the original sources, whose accuracy and authority they for the most part accepted. The second period, from 1820 to 1950, was systematic and critical. Scholars stressed the need for new and reliable editions of the sources, for which their own works were substitutes rather than supplements. A third period began in 1950 and was marked by hermeneutics and an interest in the history of ideas. Medieval writers were increasingly regarded as artists and ideologues, whose works had to be interpreted by scholars. Recently there has been a special concern with the history of texts, of which every version, however unoriginal or inaccurate by previous standards, is seen as a reflection of the needs and interests of the authors and of the time at which they wrote. Medieval history, seen from this point of view, is defined by those who write it, in the past as well as in the present, and a subject that no one has studied, like an unexcavated archaeological site or an unknown manuscript, hardly exists until it is recognized by scholars and forced to yield its secrets.

This volume deals with a group of scholars who have explored various aspects of the history of Europe between about 500 and 1500. Like most explorers, they did not all look for, or find, the same thing, and depending on where and how they looked, they came up with different discoveries and saw the Middle Ages in different ways. A few had almost no idea of the concept of the Middle Ages as a distinctive period; some accepted and liked it, while others consciously rejected it. Jean Mabillon, though he was keenly aware of the change from paganism to Christianity, saw no break in continuity in the monuments from antiquity to the Middle Ages and therefore dated some twelfth-century works of art three-to-five centuries too early. Edward Gibbon made the case for continuity in *The Decline and Fall of the Roman Empire*, where he treated the entire period down to the fifteenth century in terms of what went before and saw it as middle "at different times and at different rates in different places and with respect to different things." Henri Pirenne argued for change in *Mohammed and Charlemagne*, but for him the ancient world came to a close not with the end of the western Roman Empire in the fourth or fifth centuries but in the eighth, when the Muslim conquests turned the Mediterranean from a Roman into an Arabian lake. At the other end of the Middle Ages the idea of the Renaissance, especially as it was formulated by Jacob Burckhardt in the nineteenth century, came under attack, on the one hand in works like *The Renaissance of the Twelfth Century* by Charles Homer Haskins, who found many of the characteristics of fifteenth-century intellectual life in the twelfth, and on the other by scholars like Lynn Thorndike, who questioned the very idea of a Renaissance. Many medieval historians are not concerned with these questions, however, and study particular regions, periods, or problems without asking what, if anything, makes them distinctively medieval. Readers of this volume should not look for any consistent interpretations or conclusions about medieval history.

The criteria in selecting scholars for inclusion were not only eminence and influence but also variety, in order to illustrate the many approaches to the study of medieval history since the seventeenth century. The twenty-three historians whose biographies are included here come from nine modern nations: six from England (including three women, to whom I shall return), four from America, three each from France and Germany (including one from modern Poland), two each from Austria (as was) and Belgium, and one each from Italy, Russia, and Spain. Ten were native English-speakers, six spoke German (including George Ostrogorsky, who was born in Russia, trained in Germany, and taught in Yugoslavia), five spoke French (unless Jean Bolland's native language was Flemish), and one each spoke Italian and Spanish. The only major European countries not represented in this first volume, outside of eastern Europe, are the Netherlands, Switzerland, Portugal, and the Scandinavian nations.

These men and women represent a wide variety of divisions within medieval history. The only generalist among them is Gibbon, who covered, according to the standards of his day, the entire history of the period, and even he omitted many topics that are now regarded as important. Salo Baron, Ostrogorsky, and Gustave von Grunebaum also attempted to be generalists within their respective fields of Jewish history, Byzantium, and Islam, though Ostrogorsky and von Grunebaum were primarily concerned respectively with institutions and with culture. Bolland and Mabillon were ecclesiastical historians, who worked on saints and monasticism and on the associated problems of the criteria for assessing the reliability of historical sources. Henry Lea was likewise an ecclesiastical historian, who studied the institutions of the medieval church, especially the Inquisition, in the New World as well as the Old. L.A. Muratori was interested in the history of Italy, above all in gathering and publishing its medieval sources. Georg Waitz, William Stubbs, Claudio Sánchez-Albornoz, and Pirenne were also national historians, respectively of Germany, England, Spain, and Belgium. The influence of their nationalism on their historical writings will be assessed later, but they were all concerned to discover and explain the roots of modern national states in the Middle Ages. F.W. Maitland, Eileen Power, and Dorothy Whitelock worked almost exclusively on the history of England, and Léopold Delisle on France. Though Delisle's study of manuscripts carried him into many fields, including diplomatics and palaeography, his single most outstanding book was on the agriculture and agricultural classes of his native Normandy during the Middle Ages.

Many of these scholars, especially those who studied ecclesiastical and economic history, reached across national frontiers, but comparative history was not fully established until the twentieth century, together with interdisciplinary history, which crossed the boundaries between established academic fields. Henry Adams, perhaps because he was an American and did not regard himself as a professional scholar, was a pioneer in this regard, especially in *Mont-Saint-Michel and Chartres*, where the study of art and architecture is integrated into the history of ideas and religion. Haskins, whose *Normans in European History* and *Norman Institutions* appeared in 1915 and 1918 respectively, studied the Normans on both sides of the Channel and in Sicily and drew on sources from all over Europe in his work on the history of culture and science. Comparative medieval history came into its own in the work of Marc Bloch, who in spite of his personal loyalty to France described himself as an historian of "comparative European societies." His *Société féodale*, of which the two parts were published in 1940 and 1941, though superseded in some respects, is still a classic comparative account of medieval feudalism. Percy Schramm and Ernst Kantorowicz, though each in his own way a German nationalist, were also international and comparative in their studies of the symbolism and ideology of rulership, and Thorndike and Beryl Smalley show the increasing internationalism in the field of intellectual history.

This is a varied group of scholars, therefore, and it is fair to say that many medievalists might not agree with the list of twenty-three historians who were chosen for inclusion here. They should remember first, however, that some of the scholars who have most influenced the study of medieval history, and might therefore have qualified for inclusion, such as Giovanni Baptista Vico, Leopold von Ranke, Jacob Burckhardt, Johan Huizinga, and Fernand Braudel, were not primarily medievalists. Arnold Toynbee, too, started life as a Byzantinist and wrote a large book on the emperor Constantine Porphyrogenitus, but he is not best known for his work in medieval history. The questioners should look, second, at the other volumes in this series, which will include scholars in the areas of medieval literature, philosophy, theology, architecture, and music. The lines between these fields and history are less marked in medieval studies than in other historical periods, and a number of scholars who might have been in this volume, including Marie-Dominique Chenu, Hippolyte Delehaye, Pierre Duhem, Ramón Menéndez Pidal, and André Wilmart, will be found in other volumes. It is nonetheless undeniable that some fields are not well represented, especially those that cut across established academic disciplines, such as archaeology and the so-called *Hilfswissenschaften* or auxiliary sciences, which are represented here only by Mabillon and Delisle. There is not even a passing reference to the great palaeographer Ludwig Traube, whose students helped to make the United States a center for the study of medieval palaeography, and only a few to Charles du Cange, whose dictionaries of medieval Latin and Greek are still indispensable to medievalists in almost all areas of study.

I make these points not to criticize but to emphasize that some difficult, and occasionally painful, decisions had to be made in choosing scholars for inclusion in this volume and that the selection of one inevitably involved the exclusion of another, who might be equally or more distinguished in some particular field of work. There would be general agreement, I think, on only about half of the names, beginning with Mabillon, Muratori, Gibbon, Maitland, Pirenne, and Bloch. Haskins still has a very high reputation in Europe as well as in America, where he was a notable teacher and administrator. Close after these, probably as much owing to their influence as to the scholarly originality of their works, would come Waitz, Stubbs, and Delisle, though there were other medieval historians in Germany, England, and France in the nineteenth century, such as Wilhelm von Giesebrecht, Edward Augustus Freeman, and Achille Luchaire, who could have represented the same developments. To Europeans and perhaps to some Americans, the most surprising inclusion is probably Henry Adams, who was at best a part-time medievalist and whose works on the Middle Ages are not highly esteemed by professional scholars. Through his writing and teaching, however, he exercised a deep influence on historical studies in the United States.

Many of the historians included here stand for a particular school, subject, or trend in the study of medieval history and should be seen in relation to other scholars who are perhaps only slightly less celebrated. Bolland, for instance, belonged to a group which included Heribert Rosweyde, Godefroid Henskens, and above all Daniel Papebroch, who was in many respects more learned and accomplished than Bolland, who is better known primarily because he gave his name to the group of Jesuits responsible for producing the *Acta Sanctorum* and, later, the *Analecta Bollandiana* and *Subsidia hagiographica*. Mabillon is the most eminent of a group of French scholars, which included Étienne Baluze and (somewhat later) Edmond Martène and Bernard de Montfaucon, upon whom medievalists still depend for the standard editions of many basic texts. There is no representative at all in this volume of the English antiquarian school of the seventeenth and early eighteenth century, such as William Dugdale, whose *Monasticon* is still fundamental for the study of monasticism in England, and Thomas Madox, the author of the *Formulare* and *History of the Exchequer*. George Hickes and Humfrey Wanley, however, will appear in the volume on literature.

The selection becomes increasingly difficult in the nineteenth and twentieth centuries. Michele Amari opened up, and is still an outstanding authority on, the field of Arabic-Sicilian studies, and Giesebrecht, Freeman, and Luchaire have already been mentioned for their contributions to the medieval history of, respectively, Germany, England, and France. For the twentieth century, the names of Frank Stenton, F.M. Powicke, Helen Cam, and David Knowles come to mind for England; Ferdinand Lot and Louis Halphen for France; François-Louis Ganshof for Belgium; and Americo Castro for Spain. Paul Vinogradoff, who was Russian but lived in England, worked on English medieval history; the Byzantinist A.A. Vasiliev came from Russia to America; and the Americans Harry Wolfson and Schlomo Goitein were preeminent in the field of Jewish medieval history. This list of names could easily be extended, but enough have been mentioned to show that there are no clear criteria for inclusion and that many scholars had to be omitted in order to allow space for those whose biographies are published here.

A small but significant group is formed by women, of whom all of those included in this volume were English and born between 1889 and 1905. They came from middle-class families, with no tradition of learning or higher education. Eileen Power's father was a stockbroker; Dorothy Whitelock came from an established but apparently modest Yorkshire family; and Beryl Smalley's father was a Manchester businessman. They all reacted to some extent against their families by going to university—Power and Smalley also by their left-wing political views, and Smalley by converting to Roman Catholicism—but we must look beyond this to explain their exceptional distinction in the field of medieval scholarship. One factor was the existence in England, unlike the Continent, of institutions devoted to the higher education of women, who were excluded from most universities and colleges. Power and Whitelock attended, respectively, Girton and Newnham Colleges in Cambridge, and Smalley was at St. Hilda's College, Oxford. The high standards of these colleges, combined perhaps with their somewhat embattled position in predominantly male universities, contributed to bringing out the best in these young women. A second and, to my mind, no less important factor was the existence in England of a number of distinguished female medievalists, including the iconographer and art historian Anna Jameson, Alice Green, Mary Bateson, and Kate Norgate in the nineteenth century, and, more recently, Helen Cam, who taught medieval history first at Cambridge and later as one of the first female professors at Harvard. The United States also had a tradition of female medieval historians, such as Norma Adams, Margaret Hastings, and Bertha Putnam.

With regard to the male scholars, only the first three came from relatively humble origins. Bolland's family was simple, and the fathers of Mabillon and Muratori were, respectively, a poor farmer and a copper worker who also farmed and ran a small shop. These three owed their education and advancement to the church. Bolland and Muratori attended Jesuit colleges and Mabillon, the seminary at Reims. Together with Stubbs, who was the son of a Yorkshire solicitor and also had to make his own way, they are the only clerics in the group. The remainder (aside from one whose family is not mentioned) all came from the business or professional middle class, with the possible exception of Adams, who might, as a member of an old and wealthy Boston family and as the great-grandson and grandson of presidents of the United States, be considered an aristocrat. Gibbon, in spite of his pretensions, was the grandson of a director of the failed South Sea Company, and Waitz, Pirenne, Schramm, Kantorowicz, and von Grunebaum all came from commercial and business backgrounds, as did Lea, whose family ran a successful publishing house in Philadelphia. Delisle's father was a doctor; Thorndike's father was a Methodist minister from a modest family with deep New England roots; Sánchez-Albornoz's father was a politician; and the fathers of Haskins and Ostrogorsky were both teachers. Only Maitland and Bloch came from families with any serious intellectual pretensions. Maitland's grandfather was the medievalist Samuel Roffey Maitland, whose *Dark Ages* can still be read with profit, and his father was a civil servant. Bloch's father was a well-known Roman historian. It is hard to see any pattern in this variety, though the sample is admittedly small, and no single factor in the background of these scholars seems to have pointed them in the direction of medieval history or to have presaged their future distinction.

The same is true of their training and education. Bolland, Mabillon, and Muratori apparently all showed early promise, but Gibbon was a sickly youth who dropped out of Magdalen College, Oxford, after only fourteen months and subsequently looked back on his university career with dislike. Beryl Smalley got a second-class degree in her finals at Oxford—a setback that might have destroyed the career of a lesser scholar. Lea was educated at home in preparation for entering the family publishing house and came to study medieval history almost by accident. Haskins and Sánchez-Albornoz, on the other hand, were clearly precocious students, if not prodigies, and took their doctorates, respectively at Johns Hopkins University and the University of Madrid, when they were nineteen and twenty-one years of age. The remainder seem to have followed a relatively normal course of higher education for able young scholars in their respective countries. Waitz took his doctorate at Berlin; Schramm, Kantorowicz (after periods at Berlin and Munich), and Ostrogorsky were at Heidelberg, which must have been an exciting place for historians in the early 1920s. Delisle and Bloch took their degrees respectively at the École des Chartes and the École Normale Supérieure in Paris; Pirenne at Liège, after periods of study in Paris and Berlin; Thorndike at Columbia, where he was trained in the "scientific presentation of history"; and Baron and von Grunebaum at Vienna. Higher degrees were not usual in England or America in the nineteenth century. Adams took no doctorate. Stubbs, Maitland, Power, and Whitelock also had no earned higher degree in history, and Smalley, after her disappointing start, was the only one of the English scholars to go on to a doctorate.

It is hard to judge from looking at their credentials and occupations which of these scholars can be considered professional historians in the sense of belonging to a group with a recognized obligation to promote a specialized field of knowledge through research, writing, and teaching and with a certain autonomy and control over its membership through a system of certification and degrees. Bolland, Mabillon, Muratori, and Gibbon would almost certainly not have considered themselves professional historians in this sense, though each of them spent most of his life studying history. The definition of a historian was broad in the eighteenth century, and even a philosopher like Gottfried von Leibniz compiled an important collection of medieval source material and corresponded with Muratori about the genealogy of the house of Hanover. Stubbs was a clergyman before he was a professor and did little historical work after he became a bishop. Delisle was a librarian and administrator. Lea and Adams were private scholars or amateurs, in the old sense of those who cultivate a particular pursuit or study out of personal taste or interest. This freedom was in many ways a scholarly advantage and allowed them to follow unconventional lines of work. Lea was described by Maitland as "one of the very few English-speaking men who have had the courage to grapple with the law and the legal documents of continental Europe." G.G. Coulton also admired Lea, but said of Adams that "his elaboration of style and his rather pretentious allusiveness often cover a somewhat superficial knowledge of original sources." Yet *Mont-Saint-Michel and Chartres* is more widely read today, at least in the United States, than Coulton's writings.

Waitz, who lived from 1813 to 1886, was the first among the historians whose lives are published here who can be called a professional, not yet in the sense of belonging to a self-conscious and autonomous group, but as a scholar who received formal academic training, occupied himself with historical research and writing, and helped to raise a future generation of scholars. Maitland, although he was trained as a lawyer and held no higher degree in history, can also be considered a professional because he was a Reader and later a Professor of Law at Cambridge and occupied himself with teaching history as well as with writing historical works and editing medieval texts. By the time he died, in 1906, the study of history was fully professionalized on both sides of the Atlantic. All the scholars here who were born after 1850 were clearly professionals, including Sánchez-Albornoz, who in spite of his political activities took a doctorate in history and was associated for most of his life with universities and research institutes both inside and outside Spain. It is worth considering, however, while reading this volume, the results of professionalization, which shelters behind a concern for scholarly standards and the public interest but which has, at the same time, tended to enclose history in an academic straitjacket and to cut historians off from contact with the outside world and with other scholarly disciplines.

Many of the early scholars discussed here were involved in public affairs. Bolland, Mabillon, and Muratori, in spite (or perhaps because) of their clerical status, all turned their talents to the needs of their times. The Bollandists and Mabillon served the church, and especially the papacy and Roman curia, since the need for reliable editions of the lives of the saints and of ecclesiastical documents, which may not seem pressing today, was of central importance in the seventeenth century, in order to ward off the attacks not only of Protestants but also of educated Catholics who ridiculed the uncritical use of corrupt and forged texts. Mabillon's *Traité des études monastiques*, which was published in 1691, dealt with a central issue in the contemporary reform of monasticism, and the authenticity of the documents in the *Histoire généalogique de la maison d'Auvergne*, in which Mabillon was involved with Baluze, touched on the claims of Louis XIV to the throne of France. Muratori served the interests of his patron, the duke of Modena, both as an archivist and librarian and also in his historical writings, such as his history of the family of Este and his research supporting the duke's claims to the city of Comacchio. Muratori worked "only for the glory of Italy," he said, and believed that the origins of modern Italian civilization lay in the Middle Ages rather than in classical antiquity or in the Renaissance.

Most of the nineteenth-century historians were nationalists, and their writings were influenced by their desire to serve national interests. Waitz was deeply involved in contemporary German politics and "an active supporter of liberal constitutionalism." Though he was opposed in principle to the politicization of history, his "national-political orientation," as it is called here, can be seen in his emphasis on the Germanic character of medieval kingship. His *Verfassungsgeschichte* was in many ways a model for Stubbs's

Constitutional History, which treated the history of liberty in England "with a sense of providential destiny" and contrasted English liberty, which derived from the free institutions of the Germanic settlers, with French despotism. Stubbs regarded the study of English medieval history as an essential preparation for life in the modern world. The later rejection of the Stubbsian view of history was to some extent the result of an overexposure of two generations to Stubbs's works and a reaction against the Victorian views they so confidently embodied. Adams shared an admiration for Germany with many American intellectuals of his day and emphasized the importance of Germanic influence, or Teutonism, as he called it, in his *Essays in Anglo-Saxon Law* and in *Mont-Saint-Michel and Chartres*, which is described here as "a work of North American, or even national literature, rather than an historical inquiry." Delisle, on the other hand, disliked Germany, especially after the Franco-Prussian War. His ignorance of German is astonishing in a scholar who contributed so much to disciplines in which German scholars excelled. Many English scholars turned against Germany after the First World War, as did Pirenne, whose view of the collective tendencies of urban, economic, and social developments, as contrasted with political and cultural history, was inspired by his desire to find unifying elements in the history of his native Belgium.

The historians of the late nineteenth and twentieth centuries sought somewhat calmer intellectual waters, and their works were less conspicuously influenced by nationalism. Though Maitland worked almost exclusively on English legal history, his writings were not nationalistic, and he argued, against Stubbs, that the church in medieval England was fully part of the international church. Of the twentieth-century scholars, Sánchez-Albornoz was involved in public affairs, serving first as minister of state and vice-president of the Cortes in the Second Spanish Republic and later as president of the Spanish Republican government in exile. He sought in his historical writings to show the distinctive character of medieval Spain and to deny the contribution of the Islamic and Jewish elements. Haskins, in spite of his involvement in the Versailles peace conference and in the development of higher education in America, was comparatively uninfluenced by nationalistic concerns in his historical work. The same is true of Marc Bloch, and the reader of *La société féodale* would have little reason to suspect that the author was soon to write *L'étrange défaite* and lose his life in the French resistance. The early work of Kantorowicz, especially his biography of Frederick II, can be fully understood only in the light of German history after the First World War, but German nationalism is hardly apparent in his later works, written after he went to America. The lives of Schramm, Baron,

Ostrogorsky, and von Grunebaum, of whom all but one were forced to leave their native countries, were also profoundly influenced by the political events in Europe in the 1930s and 1940s. It may be that the interest in political imagery and symbolism of Schramm and Kantorowicz, and also perhaps of Smalley, was related to the history of their times and to a growing concern for the "rites of power," but none of them put their pens specifically at the service of political causes, and for the most part they separated their scholarly work from their outside activities and interests.

The principal forms of expression for these scholars were writing and teaching. Waitz and Stubbs were both notable teachers. Adams during his few years of teaching at Harvard helped to reorganize the structure of undergraduate and graduate instruction in history. Pirenne and Haskins both trained generations of students in their respective countries. Several of them also wrote textbooks and works addressed to a public outside the halls of academe. Thorndike's *History of Medieval Europe* and *Short History of Civilization* were widely used in American classrooms; Eileen Power wrote history books for children and reached a large audience through *Medieval People* and her radio broadcasts; and even Beryl Smalley, who was in some respects a scholar's scholar, wrote a more popular book on *Historians in the Middle Ages* for students and "the general reader."

It is somewhat dispiriting today to consider the energy and productivity of many of these scholars. The mind boggles at the sheer labor, even taking into account the help of colleagues and assistants, that went into copying out in long-hand the huge folio volumes of the *Acta Sanctorum*, of which the first eighteen volumes, covering January through May, were produced in forty-five years—an average of two and a half years per volume—or of Mabillon's *Annales* and *Acta sanctorum ordinis sancti Benedicti* and Muratori's *Scriptores* and *Antiquitates*. The six quarto volumes of Gibbon's *Decline and Fall* were published between 1766 and 1788, and Lea produced eighteen substantial octavo volumes, and various incidental works, in the course of a career largely devoted to business and civic affairs. Waitz's published oeuvre is described here as "of astonishing size and scope"; Stubbs is said to have had "almost superhuman" powers of work; and Delisle's enormous bibliography fills an entire volume.

These figures fall off a bit in the later nineteenth and twentieth centuries, except for writers like Pirenne, Thorndike, and Baron, who devoted much of their energies to multivolume works on particular subjects. By a rough count Maitland wrote his six books on medieval history, plus three volumes of collected papers and several posthumous works; Haskins wrote four, plus two volumes of collected studies; Bloch wrote five, not including several posthumous publications; Power, five; Sánchez-Albornoz, nine, of which two were in three volumes and one in two; Schramm, eight, plus five volumes of collected articles; Kantorowicz, four, plus a volume of selected studies; and so on—all respectable in comparison with other members of the profession but for the most part not exceptional, and relatively little in comparison with the prodigious efforts of their predecessors. The only twentieth-century medievalist known to me who could begin to rival some of the earlier scholars in productivity is Jean Leclercq, who was still living when these volumes were planned and was not therefore considered for inclusion.

It may legitimately be objected that these crude statistics take no account of nonmedieval works or those written in collaboration with other scholars, nor of articles and above all of editions of texts, which present an interesting problem in the historiography of medieval history. Bolland, Mabillon, and Muratori, all of whom lived in Mortenson's first, or antiquarian, period in the history of medieval historiography, were above all editors, and their own writings mostly, though not exclusively, arose out of their work on texts. Waitz started his career editing texts at the Monumenta Germaniae Historica, where he returned as president in 1875 and again devoted himself to the publication of texts. Stubbs was for many years primarily a text editor, and the editions he made for the Rolls Series, and their introductions (which were published together in 1902), have stood the test of time as well, and in some respects better, than the *Constitutional History*. Delisle edited countless texts and documents in the course of his work on medieval manuscripts, and modern scholars are still in his debt for important discoveries and publications. Maitland was a pioneer in the editing of legal texts, many of which appeared, with valuable introductions, in the publications of the Selden Society, which he helped to found. Gibbon, Lea, and Adams edited no medieval texts, so far as I know, and after Maitland text editing tended to pass out of the mainstream of professional historical training and activity. Pirenne and Thorndike both produced a few editions of texts, but they are better known for their monographic works, and though some twentieth-century scholars, like F.A. Schmitt and Jean Leclercq, devoted themselves to preparing new editions of major medieval writers, they never held established academic positions. Thorndike is significantly described here as having "served time as an editor of texts—a slow, demanding, and tedious activity that garners few professional rewards and little recognition outside a small circle of colleagues." This would never have been written about Mabillon or Muratori, or even about Waitz, Stubbs, and Maitland. For them textual editing was a basic part of their work and won not only prestige in the scholarly world of their time but also a place in this volume. This decline in the esteem accorded to the editing of texts in the professional historical community is in part a result of a perceived progress of medieval studies from the time when reliable text-editions were the primary requirement for research. It also reflects the specialization of scholarship and the declining role of philology—once the mother of history—in the training of historians. Text editing is now commonly considered the task of philologists and literary scholars rather than historians, whose primary work is interpreting rather than editing texts. The standards for editing have at the same time risen so high that they are self-defeating, and it is almost impossible now for a scholar working alone to produce a critical edition of a long text with many manuscripts, such as the letters of Peter of Blois. It would take the better part of a century to produce today a single volume of the *Acta Sanctorum*, of which the early volumes, in spite of their faults, are still of great service to scholars. Now that there is a new interest in the history of texts, scholars may reassert the value of text editing in historical training and the need not only for comprehensive critical editions but also for practical working texts designed for the use of historians.

Through the lives and work of these twenty-three outstanding scholars it is thus possible to see the development of the study of medieval history over the past three hundred years and, to some extent, the changing concept of the Middle Ages, which have been seen and presented in many ways. For some scholars the Middle Ages were embodied in the church or in particular peoples or national states; for others they lay in institutions and laws and in economic and social structures; more recently they consisted of the ideas, concepts, attitudes, and symbols that controlled the way people thought and behaved. Some newer developments are not represented here because their leading practitioners are still alive and active. Cliometrics, for instance, have thrown light on many previously hidden aspects of social history, such as family structure and social mobility, and psychology and anthropology have contributed to understanding the inner lives of men and women in the Middle Ages. In some respects the study of medieval history has come a full circle, and some subjects, such as hagiography and religion, which were long considered marginal by constitutional and institutional historians, are now back in the center. The religious dimensions of the Crusades, for instance, are again taken seriously, and the texts published by the Bollandists and by Mabillon are being studied for the light they throw on medieval values and attitudes.

These lives also throw light on the growing professionalization of the study of history, especially in the nineteenth century, and on the systematization and narrowing of scope in the training of historians. The rules for the critical evaluation of medieval texts and documents that were developed in the seventeenth and eighteenth centuries are as true now as then, and the system of seminars used in German universities in the nineteenth century has spread all over the world. The lives show something, too, of the varying interests that have attracted, and continue to attract, young scholars to the study of the medieval history. For some it is the changes and differences from the modern world and for others the continuities and resemblances. Gibbon saw the Middle Ages as the end of the ancient world and of all it stood for, and Henry Adams was inspired by a sense of estrangement and alienation to see them in contrast to the present. For Muratori, on the other hand, and also for Waitz and Stubbs, the Middle Ages were in continuity with the modern world. For them the study of medieval history was a vital involvement with themselves and with the problems of their own world.

It is a source of pride for medieval historians that the works of scholars who lived many years ago are still of interest and value. In modern history even recently published books are often considered out-of-date and of use only as evidence of the views that prevailed at the time they were written. In medieval history, however, almost every decade since 1700, and beyond (as Maitland said of Domesday Book), saw the publication of works that are still of scholarly importance. Their writers naturally made mistakes, of both fact and interpretation, and they need to be challenged and corrected, as do modern historians, but through the information they provide and the questions they ask—and also through their mistakes, which often serve as a springboard for further work—they contribute to an understanding of a past that is both theirs and ours, and they opened doors that might otherwise have remained closed. There is a sense of excitement in reading an old work on medieval history and in seeing what its author had to say about the period and people in which we ourselves are involved, and some of the same sense of excitement can be found in the biographies in this volume.

BIBLIOGRAPHICAL NOTE

It is my intention in this introduction to draw some general conclusions and suggest some tendencies in the development of the study of medieval history, not to summarize the biographies, or to criticize them, though I have some disagreements. Unless otherwise indicated, the information and quotations are taken without specific acknowledgement from the biographies. A decision was made early in the planning of this volume to limit the number of entries, in order to allow sufficient space for each biography, and (for obvious reasons) to include no living scholars.

The discussion of the history of the idea of the Middle Ages, in the first and third paragraphs, is based primarily on Wallace K. Ferguson, *The Renaissance in Historical Thought: Five Centuries of Interpretation* (Boston: Houghton Mifflin, 1948), especially pp. 73–77; Herbert Weisinger, "The Renaissance Theory of the Reaction Against the Middle Ages as a Cause of the Renaissance" (*Speculum* 20 [1945]: 461–

67); Donald R. Kelley, *Foundations of Modern Historical Scholarship: Language, Law, and History in the French Renaissance* (New York: Columbia University Press, 1970), who remarked (p. 302) on the humanists' obsession with the problem of "origins"; May McKisack, *Medieval History in the Tudor Age* (Oxford: Clarendon, 1971); and for the eighteenth century, the works cited by Peter Gay, *The Enlightenment: An Interpretation: The Rise of Modern Paganism* (New York: Knopf, 1966), pp. 489–90, especially Herbert Weisinger, "The Middle Ages and the Late Eighteenth-Century Historians" (*Philological Quarterly* 27 [1948]: 63–79), and Jacques Vanuxem, "The Theories of Mabillon and Montfaucon on French Sculpture of the Twelfth Century" (*Journal of the Warburg and Courtauld Institutes* 20 [1957]: 45–58).

The quotations about Lea and Adams cited on p. xx are taken from Charles Homer Haskins, *Studies in Mediaeval Culture* (Oxford: Clarendon, 1929), p. 258, and G.G. Coulton, *Five Centuries of Religion*, 2nd ed., vol. 1 (Cambridge: Cambridge University Press, 1929–50), 521.

On the professionalization of history in the nineteenth century and the influence of nationalism (pp. xx–xxii), see the articles by Doris S. Goldstein, "History at Oxford and Cambridge: Professionalization and the Influence of Ranke" (pp. 141–53); Dorothy Ross, "On the Misunderstanding of Ranke and the Origins of the Historical Profession in America" (pp. 154–69); and Wolfgang Mommsen, "Ranke and the Neo-Rankean School in Imperial Germany: State-oriented Historiography as a Stabilizing Force" (pp. 129–40), in *Leopold von Ranke and the Shaping of the Historical Discipline*, edited by Georg G. Iggers and James M. Powell (Syracuse: Syracuse University Press, 1990).

PHOTOGRAPH CREDITS

Jean Bolland and frontispiece,
courtesy Richard Collin, Antwerp

Jean Mabillon, after a contemporary
engraving by P. Giffart

Lodovico Antonio Muratori,
courtesy Museo di Roma

Edward Gibbon,
courtesy Patricia Craddock,
with thanks to the British Library

Georg Waitz,
courtesy State Historical Library,
Schleswig-Holstein, photograph
by Stromfeld, Göttingen,
Altier Urbans, Kiel, 1927

William Stubbs,
courtesy James Campbell

Henry Charles Lea, courtesy Lea
Library, University of Pennsylvania

Léopold Delisle,
courtesy Damian Andrus

Henry Adams,
courtesy Massachusetts
Historical Society

Frederic William Maitland,
courtesy Robert Brentano

Henri Pirenne, courtesy
Jacques-Henri Pirenne

Charles Homer Haskins,
courtesy Houghton-Mifflin

Lynn Thorndike,
courtesy Peter Riesenberg

Marc Bloch,
courtesy Daniel Bloch

Eileen Power, courtesy the
Estate of Eileen Power and
The Mistress and Fellows,
Girton College, Cambridge

Claudio Sánchez-Albornoz y
Menduiña, courtesy
Nicholas Sánchez-Albornoz

Percy Ernst Schramm,
courtesy Dr. Gottfried Schramm

George Ostrogorsky,
courtesy Mrs. George Ostrogorsky

Ernst H. Kantorowicz,
courtesy Lucy Cherniavsky

Beryl Smalley,
courtesy Suzanne Pinsent

Salo Wittmayer Baron,
courtesy Norman Roth

Gustave E. von Grunebaum,
courtesy Mrs. Gustave von
Grunebaum

Dorothy Whitelock,
courtesy British Academy

Contributors

RUTHERFORD ARIS
University of Minnesota

JÁNOS BAK
Central European University,
Budapest College

DAVID BATES
University of Glasgow

ROBERT L. BENSON
AND LOREN J. WEBER
University of California,
Los Angeles

ROBERT BRENTANO
University of California,
Berkeley

JAMES CAMPBELL
Worcester College,
Oxford University

GILES CONSTABLE
Institute for Advanced Study
Princeton

PATRICIA CRADDOCK
University of Florida

CAROLE FINK
Ohio State University

ELLEN JACOBS
Université du Québec à
Montréal

BARIŠA KREKIĆ
University of California,
Los Angeles

ROBERT E. LERNER
Northwestern University

HENRIETTA LEYSER
St. Peters College,
Oxford University

HENRY LOYN
Penarth, South Glamorgan

BRYCE LYON
Brown University

KARL F. MORRISON
Rutgers, The State University
of New Jersey

SUSAN NICASSIO
University of Alabama

EDWARD PETERS
University of Pennsylvania

JAMES F. POWERS
Holy Cross College

FRANZ ROSENTHAL
Yale University

NORMAN ROTH
University of Wisconsin,
Madison

MICHAEL H. SHANK
University of Wisconsin,
Madison

DONALD SULLIVAN
University of New Mexico

SALLY VAUGHN
University of Houston

MEDIEVAL SCHOLARSHIP

Jean Bolland

(1596–1665)

and the Early Bollandists

Donald Sullivan

Jean Bolland was born on 11 August 1596 into a family of modest means in the Flemish village of Bolland in what is now the province of Liège. His name is synonymous with the *Acta Sanctorum* and with the small group of scholars, the "Bollandists," whom he organized into a society for a vast enterprise, a new edition of the lives of the Christian saints. This work, the *Acta Sanctorum*, composed in accordance with the most rigorous standards, was in its inception and its most formative early period the achievement of Bolland and three fellow Jesuits in what is now Belgium, then part of the Spanish Netherlands. The initial impetus to the venture came just after 1600 from the Jesuit Heribert Rosweyde; it received its permanent focus and structure a generation later from Bolland; it was then carried forward over the rest of the century by Bolland's associates Godefroid Henskens (Henschenius) and Daniel Papebroch.

Bolland lived at a time when the academic study of medieval history was in its infancy. He entered the Jesuit novitiate at Malines in 1612. After six years of philological studies and seven years of philosophy and theology at Jesuit schools Bolland was ordained in 1625. Over the next five years he served as prefect of studies at the Jesuit college of Malines, where he learned of Rosweyde's work in hagiography.

Hagiography, defined as the written memorials of the saints and their cults, began in the liturgical calendars of the early church. It did not become a historical "science" until the seventeenth century. These sketches of the acts of the martyrs were presented for the edification of the faithful. Virtues and miracles attributed to the holy men and women were recounted above all for their inspirational value. Although the volume and variety of hagiographic literature expanded continuously over the medieval centuries, the historical accuracy and plausibility of this material, given its basic purpose, remained of minimal concern. By 1500 the hagiographic tradition bequeathed by the Middle Ages seemed less and less adequate when measured against the exacting criteria for evaluating classical texts devised by Italian humanists from Petrarch on. Fifteenth-century humanists like Lorenzo Valla and Angelo Poliziano had applied their mastery of the classical languages and of history to establish the authenticity and reliability of ancient Greek and Roman texts. The close philological analysis of sources had become a hallmark of humanist scholarship.

Inspired by this tradition, northern humanists like Erasmus had early in the sixteenth century focused increasingly on the glaring discrepancies they observed between the humanist methodology, with its dispassionate striving for accuracy and for good Latin style, and the often crudely written, highly embroidered tales of Christian saints in the medieval compilations. By far the best known of these collections was the *Golden Legend*, completed about 1260 by the Italian Dominican Jacobus de Voragine. He had gathered a large number of pious stories and legends about the saints, intended primarily to edify rather than impart information. Anecdotal and filled with vivid tales of miracles and heroic deeds, the *Golden Legend* was the most popular book of saints' lives for well over two centuries after its appearance. Over two hundred manuscripts of the work survive from the late-medieval period, and more than 150 printed editions were published between 1470 and 1500 in all the major European languages.

After 1500 the *Golden Legend* declined dramatically in public esteem. A major reason was its hostile reception by Erasmus and his fellow humanists. After 1520 came the Protestant rejection *in toto* of the cult of the saints. The combined effect of these assaults proved devastating to what had been a central element of medieval popular religion. The Spanish Erasmian Juan Luis Vives noted in 1531 that "the *Golden Legend* was written by a man with a mouth of iron and a heart of lead" (Vives, *Opera Omnia*, 6: 108). He added, "What could be more abominable than this book?" It was not only the pious fictions in the *Golden Legend* that affronted Vives but its "extremely squalid" Latin style and its "heavily polluted" language (*ibid.*: 109).

In the world of the late Renaissance and the early Reformation, then, there were few to defend either the *Golden Legend* or indeed the whole medieval approach to hagiography. It was only in the Counter-Reformation era after 1550 that a resurgent Catholic scholarship sought to meet the humanist and Protestant challenges to the cult of saints. It did so by assimilating something of the humanist concern with the critical examination of sources.

It was in this new atmosphere that two multivolume editions of saints' lives appeared in the late sixteenth century. Both the Italian bishop Luigi

Lippomano and the German Carthusian Laurent Surius filtered out much of the manifestly legendary or otherwise questionable material that abounded in the *Golden Legend* and similar medieval compendia. Yet neither work met the standards of the new scholarship. By making the edification of the reader the overriding purpose of the narratives they incorporated much that was dubious and even spurious, including flowery orations and sermons. Although generally superior to Lippomano's approach, Surius's method frequently altered the style of the sources in the interest of greater devotional impact. By 1600 much still remained to be done if the study and writing of saints' lives were to achieve respectability among scholars.

The Flemish Jesuit Jean Bolland established hagiography as a scholarly discipline. Grounded in the historical-critical method and the command of languages, this "scientific" hagiography dates only from the early seventeenth century. The immediate inspiration came from Bolland's fellow Jesuit, the Dutch scholar Rosweyde. Born at Utrecht in 1569, Rosweyde entered the Jesuit novitiate in 1588 and completed his higher education at the French Jesuit college at Douai, where he was awarded the M.A. degree in 1591. A revised curriculum policy for most Jesuit colleges, including Douai, had been implemented in 1586. The new *ratio studiorum* included core courses in the humanities in which the study of classical Latin and Greek literature was prescribed for the abler students. This entailed the close critical analysis of selected writings in a fashion similar to the modern French *explication de textes*. Rosweyde acquired at Douai a thorough philological training. He also became so fascinated with church history and the documents that related to it that he spent his leisure moments exploring manuscript holdings in the monasteries around Douai, ferreting out interesting documents and copying many of them for future use. He found especially appealing the old manuscripts of saints' lives, where he encountered a spare, direct style in sharp contrast with the garrulous, highly colored accounts related in the recent editions of Lippomano and Surius, not to speak of the *Golden Legend*.

Ordained in 1599, Rosweyde was assigned to teach philosophy and theology at the Jesuit college in Antwerp. He soon became prefect of studies supervising the curriculum of the school. In 1603 a visiting Jesuit official asked him for suggestions of suitable projects that the order might encourage to enhance the Jesuit mission in the province. Rosweyde responded that he had been appalled to find hagiographic stories that not only defied belief but challenged certain teachings of the church. He considered it intolerable to nourish piety with fables. He noted, however, that the monastic libraries of Flanders alone contained some extraordinary manuscripts that, if published, could counteract the fanciful and often apocryphal narratives that plagued the popular compendia.

Authorized to proceed with this task, Rosweyde began to collect manuscripts and books from monastic archives throughout the southern Netherlands. In 1606 he was released from his teaching duties to pursue his project full time. The following year he drew up a detailed prospectus for an ambitious research plan. The project would entail some eighteen folio volumes to be called the *Acta Sanctorum*. Upon receiving a copy of the prospectus in Rome, the eminent Cardinal Bellarmine remarked wryly that "this man counts on living another two hundred years" (Kurth, 298).

Rosweyde intended that the bulk of the documents would encompass previously unedited lives of saints along with others reedited according to more critical scholarly principles. He projected some thirteen hundred biographical accounts based on the best texts and manuscript sources he could find. In the remaining volumes he would provide the historical context of each life, including its cult, and assess the overall reliability of the account. This approach, he contended, would achieve a healthier and better informed veneration of the saints. But distracted by other duties and undertakings Rosweyde never got beyond the initial stages of his vast plan. His death in 1629 left the strong possibility that the whole venture would be abandoned by Jesuit administrators with more practical priorities.

Rosweyde's undertaking, however, had roused widespread interest and in 1630 Bolland's superiors dispatched the thirty-three-year-old Jesuit to Antwerp to evaluate Rosweyde's collection and recommend a course of action. Bolland concluded not only that the *Acta Sanctorum* project was feasible but that he would assume the task himself, given two conditions: first, Bolland could change Rosweyde's plan if he thought it necessary and, second, he would have exclusive access to all the manuscripts, books, and other materials left by Rosweyde. When these terms were accepted, Bolland entered at once upon what became his life's work.

Bolland determined to expand Rosweyde's outline far beyond the prospectus that had so astounded Cardinal Bellarmine. Rosweyde's searches had been limited almost exclusively to the southern Netherlands and parts of northern France. Bolland decided to include all the saints venerated throughout the world; in effect he envisaged a world history of Christian sanctity, as would be reflected in the very title of the series, Acta Sanctorum quotquot toto orbe coluntur (All the Acts of the Saints Extant in the World). Rosweyde had intended to publish only original texts at first, reserving to the concluding volumes the commentaries and annotations designed to interpret the texts and resolve particular problems in them. Bolland decided to preface each document with a brief inquiry into its authorship, textual history, and credibility, as well as explanatory notes. He arranged the *vitae* to correspond to the order of the church's daily liturgical calendar. Each volume would be organized according to the months of the liturgical year. The *vitae* and materials relating to them would be grouped under the saint's feast, usually the purported date of death.

The preparation for the first volume of January proceeded. Bolland's first major task was to determine the saints whose *vitae* would be included. To this end he drew up a double list of names to be placed before each day of the liturgical calendar. One contained those judged acceptable on the grounds indicated above; the second was of those which for specified reasons were excluded, either entirely or simply for consignment to another day. Following the text of the saint's life, the cult was also to be discussed, including the festivals, pilgrimages, relics, and miracles associated over time with this veneration. Bolland, like Rosweyde, was determined to let the *vitae* speak for themselves. Each biography would be allowed to display both the saint's foibles and achievements. The *Acta Sanctorum* would exhibit a clear shift from the telling of a story primarily for its devotional effect to the careful editing of the texts in which the story was embedded.

Bolland avoided polemics, but like Rosweyde he deplored the pious fictions that "cause the learned . . . to ridicule and despise the lives of the saints themselves" (*Acta SS*, vol. 1, Januarii, xix). He refused to attack the *Golden Legend* or similar collections, for, as he noted at one point, "there is no need to follow the streams, having found the source" (*ibid.*, xx). Discovery of the earliest, most authentic version of a *vita* precluded the need to rely on derivative sources.

But by 1635, some five years after assuming the editorship of the project, Bolland found to his dismay that he was not much closer to realizing its completion than Rosweyde had been at his death. Through Bolland's efforts the inventory of documents collected had in fact more than quadrupled. Since his other responsibilities made it unlikely that this situation would change, Bolland requested, and received, a young assistant named Godefroid Henskens (1601–1681), whose subsistence would be provided initially by a generous local Benedictine abbot enlisted by Bolland. Henskens (known as Henschenius), one of Bolland's prize Latin students at Malines, had entered the Jesuit order in 1619 and taught Latin and Greek at schools in Flanders before joining Bolland in 1635. He would be associated with the *Acta Sanctorum* for the remaining forty-six years of his life. It was Henschenius who prepared much of the material in the first twenty-four volumes of the *Acta Sanctorum*, through the seventh volume for May.

Before Henschenius's arrival Bolland had virtually completed preparation of the materials for the January volume. He had also found a publisher. Bolland assigned Henschenius the saints for February and gave him full discretion as to how to proceed. When Henschenius submitted for approval the first segment of his researches on the saints of February, Bolland professed himself amazed at their quality. Bolland had confined his own preliminary remarks mainly to noting the location of the manuscripts used, followed by some brief annotations and lists of variant readings. Henschenius's much fuller commentaries sought not only to identify problems and difficulties in the texts but to explain them systematically. To this end Henschenius drew on disciplines like geography, chronology, history, and philology. His detailed commentaries on the lives and cults of the early-medieval saints Amand and Vaast turned into extended critical dissertations. His procedure was to compare every biography he could find bearing on the saint. Then, applying the resources of history and philology, he sought to explain, step by step, the obscure passages in the texts.

Henschenius's accomplishment led Bolland to make the critical dissertation a permanent feature of the *Acta Sanctorum*. Meanwhile the self-effacing Bolland, recognizing the clear superiority of Henschenius's innovation, asked his protégé to apply the same thorough scholarship to the volumes for January already prepared by Bolland. The *Acta Sanctorum*, now a genuine collaboration, gained much in the quality and usefulness of the scholarship. The two volumes for January, as published in 1643, comprised some twenty-three hundred pages, including tables and explanatory articles. It required another fifteen years, to 1668, to bring the three volumes for February to print. No previous hagiographic work had come close to the scope and erudition of the first Bollandist volumes. The project, now known as the Bollandist series, quickly won international acclaim among scholars, including many Protestants prepared to recognize its scholarly objectivity.

In 1659 Pope Alexander VII invited Bolland to Rome, where his great project would be formally honored and the rich source collections of the Vatican Library opened to him. Too ill to make the trip himself, Bolland sent Henschenius, joined now by a young scholar, Daniel Papebroch (1682–1714), recently added as the third member of the little community. Born at Antwerp, Papebroch had become a Jesuit at eighteen, and like Henschenius he excelled in the humanities course at Malines, with its strong philological orientation. Papebroch was thirty-one when he became a Bollandist in 1659. He would continue in that service for fifty-five years to his death and would be acknowledged in many ways as the most talented of the early Bollandists.

In 1660 Henschenius and Papebroch set off in response to Pope Alexander's invitation. They took advantage of the journey to Rome and back, from July 1660 to late October 1662, to visit over fifty libraries and archives across western Germany, Italy, and France, gathering masses of material for future volumes of the *Acta*. They were welcomed at virtually every stop. The larger libraries made copyists available to assist them in the task of transcription. To the hundreds of books, manuscripts, and assorted documents assembled by Roseweyde and expanded prodigiously through Bolland's Europe-wide contacts, Henschenius and Papebroch added over fourteen hundred new acts of saints, and uncounted collateral documents. By the latter seventeenth century the Bollandist library in the Jesuit house at Antwerp became an unparalleled repository of hagiographic materials.

Jean Bolland died on 12 September 1665, three years before the volumes containing the saints for March were ready for publication. His preeminent role in the genesis of the *Acta Sanctorum* had been recognized as early at 1641 by the Jesuit-General in designating the community of scholars "Bollandists." While some believed that his honor belonged more properly to Rosweyde, it was Bolland who had at a critical point breathed life into a moribund project and then marshalled the resources in people, in documents, and in material support to bring the venture to its first fruition. He also set the basic format of the series, the collegial atmosphere, and the spare style of operation that would henceforth characterize it.

The responsibility for completing the task now fell to Daniel Papebroch, who began to demonstrate the mastery of history and philology that would place him in the first rank of seventeenth-century scholars. With Henschenius long ailing prior to his death in 1681, Papebroch wrote most of the biographies for the eighteen volumes covering March through early June. One of Papebroch's insights was the realization that the oldest source was not invariably the best source. The quality of each document had to be examined carefully for authenticity and accuracy, regardless of its place in the process of transmission. The French Benedictine Maurists applied this point to great advantage in their own massive editions of medieval sources during the late seventeenth century. Further, in the first volume for April, published in 1675, Papebroch demonstrated in an extensive historical essay on the lists of popes how the most tangled problems of chronology could be resolved through patient and imaginative detective work. He sought invariably to demonstrate the relevance of such studies to the main purpose of elucidating the lives and cults of the saints.

Having discovered in a monastic archive a charter attributed to the seventh-century Merovingian King Dagobert I, Papebroch determined to devise some general rules and principles for establishing the authenticity of such documents. This treatise, appearing at the beginning of the second volume of the saints for April (1675), asserted, among other conclusions, that a large number of charters relating to the Benedictine abbeys of Saint-Denis and Corbie were very likely forgeries. This roused great apprehension among Benedictines, many of whose other houses traced their beginnings and their privileges to documents that could also by Papebroch's criteria be called into question.

Jean Mabillon of the Benedictine Congregation of St. Maurus was delegated to respond to the Bollandist challenge. Recognizing that the credibility of an entire class of documents was at issue, Mabillon examined hundreds of charters and diplomas to establish clear standards for separating the genuine from the dubious. Published in 1681 as the *De Re Diplomatica*, these studies provided for the first time scholarly principles for evaluating medieval manuscript charters and documents of all varieties, based on such characteristics as style, writing, form, and dating of a document, as well as its signatures and seals. A science of diplomatics had been created. Mabillon showed Papebroch's essay to have skimmed the surface of such issues and to have seriously overgeneralized in its criticism of monastic charters. Papebroch readily acknowledged the supreme achievement of Mabillon and the inadequacy of his own treatise. Mabillon in turn praised Papebroch's initiative as having inspired the *De Re Diplomatica*. The two scholars maintained their friendship and shared interests through an extensive correspondence.

A second episode of this period, however, had no such agreeable outcome for Papebroch. It was his intellectual integrity and refusal to let a dubious tradition go unchallenged that led to a grinding dispute with the Carmelites, who traced the foundation of their order to the prophet Elias (Elijah). Commenting in his April volume on the life of Saint Albert of Jerusalem, author of the Carmelite rule, Papebroch had found no evidence to support the connection of the order with Elias. The infuriated Carmelites launched a crude pamphlet war against Papebroch and appealed their case to higher authority. In 1695 the Spanish Inquisition, with jurisdiction over Flanders, found in favor of the Carmelites, declaring heretical all volumes of the *Acta Sanctorum* published to that point. Papebroch was devastated. The judgment against the *Acta* was lifted in major part only in 1715, a year after his death.

The Bollandist achievement and influence would nonetheless be secure. Despite a generation-long disruption in the era of the French Revolution, the program has continued along the lines laid by its founders. The sixty-seventh volume containing the saints of 9 and 10 November appeared in 1925, a supplementary volume in 1940. Other tomes are forthcoming through the labors of five Belgian Jesuits in a Brussels setting far different from the cramped attic quarters of the first Bollandists in Antwerp. Yet the disruptions of World Wars I and II and the expansion of the project to include lives in Georgian, Armenian, Arabic, Coptic, and Ethiopian have complicated the task of the modern Bollandists.

Bolland, Henschenius, and Papebroch had formed a team of genial, unassuming scholars whose collective service, spanning the years 1630 to 1714, had given the program a remarkable continuity from the outset. This continuity was particularly important in light of the contemporary absence of systematic catalogs of manuscripts. Even the finest libraries lacked adequate records of their holdings. Because of the time needed to identify pertinent materials, and the difficulties of travel and communication generally, the early Bollandists often had to settle for publishing their best single copy of a text, to which they simply added a few variant readings. Their textual commentaries sought to fill in the historical background of a given saint's life, with a brief technical description of the text itself. Close attention was devoted to establishing, where possible, its provenance, date and authorship, and history of transmission.

At the outset of the first volume for March Daniel Papebroch expressed most completely the early Bollandists' principal criteria in establishing hagiography as a scholarly discipline:

> Bolland and his successors consider it an inflexible rule not to cite any evidence they have not themselves independently established. They find it necessary to substantiate the date [and] the credibility . . . of the authorities on whose testimony they relied. They intend to evaluate all the details that might illuminate the life of a particular saint. No town or village is considered too obscure, no people too insignificant, no country too remote when it involved [tracing] the stages of devotion accorded a saint's memory. As possible, they try to explain all the barbarisms of the text by consulting books and manuscripts, by corresponding with scholars, [and] by appealing to friends who have been found in almost every country. They are less concerned with writing a general history of the church or of great nations. . . . Their main object is to throw light on the origins and growth of the diocese, towns, monasteries, and religious orders. . . . They must collate in minute detail several manuscripts and write many letters in order to clarify a difficult passage. . . . Besides, the published

texts are only a small part of the collection. Without the commentaries, the annotations, the notices on saints whose lives were lost, or never written, and [without] the scant data from casual references . . . the texts alone would scarcely have filled one volume (*Acta SS*, vol. 1, Martii, xx).

On this basis the Bollandist tradition took shape, including the principles and methods to be applied in the explication of texts in their historical settings. A direct consequence of this procedure was the accumulation of enormous amounts of new information relating not only to early Christian history but to medieval religion generally and to the broader history of the Middle Ages, Byzantine and western. Despite occasional excesses and lapses in judgment the labors of the early Bollandists placed the specialized study of saints' lives on a foundation that could inform as well as inspire. The Bollandist approach would have a decisive impact, direct and diffused, on the study of the Christian saints, most of whom lived within the medieval centuries.

Finally, since the church had been so pervasive a presence in the Middle Ages, the study of religion not surprisingly entailed the encounter with much else as well. To understand the milieu of a particular saint the Bollandists found it necessary to examine local politics, geography, folklore, language, and law.

The Renaissance passion for a return *ad fontes* had been restricted largely to the culture of the pre-Christian classical world. The Protestant reformers had focused above all on the apostolic era of early Christianity. Early-modern scholars like the Bollandists, benefiting from the critical insights and methods of the humanists, had moved on to validate major segments of medieval history, beyond hagiography, as fitting objects of study. Their achievement was rooted in the happy marriage of philology and history to make more credible the story of Christian sanctity. In the process they managed to provide the scholarly community, and students of the Middle Ages generally, with an immense compilation of carefully edited sources from the medieval period. Advancing along paths opened by scholars like the Jesuit Bollandists and the Benedictine Maurists, subsequent generations, including the later Bollandists, would steadily broaden and deepen the historical knowledge of that vast expanse of European civilization that lay between the ancient and the modern eras.

SELECTED BIBLIOGRAPHY

Full bibliographies of the works of Rosweyde, Bolland, Henschenius, and Papebroch appear in Carlos Summervogel, S.J., ed. *Bibliothèque de la Compagnie de*

Jésus. 14 vols. Brussels: Schepens, 1890–. Bolland's works are listed in vol. 1, cols. 1624–75; Henschenius: vol. 4, cols. 282–83; Papebroch: vol. 6, cols. 178–84; Rosweyde: vol. 7, cols. 190–207.

Works [The Early Bollandists to 1714: Bolland, Henschenius, Papebroch]
Acta Sanctorum. Ed. Jean Bolland et al. 67 vols. Antwerp: J. van Meurs; Brussels: Royal Publishing House, 1643–1940. On Jean Bolland's rationale for the project see beginning of vol. 1 for January: "Prefatio generalis" (1643). On Bolland's contribution see Papebroch, "De vita virtutibus et operibus Joannis Bollandi," at beginning of vol. 1 for March (1668), where Rosweyde's significance is also noted. On Henschenius's contribution see Papebroch, "De vita . . . Godefridi Henschenii," at beginning of vol. 7 for May (1688). On Papebroch's contribution see Jean Pien, "Historia de vita, gestis, operibus ac virtutibus R.P. Danielis Papebrochii," at beginning of vol. 6 for June (1717).

LETTERS AND PAPERS
Personal papers, correspondence, and travel accounts bearing on the hagiographic labors of the early Bollandists are located (since 1905) in the Bollandist Library at the Jesuit College of St. Michael in Brussels.

Sources

Aigrain, René. *L'hagiographie: ses sources, ses méthodes, son histoire*. Chapter 4. Paris: Bloud and Gay, 1953.

Analecta Bollandiana. Paris and Brussels: Société des Bollandistes, 1882–.

Bil, A. de. "Bollandistes." In *Dictionnaire d'histoire et de géographie ecclesiastique*. Vol. 9, cols. 618–35. Paris: Letouzey, 1937.

Blumenfeld-Kosinski, Renate, and Timea Szell, eds. *Images of Sainthood in Medieval Europe*. Ithaca, N.Y.: Cornell University Press, 1991.

Boureau, Alain. *La légende dorée: le système narratif de Jacques de Voragine*. Paris: Cerf, 1984.

Carnandet, Jean-Baptiste, and J. Fèvre. *Les Bollandistes et l'hagiographie ancienne et moderne: études sur la collection des Actes des Saints, précédées de considérations générales sur la vie des saints et d'un traité sur la canonisation*. Lyon: Gauthier, 1866.

Coens, Maurice. *Recueil d'études bollandiennes*. Brussels: Société des Bollandistes, 1963.

———. "Heribert Rosweyde et la recherche des documents." *Analecta Bollandiana* 83 (1965): 50–52.

Dehaisnes, Chrétien C.A. *Les origines des "Acta Sanctorum" et les protecteurs des Bollandistes dans le nord de France*. Douai: Dechristé, 1869.

Delehaye, Hippolyte. *Cinq leçons sur la méthode hagiographique*. Brussels: Société des Bollandistes, 1934.

———. *Les légendes hagiographiques*. 4th ed. Brussels: Société des Bollandistes, 1955. Translated as *The Legends of the Saints* by Donald Attwater. New York: Fordham University Press, 1962.

———. *L'oeuvre des Bollandistes à travers trois siècles 1615–1915*. 1920; 2nd ed., Brussels: Société des Bollandistes, 1959. Translated as *The Work of the Bollandists Through Three Centuries, 1615–1915*. Princeton, N.J.: Princeton University Press, 1922.

De Smedt, Charles. "Bollandists." In *The Catholic Encyclopedia*. Vol. 2, pp. 630–39. New York: Encyclopedia Press, 1907.

———. "Les fondateurs de Bollandisme." In *Mélanges Godefroid Kurth: recueil de mémoires relatifs à l'histoire, à la philologie et à l'archéologie*. Vol. 1, pp. 195–303. Paris: Champion, 1908.

Elliott, Alison Goddard. *Roads to Paradise: Reading the Lives of the Early Saints.* Hanover, N.H.: University Press of New England, 1987.

Gaiffier, Baudouin de. "Lettres des Bollandistes à L.A. Muratori." *Rivista di storia della chiesa in Italia* 4 (1950): 125–36.

———. "Hagiographie et critique: quelques aspects de l'oeuvre des Bollandistes au XVIIe siècle." In his *Études critiques d'hagiographie et d'iconologie*, pp. 289–310. Brussels: Société des Bollandistes, 1967.

———. "Mentalité de l'hagiographie médiéval." *Acta Bollandiana* 86 (1968): 391–99.

Galatariotou, Catia. *The Making of a Saint: The Life, Times and Sanctification of Neophytos the Recluse.* Cambridge: Cambridge University Press, 1991.

Grafton, Anthony. *Defenders of the Text: The Traditions of Scholarship in the Age of Science, 1450–1800.* Cambridge, Mass.: Harvard University Press, 1991.

Head, Thomas. *Hagiography and the Cult of Saints: The Diocese of Orleans, 800–1200.* Cambridge: Cambridge University Press, 1990.

Heffernan, Thomas J. *Sacred Biography: Saints and Their Biographers in the Middle Ages.* New York: Oxford University Press, 1988.

Jacobi a Voragine. *Legenda aurea, vulgo Historia lombardica dicta.* Edited by Theodor Graesse. 2nd ed. Leipzig: Arnold, 1850. Translated as *The Golden Legend: Readings on the Saints* by William Granger Ryan. 2 vols. Princeton, N.J.: Princeton University Press, 1993.

Kleinberg, Aviad M. *Prophets in Their Own Country: Living Saints and the Making of Sainthood in the Later Middle Ages.* Chicago: University of Chicago Press, 1992.

Knowles, Dom David. "The Bollandists." In his *Great Historical Enterprises: Problems in Monastic History*, pp. 1–32. London: Nelson, 1963.

Lechat, Robert. "Les 'Acta Sanctorum' des Bollandistes." *Catholic Historical Review* 6 (1920): 334–42.

Palmieri, Aurelio. "The Bollandists." *Catholic Historical Review*, n.s., 3 (1923): 341–57.

Peeters, Paul. *L'oeuvre des Bollandistes.* Brussels: Duculot, 1960.

Pitra, Jean Baptiste. *Études sur la collection des Actes des saints par les . . . Jésuites Bollandistes.* Paris: Lecoffre, 1850.

Pullapilly, Cyriac K. *Caesar Baronius: Counter-Reformation Historian.* Notre Dame, IN.: University of Notre Dame Press, 1975.

Reames, Sherry L. *The "Legenda Aurea": A Reexamination of Its Paradoxical History.* Madison: University of Wisconsin Press, 1985.

Tougard, Albert Eugène Ernst. *De l'histoire profane dans les actes grecs des Bollandistes: extraits grecs, traduction française, notes, avec les fragments laissés inédit par les Bollandistes.* Paris: Didot, 1874.

Van Caenegem, R.C. and F.L. Ganshof, eds. *Guide to the Sources of Medieval History.* 2nd ed. Amsterdam and New York: North Holland, 1978.

Vives, Juan Luis. *Joannis Ludovici Vivis Valentini Opera Omnia.* 8 vols. Valencia: Montfart, 1782–90.

Wilson, Stephen, ed. *Saints and Their Cults: Studies in Religious Sociology, Folklore and History.* Cambridge: Cambridge University Press, 1983.

JEAN MABILLON

(1632–1707)

Rutherford Aris

You may still visit the place where Jean Mabillon, historian and virtual founder of the sciences of palaeography and diplomatics, was born and grew up. In a row of houses that look out on a farmyard just east of the church in the village of Saint-Pierremont in the Ardennes is a door that has a little marble plaque over it bearing the words: "JEAN MABILLON. NÉ LE 23 NOVBRE 1632." The village is far from any tourist route, and the attempts of enthusiasts to make it an attraction to a public that knows "Mabillon" only as the name of a Paris subway station have been doomed to failure.

The son of a peasant farmer, Mabillon was his mother's fifth child (the first three dying in infancy, the fourth a daughter of whom nothing is known); a brother ten years his junior became a soldier and later a merchant. As a boy Mabillon showed promise, learning quickly from the local teacher and getting the rudiments of Latin from his uncle, the curé of Neuville, until the latter left for Condé-sur-Marne. His uncle's death a year or two later, from a beating administered by the brothers of a girl with whom he was cohabiting, seems to have confirmed Mabillon's intention to embrace the monastic life rather than the secular priesthood. But by this time he had been sent to the Collège des Bons-Enfans in Reims, where he made steady progress during the years 1644–50. He then moved on to the seminary for a year of philosophy and two of theology, becoming *maitre ez arts* in July 1652. Meanwhile his life as a religious had begun. In January 1651 he was confirmed and received the clerical tonsure; in August 1653 he was received at the monastery of Saint-Remy as a postulant and in September put on the Benedictine habit; on 6 September 1654 he made his monastic profession.

Mabillon's next six years were marred by an illness of violent headaches and overwhelming weakness. His superiors sent him first to Nogent and in 1658 to Corbie, where he served as porter and cellarer but was not connected in any official way with the great library whose books (by the translation of 1638) had so enriched the library of Saint-Germain-des-Prés, in which Mabillon was to do his lifework. His illness did not prevent his progress to the priesthood, and he was ordained at Amiens on 27 March 1660. At Corbie his health improved, and he developed a lively devotion to Saint Adalhard, in whose honor he composed a hymn.

After his recovery Mabillon was sent to Saint-Denis as treasurer, catechist, and preacher (July 1663), but he was not to be there long. A year later Luc d'Achery, the leader of Maurist scholarship and intellectual activity, drew him to the center of the Congregation of Saint-Maur, the Parisian house of Saint-Germain-des-Prés, where he was to spend the remaining forty-three years of his life. The monastery, thanks to the influence of d'Achery and his like, was in a healthy state, with the Rule strictly but sensibly observed and the duties organized so as to promote literary enterprises. At the same time there was considerable contact with scholars outside the monastery. Dom Luc, an invalid confined to the infirmary, was at home to his learned confreres on "certain days," particularly after vespers on Sunday, and this brought Mabillon together with such scholars as Michel Germain, Thierry Ruinart, Charles du Fresne du Cange, Jean Baptiste Cotelier, Étienne Baluze, Antoine Faure, Émery Bigot, and Eusèbe Renaudot. Other leading intellectuals, notably Jacques Bénigne Bossuet, would come from time to time when in Paris. Emmanuel de Broglie has painted a group portrait in *Mabillon et le société de l'abbaye de Saint-Germain-des-Prés.* Twenty-six years before Mabillon's arrival the authorities, concerned about the dangers of war to which the location of Corbie continually exposed its library, arranged for some 400 manuscripts to be brought to the comparative safety of Paris and were persuaded that the best place to keep them was in the library of Saint-Germain-des-Prés. An outstanding resource, the library was cared for in a manner worthy of its contents, for we read of a regular check and spring-cleaning in March of each year to which the librarian summoned a contingent of helpers from the community.

Here Mabillon spent his remaining years in a life of scholarship that was to earn him the reputation of "the most learned man in the kingdom." (So was he introduced to Louis XIV by Michel le Tellier, thinking to pique Bossuet, his co-presenter; Bossuet quickly interjected, "The archbishop of Reims should have added: and also the most humble" [Tassin, 210]. Both epithets were true, insofar as superlatives are meaningful.) It might be thought an isolated, peaceful, and sedentary life were it not for Mabillon's vast correspondence, the polemics that his scholarship generated, and his literary journeys. Of his correspondence eleven folio volumes survive in the Bibliothèque Nationale (MSS fr. 19649–59), survivors of a fire at

Saint-Germain in 1794, yet still providing 1,856 items for Henri Leclercq to list in a 130–page appendix to his biography (1953–57). Mabillon's *voyages littéraires* played an important role in his life and work, for they set the exemplary tone and style for all future scholars. Considerations of space prevent my mentioning more than an occasional highlight of his bibliographical discoveries. His three principal journeys, the *Iter Burgundicum*, the *Iter Germanicum*, and the *Iter Italicum*, are extensively treated by Leclercq and de Broglie. On these travels he met many of his correspondents and brought back information useful for his work from nearly every port of call.

After the publication of the *De Re Diplomatica* (1681) and ten years after his first bibliographical voyage to Flanders with Claude Estiennot in July 1672, Mabillon set out with Michel Germain for Burgundy on 16 April 1682. Their route lay through Melun and Montereau-sur-Yonne, Sens and Joigny, to Auxerre, where they took down some details from a manuscript on the usage of Saint-Victor (Paris). They spent four days in Dijon, visiting the magnificent church of Saint-Bénigne and examining the treasures of Robert Bouhier and Philibert de Marre, two prominent citizens with outstanding libraries. Among these was a martyrology of Bede's composition in a small Caroline hand that Mabillon judged to be seven hundred years old and which can be seen today in the library of the Faculté de Médecin in Montpellier (MS lat. 410).

Leaving Dijon, the two travelers went southwest to Saint-Jean-de-Losne, and found refuge from the frequent rains at Cîteaux, of whose library Mabillon notes eight works. At Saint-Emiland the parish priest raised their eyebrows by assuring them that the tombs in the middle of the raised cemetery that graces the village to this day had tumbled out of the air when Saint Milan prayed to receive the bodies of crusaders slain by the Saracens. They came to Autun on the eve of the Feast of the Ascension (6 May) and took a lively interest in the city, the churches, and the manuscripts and charters; Mabillon recorded the colophon of the Gundohinus Gospels and noted a charter of Odo's whose seal was in perfect condition and matched a reproduction in the fifth book of *De Re Diplomatica*. During the four days at Cluny they experienced an earthquake "quo magna pars Franciae concussa est"—small exaggeration, since quakes were recorded from the Savoy and Provence to Alsace and Champagne throughout early May. They made extensive notes on items in the library and cartulary and on the notable discovery of a calendar of the church at Carthage in the binding of a copy of Jerome's commentary on Isaiah.

Mabillon and Germain left Cluny for Lyon via Mâcon, Bourg, and

Brou. Mabillon seems to have been curiously ignorant of the manuscript riches of Lyon, for after commending the amenities of the city he says they did not stay longer because it lacked "veterum librorum monumenta," the whole point of their journey. Souvigny, Charité-sur-Loire, and Fleury-sur-Loire proved to be unfruitful, though at Fleury Mabillon did transcribe some prayers and the archives yielded an autograph of Louis V dated 979.

The following year Mabillon went through parts of what is now northern Switzerland, Austria, and southern Germany, on a journey financed by Jean Baptiste Colbert, statesman and financier, from the royal purse. This was a greater undertaking, for he was ignorant of German, and relations between France and Germany were unsettled. It was on a detour from their way to Basel that Mabillon made the capital discovery of the Luxeuil Lectionary (Paris, B.N. lat. 9427). Though welcomed and at home in the monasteries where they for the most part stayed, Mabillon did not take kindly to many aspects of the country inns in which they had from time to time to lodge. He complained of the flies, the nauseating odor of tobacco, the short beds that made sitting up preferable, and even the bread—"black and full of bran" (*Iter Germanicum*, 17). In spite of difficulties that plagued them throughout the German voyage and that stemmed from the political situation, they traveled on through Muri and Einsiedeln to Saint-Gall, where they saw Orosius's *History*, Avitus's *Poems*, Quintilian's *Institutions*, a manuscript of Alcuin with a colophon dating it to 806, and where they were given a copy of the famous Plan of Saint-Gall. At Saint-Gall they had the leisure to examine much diplomatic material before moving on to Kempten, another Benedictine house isolated like Saint-Gall in a Protestant city. The next major discoveries were made in Regensburg, where at Saint-Emmeram's they saw some of the treasures of the monastic library, including the Gospel Book of Charles the Bald (Munich, Bavarian State Library Clm. lat. 14000), written in 870, which Mabillon declared to be one of the most beautiful he had seen in his life.

From Regensburg they went to Salzburg, then turning toward Seeon, Attel, Rott, Tegernsee, and Benediktbeuern. Though meeting with obstruction and animosity from the librarian, they nevertheless discovered a letter of Charlemagne in a manuscript of homilies and some material on two Lyonnais martyrs. Having thus made the best use of a brief and unfriendly encounter, the travelers continued the next day to Munich.

Their next major stop was the Cistercian house at Salem, in whose library they found a treatise of Ratramnus, *De Perceptione Corporis et Sanguinis Domini*. At Überlingen they had intended to stay at the Benedictine house in the suburb of Petershausen but were warned that the authorities had received instructions to question straitly a suspicious party of two French Benedictines and an interpreter who had been reported to be traveling throughout Germany, for what purpose no one knew. They moved on without delay to Reichenau, where Mabillon recorded the inscription on the tomb of Charles the Fat and noted having seen a *Patrum Expositiones in Orationem Dominicam* with various confessions of faith, an address by Symmachus to Theodosius, and the homilies of Paul the Deacon. On 1 October they arrived in Strasbourg, greatly rejoicing to be back on French soil but acknowledging how well they had been received during their ten weeks in Germany. Their road now lay through Molsheim, Saint-Dié, Moyenmoutier, Saint-Mihiel, Verdun, Sedan, Charleville (where a happy coincidence allowed them to give Le Tellier an account of their journey), Reims, Laon, Soissons, and Meaux (where they paid their respects to Bossuet). And so to Paris and Saint-Germain-des-Prés after nearly four months on the road. At Freiburg Mabillon had learned of the death of Colbert and celebrated a mass for the repose of his soul. At the conclusion of his *Iter Germanicum* he pays tribute to the patron of his travels: "Quantum publica res litteraria illustrissio Colberto debeat . . . Maximum enim existimo quaestum memorem gratumque agnosci" (What a debt the literary public owes him . . . for I reckon that to be remembered gratefully is the greatest of riches).

Mabillon's *Iter Italicum* was by far the longest of his travels and the most official. Funded from the royal purse, he was to buy books and manuscripts for the Royal Library, as well as pursue his own studies. In those fifteen months (1 April 1685–2 July 1686) he purchased and sent back 2,192 books and manuscripts costing 6,096 francs (Leclercq [1931], cols. 553–56). So preoccupied with Christian monuments was he that the *Iter Italicum* contains even fewer of the asides on the scenes through which he passed than do the *Burgundicum* and *Germanicum*, where they are already rare enough. He seems, says Leclercq, "to have forgotten the pagan dead and to have been oblivious to the living" (*ibid.*, 537), and it is only from Dom Germain's correspondence that we get a glimpse of some of the political intrigue and personal jealousy that came to light during the enterprise.

Only the briefest account of Mabillon's journey through Italy with Germain as companion can be given here. Holy week found them in Turin, where their participation in the liturgy left little time for study. In Milan the Prefect of the Ambrosiana showed them his treasures, which included the great Leonardo volume and the sixth-century Josephus on papyrus (Cimelio 1), whose script Mabillon compared with that of some of the Ravenna charters he had published in the *De Re Diplomatica*. Mabillon spent some time in the Ambrosiana, took an interest in the Milanese liturgical patavinities (a literary style particular to the region), and visited Caravaggio and Arona on Lake Maggiore.

The next leg of their journey took them through Bergamo, Brescia, Verona, Vicenza, and Padua to Venice, a week of travel with quite a few literary observations, such as of the 1436 copy of *De Imitatione Christi* in which someone had altered the title page to "Gerson, alias Thomae de Campis." During their ten-day stay in Venice Mabillon learned of the death of Luc d'Achery, "quem patris loco semper ego suspexeram" (whom I have always regarded as a father).

Mabillon's first sojourn in Rome lasted four months and gave him time for a great deal of study even though he was in demand for other things, including a round of social obligations that put heavy demands on his none too robust constitution. His attention was riveted by the Vatican Library's collection, but there were others, public and private—such as that of Queen Christina of Sweden—that he wanted to see or was asked to examine. Leafing through the catalog of one library, he found the entry *Ciceronis liber de republica*, but his excitement was brief, for it turned out to be the first Philippic; it was a century and a half before Angelo Mai's great discovery of the *De Republica* itself.

In mid-October Mabillon and Germain left for a month's visit to the south, taking the Appian Way through a poverty-stricken Latium to the lively city of Naples—"Fragmentum caeli delapsum in terram" (a bit of heaven come down to earth). They were well treated, Mabillon's reputation standing almost higher there than in Rome. As well as seeing the monuments and libraries of the city, they made expeditions to Cava, where the monastic library yielded several notable items, some of them in Beneventan.

The high point of the return journey to Rome was Montecassino, where they saw a Liber Scintillarum of extracts from the church fathers; a volume of lesser works of Gregory; a martyrology with a later footnote adding Thomas Aquinas's natal day, with the reminder that "primo Casinesis monachus factus" (he was in the first instance a Casinese monk); Palladius's *De Re Rustica*, and the Frontinus's *De Aquaeductibus* that Poggio Bracciolini had discovered. More than a score of manuscripts are mentioned in the eleven pages of the *Iter* that cover the return to Rome.

During the final two months of study in Rome Mabillon was called on to make his report on a question on which the Sacred Congregation of the Index had consulted him: whether Isaac Vossius was heretical in holding that the flood was not universal. Mabillon's report, found posthumously among his papers, gives a unique insight into this otherwise closed proceeding. He concluded that, though Vossius was at variance with all the fathers, Augustine and Thomas Aquinas had held that scripture was not always to be read in a completely literal sense and that therefore Vossius's opinion could be tolerated. Vossius's *De Vera Aetate Mundi* was nevertheless put on the Index and remained there until 1900.

Mabillon and Germain spent their final months in Italy in Florence, from where they visited the great libraries in the surrounding area and enjoyed the friendship of the Florentine scholar, Antonio Magliabechi; in Bologna, where they saw the fifth-century Lactantius; and in Genoa, from which they made a side trip to Bobbio and discovered the *Missale Bobbiense*. The *Museum Italicum*, of which the first part is a full account of the journey, appeared in 1687.

Mabillon's last major journey, to Alsace and Lorraine (20 August to 10 November 1696), was written up by his companion Thierry Ruinart as the *Iter Lotharingicum*. Their farthest point was Strasbourg, where Mabillon's religious tolerance is apparent by his having visited not only the cathedral and its library but also the Lutheran seminary, where he and Ruinart attended a Lutheran service. At Toul they went to the synagogue for the Feast of Tabernacles, which Ruinart describes in detail. Lesser journeys to Tours and Angers in 1698, Champagne in 1699, and Normandy in 1700 were undertaken to answer queries or confirm points in his diplomatic work, for he intended to bring out a second edition of *De Re Diplomatica* though he did not live to achieve this. His visit to Fleury and Clairvaux in 1701 was as much a pilgrimage in honor of Saint Benedict and Saint Bernard as a literary journey; Ruinart describes Mabillon, greatly moved on coming in sight of Clairvaux, descending from his horse and continuing on foot. Mabillon celebrated mass daily at Saint Bernard's tomb, using the same chalice that the Melifluous Doctor had used on his own travels. Mabillon's daily prayer was that he might have the strength to take the *Annales* of his order up to the death of Saint Bernard—a request that was granted to him.

The writing of the *Annales* was Mabillon's last major undertaking. He had had it in mind since 1670, began actively to work on it in 1693, and occupied himself with it for the remainder of his life, the first volume coming out in 1703. It was material for this work that he sought on his later travels. His studies, writing, and correspondence continued unabated, but his health declined. In 1701 Louis XIV appointed him an honorary member of the Académie des Inscriptions, a newly created class of membership. Though appreciative of the honor, Mabillon was not an enthusiastic academician, attending fewer and fewer meetings as the years went on. His last journey was made in 1703, a trip of about two months, principally to Reims, where he was entertained by the archbishop, Le Tellier, but also to Saint-Pierremont, where he visited his 112-year-old stepmother. In 1704 he published a supplement to the *De Re Diplomatica*, evoking another flurry of controversy.

At the beginning of December 1707 Mabillon became ill during a visit to the convent of Chelles and was laid up there for a week, returning only after a doctor had been sent out from Paris. Five years before he had written his tract on Christian death, and now he was being tested. He was not found wanting; for he endured considerable suffering with patience and fortitude until on Tuesday, 27 December, the Feast of his patron Saint John the Evangelist, he died. By the order of Pope Clement IX the tradition of anonymity of Benedictine burial was breached, and Mabillon's grave was marked with his name. In 1799, when the chapel, which in the Revolution had been turned into a saltpeter factory, was to be torn down to make way for a road, the abbot requested that Mabillon's remains might be removed to the Musée des Monuments Français. They were translated again in 1819 to Saint Benedict's Chapel on the south side of the church of Saint-Germain-des-Prés, where they now lie together with those of Montfaucon and Descartes.

When Mabillon first arrived in Saint-Germain in July 1644, his primary task had been to take over the editing of the complete works of Bernard of Clairvaux, a project that had been left adrift by the sudden death of Dom Chantelou. Completed in three years, it appeared in two folio volumes in 1667 under the title *Sancti Bernardi abbatis primi Clarevallensis opera omnia, post Horstium denuo recognita, aucta, et in meliorem ordinem digesta, necnon novis praefationibus, notis et observantionibus, indicibusque copiosissimmis locupletata et illustrata.* It was well received, showing, as one critic put it, "such exactitude, insight, judgment, and erudition in a first publication that it was clear that the author was destined to take a considerable place among the savants of his age" (Leclercq [1931], col. 451). Saint Bernard's works appeared in a nine-volume octavo edition the same year and in editions that Mabillon revised in 1690 and 1701. Also in 1667 d'Achery and Mabillon sent out a letter seeking subscriptions to a work for which d'Achery had long been acquiring material, an *Acta Sanctorum* of the Benedictine order. With Mabillon's help this was prepared for publication, and the nine volumes appeared between 1668 and 1701, covering the period A.D. 500–1100. A tenth volume of material prepared by Mabillon was never published. As with the works of Saint Bernard copious indexes, footnotes, prefaces, and introductions were provided; one critic welcomed it not simply as a collection of monastic histories but as an illumination of one of the more obscure areas of ecclesiastical history, whose prefaces alone would assure the author of "une gloire immortelle." Not all his brethren were as complimentary, however, and Mabillon's critical methods and probity as a historian were attacked from the publication of the first volume. He was accused of betraying the order by rejecting many accepted saints and favorite legends and by not omitting some of the faults of those he did include. Mabillon's characteristically mild but firm reply soon won over the majority of his critics—including, fortunately, his superiors—but two, Dom Bastide and Dom Mége, pursued him in private and public, with venom and with volume. A vast amount of material in the Archives Nationales and the Bibliothèque Nationale has yet to be exhumed, and most of it is perhaps best allowed to rest in peace; but one item deserves mention. During the period 1673–77 Mabillon wrote a *Mémoire pour justifier le procédé que j'ay tenu dans l'édition des Vies de nos Saints*. In it he claimed to have been obliged to discuss the true and the doubtful saints and to have done so by the just application of historical principles, which he then outlined. He used this memoir in preparing a reply to the formal complaint submitted in 1677 by Dom Bastide to the Chapter General of the Congregation. Mabillon's *Résponse aux remarques que le R.P. Bastide a faites sur le préface du IVme siècle bénédictin* satisfied the Congregation at its meeting the following year at Fleury-sur-Loire. Mabillon was justified, and it was ordered that the controversy should cease, but what it had cost him only those of his temperament who have been involved in such polemics can judge.

A different controversy gave birth to the work that first springs to mind when the name of Mabillon is mentioned, his *De Re Diplomatica*. Another group of scholars concerned with critical hagiography was the Bollandist wing of the Society of Jesus, which was engaged in compiling a comprehensive *Acta Sanctorum*. Daniel Papebroch, a Dutch Bollandist, took up the question of the authenticity of early charters in the late 1670s and came to some damning conclusions on the basis of a number of rules that he had set up. Some of these rules (e.g., that the appearance in a charter of the invocation *In nomine Patris et Filii et Spiritus Sancti* is the sole authentication for the Merovingian period and the first two Carolingian reigns) were incorrect, and others, partially correct, were based on insufficient evidence. Mabillon was later to give him credit for having been the first to attempt anything of this sort, but Papebroch was altogether too severe, and his sweeping judgments were inadequately based. When in the preface to the April volume of the *Acta Sanctorum* he claimed that not one of the charters of Saint-Denis was authentic, he caused considerable stir in the Benedictine community, and Mabillon was called upon to reply.

In his hands this was no merely chauvinistic counterattack but an opportunity to examine the whole question of diplomatics. In less than six years he assembled and organized a mass of evidence—no small feat, even allowing for the faithful help of Germain and the contact that he had with du Cange and others. The resulting treatise was published in 1681 under the title *De Re Diplomatica libri VI in quibis quidquid ad veterum instrumentorum antiquitatem, materiam, scripturam et stilum.* . . . In 1704 Mabillon published a supplement that included replies to some of the criticisms that had been raised—not too kindly in some quarters—and he was working on a second edition at the time of his death. This was published in 1709 by Ruinart, and a third edition (no more than a reprint) was published in Naples in 1789.

Papebroch was among the first to see and acknowledge the virtues of Mabillon's work. He wrote on 20 July 1683:

> I can tell you that the only satisfaction I have from having written on this matter [i.e., diplomatics] is that it has given you occasion to publish so accomplished a work. True, I felt some chagrin on first reading your book at seeing myself so completely refuted; but then the usefulness and beauty of so valuable a work overcame my shortcomings and, filled with joy at seeing the truth brought to light so clearly, I called on my associate . . . . For this reason do not hesitate, whenever you have opportunity, to let people know that I am completely converted to your position. I ask you to count me as a friend, who am not very learned, but always ready to learn [Mabillon (1724), 459–60].

Such a letter deserved and got an equally large-hearted reply. Mabillon wrote back:

> On my return from Germany I found the letter in which you express your feelings for my work. I cannot but admire its combination of great modesty and profound learning; indeed I have never come across the like. Where would you find a scholar who, overcome in an argument, not only acknowledges but even publicly proclaims his defeat? . . . But far from being puffed up by my success, I would rather have been the author of so modest a letter as yours than to be vainglorious about my own work. May God grant that, even as I try to follow you in the paths of knowledge, I may be worthy to follow you also in the way of Christian humility [Mabillon (1724), 460–61].

It is good to record that they remained friends and that Mabillon came to the defense of Papebroch when the Bollandists' historical enterprise was under attack.

Not all reaction to *De Re Diplomatica* was so irenical. The malicious Hadrien de Valois wrote a bitter letter to d'Achery, complaining that Mabillon and Germain had ignored his help and stolen his contributions. Germain would have willingly boxed Valois's ears, but Mabillon merely pointed out that God allowed these little humiliations to counteract the adulation they too often received.

The *De Re Diplomatica* was well printed, with a frontispiece showing Criticism at the service of Truth and Justice and a dedicatory epistle to Colbert, whose concern for scholarship Mabillon greatly appreciated. The plates, engraved by hand, were of a high standard of fidelity, as comparison with modern photographic illustration shows. In Book 1 Mabillon sought to discover the principles on which true and false could be distinguished. He first classified charters into various categories for various purposes, then referred to the use of materials and different scripts, finishing with a study of the script of a Merovingian charter with some remarks on Caroline, Lombardic, and the abbreviations known as Tironian notes. Book 2 took up some of the external features, the style, seals, subscriptions, and chronological notes. In discussing the formulas, he had to refute some of Papebroch's rules. About the rule mentioned above he says, "I have not found a single authentic royal diploma that has the invocation [*In nomine Patris et Filii et Spiritus Sancti*]; they all have a form like *Chlodoveus, rex Francorum, vir inluster...*" (*De Re Diplomatica*, bk. 2, ch. 1). Book 3 deals with certain objections to the authenticity of certain diplomas of Charlemagne and Dagobert and with the authority behind different types of charters. Book 4 contains a discussion of the French royal palaces. Book 5 is the palaeographical section, in "quo exhibentur, explicanturque specimena veterum scripturarum" (in which specimens of old writings are exhibited and explained), a series of plates with alphabets and fragments, charters from Dagobert I to Saint Louis, and some ecclesiastical charts. In Book 6 various diplomas (documents) and legal instruments are given chronologically as tests of the preceding principles. The whole is followed by appendixes and indexes. In the *De Re Diplomatica*, Mabillon set forth specific criteria for establishing more accurately the meaning and authenticity of manuscript charters, official letters, seals, and acts. Each document was to be examined systematically according to such considerations as its age, provenance, style, and writing material. *De Re Diplomatica* marks Mabillon as the founder of diplomatics as the basic discipline of medieval studies.

In 1674 a tract was published on the use of unleavened bread in the eucharist, but there was little of Mabillon the medievalist in this. His development of the collection of miscellaneous material started by Luc d'Achery under the name *Spicilegium*, however, is entirely medieval. In 1674 Mabillon formed a new collection of his hitherto unedited short writings in prose or verse or of fragmentary material and published this with notes and comments under the title *Vetera Analecta*. Four volumes appeared in the decade following 1675. In 1685 Mabillon brought out a work on the Gallican liturgy, *Liturgia Gallicana Libri III*, in the second volume of which he published the Luxeuil Lectionary, the great discovery of his *Iter Germanicum*.

The treatise on monastic studies was another of Mabillon's works that grew out of controversy that was dignified by his characteristic concentration on substance rather than personality. Armand Jean le Bouthillier de Rancé, abbot of La Trappe, was not a man to do things by halves. His conversion was striking and his reforms of the monastery at La Trappe severe. His injunctions to his flock were the fruit of his personal involvement, and he resisted for some time any suggestion of publication. But persuaded by Bossuet, de Rancé published *La sainteté et les devoirs de la vie monastique* in March 1683. Within a couple of months Bossuet was predicting that it would both do good and arouse a storm. De Rancé defined the monk as one who was vowed to God alone and dedicated solely to things eternal. He would be furnished with many helps in his development of an austere spirituality, but among these study in itself played no essential part. The Benedictines, and particularly the Congregation of Saint-Maur with its greater openness, felt themselves to be a target of de Rancé's attack, and the superiors of the Congregation turned to Mabillon. His reply was pointed: the Council of Trent, he argued, had insisted that the Benedictine schools should be for students from without but that there was a need for instruction within, and therefore a retrenchment of studies would be contrary to the spirit of the church. De Rancé responded in his *Éclarissements* of June 1685 with the reaffirmation that study contributes nothing to the love and service of God.

The controversy simmered long, with various figures getting into the fray, not always in the same elevated tone as Mabillon's. With some reluctance Mabillon eventually set about to publish his own treatise, *Traité des études monastiques, dédié aux jeunes religieux bénédictines de la congrégation de Saint-Maur*, which appeared in June 1691. In the introduction Mabillon paid tribute to de Rancé and his intentions but went on in the first part to demonstrate the value of study, to which the whole monastic tradition was favorable. He quoted the comments of various teachers on the Rule, cited the example of Stephen, third abbot of Cîteaux, and his biblical studies; Anselm's injunction to his disciple Maurice to read Virgil; and Saint Bernard's commendation in one of his sermons of the Song of Songs. He agreed with de Rancé that everything the monk did in the way of work should contribute to the life of prayer and be directed only to the glory of God, but he claimed that for some monks study could do precisely this. In the second part Mabillon laid out a course of study encompassing scripture, the fathers, the councils, canon and civil law, theology, sacred and profane history, belles lettres, and manuscripts. Diplomatics had a place, but numismatics could too easily be a diversion and was best left to the secular. The long and intricate controversy came to a peaceful conclusion, at least as far as the principals were concerned, when they met face to face in May 1693. The debate is relevant to Mabillon the medievalist, since his arguments drew so extensively on his knowledge of the Middle Ages, the depth of which gave his position its authority.

It was probably about this time that Mabillon wrote down his *Réflexions sur les prisons des ordres religieux*. Though informed by his knowledge of history, it grew more particularly from his common sense and largeness of heart. He pointed out how self-defeating extreme severity of punishment could be and how self-contradictory were some of the ecclesiastical practices. In the jails of the state, whose raison d'être was the maintenance of public order, mass was celebrated; in the monastic prison, whose purpose was the saving of a soul, mass was denied the sinner. The prisoners were isolated in idleness, without friend or counselor: how could such a regime conduce to repentance? These reflections probably grew out of an experience in which a young monk, Denis de La Compagne, took advantage of Mabillon's simplicity and under a profession of piety won his confidence. Mabillon's intercession obtained a mild penance the first time Denis fled the monastery, but he proved a chronic backslider, and when Denis was arrested in May 1691 even Mabillon's pleas could not stay a sentence of fifteen years in the prison and five in the monastery of Mont-Saint-Michel.

In the matter of the house of La Tour d'Auvergne Mabillon stumbled badly. He, Ruinart, and Étienne Baluze were called in to authenticate some documents, allegedly of the eleventh century, that were favorable to the claims of the house of Bouillon. These were supposed to have come from the cartularies of the church of Saint-Julien of Brioude in Auvergne and to prove that Geraud de La Tour, the first of that name, was lineally descended from Acfred, the first of that name, duke of Guyenne and count of Auvergne. The documents were brought to the abbey by a certain Jean-Pierre de Bar, an assistant to the late genealogist Jean du Bouchet. Examined at Saint-

Germain-des-Prés in the summer of 1695, they were given a clean bill of health, in spite of the curious circumstances in which they had come to light and the fact that they were not original titles but only cartulary entries. Much of the criticism that was aroused seems to have been written off as envy, and it was answered inadequately, as when Baluze in 1698 published his *Letre* [sic] *de Monsieur Baluze pour servir de responses á la Cour de Boullion d'aujourd'huy descendent en ligne direct et masculine des anciens ducs de Guyenne et comtes d'Auvergne.* Eventually it was found that these documents had been forged by de Bar, who confessed to it in the Bastille in 1700. Mabillon, Ruinart, and Baluze persisted in their belief that de Bar's confession had been obtained under duress and that the documents were "bons et très véritables" (Loriquet, 265). It is difficult to understand this persistence, which was fatal to the reputation of Baluze and did nothing for those of Ruinart and Mabillon.

Mabillon's critical stature shows up better in the questions surrounding the cult of unknown saints. The late seventeenth century had a hunger for relics, and Rome, deluged with requests from all over Europe, seemed happy to satisfy it. Any old bones dug up from the neighborhood of a catacomb qualified, with no regard for the lack of evidence that it was the tomb of a Christian, let alone a meritorious one. This "inépuisable générosité" (Leclercq [1931], col. 609), had been remarked with disapproval by Mabillon when in Rome, and on his return he mentioned it to friends. But the receipt by a Parisian church of a martyr's head, which competent surgeons judged to be that of an animal, moved him to take up the question of authentication seriously. In 1691 he wrote a dissertation on the cult of unknown saints that circulated privately. Moderate as always in tone and showing all deference to the Congregation of Rites, it nevertheless raised hackles in Rome when in 1696 he sent it to Cardinal Colloredo. Colloredo himself asked Mabillon not to publish, but in 1698 it appeared under the transparently pseudonymous title of *Eusebii Romani ad Theophilum Gallum Epistola de Cultu Sanctorum Ignotorum.* An instant success, it went through five editions in Paris and was reprinted in Brussels, Tours, Grenoble, and Utrecht. In Rome, however, it met with less approval and would probably have been condemned but for the intervention of Pope Clement, who persuaded Mabillon to make some of his points a little less directly. This Mabillon felt he could do without conceding any principles, and the work finally appeared with Clement's approval. Both texts and much of the correspondence can be found in the *Ouvrages Posthumes* (1: 213–364).

Another major textual project was the edition of Saint Augustine's works by Mabillon's Maurist brethren Doms Blampin, Constant, and

Guesnié. Publication of the tenth volume fanned the embers of a controversy into the flames of attack and counterattack; an anonymous pamphlet condemned some of the readings as pro-Jansenist, favoring Jansen's reading of Saint Augustine's theology of grace—that special grace is needed to keep the commandments and that it is irresistable. Mabillon, who had been of some incidental help to the editors along the way, was called to their defense and wrote a general introduction in which, to quote Dom David Knowles, "the teaching of Augustine on grace was set out with lapidary precision and in which principles were established for its technical expression" (Knowles, 235). In 1700 the Holy Office impartially condemned both sides in the pamphlet war, and Mabillon's introduction was published in the eleventh volume.

Mabillon's last great project was the *Annales Ordinis Sancti Benedicti*, which was in his mind during his literary journeys and was the main preoccupation of his last years. In 1703 the *Tomus Primus complectens libros* XVIII *ab ortu S. Benedicti ad annum* DCC *cum duplici appendice et indicibus necessariis* was published and was followed by the second volume, covering the years 701–849, in 1704; the third, from 850–980, in 1705; and the fourth, dealing with the period 981–1066, in 1707. Mabillon left well-prepared material for the annals down to the death of Saint Bernard, and the work was taken over by Ruinart, who left the fifth volume (1067–1116) ready for publication when he died in 1709, though it did not appear until four years later.

MONACHUS STI BENEDICTI / PAUPER CASTUS HUMILIS / ERUDITIONE CLARAVIT / SIC DOLET IUVARE / PIETATEM SCIENTIA / SCIENTIAM PIETATE. So reads the inscription on the wall of the church in which Mabillon was baptized and catechized, and though there is an element of *de mortuis* in any such memorial, seldom has there been less *nisi bonum* to omit or so many *bona* to be summarized so aptly. For Mabillon's scholarship was integral with his vocation and cannot be understood apart from it. It gave him the confidence in truth that allowed him to put forward his theses with definiteness but without assertiveness and to take a position in controversy with firmness but without rancor. His attitude is well expressed in the dedicatory epistle of the work for which he is best known, *De Re Diplomatica*, where he wrote:

> Be it far from me to arrogate to myself the role of master in this matter. For in the republic of letters we are all free. Laws and rules may be proposed by anyone, but no one should impose them. Those that are in accord with truth and right judgment will prevail; if they fail,

they will be properly rejected by those with learning and discernment [*De Re Diplomatica*, 7].

Blessed with the most favorable conditions for study—resources, patronage, collegial support—Mabillon was nevertheless indefatigably industrious, producing over forty works, many of them of no small size.

As Leclercq (1931) remarks, the key to Mabillon's character was his simplicity—not the naiveté or gullibility that the contemporary mind often associates with this virtue but the absence of secondary motive or concealed interest. Given the peculiar stature that he attained and the relatively open structure of the Maurist Congregation, he could have carved out a niche for himself on the margin of true monastic life, but he refused to do anything of the sort, declining with finality the royal pension that Colbert offered him. His observance of the monastic discipline was straightforward, without frills or excesses, and he remained uncorrupted by the approval of the powerful and by his contacts with the worldly.

Most of his studies, whether in liturgics, hagiography, history, or textual editing, had a bearing on the understanding of the Middle Ages. But two of the most important tools of the medievalist, the ancillary sciences of palaeography and diplomatics, he forged virtually singlehandedly. It was a case not of his never having put a foot wrong but of his having stepped out so surely in the right direction that those who followed were not seriously misled by his occasional stumble. He was capable of mistakes and confusions, as when he lumped together early Corbie and Beneventan scripts, and his authority may have perpetuated misapprehensions, such as the name "Lombardic" for the south Italian minuscule. Mabillon would have rejoiced in the advances of palaeographic knowledge, for by these he would have been corrected. But few subjects have been born with principles that have held up under constant use so well formulated: the principle of testing rules by actual observations (*Praevalent istae, si veritate ac recto judicio fulciantur* [Those will prevail that are supported by fact and right judgment]); the value of good facsimiles (*Rectius docent specimena quam verba* [Specimens are more instructive than words]); the importance of the overall impression (*Non ex sola scriptura, neque ex uno solo characterismo, sed ex omnibus simul de vetustis chartis pronunciandum* [Ancient charters are not to be judged only by the script or by a single characteristic but by all features taken together]). All these are to be found in Mabillon's first explorations, and all are in use at the frontiers of palaeography today.

Mabillon has been called the greatest of monastic historians, singular both in learning and impartiality. His modesty would have shaken such epithets off like loose feathers from a rousing falcon. But he could not have denied the range or acuity of his vision. No theoretician, he held that history was the disciplined discovery of just what had happened and the disinterested summing up of the facts as a judge might sum up for the jury. "If he [i.e., such a judge] is honest," he wrote (quoted by Knowles), "he must present as certain things certain, as false things false, and as doubtful things doubtful; he must not seek to hide facts that tell against either party to an issue. Piety and truth must never be considered as separable, for honest and genuine piety will never come into conflict with truth."

SELECTED BIBLIOGRAPHY

Works

BOOKS

Acta Sanctorum Ordinis S. Benedicti. 9 vols. Paris: Billaine, 1668–1701.
De Re Diplomatica libri VI. 6 vols. Paris: Billaine, 1681–1704. Supplement. Paris: Robustel, 1704.
Museum Italicum: sev Collectio veterumscriptorum ex bibliothecis italicis. 2 vols. Paris: Martin, Boudot and Martin, 1687–89.
Traité des études monastiques. Paris: Robustel, 1691.
Annales Ordinis Sancti Benedicti. . . . 6 vols. Paris: Robustel, 1703–39.
Vetera Analecta: sive Collectio veterum aliquot operum & opusculorum omnis generis, carminum, epistolarum, diplomatum, epitaphiorum, & c: cum itenere germanico. Paris: Apud Montalant, 1723. Facsimile reprint. Farnborough: Gregg, 1967.
Ouvrages Posthumes de D. Jean Mabillon et de D. Thierri Ruinart. 3 vols. Edited by D. Vincent Thuillier. Vol. 2 includes *Iter Burgundicum.* Vol. 3 includes *Iter Litterarium in Alsatiam et Lotharingiam, anno 1696.* Paris: Babuty, 1724.
Annales. A partial translation of Mabillon's Preface of vol. 3, in *A Preface of Mabillon* by Dom David Knowles. *Downside Review* 36 (1919): 53–57.
De Re Diplomatica. Partial translation by Richard Wertis in *Historians at Work*, vol. 2, edited by Peter Gay and Victor G. Wexler, pp. 161–98. New York: Harper and Row, 1972.
Brèves réflexions sur quelques règles de l'histoire. Preface and notes by Blandine Barret-Kriegel. Paris: POL, 1990.

LETTERS AND PAPERS

The Bibliothéque Nationale has the most comprehensive collection: MSS lat. 11866, 11902, 12089, 12301, 12777–80, 13067, 13119, 13120, 14187; fr. 17693–700, 19649–59. Thuillier prints many letters in *Ouvrages Posthumes* (see above). For other letters in print see below under *Sources*, especially Valery, Leclercq's article and biography, and de Broglie.

Sources

Barret-Kriegel, B. *Jean Mabillon.* Paris: Presses Universitaires de France, 1988.
Bauckner, A. *Mabillons Reise durch Bayern im Jahre 1683.* Munich: Wild, 1910.
Bergkamp, Joseph Urban. *Dom Jean Mabillon and the Benedictine Historical School of Saint-Maur.* Washington, D. C.: Catholic University Press, 1929.
de Broglie, Emmanuel. *Mabillon et la société de l'abbaye de Saint-Germain-des-Prés à la fin du dix-septième siècle 1664–1707.* 2 vols. Paris: Plon, Nourrit, 1888.

Didiot, Henri. *La querelle de Mabillon et de l'Abbé de Rancé*. Amiens: Rousseau-Leroy, 1892.

Heer, Gall. *Johannes Mabillon und die schweizer Benediktiner*. St. Gallen: Leobuchhandlung, 1938.

Ingold, A.M.P. "Mabillon en Alsace." *Revue catholique d' Alsace* 20 (1901): 484–86, 731–32, 801–06; 21 (1902): 114–19, 214–30, 277–87.

Jadart, Henri. *Dom Jean Mabillon (1632–1707) étude suivie de documents inedits sur sa vie, ses oevres, sa memoirs*. Reims: Deligne and Renart, 1879.

Knowles, Dom David. "Jean Mabillon." In his *Historian and Character and Other Essays by David Knowles, Collected and Presented to Him by His Friends, Pupils and Colleagues on the Occasion of His Retirement*, pp. 213–39. Cambridge: Cambridge University Press, 1963.

—. "The Maurists." In his *Great Historical Enterprises: Problems in Monastic History*, pp. 33–62. London: Nelson, 1963.

Leclercq, Dom Henri. "Mabillon." In *Dictionnaire d'archéologie chrétienne et de liturgie*, edited by Dom Fernand Cabrol, vol. 10, part 1, pp. 427–723. Paris: Letouzey and Ané, 1931.

—. *Mabillon*. 2 vols. Paris: Letouzy and Ané, 1953–57.

Loriquet, [Charles?]. "Le cardinal de Bouillon, Baluze, Mabillon et Th. Ruinart, dans l'affaire de l'Histoire générale de la Maison d'Auvergne." *Travaux de l'Academie Imperiale de Reims* 47 (1867): 265–308.

Martène, Edmond. *Histoire de la congregation de Saint-Maur*. 9 vols. Paris: Picard, 1928–43.

Mélanges et documents publiés à l'occasion du 2e centenaire de la mort de Mabillon. Liguge: Abbaye de Saint-Martin; Paris: Veuve Poussielque, 1908.

Raguet, Gilles-Bernard. *Histoire des contestations sur la Diplomatique avec l'analyse de cet ouvrage composé par Jean Mabillon*. Paris: Delaulne, 1708. [Authorship also attributed to J.-P. Lallemont and P. Germon.]

Ruinart, Thierry. *Abrégé de la vie de dom Jean Mabillon, prêtre et religieux bénédictin de la congrégation de Saint-Maur*. Paris: Muguet and Robustel, 1709. Translated into Latin by Dom Claude de Vic (1713).

Tassin, Dom René Prosper. *Histoire littéraire de la congrégation de Saint-Maur y ordre de s. Benôit, où l'on trouve la vie et les travaux des auteurs qu'elle a produits depuis son origine jusqu'à présent*. Brussels: Humblot, 1770.

Valery, M. *Correspondence inédite de Mabillon et Montfaucon avec l'Italie*. 3 vols. Paris: Labitte, 1846–47.

Lodovico Antonio Muratori

(1672-1750)

Susan Nicassio

Lodovico Antonio Muratori, who not only achieved the first scholarly re-evaluation of Italian history (Noether, 65) but also transformed the study of the Middle Ages and laid the groundwork for a new approach to history as a discipline, was born a subject of the duke of Modena in the provincial town of Vignola, Italy, in 1672. Muratori's father worked in copper and kept a small shop and a farm. Ambitious for his son, he knew where money and advancement could be found—in the law. But he had to contend with the eager, wide-ranging intellect of a boy who could never limit himself to one narrow field of studies. Worse, he seemed to have little interest in wealth or power, and although he would achieve early and lasting fame as a scholar, he lived simply and (except for a few years in Milan) remote from the great capitals of Europe, the obedient servant of his duke and his church. In his 1721 autobiographical letter to Count Porcìa (Soli-Muratori; Falco and Forti, bk. 1, 4–38) Muratori recalled that as a boy he had a quick mind, a good memory, and a "dangerous" attraction to letters, to the point of reading Madame de Scudéry's adventure stories at the dinner table. Despite, or maybe because of, his own attraction to such things he never really approved of light entertainment (his motto was "The best recreation is a change of work") and frowned on opera and popular theater as frivolous.

At the age of thirteen he was sent to the Jesuit school in the capital city of Modena, where he studied letters, and then to the University of Modena, where he received degrees in philosophy (1692) and law (1694). It was at this time that he came under the influence of one of the major intellects of the period, Benedetto Bacchini (1651–1721). Bacchini, a Benedictine, was a friend of Jean Mabillon and the Maurists, editor of the *Giornale de' letterati* of Parma and Modena (1686–97), librarian to Rinaldo I (Este), and a distinguished historian in his own right. As the teacher of both Scipione Maffei and Muratori, Bacchini was one of the most important connections between Maurist erudition and the new Italian culture that was taking shape in the early eighteenth century (Falco and Forti, bk. 1, 13–14). Working in the scholarly tradition of Bacchini, Muratori would go on to produce voluminous, accurately documented histories, leavened by enthusiasm and a dedication to unbiased history written from a secular point of view.

At the turn of the eighteenth century Italy provided the young scholar with a stimulating intellectual environment. The "crisis of the European mind" identified by Paul Hazard was well under way; Ancients and Moderns quarreled at sword point (or, at least, sharpened pen point) all over Europe. Italians, keenly aware of their decline from dominance to stagnation after the Renaissance and Counter-Reformation, struggled to recreate Italian culture. Literary journals and scientific academies sprouted up in every court and town, and Bacchini's *Giornale de' letterati* made Modena at least briefly a nodal point of Italian letters. Just down the road from Modena was the great cultural center of Bologna, and between the two the teenaged Muratori began what Giorgio Falco has called his "vagabondaggio," the rambling journeys among the many fields of learning that would continue for the rest of his life.

In these last years of the seventeenth century Muratori began to form the networks that would enable him to collect the documents he would need in order to discover and redefine the origins of his civilization. He corresponded with virtually every European literary and intellectual figure of his day; this correspondence is still in the process of being collected.

During his student days Muratori decided against pursuing his studies in the law. Influential friends in Modena introduced him to the Borromeo family of Milan, and in February 1695 he was appointed a doctor of the Ambrosiana. Surrounded by the treasures of this great library, he began his scholarly career in Milan in 1697 with a volume focusing on documents of the early history of Christianity in Italy. He was to produce five volumes in this series (*Anecdota quae ex Ambrosianae Bibliothecae Codicibus*). Shortly after arriving in Milan he was ordained a priest (with a dispensation because he was under the canonical age).

In Milan the poet Carlo Maria Maggi introduced Muratori to Italian literature and inspired a lifelong passion for the cultural reformation of Italy. Apostolo Zeno proposed that he and the young Modenese scholar collaborate on a collection of documents in Italian history, similar to collections then being made in several European states. Zeno later abandoned the project, but Muratori eventually took it up as *Rerum Italicarum Scriptores*.

In 1700 Rinaldo I, duke of Modena and Muratori's "natural prince," summoned him back to Modena to oversee the reorganization of the ducal library, the Biblioteca Estense. Rinaldo's interest was more political than cultural: he hoped that the coming wars over the Spanish succession would provide Modena with the opportunity to gain territory, and he wanted documentation to support his claims. But the wars did not go well for Modena, and French troops occupied the city from 1702 until 1707. Deflected from his major interests by the difficulties of living and working in an occupied city, Muratori, incapable of idleness, turned to reflections on literary and cultural reformation. This interest strengthened his desire to reform Italy and Italian life, the driving force for most of his work.

With his return to Modena Muratori became the diligent servant of his ruler. But what for a lesser mind could have meant a lifetime of drudgery turned out to be grist for the mill of his greatest works. The famous scholar Gottfried Leibniz, working on a genealogy of the house of Hanover, asked for Muratori's help in tracing the Hanoverian relationship with the house of Este. Tradition had placed the origin of great families in Rome or Troy, but Muratori, trained by Bacchini, looked instead to the documentary evidence in the Middle Ages. The collaborative effort was never completed, but Muratori's part of the project was to become the *Antichità estensi ed italiane*. By the time he completed the first edition of this genealogical study, he was already planning what he then thought of as two appendixes. Over the years these "appendixes" would grow into two of his greatest works: the twenty-seven volumes of medieval sources on which his reputation now rests, *Rerum Italicarum Scriptores*, and a series of essays on medieval Italy, *Antiquitates Italicae Medii Aevi*. Between 1708 and 1720 research on a land dispute between the Este and the papacy over the little city-state of Comacchio led Muratori deeper into the records of the Middle Ages.

It would be a distortion of the man's life and work to overlook his religious thought. Muratori does not conform to the stereotype of the eighteenth-century cleric. Pious and orthodox, he appears to have considered his faith as the wellspring of all of his work. While he disapproved of emotional excess in popular religion, he yearned for a parish of his own, and in 1716 he finally achieved his goal. Despite its name the parish of Santa Maria Pomposa was located in the poorest district of Modena, and the church itself was in such a state that Muratori had to spend two thousand sequins of his own money to repair it. In the early 1720s, while working as a parish priest, he formulated his ideas on charity, founding the Charitable Companionship and writing *Della carità cristiana*.

The death of the Jesuit Paolo Segneri moved him to write a biography and edit a collection of his friend's spiritual exercises, *La vita del padre*

Paolo Segneri and *Esercizi spirituali*. Although a determined enemy of the baroque spirituality of the Jesuits (*Dei superstitione*), Muratori admired the order's missionary and spiritual fervor. In 1743 he published the first part of a study of the Jesuit missions in Paraguay, inspired by letters from the Modenese Jesuit missionary Gaetano Catteneo (*Il cristianesimo felice*).

Throughout his career Muratori affirmed that while the church's authority in spiritual matters was absolute, it in no way limited either the scholar's right of rational criticism or the state's right to jurisdiction over civil and temporal matters in which the church might be involved. This intellectual stand, as well as the Modenese attachment to the empire, put him into the neo-Ghibelline camp, with those who look to the empire rather than to the pope as a focus of Italian political life. It also left him open to (unjustified) charges of Jansenism, which plagued him throughout his life and continued after his death. A form of Catholic pietism, Jansenism stressed man's innate depravity and veered too close to Calvinism to be orthodox. But what Muratori's enemies interpreted as Jansenism might be better described as a distaste for religious emotionalism combined with a tendency toward Catholic illuminism, a rationalism in the service of rather than inimical to revealed truth. He wanted the physical and social care of the poor to take precedence over the construction and decoration of churches; he opposed spending money on masses rather than on charity; he supported the state over the church in nonspiritual matters. His ideas on religious reform were summed up in his treatise on moderation in Christian devotions, *Della regolata devozione de'cristiani* (1743).

By 1721 Muratori was famous throughout Europe as a scholar, philosopher, and religious and civil reformer. The next twenty years saw him at the height of his mature scholarship. He published his major works on the Middle Ages, a history of Italy (*Annali d'Italia*), important treatises on civil and religious reform, and several less enduring works on the philosophy of knowledge.

When the French "grand tourist" Charles de Brosses visited Italy in 1740, he made a special trip to see the saintly old scholar and found him working diligently in the icy depths of the Estense library. Muratori continued working to within a few days of the end, and died, as he had hoped he would, "with his hand on the plow" in January 1750.

The volume of Muratori's work is phenomenal, encompassing hundreds of books on poetry, literature, and general culture; pastoral philosophy and Christian dogma and ritual; epistemology; social, civic, and administrative reform; history, biography, and genealogy; economics and education. There is, however, one unifying theme to Muratori's lifework. As he wrote to a collaborator in 1722, "We are not working so hard in order to harm anyone, nor to praise others, but only for the glory of Italy" (Muratori to G.A. Sassi, 17 December 1722, *Epistolario* 6: 2302). His enthusiasm and capacity for hard work, his tough-minded modesty, his multidisciplinary passions, his fertile combination of piety and reason—all came together in the service of his beloved Italy. His search for the origins of Italian civilization led not to the classical age or to the church but to the musty, neglected, hitherto despised records of the Middle Ages. Among the inspirations for Muratori's medieval studies were the rich tradition of Maurist historiography to which he was introduced by Bacchini, the Ambrosian records in Milan with which he came into contact between 1695 and 1700, the abortive Zeno project to collect the documentary sources of Italian history, the Leibniz collaboration on the joint genealogies of the Este and Brunswick dynasties, his research into the Este claim on Comacchio, and his archival research between 1714 and 1717.

The Muratorian oeuvre is complicated by his habit of undertaking several projects at the same time, sometimes related but often quite different. In addition he began some projects and then set them aside for years, either because of outside interference, such as wars or ducal commissions, or for want of a patron to pay for them, or because of personal reasons, such as illness or the deaths of friends. And while Muratori wrote extensively for publication, he also carried on a vast, important correspondence (*Epistolario*), still in the process of publication. The bibliography (after a few student works) begins in 1697 with the *Anecdota*, the first of a five-volume series of Latin and Greek essays on manuscripts found in the Ambrosian library.

During his five years in Milan Muratori became convinced that the regeneration of Italy had to be based on a revival of Italian culture in the broadest sense. He was influenced, as were all European thinkers at the end of the seventeenth century, by the splendors of French cultural dominance. This both excited his admiration and inspired a determination to rescue Italy from her humiliating decadence. Carlo Maria Maggi encouraged two of Muratori's early literary works, his plan for a republic of letters (*Primi disegni della repubblica letteraria*) and his essay on poetry (*Della perfetta poesia*). Maggi's death in 1699 moved Muratori to publish a biography and a collection of his friend's writings.

In the first decade of the new century he began two works. *Riflessioni sopra il buon gusto* was a plea for simplicity of language and clarity of purpose in the regeneration of Italian arts and sciences; *De Ingeniorum Moderatione in Religionis Negotio* was a consideration of religious culture.

As early as the 1690s Muratori had corresponded with Zeno about a collection of documentary sources in Italian history. The collaboration with Leibniz and researches into the origins of the Este family began after Muratori's return to Modena and led eventually to *Antichità estensi ed italiane*. This work would later expand into his grand project, a complete picture of Italian life over the thousand years between the fall of Rome and the Renaissance (*Rerum Italicarum Scriptores* and *Antiquitates*). In the meanwhile (1708) his duke directed him to prove the Este claim to the city of Comacchio, a project that involved the analysis of a variety of medieval documents. Finally, between 1714 and 1717, he toured the archives of northern and central Italy, combing them for documents to supplement his collection.

The first volume of *Antichità estensi ed italiane* was an outgrowth of the Este genealogy work, but it was even then in the process of expanding. The document collection proposed as an appendix grew to a twenty-seven-volume series, *Rerum Italicarum Scriptores* (1723–38). This seminal work is a mosaic made up of over 2,000 sources—laws, public acts, diplomatic documents and correspondence, chronicles, codexes—all painstakingly transcribed and collected. These came to Muratori from many parts of Italy: from Milan, the codexes of the Ambrosian library; from the Veneto, the chronicle of Ferreto and the Cortusi Codex; from Lombardy, *De Laudibus Civitatis Ticinensis*; from the Romagna, the histories of Ricobaldo; from Tuscany, Manetti's *Historia Pistoriensis* and the chronicles of Gorello Aretino; from the Marches, the codex *De Proeliis Tusciae*; from Turin, the chronicle of Novelesa; from Bologna, the chronicle of Borselli; from Naples, Tristano Caracciolo's *Opuscola Historica*; from Sicily, Bartolomeo Neocastro's *Historia Sicula*. There were, however, limits. Muratori took little interest in evidence provided by coins, seals, inscriptions, or medieval monuments and art. Although he intended to discuss Italian culture in its entirety, the vast majority of his documents came from the north, primarily from Lombardy, Emilia, and Tuscany. And although he described the work as dealing with the period from 500 to 1500, in practice he stressed the High Middle Ages and took little interest in events before 1000.

The *Rerum Italicarum Scriptores* was more than a collection of unpublished sources. With Muratori's dedication to accuracy and truth, and his vision of a new, civil history of Italy rooted in the common reality of the Middle Ages, the *Rerum* became a history of medieval Italy told through documentary sources.

The second proposed appendix to the *Antichità* became a six-volume collection of "dissertations" based on the documentary sources. These appeared between 1738 and 1742 as *Antiquitates Italicae Medii Aevi*, and the essays were later translated into Italian and published posthumously in 1751 (*Dissertazioni sopra le antichità italiane*). This was a sprawling, monumental work organized by topic and by chronology. The seventy-five essays are designed to present the whole range of Italian life between 500 and 1500, though in effect, as with the *Rerum*, most of the documents came from the north, and he took little notice of events before 1000. He hoped to create a resource that would be for the Middle Ages what the great manuals on Greek and Roman antiquity were for the classical world. Falco and Forti see this work, considered by many to be Muratori's masterpiece, as the point of origin of a wide range of scholarly disciplines, and the high point of Italian scholarship in the eighteenth century.

Between 1744 and 1749 Muratori wrote a history of Italy, the *Annali d'Italia*, originally conceived as a civil history in the Renaissance style based on chronicles and documentation. In its final form it covers the period from the Renaissance to 1748. Although the *Annali* tends to be disorganized and lacking in a central theme, it is simply and colorfully written and like his medieval studies presents a broad history of culture based on the thesis that the past should enlighten the problems of the present. Other antiquarian works include the series of writings on the Este claim to Comacchio (most published between 1712 and 1714) and his monumental collection of inscriptions, the *Thesaurus*, published between 1739 and 1743.

Among the large body of Muratori's writings on religious and philosophical topics the most important are *Carità cristiana* (1723), an influential examination of poor relief and Christian charity; *Il cristianesimo felice* (1743 and 1749), a laudatory study of the economic, social, and religious work of the Jesuits in Paraguay; and his culminating work on the practice of religion, *Della regolata devozione de'cristiani* (1747), an enlightened plea for moderation and simplicity in Christian worship.

One of Muratori's duties as servant of the duke of Modena was to provide an outline of moral philosophy for the benefit of Francesco, heir to the ducal throne (*Rudimenta Philosophiae Moralis pro Principe Francesco Maria Estensi*, 1713). His interest in moral philosophy and in the education of the young led him to write a simple guide to the subject *La filosofia morale*, in 1735. But his philosophical interests were not limited to teaching the young; he wrote works on epistemology, wrestling with the paramount intellectual and philosophical issues of his day and attempting to reconcile rational Christianity with the limitations of human understanding (*Della forza della fantasia umana* and *Della forza dell'intendimento umano o sia il pirronismo confutato*, both Venice, 1745).

As a reformer Muratori was interested in all aspects of civil life, and he wrote on government and political philosophy. The most important works are a treatise on the management of the plague, *Del governo della peste* (1714), widely reprinted as a guide to city management and public health, and *Dei difetti della giurisprudenza* (1742), a plea for legal reorganization and codification that would do away with the tangle of laws and lawyers. Perhaps the most interesting of these civic writings was published shortly before his death. *Della pubblica felicità*, the culmination of his political and social philosophy and fruit of a lifetime's examination of the origins and nature of civil life in Italy, provides detailed instructions on how a state should be run in order to achieve the "first duty of the good prince: public happiness."

Although there is much that is unique about Muratori, he is clearly indebted to at least two traditions of scholarship: the Benedictine ecclesiastical historians exemplified by Mabillon and the Maurists and the Italian secular historians of the Renaissance and Baroque, from Guicciardini and Machiavelli to Carlo Sigonio.

The seventeenth century saw the emergence of industrious, productive Catholic scholars who delved into archaeological and documentary records in the confident expectation that the unvarnished truth about the Middle Ages would be the best defense of the Catholic faith against the challenges of Protestantism. To this end they turned to painstakingly researched, unbiased, accurate documentation. By the eighteenth century the certainty that historical fact would inevitably support church doctrine had dissolved under the attacks of Jansenists, Cartesians, and freethinkers. But by then Baconian and Galilean scientific tradition had made experiment and research fashionable, and historians began to look to documents to assume the function that experiment filled for the physical sciences.

Muratori, completing the work of the Benedictine historians, was perhaps the most ambitious, energetic, and productive of the preilluminist scholars. He shared Mabillon's insistence on accurately transcribed and analyzed documents, as well as the Frenchman's industry, modesty, and gentleness of character. But unlike the Benedictines Muratori was interested not only in ecclesiastical history but in the human condition in all of its aspects, social, political, economic, and religious.

The Modenese scholar was also heir to the Italian secular historiography of the Renaissance, although unlike Machiavelli, Guicciardini, and the Renaissance historians, he looked to the Middle Ages rather than to classical Rome for origins and models. In this he is clearly in the tradition of his fellow Modenese Carlo Sigonio, whose work on Lombard Italy was the only work of sixteenth-century Italian scholarship to find the origins of modern Italy in the medieval rather than in the classical period.

As early as the Este genealogy Muratori had established what would be the major themes of his work: that it was in the "middle ages" between the fall of Rome and the Renaissance that the true origins of modern Italian civilization lay; that it was here, among the barbarian tribes, that one would have to seek for the roots of the tangled and troublesome relations between the Christian church and the civil state; and that for all its turbulence the Middle Ages was not only an important but also a positive and fruitful era. In particular he put a positive value on the culture of the Goths and the Lombards, those "barbarians" so despised by classical Rome and by the church.

While he was fascinated with the Middle Ages, and saw there the true (rather than the imaginary) origins of modern civilization in general, and *italianità* in particular, Muratori was a man of the eighteenth century. His study of the medieval period was a conscious reaction against the baroque but without any trace of romantic attachment to the Dark Ages. In fact he did not care for medieval art or architecture and firmly disapproved of anything that smacked of medieval superstition or religious emotionalism. Muratori's byword was "good taste" (*buon gusto*), by which he meant usefulness and a healthy good sense in the face of the realities of life, thought, and faith. In its simplicity and clarity this "good taste" was one of the principal virtues that he believed critical historical thought could contribute to understanding.

Emiliana Noether and others see the eighteenth century and the work of Muratori as a turning point in the creation of an Italian consciousness that transcends regional differences. After Muratori Italian scholars no longer looked nostalgically back toward the internationalist, imperialist Roman Empire; they began to anticipate a new Italy built on the basis of its medieval city-states and the civilization of the Lombard and Gothic "barbarians."

By the time he wrote the seventy-five dissertations that make up the *Antiquitates*, Muratori had clearly abandoned a simple, chronological, or antiquarian approach to the past in favor of a global vision of the history of civilization. He saw the past not as a series of public acts by public persons to be arranged chronologically but as a place in which the historian could search for the origins of human conditions and problems by analyzing past societies, institutions, and cultural and economic relationships. His interest in the evolution of virtually all social institutions led him to the conviction that change is a slow process rooted in institutions rather than in individuals, a process in which modification and instability are the norm.

Much in Muratori seems incongruously modern, such as his fascination with technology and the mechanics of everyday life (what we would now call material civilization and social history) and his interest in linguistics and etymology. The result of his wide range of interests is often an apparent jumble of information, but it is a "jumble" through which we can trace the origins of a number of modern disciplines.

Muratori has a secure place in religious history as a Christian illuminist, who while impeccably orthodox in spiritual matters nevertheless looked to reason and to freedom of enquiry for truth. Hostile to superstition and obscurantism, he insisted that in all matters excepting faith truth can be found by reason, experiment, and free enquiry.

His influence extended far beyond Italy, and even beyond the Catholic world. Denis Hay (*L.A. Muratori, storiografo*, 323–39) identifies the *Antiquitates* as the "best early example" of a whole new historiographical technique, one that would lead in the end to the analytical professional history that developed in the later nineteenth century and on which our present discipline rests. In developing this new, critical, and sophisticated historiography Muratori clearly influenced the British historian-philosophers of the Enlightenment. During David Hume's tenure as librarian of the Advocates' Library in Edinburgh it contained sets of the *Annali*, the *Antiquitates*, the *Rerum Italicarum Scriptores*, and thirteen of Muratori's other works; that dogged old anti-Christian Edward Gibbon acknowledged Muratori as "my guide and master in the history of Italy" and praised him as "a diligent and laborious writer" despite his Catholicism.

Muratori remains a reliable guide to the authenticity of texts, thanks to his insistence on going back to the original rather than working from copies and, where that was impossible, on examining all available transcriptions in order to arrive at an authoritative text. Much of his correspondence deals with this search for all the alternative versions of a document and with his relentless tracking down of references and scraps and codexes tucked away in remote archives. Letter after letter is testimony to the long, difficult, and frustrating work of wheedling manuscripts from busy scholars, suspicious librarians, uncooperative princes, and hostile clerics and to the constant interruptions by wars, sickness, and the vagaries of the post.

Muratori was the central Italian scholar of the eighteenth century, the man through whom all the lines of the scientific and literary network passed. His work had profound implications for the modernization of history as a discipline and in particular for the scientific study of the Middle Ages. The clarity of his vision and the scope of his interests opened up new areas of history, linguistics, and humanist studies that are still being fruitfully explored.

SELECTED BIBLIOGRAPHY

Only Muratori's major works on the Middle Ages are included here, along with the most important of his writings on cultural and religious topics. A good bibliography can be found in Falco and Forti, bk. 1, xxxiv-xlv. *Erudizione e storia in Ludovico Antonio Muratori* includes a detailed bibliography of the Comacchio controversy (Bertelli, 468–82); and although *La vita di Ludovico Antonio Muratori* (Schenetti, 158–61) is written in a popular style, it includes a useful chronology of his works (see *Sources* below).

Works

BOOKS

Anecdota, quae ex Ambrosianae Bibliothecae codicibus nunc primum eruit, notis ac disquisitionibus auget Ludovicus Antonius Muratorius. 4 vols. Vols. 1 and 2, *Anecdota Latina,* Milan: Malatestae, 1697 and 1698: Vols. 3 and 4, Padua: Manfrè, 1713.

Primi disegni della repubblica letteraria d'Italia rubati al segreto e donati alla curiosità di altri eruditi da Lamindo Pritanio. Naples [in fact, Venice]: 1703.

Della perfetta poesia italiana spiegata e dimostrata con varie osservasioni e con vari giudizi sopra alcuni componimenti altrui. Modena: Soliani, 1706.

Delle riflessioni sopra il buon gusto nelle scienze e nelle arti. Part 1, Venice: Pavino, 1708. Parts 1 and 2, Naples: Reynaud, 1715.

Anecdota grâeca quae ex mss. codicibus nunc primum eruit, latio donat, notis, & disquisitionibus auget Ludovicus Antonius Muratorius. Padua: Manfrè, 1709.

Piena esposizione dei diritti imperiali ed estensi sopra la città di Comacchio. Modena: Soliani, 1712.

Raccolta di tutto ciò che è uscito alle stampe fino al giorno d'oggi sulla controversia di Comacchio tanto per parte della Santa Sede che per parte del signor duca di Modena. Frankfurt: 1712; 2nd ed., 1713.

Rudimenta philosophiae moralis pro principe Francesco Maria Estensi. Modena: Soliani, 1713.

Del governo della peste e delle maniere di guardarsene . . . diviso in politico, medico ed ecclesiastico. Modena: Soliani, 1714.

De ingeniorum moderatione in religionis negotio. Paris: Robustel, 1714.

Ragioni della serenissima casa d'Este sopra Ferrara confermate e difese in risposta al Dominio temporale della Sede Apostolica. Modena: Soliani, 1714.

Delle antichità estensi ed italiane. Part 1, Modena: Ducale, 1717. Parts 1 and 2, Modena: Ducale, 1740.

Della carità cristiana in quanto essa è amore del prossimo. Modena: Soliani, 1723.

Rerum italicarum scriptores ab anno aerae cristiane quingentesimo ad millesimum quingentesimum, quorum potissima pars nunc primum in lucem prodit ex Ambrosianae, Estensis aliarumque insignium bibliothecarum codicibus L.A.M. Serenissimi ducis Mutinae Bibliothecae praefectus collegit, ordinavit ed praefationibus auxit. . . . Vols. 1–24, Milan: Società Palatina, 1723–38. Vol. 25, 1751.

Vita Caroli Signoii praemissa eiusdem operibus. Vol. 1 of *Caroli Signoii mutinensis Opera Omnia.* Milan: Argelati, 1732.

La filosofia morale esposta e proposta ai giovani da L.A.M. Verona: Targa, 1735.

Antiquitates italicae Medii Aevi sive dissertationes de moribus, ritibus, religione, regimine, magistratibus, legibus, studiis literarum, artibus, lingua, militai,

43

nummis, principibus, libertate, servitute, foederibus aliisque faciem et mores italici populi referentibus post declinationem Romani Imperii ad annum usque MD . . . auctore L.A.M. 6 vols. Milan: Società Palatina, 1738–42.

Novus thesaurus veterum inscriptionum. 4 vols. Milan: Società Palatina, 1739–43.

Dei difetti della giurisprudenza. Venice: Pasquali, 1742.

Il cristianesimo felice nelle missioni de'Padri della Compagnia di Gesù nel Paraguai descritto da L.A.M. Part 1, Venice: Pasquali, 1743. Part 2, 1749.

Annali d'Italia dal principio dell'era volgare sino all'anno 1500. 3 vols. Milan [in fact, Venice]: Pasquali, 1744.

Annali d'Italia dal principio dell'era volgare sino all'anno 1749. 12 vols. Milan [in fact, Venice]: Pasquali, 1744–49.

Della forza della fantasia umana. Venice: Pasquali, 1745.

Delle forze dell'intendimento umano o sia il pirronismo confutato. Venice: Pasquali, 1745.

Della regolata divozione de'cristiani. Venice: Albrizzi, 1747.

Della pubblica felicità, oggetto de'buoni principi. Venice: Albrizzi, 1749.

Dissertazioni sopra le Antichità italiane già composte e pubblicate in latino dal proposto L.A.M. e da esso poscia compendiate e trasportate nell'italiana favella. Opera postuma data in luce dal proposto G.F. Soli-Muratori. 3 vols. Milan [in fact, Venice]: Pasquali, 1751.

Scritti inediti di Lodovico Ant. Muratori, II edizione coll'aggiunta di LXIV lettere, edited by Corrado Ricci. Parts 1 and 2. Bologna: Zanichelli, 1880.

Scritti autobiografici: L.A.M., scritti autobiografici, edited by Tommaso Sorbelli. Vignola: Comitato Vignolese per le Onoranze a Lodovico Antonio Muratori, 1950.

Opere di Ludovico Antonio Muratori. Books 1 and 2 of *Dal Muratori al Cesarotti,* vol. 44 of *La letteratura italiana, storia e testi,* edited by Giorgio Falco and Fiorenzo Forti. Milan: Ricciardi, 1964.

LETTERS AND PAPERS

Campori's work, although incomplete, remains the best collection of Muratori's correspondence. Several editions of Muratori's letters were collected in the last century. There is now an ongoing project to publish a complete collection of the letters from Muratori's correspondents, which when completed will be an invaluable supplement to Campori's collection.

The most important repository of Muratori's unpublished works is the Archivio Soli-Muratori, in the Estense Library in Modena. Some other documents can be found in the Aedes Muratoriana, the Muratorian museum located in the old parish church of Santa Maria Pomposa in Modena. Aedes Muratoriana also publish essays on Muratorian study.

Epistolario di Lodovico Antonio Muratori. Edited by Matteo Campori. 14 vols. Modena: Società Tipografica Modenese, 1901–22.

Sources

Archivio Muratoriano: studi e ricerche in servizio della nuova edizione dei "Rerum Italicarum Scriptores" di L.A. Muratori. Città di Castello: Lapi, 1904–22.

Bellini, Luigi. *Comacchio nell'opera di L.A.M.* Rome, 1950.

Bellotti, Michele. *Opere del proposto Lodovico Antonio Muratori, già bibliotecario del serenissimo signore duca di Modena.* 19 vols. Arezzo: Bellotti, 1767–73.

Bertelli, S. *Erudizione e storia in Ludovico Antonio Muratori.* Naples: Nella sede dell' Istituto, 1960.

Bertoni, G. *Il concetto della storia e l'opera storiografica di L.A. Muratori.* Modena: Orlandini, 1922.

————. *L.A. Muratori*. Rome: Formíggini, 1926.

Cochrane, Eric. "The Settecento Medievalists." *Journal of the History of Ideas* 19 (1958): 35–61.

Fubini, Mario. *Dal Muratori al Baretti: studi sulla critica e sulla cultura del settecento*. 2nd ed. Bari: Laterza, 1954.

L.A. *Muratori, storiografo*. Vol. 2 of *Atti del Convegno Internazionale di Studi Muratoriani*. 5 vols. Florence: Olshki, 1975–79.

Ludovico Antonio Muratori nel secondo centenario della morte. With essays by R. Cessi, G. Falco, and A.C. Jemolo. Rome: Accademia Nazionale dei Lincei, 1950.

Miscellanea di studi muratoriani: atti e memorie del convegno di studi storici in onore di L.A. Muratori, tenuto in Modena 14–16 Aprile 1950. Modena: Deputazione di Storia Patria per le antiche Provincie Modenesi a Modena, 1951, and 1963.

Muratoriana. Modena: Centro di Studi Muratoriani, 1951.

Noether, Emiliana P. *Seeds of Italian Nationalism, 1700–1815*. New York: Columbia University Press, 1951.

Nonis, Pietro. *L.A.M. e il pensiero medioevale*. Milan, 1959.

Ponzelli, Giuseppe, ed. *Raccolta delle opere minori di Ludovico Antonio Muratori*. 22 vols. Vols. 1–3, Naples: Ponzelli; vols. 4–22, Alfano, 1757–64.

Schenetti, Matteo. *La vita di Lodovico Antonio Muratori, ricavata dal suo epistolario e pubblicata nella ricorrenza del III centenario della nascita*. Turin: Marietti, 1972.

"Scritti sul Muratori." *Convivium*. Special edition. Turin: SAI, 1950.

Soli-Muratori, Francesco. *Vita del proposto Lodovico Antonio Muratori già bibliotecario del serenissimo signor duca di Modena descritta dal proposto Gian Francesco Soli Muratori suo nipote*. Venice: Pasquali, 1761.

Sorbelli, Tommaso. *Bibliografia muratoriana*. 2 vols. Modena: Società Tipografica Modenese, 1943–44.

EDWARD GIBBON

(1737–1794)

Patricia Craddock

Edward Gibbon, author of *The History of the Decline and Fall of the Roman Empire*, was born on 8 May 1737 (N.S.), the first and only surviving child of parents deeply engrossed in a "love tale at . . . Putney" (Gibbon [1966], 19). His birth came just too late to persuade a stern grandfather to forgive the young lovers for a marriage he had disapproved of and to make a will more favorable to his only son, Gibbon's father. The grandfather (an ex-director of the notorious South Sea Company who remained well-to-do despite the punitive measures taken against the directors when the "bubble" burst) had died in December 1736, and the shadow of his disapproval and of his austere brand of Anglicanism hung over Gibbon's childhood. Gibbon was often desperately ill as an infant and had only brief intervals of health as a boy. His mother, absorbed in her husband and numerous pregnancies (followed within days or months by the deaths of the infants), had little time for him. Her place was filled by one of "the world's perfect aunts" (Low, 24), her sister Catherine Porten, "the true mother of my mind as well as of my health," Gibbon called her gratefully (Gibbon [1966], 36). She instilled in him a delight in reading, especially in tales of life exotic in time or place. Early favorites were the *Arabian Nights* and Pope's *Homer*.

Though neither aunt nor nephew knew a foreign language, they did not content themselves with storybooks, and they were not passive readers. He "seriously disputed with [his] aunt on the vices and virtues of the Heroes of the Trojan War" (Gibbon [1966], 37). She was "more prone to encourage than to check, a curiosity above the strength of a boy" (Gibbon [1966], 37), the mental strength, that is, for a boy too weak and ill to join in the usual childhood sports. "The Dynasties of Assyria and Egypt were my top and cricket-ball," Gibbon remembered (Gibbon [1966], 43).

His aunt, however, could not give Gibbon a gentleman's education. A brief interval at a preparatory school at Kingston-on-Thames taught him that he could be punished by his peers for the "sins of his Tory ancestors," and with "many tears and some blood, [he] purchased the knowledge of the Latin syntax" (Gibbon [1966], 33). This schooling was interrupted by his usual illnesses and terminated by the death of his mother. He was not yet ten, and his father's passionate grief was a stronger memory than that of his mother herself. He was not sent back to school, nor was he taken with his father to the country, to which the elder Gibbon retired; he was left with his aunt, in her father's house in Putney. It was a high spot in young Edward's education, for it "unlocked the door of a tolerable library," and he "turned over many English pages of Poetry and romance, of history and travels" (Gibbon [1966], 37).

But school was still necessary, despite the boy's sophistical arguments against learning languages and despite his aunt's precarious finances. Gibbon's aunt after her father's bankruptcy had need to support herself and her parents. She combined her goals by undertaking to provide room, board, and care for scholars at Westminster School, starting with her own nephew. She made a success of this career, earning enough money not only to buy outright the boarding house she maintained but to retire with a comfortable income. From January 1748 to January 1751, when he was almost fourteen, Gibbon attended Westminster in the intervals of his illnesses. At one point his life was despaired of; at another he suffered a "strange nervous affection which alternately contracted [his] legs, and produced without any visible symptoms the most excruciating pain" (Gibbon [1966], 39). As he moved from the fourth form to the third, he began to manifest the talent for friendship that was along with scholarship the great joy of his life; but he could not really endure the rigors of public-school life, even with the advantage of his aunt's care. A few temporary tutors were tried, and his voracious reading continued.

With puberty his health problems vanished, and his father, desperate, sent the precocious fourteen-year-old to Magdalen College, Oxford. Gibbon was ever afterward indignant about the waste of time and intellectual energy he suffered in his fourteen months there, but it was to Oxford he owed the most fortunate error of his life: he "bewildered" himself into "the errors of the Church of Rome" (Gibbon [1966], 58) and was exiled by his father to Protestant Switzerland.

In Switzerland, in addition to losing his new faith and most of his old, he spent the most important five years of his youth. Under the friendly tutelage of a minister, Daniel Pavillard, Gibbon learned French and Latin thoroughly, encountering many scholarly and philosophical books that influenced his subsequent career. It was here that he began to write what would become his first published book, the *Essai sur l'étude de la littérature*, and in effect initiated his public scholarly career by engaging in Latin correspondences about textual questions with several scholars. Switzerland likewise provided him with a social milieu in which he felt comfortable and welcome. He became acquainted with one of his two most important lifelong friends, Georges Deyverdun, and he fell in love (seriously enough to wish to marry, for the first and probably only time in his life) with Suzanne Curchod, later Madame Necker.

At the age of twenty-one Gibbon was recalled to England, where in exchange for his agreement to break the entail on the family estates he received an independent allowance in the form of an annuity. The amount, £300, was enough for him to begin acquiring the scholarly library essential to his work—he always remembered "the joy with which [he] exchanged a bank note of twenty pounds for the [first] twenty volumes of the Memoirs of the Academy of Inscriptions" (Gibbon [1966], 97) when he received his first quarter's allowance. But it was hardly enough to live on in London as a gentleman of Gibbon's rank and fashion, and it certainly would not permit him to marry and carry on scholarship, much less fashion, at the same time. He approached his father for permission to marry his Swiss love. The elder Gibbon made it clear that if he did so he would have no provision but his annuity; moreover his father would be hurt and offended, hurried to the grave by his son's callousness. This emotional and financial blackmail worked: Gibbon "sighed as a lover . . . obeyed as a son" (Gibbon [1966], 85n). His sufferings were more profound and prolonged than his later insouciant account suggests, but he was helpfully distracted by progress on his book and piqued by reports from Lausanne that the lady was consoling herself.

The *Essai* was the first of Gibbon's attempts to reconcile the virtues of the *érudits*, the *philosophes*, and the ancients (Momigliano, 40–55; Levine, 47–62). He defended the antiquarian study of the ancients as necessary, or at least valuable, to the development of the "philosophic spirit": for Gibbon the contextual knowledge provided by these scholars—some of whom he conceded were mere drudges but others of whom inquired and judged with a critical spirit—allowed contemporary readers to acquire the eyes of a different age when they encountered the writings of the past. Such a perspective not only helped to free readers from excessive confidence in the views and values of their own age but gave them access to experiences and information that were lacking in their own time and place.

The *Essai* was completed and published while Gibbon, with his father, was enjoying or suffering an unexpected foray into the active life of the South Battalion Hampshire Militia, which they had joined in May 1760. For more than two years Gibbon combined the role of captain and acting executive officer of an independent military unit of 476 officers and men, with that of budding scholar. In this period he taught himself to read Homer; more significantly he resolved to be a historian, though he did not as yet choose a subject. In his later view the "Captain of the Hampshire grenadiers (the reader may smile) has not been useless to the historian of the Roman Empire" (Gibbon [1966], 117).

The *Essai* was published in 1761 to some applause in France but to little notice in England. Its success abroad led the young scholar to depart for Paris on a belated grand tour, after the militia was disbanded, with high hopes of being recognized as both a gentleman and a man of letters. In Paris he studied "the world," but he also read Jean Mabillon and Bernard de Montfaucon, though he mastered only their results, not their methods. Despite his religious liberation, he was taken aback by the "intolerant zeal of the philosophers and Encyclopaedists" in Paris (Gibbon [1966], 127). By his own account "the most pleasing connection which [he] formed in Paris [was] the acquisition of a female friend by whom [he] was sure of being received every evening with the smile of confidence and joy . . . Madame Bontems" (Gibbon [1966], 127). Nineteen years older than Gibbon, she astonished him by being an author who did not parade her celebrity or ability. She was seriously religious without losing either her charity toward heretics and sinners or her good humor. When he returned to Paris in 1765, on his way back to England, she may have extended still more generous favors to him (Baridon, 128).

In April 1763 Gibbon left for Lausanne, where he spent the summer and winter preparing himself for his trip to Italy by compiling a study of its geography and history as represented in the ancient authors. In this period and during his Italian journey itself Gibbon kept notes on his reading and wrote essays on many literary and scholarly subjects; some showed his great interest in Roman history, but many dealt with medieval subjects. His original intention indeed was to choose for his first major historical study one of two favorite subjects, significantly both medieval: "the history of Swiss liberty" and Florence under the Medicis. He also formed the second of the two great friendships of his life, with a fellow Englishman, John Holroyd, who became Gibbon's adviser in all matters of "business."

In Italy Gibbon found his subject. Entering the Rome of the popes in 1764, he was "overcome by a dream of antiquity" (Gibbon [1961], 225). In his own famous account, echoed at the end of *Decline and Fall*, "It was at Rome, on the fifteenth of October 1764, as I sat musing amidst the ruins of the Capitol while the barefoot fryars were singing Vespers in the temple of Jupiter, that the idea of writing the decline and fall of the City first started to my mind" (Gibbon [1966], 136). Confined at first to the fortunes of the city, his subject from the beginning encompassed both imperial and medieval Rome; but it was only after two anonymous publications, *Mémoires littéraires* and *Critical Observations*, and some abortive attempts at several other projects (including the Swiss history), and with the financial and emotional freedom made possible by his father's death, that he actually began writing *Decline and Fall*.

The first volume appeared with great success in 1776. During the years of its composition Gibbon had become a member of Parliament in 1774 and a silent supporter of Lord North's government, at first in a seat given him by his cousin and later in one provided by North. In 1779 he became Lord of Trade (a near sinecure appointment with nominal oversight of colonial trade) and an occasional pamphleteer, first in defense of his own work (the *Vindication of . . . Chapters XV and XVI*, January 1779), and then of the government's (*Mémoire justicatif*, October 1779). Volumes 2 and 3 were written during these years of public activity, and published in 1781. When North's government fell, Gibbon lost his seat and chose to retire to Lausanne (1783), where his income would go much farther, especially since he could share a house recently inherited by his longtime friend Deyverdun. There he completed the last three volumes, returning to England for a lengthy visit to publish them in 1787–88.

After the publication of the last three volumes Gibbon returned once more to Lausanne, where he lived most of the remainder of his life very happily. He turned his hand to many projects after completing the history but finished none to his own satisfaction, not even his memoirs, which after his death were compiled by Holroyd, now Lord Sheffield, into a single whole (from the six drafts Gibbon had written) and published as the centerpiece of Gibbon's posthumous *Miscellaneous Works* (2 vols., 1796; 5 vols., 1814). Also included in this collection was another incomplete project of interest to medieval historians, the *Antiquities of the House of Brunswick*, which incorporated much of the medieval Italian material Gibbon had accumulated while preparing *Decline and Fall* but foundered like the Swiss history when he began to require materials in German.

His final return to England, in May 1793, was made in an effort to comfort the Sheffields when Lady Sheffield died. While there, following surgery for an enormous swelling in his groin that he had neglected for years, he died at age fifty-six on 16 January 1794. Despite his ill health he had just made an enthusiastic beginning on another kind of scholarly contribution, an edition of the medieval English historians, for which he wrote a preface *cum* prospectus. This project was to have been a collaboration between him and a young scholar named John Pinkerton, who would have done the actual editing. Gibbon was to provide introductions and commentaries.

When Gibbon began thinking about writing medieval history, he "periodized" the "memorable series of revolutions, which, in the course of about thirteen centuries, gradually undermined, and at length destroyed, the solid fabric of [Roman] greatness," as follows:

> The first . . . from the age of Trajan and the Antonines . . . to the subversion of the Western Empire, by the barbarians of Germany and Scythia . . . [was] completed about the beginning of the sixth century. . . . The second . . . may be supposed to commence with the reign of Justinian who by his laws, as well as by his victories, restored a transient splendour to the Eastern Empire. It will comprehend the invasion of Italy by the Lombards; the conquest of the Asiatic and African provinces by the Arabs, who embraced the religion of Mahomet; the revolt of the Roman people against the feeble princes of Constantinople; and the elevation of Charlemagne, who, in the year 800, established the second or German Empire of the West. . . . [The] last and longest [extends] . . . from the revival of the Western Empire till the taking of Constantinople by the Turks and the extinction of a degenerate race of princes, who continued to assume the titles of Caesar and Augustus, after their dominions were contracted to the limits of a single city. . . . The writer . . . w[ill] find himself obliged to enter into the general history of the Crusades, as far as they contributed to the ruin of the Greek empire; and he w[ill] scarcely be able to restrain his curiosity from making some enquiry into the state of the city of Rome during the darkness and confusion of the middle ages [*Decline and Fall*, ed. Bury, 1: xxxix-xl].

Gibbon revised this scheme in large ways and small, as over the course of twelve more years he completed his history. At the beginning of the last two volumes, after his "age of Justinian" was complete with accounts of Roman law and of the religious controversies and conflicts over the doctrine of the Incarnation in which Justinian involved himself, Gibbon proposed a revised structure for the remainder of his task, preferring, he said, to "group . . . my picture by nations; . . . the seeming neglect of Chronological order is surely compensated by the superior merits of interest and perspicuity" (Gibbon [1966], 179). In youth he had objected to Voltaire's topical arrangement in *Siècle de Louis XIV*, although he admired that work because different matters "are all connected in human affairs, and as they are often the cause of each other, why seperate [sic] them in History?" (Gibbon [1929], 129). On the other hand he was enthusiastic about the method of Robert Henry's then recent (and now forgotten) history of Great Britain, which was topical but narrative within the topics (Gibbon [1956] 3: 223, with note). This was Gibbon's practice in the remainder of his medieval history, which proceeds narratively and even chronologically but which is conceived as a number of parallel narratives, with a few atemporal analyses interspersed. As a result the same year and even the same events may be discussed in several chapters even as the history gradually moves forward to 1453, and the temporal framework is often violated in both directions. Gibbon conceives of the "middle" ages as medial at different times and at different rates in different places and with respect to different things.

Gibbon's new plan for the remainder of *Decline and Fall* called for a chapter devoted to the "revolutions of the [Greek] throne" from Heraclius to the "Latin conquest," a "tedious and uniform tale of weakness and misery," but included because it is "*passively* [Gibbon's emphasis] connected with the most splendid and important revolutions which have changed the history of the world" (*Decline and Fall* 5: 183–85). He posits that "such a chronological review will serve to illustrate the various arguments of the subsequent chapters; and each circumstance of the eventful story of the barbarians will adapt itself in a proper place to the Byzantine annals" (*ibid.*). In addition to this chronological survey he promises analytical chapters on the internal state of the empire and "the dangerous heresy of the Paulicians, which shook the East and enlightened the West" (*ibid.*). He will arrange topically his discussion of "the world in the ninth and tenth centuries" (*ibid.*), enumerating the nations to be discussed: the Franks (Chapter 49), the "Arabs or Saracens" (Chapters 50–52), the Bulgarians, Hungarians, and Russians (Chapter 55), and on through the nations of the West. He will treat the Moguls, Tartars, and Turks last. Gibbon's topical arrangement will include two additional subjects: "the [religious] schism of the Greeks will be connected with their last calamities, and the restoration of learning in the Western world. I shall return from the captivity of the new, to the ruins of ancient Rome (Chapters 69–71); and the venerable name, the interesting theme, will shed a ray of glory on the conclusion of my labours" (*ibid.*).

But in the text itself, before he even arrives at the conclusion of the "first part" of his original plan with the last of the western emperors, he marks strongly a chronological division, a sense that a new age had begun in the first part of the fifth century. He singles out from the "insipid legends of ecclesiastical history" the story of the Seven Sleepers who fell asleep in the reign of Decius and awoke in that of Theodosius the younger:

> We imperceptibly advance from youth to age, without observing the gradual, but incessant, change of human affairs, and, even in our larger experiences of history, the imagination is accustomed, by a perpetual series of causes and effects, to unite the most distant revolutions. But . . . if it were possible, after a momentary slumber of two hundred years, to display the *new* world to the eyes of a spectator, who still retained a lively and recent impression of the *old*; his surprise and his reflections would furnish the pleasing subject of a philosophical romance. The scene could not be more advantageously placed than in the two centuries which elapsed between the reigns of Decius and of Theodosius the younger. During this period, the seat of government had been transported from Rome to a new city, [Constantinople] . . . and the abuse of military spirit had been suppressed by an artificial system of tame and ceremonious servitude. The throne of the persecuting Decius was filled by a succession of Christian and orthodox princes, who had extirpated the fabulous gods of antiquity; and the public devotion of the age was impatient to exalt the saints and martyrs of the Catholic church on the altars of Diana and Hercules. The union of the Roman empire was dissolved; its genius was humbled in the dust; and armies of unknown Barbarians, issuing from the frozen regions of the North, had established their victorious reign over the fairest provinces of Europe and Africa [*Decline and Fall* 3: 439].

Gibbon's history of this new phase is well established before his original "first period" ends in Chapter 36 of Volume 3. It is in Volume 3, for example, that he treats what Santo Mazzarino calls the "Stilicho problem." Mazzarino credits Gibbon, "the greatest of the Enlightenment historians," with achieving a positive view of the minister and general Stilicho (d. 408), in opposition to the Augustinian position (Mazzarino, 313). But Enlightenment historiography—and hence Gibbon—Mazzarino believed, could appreciate only the character, not the age, of Stilicho, because its attention centered on the transition from an age of faith to an age of reason. It therefore could not appreciate a more important conflict, that between a supranational idea like that of the Roman Empire and the emergence of nations, "the empire's successors and [yet] its continuation" (*ibid.*). Gibbon, however, clearly distinguishes himself from Enlightenment historiography of the "school of Voltaire" by, among many other means, recognizing and being concerned with precisely this problem, as Giorgio Falco pointed out: the loss of the distinctive set of qualities that characterized Roman civilization, and the compensations for that loss.

From the beginning of the history Gibbon had known that his subject was as much the rise of a new world order as the dissolution of an old: "The [imperial] Roman world was indeed peopled by a race of pigmies, when the fierce giants of the north broke in and mended the puny breed. They restored a manly spirit of freedom; and, after the revolution of ten centuries, freedom became the happy parent of taste and science" (*Decline and Fall* 1: 64). Gibbon's subject is neither the pygmy world nor the mended one but the ten centuries in between.

Falco's *La polemica sul medio evo* (1933) contains one of the most extended considerations of Gibbon as medieval historian. Two chapters (150 pages) are devoted to Gibbon, who is credited with offering, "perhaps for the first time" (despite his acknowledged debt to both Voltaire and Robertson, on whom he improves in complementary ways, according to Falco), "a full narrative of the Middle Ages, distinguished from universal history, irradiated by an idea" (Falco, 191). For Falco Gibbon's main faults in the final volumes of the history are a lack of organic unity and a static method. He concedes, however, that it is not altogether regrettable that Gibbon failed to sacrifice "his art and his encyclopedic learning" for the cause of organicity. Gibbon's work has become a great model of medieval history, and it behooves us to see how he configures the Middle Ages and to learn what we can from his inability to systematize all his material organically. For Gibbon, Falco argues, the ancient problem of the decline of the empire was reborn as a vague design of the decline of Romaninity, together with a sense of the progressive enlargement of "Europe" intimately connected with that decline. Hence his "impenitent wandering" from east to west, north to south (Falco, 197–98).

Falco singles out several topics in Gibbon's medieval history for special treatment, starting with religion. He cites Gibbon's fantasy of Peter and Paul returned to life and to Rome, wondering what god might be worshiped with such mysterious rites in such splendid temples. "In this fantasy is summed up his judgment on the medieval church. We can know no other Christianity than that which is seen in the unique and manifold process of history" (Falco, 206). Falco argues that Gibbon grants even Catholic Christianity qualified approval: we do not see in it moral or intellectual positions that can be admired by the philosopher; yet we may speculate that most people cannot get along with austerely rational metaphysics, and we can acknowledge that as a social institution religion, even in the form of the Catholic church, has done some good. Falco's second topic is that of competitive value systems, represented in the orientals and the orientalized empire and in the barbarians. Gibbon's norm is the laws of nature and, first, those of personal freedom.

Though it offers the advantages of order and comfort, the empire is condemned. For barbarians "the problem is simply inverted" (Falco, 220): their "freedom" depends on "misery, material and moral" (*ibid.*). In the falling empire and in the High Middle Ages Gibbon's recurrent theme is the opportunity for a better, that is, freer, society, one that arises and is lost. In the treatment of reviving constitutional states of the late Middle Ages and modern times Gibbon indicates, even beyond his sympathies, the temperateness of his democratic propensities and his conservative bent, faithful to the theory of balance of powers. He makes clear his idea of the worst government: an ecclesiastical state, which can neither secure order and comfort nor allow civil and religious liberty.

These aspects of *Decline and Fall*, however, are not unusual in its century, says Falco. The originality and fecundity of the history will appear to those who consider the historian's art and method. What it gives us is a series of great pictures of the "fundamental moments" of the Middle Ages: Constantine; Christianity and the empire; Charlemagne, Muhammad, and the Arabs; the Crusades; the Renaissance. Falco devotes an entire chapter to an appreciation, with appropriate qualifications, of these "moments" (269–340). In Gibbon, he concludes, "we could trace the thread of an organic medieval history but it would be artificial" (339). This is not Gibbon's argument. He intended to write the history of the decline and fall of all Romaninity as a political organism. He had a lively sense of the ancient world, of the unified empire that dissolved, and he studied acutely and minutely its crises; "a thousand sporadic points show a clear consciousness of the modern states: but . . . despite all the riches of information and penetration he provides, he lacks precisely an appreciation of the 'Middle Ages' as an object of study for its own sake" (Falco, 340).

Many other writers and editors have paid special attention to these and other aspects of the final four volumes of Gibbon's history without necessarily agreeing with this assessment. Anyone who closely reads the last volumes realizes that Gibbon does not portray the "decline and fall" as merely a negative process. One valuable study, that of G. Giarrizzo, goes so far as to claim that the title of *Decline and Fall* is merely occasional: its true theme is rather a product of Gibbon's lifelong interest in medieval history, "an unconscious exaltation of modern Europe, after a near tragic gestation period" (Giarrizzo, 446).

Despite this view Giarrizzo leaves much of Gibbon's medieval history undiscussed. He views the work from the viewpoint of his own agenda, as a contribution to intellectual history of the eighteenth century, not from Gibbon's, which was to give some understanding of the fate of the once Roman world. This is understandable. Even if we limit ourselves "only" to Gibbon's medieval history, his range—chronological, geographical, and topical—is enormous. Perhaps we may view his conceptual achievement as paradoxical: on the one hand to see the continuity between the ancient world and modern Europe—to see antiquity, the Middle Ages, and the modern age as parts of a single whole; on the other to respect the profound discontinuities among the stories that might be perceived in his materials, depending on the vantage point of the observer. Gibbon's readers have tended to see, whether with approval or disapproval, whichever of these perceptions interested them; and some readers who were aware of both have objected to Gibbon's "inconsistency."

Recent readers have begun to admire the honesty and richness of this complex response. Increasingly, as Gibbon worked through his history, he treated his subject as a set of distinct and parallel stories, interconnected both by influence and by analogous and contrasting motifs: such stories as those of church and state, East and West, Rome and "barbarians" both northern and Persian. Byzantium is the center of a narrowing circle preserving the Roman name but fewer and fewer features of the "Roman spirit"; beyond Byzantium, on the other hand, the excitement of human diversity can include embodiments of some features of Roman culture and spirit and improvements on others.

One recurrent inquiry in all these stories is about the interplay among major competitors for the power to define human groups: religion, politics, and economic life. Recent work, particularly a series of essays by J.G.A. Pocock, is illuminating Gibbon's development of perspectives on politics and economics derived from Machiavelli, Adam Smith, John Ferguson, and others.

More famous is Gibbon's interest in religion. The most controversial part of his history of religion, however, was that included in the final two chapters of his first volume, Chapters 15 and 16. The subject of Chapter 15, as Gibbon stated with ironic deference, is the "secondary" causes for the success of Christianity in the first three centuries A.D., which he lists as "inflexible . . . zeal," the promise of life after death, the appearance of miracles, "pure and austere morals," and a "union and discipline . . . which gradually formed an independent and increasing state in the heart of the Roman empire" (*Decline and Fall* 2: 3–4). Chapter 16, a review of the persecutions of the early Christians by the Roman emperors, offended not only by deprecating the numerical claims about martyrs and portraying their sufferings without much sympathy, but also by its real point, that even accepting "all that history has recorded, or devotion has feigned" about the early Christian martyrs, far better records make it abundantly clear that Christians have killed far more of each other (*Decline and Fall* 2: 148). Chapter 15 was regarded as still more offensive, and a spate of books and pamphlets attacking both chapters quickly appeared. The attackers attempted to refute Gibbon's historical statements; they disagreed with his explicit and implicit characterization of the early Christians as the sort of people gentlemen would not enjoy knowing, and they deplored his irony. Unused to the treatment of religious events in the same way as secular history, they were particularly offended because Chapter 15 is concerned with the Christians of apostolic times and immediately thereafter, who were as valued by Protestants as by Catholics. Gibbon even presumes to hint that there might be some fiction in the gospel accounts of the Crucifixion. When later volumes were published, in which Gibbon treats portions of church history that many Protestants were as willing to attack as he, and after he had triumphantly replied to the attackers of Chapters 15 and 16, no such outpouring of Christian anger occurred. As we have seen, moreover, his account of the medieval church is not entirely hostile. In his medieval history, then, Gibbon maintains and pursues his right to treat all religion as a human institution like any other.

All three institutions had to be considered, in Gibbon's view, in connection with the possible historical role of heroic individuals, in any sense of the word "heroic." Gibbon sees certain large historical results as affected by the existence and nature of particular individuals, but more often he sees individuals as heroic or ridiculous in the futility of their resistance to the "times." He is concerned from the beginning of the history about the fate of the individual, whether or not heroic, who is capable of thinking for himself or herself. At the height of the empire he sees this opportunity as threatened by cultural hegemony; in the disintegrating empire he sees twin perils, orientalization and decivilization. He sees the "orientalized" eastern empire as attempting to deny change and the nomadic tribes as unable to preserve it. Both threatening types essentially withdraw themselves from history.

Almost as soon as *Decline and Fall* was published, specialist historians were able to improve upon Gibbon's account of any one of his subjects, to challenge or enlarge any one of his perspectives. But he succeeded in creating an awareness of and an interest in even those aspects of his subject with which he was least sympathetic, whether it was the history of religious controversy, or the endurance of Byzantium, or barbaric heroics. Thomas Carlyle, unconsciously echoing Suzanne Necker, recommended that Jane Welsh read *Decline and Fall* because "there is no other tolerable history of those times and nations. . . . It is a kind of bridge that connects the antique with the modern age. And how gorgeously does it swing across the gloomy and tumultuous chasm of those barbarous centuries!" (Carlyle, 2: 180; Letter from Necker, in *Works*, 2: 246). Gibbon, perhaps because of the title of his great work, is seldom thought of as a historian of the medieval world. But as an inquirer into the significance that world had both in its own right and as a link to its past and future he remains not only stimulating but indispensable.

Selected Bibliography
For full bibliographies see Craddock (1987) and Norton.

Works

Books
Essai sur l'étude de la littérature. London: Becket and De Hondt, 1761. Translated as *An Essay on the Study of Literature.* London: Becket and De Hondt, 1764.
With Georges Deyverdun. *Mémoires littéraires de la Grande Bretagne, pour l'an 1767.* London: Becket and De Hondt, 1768.
————. *Mémoires littéraires de la Grande Bretagne, pour l'an 1768.* London: Heydinger and Elmsley, 1769.
Critical Observations on the Sixth Book of the Aeneid. London: Elmsley, 1770.
The History of the Decline and Fall of the Roman Empire. 6 vols. London: Strahan and Cadell, 1776–88. Modern edition, 7 vols. Edited by J.B. Bury. London: Methuen, 1896–1900. Rev. ed. 1909–14.
A Vindication of Some Passages in the Fifteenth and Sixteenth Chapters of the . . . Decline and Fall of the Roman Empire. London: Strahan and Cadell, 1779.
Mémoire justicatif pour servir de réponse à l'Exposé de la Cour de France. London: n.p., 1779.
Miscellaneous Works of Edward Gibbon, Esquire: With Memoirs of His Life and Writings, Composed by Himself. 2 vols. Edited by John, Lord Sheffield. London: Strahan and Cadell, and Davies, 1796. Rev. ed., 5 vols. London: Murray, 1814. Modern edition, *Memoirs of My Life.* Edited by Georges A. Bonnard. London: Nelson, 1966.
The Autobiographies of Edward Gibbon. Edited by John Murray. London: Murray, 1896.
Gibbon's Journal to January 28, 1763. Edited by D.M. Low. London: Chatto and Windus, 1929.
Le journal de Gibbon à Lausanne. Edited by Georges A. Bonnard. Lausanne: Rouge, 1945.
Miscellanea Gibboniana. Edited by G.R. de Beer, G.A. Bonnard, and L. Junod. Lausanne: Rouge, 1952.
Gibbon's Journey from Geneva to Rome. Edited by G.A. Bonnard. London: Nelson, 1961.

The English Essays of Edward Gibbon. Edited by Patricia B. Craddock. Oxford: Clarendon, 1972.

LETTERS AND PAPERS

Most of Gibbon's papers are in the British Library, Add. MSS 34880–34887. Some are in the Pierpont Morgan Library in New York, and collateral papers relating to the posthumous publication of his work are in the Beinecke Library at Yale University.

The Private Letters of Edward Gibbon. 2 vols. Edited by R.E. Prothero. London: Murray, 1896.

The Letters of Edward Gibbon. 3 vols. Edited by J.E. Norton. London: Cassell; New York: Macmillan, 1956.

Sources

Baridon, Michel. *Edward Gibbon et le mythe de Rome: histoire et ideologie au siècle des lumières.* Paris: Champion, 1977.

Bennett, J.A.W. *Essays on Gibbon.* Cambridge, Mass.: Bennett, 1980.

Bernays, Jacob. "Edward Gibbons Geschichtswerk: Ein Versuch zu einer Würdigung." In his *Gesammelte Abhandlungen,* edited by H. Usener, vol. 2, pp. 206–54. Berlin: Herz, 1885.

Bond, Harold L. *The Literary Art of Edward Gibbon.* Oxford: Clarendon, 1960.

Bowersock, G.W., John Clive, and Stephen R. Graubard, eds. *Edward Gibbon and the Decline and Fall of the Roman Empire.* Cambridge, Mass.: Harvard University Press, 1977.

Braudy, Leo B. *Narrative Form in History and Fiction: Hume, Fielding and Gibbon.* Princeton, N.J.: Princeton University Press, 1970.

Burrow, J.W. *Gibbon.* Oxford: Oxford University Press, 1977.

Carlyle, Thomas. *Early Letters.* Edited by C.E. Norton. Vol. 2, p. 180. London: Macmillan, 1886.

Carnochan, W.B. *Gibbon's Solitude: The Inward World of the Historian.* Stanford, Calif.: Stanford University Press, 1987.

Charrière de Sévery, M. et Mme. William de. *La vie de société dans le Pays de Vaud à la fin du dix-huitième siècle.* 2 vols. Lausanne: Bridel; Paris: Fischbacher, 1911–12.

Craddock, Patricia B. *Young Edward Gibbon: Gentleman of Letters.* Baltimore, Md.: Johns Hopkins University Press, 1982.

———. *Edward Gibbon: A Reference Guide.* Boston: Hall, 1987.

———. *Edward Gibbon, Luminous Historian, 1772–1794.* Baltimore, Md.: Johns Hopkins University Press, 1989.

Ducrey, Pierre, ed. *Gibbon et Rome à la lumière de l'historiographie moderne: 10 exposés suivis de discussions.* Geneva: Droz, 1977.

Falco, Giorgio. *La polemica sul medio evo.* Turin: Fedetto, 1933.

Geanakoplos, Deno J. "Edward Gibbon and Byzantine Ecclesiastical History." *Church History* 35 (1966): 170–85.

Giarrizzo, Giuseppe. *Edward Gibbon e la cultura europa del Settecento.* Naples: Istituto Italiano per gli Studi Storici; Turin: Einaudi, 1954.

Gossman, Lionel. *The Empire Unpossess'd: An Essay on Gibbon's Decline and Fall.* Cambridge: Cambridge University Press, 1981.

Grewal, J.S. "Edward Gibbon on Islamic Civilization." In his *Medieval India: History and Historians,* pp. 12–23. Amritsar: Guru Nanak University, 1975.

Jordan, David P. *Gibbon and His Roman Empire.* Urbana: University of Illinois Press, 1971.

Keynes, Geoffrey. *The Library of Edward Gibbon: A Catalogue.* London: Cape, 1940.

Levine, Joseph M. "Edward Gibbon and the Quarrel Between the Ancients and the Moderns." *Eighteenth Century: Theory and Interpretation* 27 (1985): 47–62.

Low, D.M. *Edward Gibbon, 1737–1794*. London: Chatto and Windus, 1937.

Lyon, Bryce. *The Origins of the Middle Ages: Pirenne's Challenge to Gibbon*. New York: Norton, 1972.

McCloy, Shelby T. *Gibbon's Antagonism to Christianity*. Chapel Hill: University of North Carolina Press; London: Williams and Norgate, 1933.

Mazzarino, Santo. *Stilicone*. Rome: Signorelli, 1942.

Momigliano, Arnaldo. "Gibbon's Contributions to Historical Method." In his *Studies in Historiography*, pp. 40–55. London: Weidenfeld and Nicolson, 1966.

Morison, J. Cotter. *Gibbon*. London: Macmillan, 1878.

Norton, J.E. *A Bibliography of the Works of Edward Gibbon*. London: Oxford University Press, 1940.

Oliver, E.J. *Gibbon and Rome*. London: Sheed and Ward, 1958.

Pocock, J.G.A. "Gibbon's *Decline and Fall* and the World View of the Late Enlightenment." *Eighteenth-Century Studies* 10 (1977): 287–303.

———. "Gibbon and the Shepherds: The Stages of Society in the *Decline and Fall*." *History of European Ideas* 2 (1981): 193–202.

———. "Superstition and Enthusiasm in Gibbon's History of Religion." *Eighteenth-Century Life*, n.s., 8 (1982): 83–94.

Rehm, Walther. "Gibbon" and "Von Gibbon zu Nietzsche." In his *Der Untergang Roms im abendländischen Denken: Ein Beitrag zur Geschichtsschreibung und zum Dekadenzproblem*, pp. 120–41. Leipzig: Dieterich, 1930.

Robertson, J.M. *Gibbon*. London: Watts, 1925.

Roussev, R. "Edward Gibbon and the History of Bulgaria." *Annuaire de l'Université de Sofia Faculté Historico-philologique* 29 (1933): 1–7.

Trevor-Roper, H.R. "The Historical Philosophy of the Enlightenment." *Studies on Voltaire and the Eighteenth Century* 27 (1963): 1667–87.

———. "Historiography 1: The Other Gibbon." *American Scholar* 46 (1976): 94–103.

White, Lynn, Jr., ed. *The Transformation of the Roman World: Gibbon's Problem After Two Centuries*. Berkeley: University of California Press, 1966.

Womersley, David. *The Transformation of The Decline and Fall of the Roman Empire*. Cambridge: Cambridge University Press, 1988.

Young, G.M. *Gibbon*. London: Davies, 1932.

Georg Waitz

(1813–1886)

Robert L. Benson
and Loren J. Weber

Georg Waitz, a leading figure in the study of constitutional history and nineteenth-century Germany's preeminent teacher of medieval historians, was born on 9 October 1813 to a German merchant family at Flensburg in Schleswig-Holstein. He became interested in historical studies after reading Barthold Georg Niebuhr's *Römische Geschichte*, which inspired his lifelong fascination with constitutional history and convinced him that legal knowledge should form the basis of the historian's training (as he later formulated in his dissertation: "nemo historicus nisi iuris cognitione imbutus"). Entering the University of Kiel as a student of law in 1832, Waitz in the following year sought a broader education in Berlin, where he studied under the jurists Friedrich Karl von Savigny and Karl Gustav Homeyer, the philologist Karl Lachmann, and the historian Leopold von Ranke. In many respects the founder of modern "critical" historical scholarship, Ranke soon became the focal point of the young scholar's education and persuaded Waitz to devote himself fully to historical studies, while at the same time inculcating in his protégé the Rankean method: reliance on original records and archival documents rather than literary sources; critical examination of documents and sources to verify their authenticity and to identify authorial bias; and the writing of history with the greatest possible moral neutrality.

Already in 1835 Waitz demonstrated his promise as a historian, winning first prize in a contest sponsored by the university for an essay on King Henry I the Fowler. After receiving his doctorate the following year, he moved to Hanover to assist Georg Heinrich Pertz at the Monumenta Germaniae Historica (MGH), the great national undertaking dedicated to the publication of the literary and diplomatic sources of German history from the Middle Ages. Waitz's activities during his six years at the MGH included the preparation of critical editions of Latin authors from the Frankish and Saxon periods as well as travels to archives throughout Germany and Europe in search of new manuscripts, sources, and documents. On one such trip in August 1837 he formed enduring friendships with three professors at Göttingen, the brothers Jacob and Wilhelm Grimm (famed for their dictionary and anthology of fairy tales) and the historian Friedrich Christoph Dahlmann. Soon thereafter Dahlmann and the Grimms together with four other professors, collectively referred to as the "Göttingen Seven," framed a protest against the revocation of the Hanoverian constitution by King Ernst Augustus; their subsequent dismissal from the university and banishment from Hanover aroused popular sympathy and placed them at the forefront of the growing liberal movement in Germany. This period's events awakened Waitz's political consciousness, and he remained thereafter an active supporter of liberal constitutionalism.

Waitz's work at the MGH won him such renown in the academic community that in 1842, at the age of twenty-eight and without either the normally necessary second thesis (*Habilitation*) or teaching experience, he received a professorship at the University of Kiel in Holstein, then under Danish sovereignty. The university considered Waitz an excellent acquisition not only as a student of Ranke but as a "son of the fatherland," a native of Schleswig-Holstein unlikely to harbor Prussian sympathies. The university's estimation of Waitz's unquestioning loyalty soon proved mistaken: in 1846, protesting what he saw as Copenhagen's growing encroachments on the duchies' rights, Waitz refused a call to serve at the National Assembly and contributed along with Johann Gustav Droysen, Kiel's other professor of history and an ardent Prussian, to a written protest against Denmark's actions. In 1847, when he received a call to a chair of history at Göttingen, Waitz, standing unfavorably with the Danish government, was inclined to accept.

Political events, however, delayed Waitz's assumption of his new chair. Early in 1848 Schleswig-Holstein rebelled against Denmark, whereupon Waitz offered his services to the provisional government of the duchies in Rendsburg and traveled to Berlin as their authorized agent. While in Berlin he learned that he had been elected as delegate from Kiel to the first National Assembly in Frankfurt. Charged with drafting a constitution for a united German state, the assembly convened in May of 1848; Waitz, with Dahlmann, Droysen, and Jacob Grimm, belonged to the right-center Casino (liberal-constitutionalist) party, favoring a union of the German states in a constitutional monarchy ruled by a Prussian emperor. Both in the greater assembly and as a key member of the constitutional committee Waitz devoted his abundant energies to the Schleswig-Holstein question and the drafting of a pan-German constitution. The Prussian king Frederick William IV, however, refused to accept either the proposed constitution or the imperial crown, and Waitz left the assembly disillusioned by its failure. Confessing sadly to having learned more in this short period than in many years of scholarly labor, Waitz like many other "parliament professors" retreated from the political arena to the world of scholarship, hoping to influence events through teaching and writing.

In the autumn of 1849 Waitz assumed his chair at the University of Göttingen, popularly known as the Georgia Augusta after its founder, where over the next quarter-century he created Germany's preeminent school of medieval historical studies. It was to this school, affectionately nicknamed the Georgia Waitzia by its students, that young men from all over Europe came to receive (according to his own student Gabriel Monod, founder of the *Revue historique*) their "scholarly baptism" from Waitz, who "exercised a sort of scholarly kingship" (Monod, 386). During his twenty-six years in Göttingen Waitz trained more scholars—primarily medievalists, but also historians in other fields and even jurists—than any other Ranke pupil, indeed more than Ranke himself. In 1896, ten years after Waitz's death, Ferdinand Frensdorff estimated that some thirty of Waitz's students still held professorships at German universities, while yet others had gone on to work for the MGH and the Historical Commission at Munich (which counted Waitz among its founders), as well as for archives, libraries, and research institutions. The majority of Germany's leading medieval historians active before 1914 had received all or part of their education at Göttingen.

Waitz was an uninspired speaker: according to one report he paid more attention to his copious notes than to his hearers. Yet his lectures, because of their thoroughness and lucidity, soon became popular and had an extraordinary effect on their hearers. Even the passionate and uncompromising Prussian historian Heinrich von Treitschke wrote with enthusiasm of hearing Waitz's "magnificent lectures" (*herrliche Vorträge*; Selle, 296). Historical training at Göttingen focused, however, less on the lectures than on Waitz's seminars or, as he preferred to call these meetings, "historical exercises" (*historische Übungen*). These took place in the study of Waitz's home on Friday evenings; while he originally hoped to limit the number of participants to ten, as demand increased he soon began to hold separate sessions for younger and for advanced students. The group openly debated the interpretation of texts or discussed each other's work. Through his seminars Waitz exercised a highly personal tutelage; it is said that when in 1874 some 155 of his former students (just under half of all his pupils) presented him with a group picture, he was still able to name each of them. In turn he received the intense respect and devotion of his protégés, not least because of his interest in their personal development. Monod attested that Waitz wanted to cultivate each student's character as well as intellect, "to form men as well as savants." He asserted on more than one occasion that "my best works are my students" (Monod, 383–84).

In 1875 Waitz moved to Berlin to succeed Georg Heinrich Pertz as president of the MGH. As principal editor and president since 1824 Pertz had guided the institute and its editorial tasks masterfully for almost a half-century, but during his final years his judgment grew erratic and he alienated some of his ablest helpers, notably the brilliant Philipp Jaffé, who had probably been the MGH's most gifted *Mitarbeiter* (scholarly staff member) in the 1850s and early 60s. In 1873, under pressure to resign, the secretive and increasingly autocratic Pertz unexpectedly laid down his office, leaving the MGH and its projects in chaos. Superior to Pertz not only in scholarship but in his ability to deal with people, Waitz soon succeeded in attracting leading scholars to the newly reorganized institute, among them Theodor Mommsen, Ludwig Traube, Theodor Sickel, and Wilhelm Giesebrecht; he also enlisted the help of many of his own best pupils. Characteristically Waitz contributed much of the labor himself: in addition to assuming responsibility for the Scriptores series of editions, he once again, as some forty years before, undertook travels to archives throughout Europe and revitalized the staid MGH journal *Archiv*, which under the title *Neues Archiv* (1876–1935) soon became one of Europe's leading scholarly journals and continues today as *Deutsches Archiv* (1937–). During the ten years of Waitz's able leadership the MGH enjoyed an active and productive period—indeed, in the opinion of the institute's official historian, Harry Bresslau: its golden age.

Waitz's seemingly boundless energy began to fail in the winter of 1886, and after losing consciousness while chairing the annual meeting of the MGH's governing board, he died in the night of 24 May, several weeks before the fiftieth anniversary of receiving his doctorate. Ranke had preceded him by a single day; having heard that Waitz was stricken, Ranke's last words inquired after the condition of his staunch friend and student: "Was macht denn der treue Waitz?"

Waitz was married twice, on his twenty-ninth birthday to Clara Schelling, second daughter of the philosopher Friedrich von Schelling, and, following Clara's death during childbirth in 1857, to the youngest daughter of General Julius von Hartmann in 1861. His fourth son, Eberhard, published an intimate biography of Waitz in 1913 in celebration of the hundredth anniversary of his father's birth.

During his long career Waitz produced an oeuvre of astonishing size and scope—the bibliography of his works assembled by his student and son-in-law Ernst Steindorff contains 743 items—encompassing a wide range of subjects and genres, including multivolume histories, a major bibliography of the sources and secondary literature for German history, more than 175 editions and a hundred textual studies, and a vast number of shorter political writings, journal articles, and book reviews. His greatest and most extensive work was the eight-volume *Deutsche Verfassungsgeschichte* or *German Constitutional History*.

It is significant that Waitz dedicated such a generous share of his energies to the study of constitutional history, which represented for him not merely a set of historical or scholarly concerns but a field of highly relevant intellectual inquiry whose conclusions had, at least in the minds of Waitz and his colleagues, weighty ramifications for contemporary political issues. By 1843, soon after assuming his chair at Kiel, Waitz had become convinced that the standard work on German constitutional law, Karl Friedrich Eichhorn's *Deutsche Staats- und Rechtsgeschichte*, relied on both inadequate and faulty use of the source material. Waitz decided to embark on a new account of German political, legal, and constitutional life based on critical and scrupulous examination of the relevant sources, an endeavor he was well prepared to undertake both as a student of Ranke and through his extensive work with primary documents at the MGH. The first two volumes of the *Constitutional History* (published 1844–47), treating the period from earliest antiquity to the end of the Merovingian era, exhibited Waitz's astonishing command of the sources. Waitz continued to work on the *Constitutional History* throughout his life: the third and fourth volumes, on the Carolingian era, appeared in 1860–61, and Volumes 5–8 (published 1874–78) brought the survey up to the middle of the twelfth century. In the years 1865–85 Waitz issued revised editions of the first four volumes, and various students reworked the last four after his death.

The *Constitutional History* exemplifies Waitz's conscious intention to write "scientific" history, free from subjective interpretation or speculation beyond the strict testimony of the sources; accuracy and precision were of greater importance to Waitz than the construction of an aesthetically pleasing narrative. The resultant work is sober and supported by massive documentation. Waitz's critics, and indeed some of his admirers, have epitomized the work as a "mass of citations" (so Karl Wilhelm Nitzsch, quoted by Grundmann, 315) or as less a history than a collection of essays that leaves readers to discover for themselves the larger connections and lines of development. Waitz has been criticized for timid adherence to the testimony of the sources and fear of drawing difficult or uncertain conclusions. Yet precisely these characteristics have afforded his work its lasting value. Whereas the politically programmatic histories of Waitz's nineteenth-century critics soon lost their worth as historical works, the *Constitutional History* established its subject as an independent area of study and provided the paradigm for all research in the field until the early twentieth century. Even today Waitz's *Constitutional History*, though superseded in many areas, remains because of its exhaustive presentation and precise critical analysis one of the discipline's standard works and a useful starting point for investigation into manifold aspects of German constitutional history.

Despite Waitz's predilection for scientific history he did not subscribe to the idealistic positivist philosophy of history, popular in his time, according to which historical phenomena were subject to invariable natural laws and reducible to rigid, or even predictive, models; nor did he believe that history could be written scientifically in the sense of the word as used in the natural sciences. Waitz was aware that, for better or worse, "every age measures the past according to its own standards," a trait that "exists necessarily in human nature" ("Jugendbriefe," 247). And in fact Waitz's political views directly influenced the premises of his *Constitutional History*. His portrayal of the early German constitution bears the imprint of the nineteenth-century liberal-constitutionalist conception, suggesting that in the earliest period of German history monarchy and public freedom, far from being antithetical institutions, worked together within a constitutional framework. Waitz's national-political orientation is also evident in his emphasis on the exclusively Germanic character of Frankish kingship, which according to Waitz already found all of its essential elements among the earliest German tribes, before Roman influence was possible. Ironically it was Heinrich von Sybel, a nationalistic Prussian historian, who challenged this latter position, maintaining in opposition to Waitz that monarchy was able to develop among the early Germans only after contact with Roman institutions. Although in the eyes of contemporaries Waitz prevailed over Sybel in the ensuing debate, later historiography has all but overturned his position. Waitz characteristically asserted that the scholarly controversy had served to deepen his friendship with Sybel.

Waitz's other major historical works, while generally overshadowed by the *Constitutional History*, deserve mention. His history of Henry I, a chronological account of the German king's reign based on exhaustive collection and comparison of documentary sources, appeared in 1837 as the first volume of the Jahrbücher des deutschen Reichs, a series edited by Ranke covering the period of the Saxon rulers. Waitz revised this work twice, in 1863 and 1885, to appear in the Jahrbücher der deutschen Geschichte, a new series inspired by that of Ranke, each volume of which gives a detailed chronological précis of a reign. Like most volumes of the Jahrbücher, Waitz's study of Henry I remains an indispensable tool of historical research. In the decade preceding the annexation of Schleswig-Holstein by Otto von Bismarck (1866), Waitz turned his scholarship to works treating the history of his native Schleswig-Holstein. The first two volumes of the *Schleswig-Holsteins Geschichte in drei Büchern*, reaching to 1660, were published in 1851–54; the planned third volume for the ensuing period never appeared, as Waitz found no opportunity to inspect the necessary archival material. Tracing the struggles of Schleswig-Holstein for independence and autonomy, the *History* aimed to contribute to the debate on the duchies' future; an abridged version, published in 1864, was widely read in Waitz's homeland. His monumental three-volume *Lübeck unter Jürgen Wullenwever und die europäische Politik* (1855–56), centering on Lübeck's revolutionary sixteenth-century mayor, still offers the best account of the period.

Waitz's great bibliographical work developed out of his lengthy teaching activity at Göttingen and his desire to provide his students with a comprehensive bibliography of the sources and scholarly literature on German history. In 1869, six years after the death of Dahlmann, Waitz published a revision of his friend's *Quellenkunde der deutschen Geschichte*, a survey of the principal sources for German history that Dahlmann had originally published in 1830 and enlarged in 1838 as an aid to his own students in Göttingen. The third edition of the work, prepared by Waitz, contained some twenty-eight hundred titles (compared with the 1838 edition's seven hundred). In 1875 Waitz introduced a further revision, which expanded to 3,215 entries, and thoroughly revised the organization of the entire bibliography in response to the growing quantity of specialized research. Yet a further edition by Waitz, comprising almost thirty-eight hundred titles and 341 pages, appeared in 1883.

The best measure of the Dahlmann-Waitz's importance is the diligence with which later scholars have labored to keep it current. A ninth edition was published in 1931, containing 16,337 titles. A tenth edition under ongoing preparation by the Max Planck Institute for History in Göttingen already comprises seven large volumes. The work is divided into two sections, the first treating general works and the second arranged chronologically; each is meticulously systematized according to subject to facilitate reference despite the bibliography's dimensions. The latest edition of Dahlmann-Waitz (or "DW," as it is referred to in the scholarly literature) may well be the world's most complete national bibliography and has become an indispensable aid to serious study in any area of German history.

Almost a fourth of Waitz's publications were editions for the MGH, ranging from one to several hundred pages; these have provided much of the source material on which medieval scholarship relies. Particularly significant from his early work under Pertz for the Scriptores series (1839–52) are editions of Widukind of Corvey's *Saxon History*; the eleventh-century universal chronicle of Marianus Scotus; the *Annalista Saxo*, a twelfth-century chronicle now ascribed to Arnold of Berge and Nienburg; and the history of the bishopric and city of Trier (*Gesta Treverorum*). The last three of these editions by Waitz remain the best available texts, and the first, now in its fifth edition from the MGH (1935), still has as its basis Waitz's original text. Due to his political preoccupations and teaching duties Waitz's editing activity for the MGH largely ceased from the early 1850s until 1872, when he published his imposing and still authoritative edition of Godfrey of Viterbo's writings, on which he had worked intermittently for over thirty years. After assuming direction of the MGH in 1875, Waitz once again devoted his energies to the Scriptores volumes, producing editions at an unprecedented pace. He also contributed significantly to the volume *Scriptores Rerum Langobardicarum et Italicarum* (1878), most notably his text of Paul the Deacon's *Historia Langobardorum*; and of the fifteen volumes in the series Scriptores Rerum Germanicarum published during Waitz's presidency at the MGH he himself prepared ten, revising the printed texts and bringing the commentaries up to current standard. Particularly worthy of mention among these latter volumes is Waitz's text of the *Gesta Friderici* by Otto and Rahewin of Freising, which in its revision from 1912 by Bernhard von Simson remains the authoritative edition of this crucial work. Waitz's countless smaller editions of monastic annals, chronicles, *gesta*, and catalogs, though individually less imposing, have greatly benefited medieval historians, especially those concerned with local history. In the fifty years between 1837 and his death Waitz contributed numerous textual studies and still useful *Reiseberichte* (reports on manuscripts and charters contained in collections throughout Europe) to the MGH journals *Archiv* and *Neues Archiv*.

Waitz's editing work at the MGH continued and refined that of Pertz, who had established the institute's fundamental requirements for editions, including the need to base the edited text on the work's entire manuscript transmission instead of a single manuscript (or *codex optimus*). Waitz helped to standardize the presentation of text and apparatus at the MGH, and his extensive searches through Europe's libraries and archives for previously unknown manuscripts ensured a firm textual basis for his editions. As a result most of Waitz's edited work, now well over a hundred years old, has not been superseded. Nevertheless, his editions do not always meet today's more demanding standards: commentaries on the text and its sources are meager by modern requirements; easily accessible manuscripts were sometimes given more weight than the quality of their text justifies; Lachmannian principles were applied without respect to other aspects of a text's manuscript transmission or form in the Middle Ages; and some of the major chronicles (e.g., the universal chronicle of Marianus Scotus and Godfrey of Viterbo's world history, the *Pantheon*) are only fragmentarily edited, a result of the MGH's earlier determination to publish only those portions of a text that were considered historically significant. That many of Waitz's editions are in need of reediting does not detract from his achievement: the quantity and quality of Waitz's edited work inspire awe in any scholar with experience editing medieval texts, especially as Waitz lacked the benefits of today's technology of photographic reproduction and comprehensive catalogs of manuscript collections.

A concluding look at some of Waitz's less extensive works will attest to the breadth of his interests and abilities. His meticulous source-critical analysis of the Chronicle of Corvey, composed jointly with Siegfried Hirsch, established the text to be a modern forgery; the essay received first prize in a competition judged by the Royal Society of the Sciences in Göttingen and appeared in 1839 as the third volume of Ranke's Jahrbücher. In 1843 Waitz inaugurated his career as political writer with the tract *Über die Gründung des deutschen Reiches*, written to commemorate the thousandth anniversary of the Treaty of Verdun. While Waitz's principal argument, that the treaty had called the German *Reich* into existence, enjoys little support among German scholars, periodically the unique significance of the year 843 is restated, most notably on the hundredth anniversary of Waitz's work by Theodor Mayer, president of the Reichsinstitut für ältere deutsche Geschichtskunde, the National Socialist incarnation of the MGH. Waitz's articles on the development of German historiography (1844–45), tracing the evolution of historical writing in Germany from its beginnings under Roman influence to the end of the Middle Ages, cast their subject in a new light. Connections established through his marriage to Clara Schelling provided Waitz with a special opportunity to collect the letters of his father-in-law's first wife, Caroline Schlegel Schelling, daughter of the Göttingen professor J.D. Michaelis and center of the early Romantic movement in Jena. Waitz's editions of the correspondence (1871–82) prompted Carl Neumann, a former participant in Waitz's seminar, to censure Waitz for publishing the letters of Caroline, the very embodiment of Romanticism, with paltry commentary as if they were "an edition of the letters of Wibald of Stavelot or a collection of Merovingian charters" (Neumann, 217).

Neumann's reproach epitomizes much of the criticism Waitz's scholarship has evoked, more often than not from politically oriented historians like those of the Prussian school, who viewed history above all as a propaganda weapon and a means to mobilize public opinion; such writers had little sympathy for Waitz's dispassionate historical accounts and readiness to concede that the evidence in any given case might admit of more than one possible conclusion. For his part Waitz struggled against the politicization of history, perhaps nowhere more forcefully than in his judgment on the controversy between the Catholic Julius Ficker and the Protestant Heinrich von Sybel. While the debate between Ficker and Sybel concerned primarily the medieval German emperors' involvements in Italian political affairs, it had ramifications for an urgent political question current at that time: since Sybel believed that the Italian policies of certain medieval emperors had deflected them from the task of state building in Germany, he opposed the incorporation of Austria into a pan-German nation. Convinced that both historians had allowed their political preoccupations to compromise their objectivity in this matter, Waitz expressed his opinion "that these questions have nothing to do with the estimation of the old empire, and that it should be endeavored in every way and by everyone that our historical scholarship should not be misled by the temper and wishes of the present" (Waitz [1896], 539).

Unlike those of his master Ranke none of Waitz's works was popular: his critical editions and massively documented histories, particularly in light of his lack of narrative flair, do not attract the lay reader or amateur historian. Yet his impact on historical scholarship, most especially but not limited to the study of medieval history, was profound and lasting. His relentless pursuit of ever greater critical acumen and knowledge of the sources, both in himself and his students, helped lay the foundations for the increasing professionalization and specialization of historical scholarship; his editions ensured that the medieval scholar was equipped with easily accessible and accurate texts; and his historical works, especially the *Constitutional History*, furnished the paradigm for further research, one that continued to guide the discipline long after his death. To these contributions should be added his extraordinary success as a teacher of medievalists and his revitalization of the Monumenta Germaniae Historica. Thus, Sybel, often Waitz's opponent in scholarly matters, could claim in his eulogy on his late colleague that during his long lifetime Waitz had been in more than one way the focus of historical research in Germany.

Works

BOOKS AND ARTICLES

Commentationis de chronici Urspergensis prima parte, eius auctore, fontibus et apud posteros auctoritate specimen. Berlin: Nietack, 1836.

Jahrbücher des deutschen Reichs unter der Herrschaft König Heinrichs I. Berlin: Duncker and Humblot, 1837. 2nd ed. Berlin, 1863. 3rd ed., Leipzig, 1885. 4th ed. as *Jahrbücher des deutschen Reichs unter König Heinrich I*, Darmstadt: Wissenschaftliche Buchgesellschaft, 1963.

With Siegfried Hirsch. *Kritische Prüfung der Echtheit und des historischen Werthes des Chronicon Corbejense*. Berlin: Duncker and Humblot, 1839.

Über die Gründung des deutschen Reichs durch den Vertrag zu Verdun. Kiel: Mohr, 1843.

Deutsche Verfassungsgeschichte. 8 vols. Vols. 1–2, Kiel: Schwers. Vols. 3–8, Homann, 1844–78.

"Über die Entwicklung der deutschen Historiographie im Mittelalter." *Zeitschrift für Geschichtswissenschaft* 2 (1844): 39–58, 97–114; 4 (1845): 97–112.

With Johann Gustav Droysen et al. *Staats- und Erbrecht des Herzogthums Schleswig: Kritik des Commissionsbedenkens über die Successions-Verhältnisse des Herzogthums Schleswig*. Hamburg: Perthes-Besser and Mauke, 1846.

Schleswig-Holsteins Geschichte in drei Büchern. 2 vols. Göttingen: Dieterich, 1851–54.

Lübeck unter Jürgen Wullenwever und die europäische Politik. 3 vols. Berlin: Weidmann, 1855–56.

Kurze schleswigholsteinische Landesgeschichte. Kiel: Homann, 1864.

Ed. *Quellenkunde der deutschen Geschichte*, by Friedrich Christoph Dahlmann. 3rd ed. Göttingen: Dieterich, 1869; 4th ed., 1875; 5th ed., 1883; 9th ed., edited by Hermann Haering, Leipzig: Koehler, 1931; 10th ed., edited by Hermann Heimpel and Herbert Geuss, Stuttgart: Hiersemann, 1965–.

Caroline: Briefe an ihre Geschwister . . . . 2 vols. Leipzig: Hirzel, 1871.

Caroline und ihre Freunde: Mittheilungen aus Briefen. Leipzig: Hirzel, 1882.

Abhandlungen zur deutschen Verfassungs- und Rechtsgeschichte. Edited by Karl Zeumer. Göttingen: Dieterich, 1896.

EDITIONS FOR THE MONUMENTA GERMANIAE HISTORICA

Widukindi Res Gestae Saxonicae. Scriptores 3 (1839): 408–67.

Mariani Scotti Chronicon. Scriptores 5 (1844): 481–562.

Ekkehardi Uraugiensis Chronica. Scriptores 6 (1844): 1–267.

Annalista Saxo. Scriptores 6 (1844): 542–777.

Gesta Treverorum. Scriptores 8 (1848): 111–260.

Gotifredi Viterbiensis Opera. Scriptores 22 (1872): 1–338.

With Ludwig Bethmann. *Pauli Historia Langobardorum: Scriptores Rerum Langobardicarum et Italicarum Saec. VI–IX*. (1878): 12–187.

Ottonis et Rahewini Gesta Friderici I. Imperatoris. Scriptores Rerum Germanicarum in Usum Scholarum. 2nd ed. Hanover: Hahn, 1884; 3rd ed., edited by Bernhard von Simson, Hanover: Hahn, 1912.

LETTERS AND PAPERS

The greater part of Waitz's *Nachlass* (papers, correspondence, notes, etc. from the years 1827–86) was brought to Russia in 1945 and returned in 1959 to the Deutsches Zentralarchiv in Potsdam. The Monumenta Germaniae Historica in Munich also possesses miscellaneous documents and letters. Minor collections of Waitz's correspondence and notes are found in the Staatsbibliothek Preussischer Kulturbesitz, Berlin; the Seminar für Mittlere und Neuere Geschichte of the University of Göttingen; and the Landesbibliothek, Kiel.

"Waitz und Pertz." Edited by Ernst Dümmler. *Neues Archiv der Gesellschaft für ältere deutsche Geschichtskunde* 19 (1894): 269–82. [Correspondence between Waitz, Pertz, and Ranke in 1836.]

"Aus Georg Waitz' Lehrjahren." Edited by Mario Krammer. *Neues Archiv der Gesellschaft für ältere deutsche Geschichtskunde* 38 (1913): 701–07.

"Jugendbriefe von Georg Waitz aus der Frühzeit Rankes und der Monumenta Germaniae." Edited by Edmund Ernst Stengel. *Historische Zeitschrift* 121 (1920): 234–55.

"Georg Waitz und Theodor Sickel: Ein Briefwechsel aus der Blütezeit der deutschen Geschichtsforschung." Edited by Wilhelm Erben. *Nachrichten der Gesellschaft der Wissenschaften zu Göttingen* (1926): 51–196.

Sources

Böckenförde, Ernst-Wolfgang. *Die deutsche verfassungsgeschichtliche Forschung im 19. Jahrhundert: Zeitgebundene Fragestellungen und Leitbilder*, pp. 99–134. Berlin: Duncker and Humblot, 1961.

Boockmann, Hartmut. "Geschichtsunterricht und Geschichtsstudium in Göttingen." In *Geschichtswissenschaft in Göttingen*, edited by Hartmut Boockmann and Hermann Wellenreuther, pp. 161–85. Göttingen: Vandenhoeck and Ruprecht, 1987.

Bresslau, Harry. *Geschichte der Monumenta Germaniae Historica*. Hanover: Hahn, 1921, pp. 522–618 and passim. [Appeared simultaneously as *Neues Archiv der Gesellschaft für ältere deutsche Geschichtskunde* 42 (1921)].

Frensdorff, Ferdinand. Article on Georg Waitz. *Allgemeine deutsche Biographie* 40 (1896): 602–29.

Fueter, Eduard. *Geschichte der neueren Historiographie*. 3rd ed. Munich: Oldenbourg, 1936, pp. 487–89.

Giesebrecht, Wilhelm von. "Worte der Erinnerung an König Ludwig II., Leopold von Ranke und Georg Waitz." *Historische Zeitschrift* 58 (1887): 181–85.

Gooch, George Peabody. *History and Historians in the Nineteenth Century*. 2nd ed. London: Longmans, Green, 1952, pp. 110–14.

Graus, František. "Verfassungsgeschichte des Mittelalters." *Historische Zeitschrift* 243 (1986): 529–89.

Grundmann, Herbert. "Gedenken an Georg Waitz: 1813–1886." *Forschungen und Fortschritte* 37 (1963): 314–17.

Hagenah, Hermann. "Georg Waitz als Politiker." *Veröffentlichungen der schleswig-holsteinischen Universitätsgesellschaft* 31 (1930): 134–217.

Jordan, Karl. "Georg Waitz als Professor in Kiel." In *Festschrift Percy Ernst Schramm zu seinem 70. Geburtstag von Schülern und Freunden zugeeignet*, edited by Peter Classen and Peter Scheibert, vol. 2, pp. 90–104. Wiesbaden: Steiner, 1964.

Knowles, Dom David. "The Monumenta Germaniae Historica." In his *Great Historical Enterprises*, pp. 63–97. London: Nelson, 1963.

Monod, Gabriel. "Georges Waitz." *Revue historique* 31 (1886): 382–90.

Neumann, Carl. *Jacob Burckhardt*. Munich: Bruckmann, 1927, pp. 215–18.

Selle, Götz von. *Die Georg-August-Universität zu Göttingen: 1737–1937*. Göttingen: Vandenhoeck and Ruprecht, 1937: 295–97.

Srbik, Heinrich von. *Geist und Geschichte vom deutschen Humanismus bis zur Gegenwart*, vol. 1, pp. 297–99 et passim. Munich: Bruckmann, 1950.

Steindorff, Ernst. *Bibliographische Übersicht über Georg Waitz' Werke, Abhandlungen, Ausgaben, kleine kritische und publicistische Arbeiten*. Göttingen: Dieterich, 1886.

Sybel, Heinrich von. "Georg Waitz." *Historische Zeitschrift* 56 (1886): 482–87.

Thompson, James Westfall, with Bernard J. Holm. *A History of Historical Writing.* 2 vols. Vol. 2, pp. 198–202. New York: Macmillan, 1942.

Waitz, Eberhard. *Georg Waitz: Ein Lebens- und Charakterbild zu seinem hundertjährigen Geburtstag.* Berlin: Weidmann, 1913.

Wattenbach, Wilhelm. "Gedächtnisrede auf Georg Waitz." *Abhandlungen der königlichen Akademie der Wissenschaften zu Berlin* (1886): 2–12.

Wriedt, Sigrid. *Die Entwicklung der Geschichtswissenschaft an der Christiana Albertina im Zeitalter des dänischen Gesamtstaates (1773–1852).* Neumünster: Wachholtz, 1973, pp. 156–77.

WILLIAM STUBBS

(1825–1901)

James Campbell

William Stubbs, after Frederic William Maitland the greatest English historian of his day and a key figure in the transformation of the role of history in English intellectual life, was born on 21 June 1825. The son of a Yorkshire solicitor, he was well educated at Ripon Grammar School, but his family circumstances became such that he could gain a university education at Christ Church, Oxford, only as a servitor, an undergraduate admitted on special, and humble, terms because of poverty. After graduating in 1848 with a first-class degree in classics, Stubbs entered the church and from 1850 until 1866 was vicar of Navestock in Essex. There he began to earn the reputation as a student of medieval history that won him in 1866 the Regius Professorship of Modern History at Oxford. During his tenure he published his greatest work, *The Constitutional History of England in Its Origins and Development*. He did little more historical work after becoming bishop of Chester in 1884; in 1888 he was translated to the see of Oxford.

During Stubbs's formative years history was a matter of deep interest to the intellectual and reading public. The most popular historian of the day was Thomas Babington Macaulay (1800–1859), and it was not for nothing that Macaulay was able complacently to observe that the demand for his *History of England* fluctuated with the demand for coal, that is to say that his work had become a commodity generally consumed. Macaulay's *History* is significant in three ways to the work and career of Stubbs. First, it presents not only a brilliantly told story but also a powerful doctrine, profoundly teleological, patriotic, and, contrary to superficial appearances, subtle: a version of the Whig myth (but it was more than a myth) of English history so developed that it had almost ceased to be Whig. Second, Macaulay laid the foundations of his epic in the medieval past. In so doing he rested largely on the work of Henry Hallam (1777–1859), the best synoptic medievalist of his day. But the study of medieval history in England was in a questionable condition at the time he wrote, because the detailed study and editing of medieval texts did not flourish as they had a century or more before. Third, Macaulay was not in a modern sense a professional historian; there could hardly be such in England, for medieval and modern history were not studied at any university. Stubbs in one way continued the work of Macaulay, in that his *Constitutional History* was the last and greatest of the works whose guiding theme was the history of liberty in England, treated with a sense of providential destiny. Stubbs was not alone, but he was preeminent in recreating English medieval scholarship on a basis of deep textual learning. Although Stubbs no more than Macaulay had been taught history as a student, he was more important than anyone else in revolutionizing the role of history in university education and in the creation of a new occupation, that of professional historian.

Stubbs's first contributions were as a textual scholar. His opportunity came through the institution of the Rolls Series in 1857, a remarkable instance of a Victorian government's patronage of learning. His first edition was that of *Chronicles and Memorials of the Reign of Richard I* (2 vols., 1864–65). Nineteen volumes later his contribution concluded with his edition of William of Malmesbury's *De Gestis Regum Anglorum* (1887–89). Little that he edited has been reedited. He put the study of twelfth-century England and of the late Anglo-Saxon church on a sure footing; all his successors are irretrievably in his debt not only for his establishment of texts but for his introductions to them, the first modern accounts of English medieval history.

Even more remarkable was his *Constitutional History*. It defies easy summary. The guiding thread is Stubbs's conviction that the roots of English liberty lay in early Germany, as it was described by Tacitus. As he saw it, the "primeval polity of the common fatherland" (Stubbs [1874], 1:12, para. 9) had a determinative influence on what came later. He did not see early German circumstances as democratic, nor would he have regarded "democracy" as a word of good omen. He did see them as participatory, nonabsolutist, embodying the spirit of freedom. Fundamental to this were courts and assemblies whose authority came from the free warriors who met in them, not from some power above. The local courts and assemblies established in Anglo-Saxon England, those of the hundred, and above all of the shire, had a determinative continuity. Above all they survived the Norman Conquest, in such a way that (to use a term Stubbs did not) the "political nation" in England was wide. Things so came about that in the late thirteenth century the local assemblies had their representatives gathered in a new general assembly, Parliament. This institution was crucial. It achieved a premature success and authority under the Lancastrian kings. Although this success later became occluded, the institution survived and made England what it was in Stubbs's day.

More than the sum of its guiding theories, the *Constitutional History* is a learned, intelligent, and idiosyncratic history of medieval England, written from the "constitutional" angle. Any student, who is familiar with the narrative (a familiarity that Stubbs took for granted) and who can allow for Stubbs's virginal indifference to economic history, can still learn far more from these three volumes than from most comparable pages of print. Stubbs's work lies in a long tradition of the interpretation of English history as that of a free constitution. Those who had written in this tradition in the past had had differing emphases. At least from the seventeenth century the constitution had been understood as something established in the distant past, not later than Magna Carta. In the eighteenth century more sophisticated views saw the constitution developing with the progress of civilization. Edmund Burke had offered a means of reconciling the two approaches, in his emphasis on the spirit, the habits of mind, infusing a people and giving a consistent temper and impulse to constitutional development through the centuries. Stubbs achieved a new synthesis, one in which his detailed examination of early institutions enabled him to give realism to a Burkean approach, and to argue for institutional as well as attitudinal continuity from the distant past. At the same time he was able to deploy the metaphor, or guiding insight, of developing self-consciousness in and of the state, in such a way as to link the ideas of continuity and of development with sophisticated complexity. He had the capacity to combine massive learning with elaborate argument, often expressed in subtle metaphor.

In this and in much else Stubbs owed a debt to Germany. The development of historical ideas and the organization of historical learning in England followed German models; the Rolls Series was related to (but as a very poor relation) the Monumenta Germaniae Historica (founded in 1819), and the *English Historical Review* (founded in 1886) follows the *Historische Zeitschrift*. The intellectual influence of Germany was particularly strong in Stubbs's formative years, and Georg Waitz's *Verfassungsgeschichte* is a model for the *Constitutional History*. Stubbs's inaugural lecture draws attention to a subject that remains neglected: the intellectual significance of the Hanoverian connection. He discusses George I (the founder of the Regius Chair) as a patron of learning and reminds us that the MGH, based in Hanover, was an enterprise to which George IV, as king of Hanover, had contributed twice as much as the king of Prussia. Two volumes of Stubbs's lectures on the history of medieval Germany were published posthumously. He left no such work on French history.

In the *Constitutional History* Stubbs goes to some lengths to explain how the French polity had become established on the wrong lines. The essence of the contrast between English freedom and French despotism was that in England Germanic invaders and settlers had brought with them free institutions, whereas in Gaul the Franks had adopted a system suitable for the government of a conquered race. Such a comparative approach was characteristic of Stubbs. For example, he drew attention to the parallels between English legislation over a long period and that of Merovingian and Carolingian rulers. In this, as in other regards, leads that he provided long ago have not been fully pursued.

Not the least important feature of Stubbs's work is its relationship to the development of history as a subject for university study. Modern, in the sense of post-ancient, history first appeared on the syllabus of an English university in 1850, at Oxford. Its study remained a mere formal requirement until 1864, when the joint-degree course in history and law became a serious concern; in 1872 history and law separated. Developments at Cambridge were approximately parallel.

At first Oxford gave only grudging recognition to history; the subject was introduced partly to fend off criticism that the university was not up-to-date, partly in the hope that it might interest students whose abilities did not measure up to the strenuous demands of more serious subjects. Essential steps for the transformation of this position had already been taken when Stubbs became Regius Professor in 1866. In some ways his effect on history teaching in the university was limited. His lectures were poorly attended, he complained, sometimes by no more than a handful of bored men.

Nevertheless, Stubbs was a powerful prophet for the central importance of history in education, as in his inaugural lecture, published later in his *Seventeen Lectures on the Study of Medieval and Modern History and Kindred Subjects* (1886). This was a characteristic performance. He begins by saying that he has "not learned the tone of authority which befits the professorial character" (Stubbs [1886], 1), yet he proceeds to speak with authoritative seriousness. His argument for the cause of modern history was complex. First, a historical training best prepared one for the political life of a citizen: partly it provided knowledge but more important was the acquisition of habits of judgment, "the faculty to be trained is judgement, the practical judgement at work among matters in which the possessor is deeply interested" (*ibid.*, 19). "Interested" is here used in the sense of "having personal concerns or commitments at stake"; and Stubbs believed that from the proper study of history could be learned a right judgment in politics. The student "finds, if his study has taught him facts as well as maxims, that the great necessity of practical judgement is patience and tolerance" (*ibid.*, 21) and that "there are few questions on which as much may not be said on one side as on the other; that there are none at all on which all the good are on one side, all the bad on the other, or all the wise on one and all the fools on the other" (*ibid.*, 20). One might have supposed that with such presumptions went aversion to party politics. On the contrary, Stubbs, on this issue following closely the views of the mature Macaulay, regarded the two great English parties as representing natural divisions: "Men are born most certainly with constitutional inclinations, some to order and others to change" (*ibid.*, 22). He did not wish men to cease to be partisans but rather to be scrupulous, disciplined, and informed in their party opinions. The pursuit of historical truth was put on a high spiritual plane. History properly considered has "something of the preciousness of something that is clearly true" (*ibid.*, 26), and it can give "a gradual approximation to a consciousness that we are growing into a perception of the working of the Almighty Ruler of the world . . . leading the world on to better, but never forcing, and out of the evil of man's handiwork bringing forth continually that which is good" (*ibid.*, 27). Thus history was not only a means of seeing that students did not go into the world "a prey to newspaper correspondents," but had a religious significance little inferior to that of theology, "the sacred sister study" (*ibid.*, 22, 24).

For Stubbs piety and progress went hand in hand. Though a Tory, he was no stranger to the ebullient optimism of his generation. It shines out in an extraordinary sentence in his inaugural lecture: "The time cannot be far off when all the records of the mediaeval world which are in existence will be in print either in full or in . . . abundant extracts; when every great Library will contain copies of them all, and when every town will contain a great Library" (*ibid.*, 14). It seems from this that he had no idea of the enormous mass of the surviving medieval public records. Stubbs was adamant that ancient history did not share the high virtues of modern history. In this he differed from Edward Augustus Freeman, his successor as Regius Professor. Ancient history he saw as a closed world, in large measure detached from contemporary circumstances. Modern history "is the history of ourselves." There is hardly one point in the Dark Age and medieval history that can be "touched without awakening some chord in the present" (*ibid.*, 17). It was this, the earlier part of modern history, that Stubbs thought most suitable for educating undergraduates. Later history was too closely related to modern controversies.

In his inaugural lecture Stubbs laid stress on the importance of constitutional history, relating the modern circumstances and institutions of a state to their distant origins. His *Constitutional History* marked him as the dominant exponent of the constitutional history of England and as a leader in the development of historical studies at Oxford and elsewhere. A significance was attached to constitutional history that it has since lost. The Oxford committee that in 1870 recommended that the study of history should be separated from that of law laid down that English constitutional history ought always to be part of the history syllabus. It is unfair but not wholly untrue to say that constitutional history, especially early constitutional history, was thus valued because it was difficult, requiring a mastery of technicalities, complicated arguments, and obscure texts. Stubbs himself provided a brilliantly chosen collection of texts in his *Select Charters* (1870). The *Charters* and the *Constitutional History* became basic to historical education. Charles Oman (1860–1946), who began to study modern history as an Oxford undergraduate in 1882, wrote that the *Charters* had "already become a sort of bible from which a candidate was expected to identify any paragraph without its context being given" (Oman, 104–05). A Cambridge tutor looking back on the period around 1880 wrote, "To read the first volume of Stubbs was necessary to salvation; to read the second was greatly to be desired; the third was reserved for the ambitious student who sought to accumulate merit by unnatural austerities—but between them they covered the whole ground. The lecturer lectured on Stubbs; the commentator educated him; the commoner boiled him down" (Tanner, 54). Something of the impact of Stubbs can be felt in George Macaulay Trevelyan's (1876–1962) account of his schooldays, when he was the earliest "history specialist" at Harrow. He was (ca. 1892) "gorging" himself on Gibbon, Macaulay, and Carlyle; what he needed was, he said, "a strict regimen of the modern type of scientific history at its best" (Trevelyan, 3, 12). He was given the *Constitutional History*. "I wrote out a full analysis of the three volumes in three massive notebooks" (*ibid.*, 12). A remarkable feature of Stubbs's achievement was that the *Constitutional History* was simultaneously a major treatise, valued wherever medieval history was studied, and a textbook. He took pains to make his work easily usable, for example, by numbering each paragraph so that references to it would not be hindered by the appearance of successive revised editions.

It was not simply as an author that Stubbs had his effect on medieval studies and historical studies in general. The Oxford history school attracted more undergraduates than did any other, including Cambridge. Owens College, Manchester, was third; but it produced only fifty-four graduates in history between 1882 and 1904. At Oxford an average of 104 men graduated with honors in Modern History between 1890 and 1894. Though not a complete success as a lecturer, Stubbs did have some undergraduate pupils who were to be of the greatest importance in the establishment of professional history and the historians' profession in England, in particular Reginald Lane Poole, Thomas Frederick Tout, John Horace Round, and Charles Harding Firth. These were among the first truly professional historians in England. Their predecessors had not studied history at a university: this is true of Hallam, Macaulay, Samuel Rawson Gardiner, Mandell Creighton, Thorold Rogers, and William Edward Hartpole Lecky. The new historians were not necessarily professional in the sense that they made their living by history; what marked them out was their detached, value-free attitude toward their subject. The Victorians had been more concerned to use the past to express and illustrate their own convictions. Stubbs was instrumental in creating a historical profession whose collective mind-set differed in major ways from his own. To a remarkable extent he had laid out the agenda for the study of English medieval history for decades to come; a high proportion of the work done in the first half of the century was essentially in completion or continuance of his.

With time and the progress of research Stubbs's views were modified; but for many decades they suffered only one frontal assault. This was from Maitland, the only English historian contemporary with Stubbs whose reputation surpasses his. Stubbs, in an appendix to the Report of the Royal Commission on Ecclesiastical Courts (1883), had argued that the canon law, though always regarded as a great authority in England, was not held to be binding in the courts. Maitland in *Roman Canon Law in the Church of England* (1898) showed this view to have been essentially wrong. This apart, no serious outright challenge to Stubbs was published until 1963. In that year Henry Gerald Richardson and George Osborne Sayles in their *The Governance of Mediaeval England from the Conquest to Magna Carta* devoted much ink and animus to an attack on Stubbs's work, not only in his *Constitutional History* but also in his editions. Much of their detailed criticism was justified; the tone and thrust of their attack were excessive. Why should two distinguished medievalists have become excited to the point of injustice by books written nearly a century before? It was because, as they saw things, "the teaching of William Stubbs has been inexpugnably dominant in English and American universities for more than eighty years" (Richardson and Sayles, v). This statement, though exaggerated, was not without force. At the undergraduate level Stubbs's command was maintained not so much through the *Constitutional History* as through the *Select Charters* that continued to be widely used in universities into the 1960s.

Thereafter this dominance melted; it had been part of a tradition, founded in Oxford in the 1860s, that saw the study of the English medieval past as a necessary part of any course in modern history. How quickly this tradition perished can be seen in a survey of courses made in 1968. All the universities founded before 1949 required a study of English medieval history; of those founded in or after 1949 none required it and only three out of the twelve made provision for it. In 1992 no candidate for the Final Honour School at Oxford offered Stubbs's *Select Charters*; in the 1950s there were still fifty or sixty each year who chose to cope with its intricate challenges and its Latin. If the reign of Stubbs was long, the end came swiftly.

Stubbs has come to seem out-of-date. He has been attacked by Sir Geoffrey Elton, for example, as being near the head of a historical tradition that errs in seeing medieval parliaments as having a serious political role. However, on this matter Stubbs has the best of it, and most of his position has been vindicated by later work, not least on the *Modus Tenendi Parliamentum*; Pronay and Taylor have shown that this treatise, written in Edward II's reign and attributing great political authority to Parliament, and in particular to the Commons, was reproduced and used in a way that makes it impossible to regard it as the kind of fantasy that Sir Geoffrey assumes it to be. Here, and very frequently, Stubbs's work, imperfect though it may be, retains value not only for its learning but for its general approach. Some of the discarding of Stubbs is due to a mistaken fear of anachronism, such that if anything in the medieval period seems too "modern" it is forthwith on that account alone dismissed.

The fullest recent account of Stubbs's *Constitutional History* is in John Wyon Burrow's *A Liberal Descent*, to which I am indebted for much that is said above. Burrow does not sufficiently take account of the extent to which Stubbs may have been right, and he does not do justice to the theological element in Stubbs's thought. But his most valuable service is to place Stubbs among the eminent Victorian thinkers and writers. He sets the *Constitutional History* beside two of the masterpieces of the day, *The Origin of Species* and *Middlemarch*, and draws out resemblances between Stubbs's modes of thought and writing and those of Charles Darwin and George Eliot. It is true that the *Constitutional History* has a subtlety, complexity, and power that should save it, though they have so far failed to do so, from the fate of discarded textbooks. Its eloquent prose with careful sentence structures and repeated use of alliteration is worth a little study by itself.

Not the least remarkable thing about Stubbs was his almost superhuman, his Victorian, powers of work. "I trust," he wrote, "if God shall spare me, to work with a good heart as long as it is called today" (Stubbs [1886], 11). Work he did: in his first ten years as Regius Professor he published ten Rolls Series volumes, a volume of *Councils and Ecclesiastical Documents Relating to Great Britain and Ireland*, the *Select Charters*, and two volumes of the *Constitutional History*. His industry and the force of his almost Gladstonian prose are intimidating. Their impact is lightened by the idiosyncrasy and humor that recur in his work, often in a veiled way. One example: in his inaugural lecture Stubbs praises his predecessor Goldwin Smith (1823–1910) for what he had done "on the behalf of Christian Faith against philosophic sciolism" (*ibid.*, 3). Superficially this is valedictory unction; it rings differently when one recalls that Smith was a leading anticlerical. As often, humor was accompanied by a capacity for self-criticism: much of the most effective criticism of Stubbs's work is his own.

Selected Bibliography

Full bibliographies of Stubbs's writings, including the Rolls Series editions not listed below, are provided in Hutton's edition of Stubbs's letters and by Shaw.

Works

Books and Articles

Ed. *Chronicles and Memorials of the Reign of Richard I.* 2 vols. London: Longman, Green, Longman, Roberts, and Green, 1864–65.

Ed. with Arthur W. Haddan. *Councils and Ecclesiastical Documents Relating to Great Britain and Ireland.* 3 vols. in 4. Oxford: Clarendon, 1869–78.

Ed. *Select Charters and Other Illustrations of English Constitutional History from the Earliest Times to the Reign of Edward I.* Oxford: Clarendon, 1870.

The Constitutional History of England in Its Origin and Development. 3 vols. Oxford: Clarendon, 1874–78. [The final edition was the sixth (1897). Reference is commonly made to the "Library Edition" of 1880.]

"An Account of the Courts Which Have Exercised Ecclesiastical Jurisdiction Before the Norman Conquest, from the Norman Conquest to the Reformation, from the Reformation to the Year 1832." Appendix to the Report of the Commission on Ecclesiastical Courts. Vol. 1, pp. 21–51. London, 1883.

Seventeen Lectures on the Study of Medieval and Modern History and Kindred Subjects. Oxford: Clarendon, 1886.

Ed. *De Gestis Regum Anglorum.* London: Eyre and Spottiswoode, 1887–89.

Historical Introductions to the Rolls Series. Edited by Arthur Hassall. London: Longmans, Green, 1902.

Lectures on Early English History. Edited by Arthur Hassall. London: Longmans, Green, 1906.

Letters and Papers

Stubbs's papers are to be found in the following collections: the Bodleian Library, Oxford; the British Library; the Lambeth Library; the Society of the Most Holy Trinity, Ascot Priory; transcripts of some or all of the letters housed at the Society of the Most Holy Trinity are in the library of Pusey House, Oxford.

Letters of William Stubbs, Bishop of Oxford, 1825–1901. Edited by William Holden Hutton. London: Constable, 1904.

Sources

Blaas, P.B.M. *Continuity and Anachronism: Parliamentary and Constitutional Development in Whig Historiography and in the Anti-Whig Reaction Between 1890 and 1930.* The Hague: Nijhoff, 1978.

Brentano, Robert. "The Sound of Stubbs." *Journal of British Studies* 6 (1967): 1–14.

Burrow, John Wyon. "'The Village Community' and the Uses of History in Late Nineteenth-Century England." In *Historical Perspectives: Studies in English Thought and Society in Honour of J.H. Plumb,* edited by Neil McKendrick, pp. 255–84. London: Europa, 1974.

———. *A Liberal Descent: Victorian Historians and the English Past.* Cambridge: Cambridge University Press, 1981.

Cam, Helen Maud. "Stubbs Seventy Years After." *Cambridge Historical Journal* 9 (1948): 129–47.

Campbell, James. *Stubbs and the English State.* Reading: University of Reading Press, 1989.

Cantor, Norman F., ed. *William Stubbs on the English Constitution.* New York: Crowell, 1966.

Elton, Geoffrey R. *The History of England.* Cambridge: Cambridge University Press, 1984.

Forbes, Duncan. *The Liberal-Anglican Idea of History.* Cambridge: Cambridge University Press, 1952.

Gooch, George Peabody. *History and Historians in the Nineteenth Century.* 2nd ed., pp. 110–14. London: Longmans, Green, 1952.

Gray, John W. "Canon Law in England: Some Reflections on the Stubbs-Maitland Controversy." In *Studies in Church History,* edited by G.J. Cuming, vol. 3, pp. 48–68. Leiden: Brill, 1966.

Jann, Rosemary. *The Art and Science of Victorian History.* Columbus: Ohio State University Press, 1985.

Kenyon, John Philipps. *The History Men: The Historical Profession in England Since the Renaissance.* London: Weidenfeld and Nicolson, 1983.

Knowles, Dom David. *Great Historical Enterprises: Problems in Monastic History.* London: Nelson, 1963.

Maitland, Frederic William. *Roman Canon Law in the Church of England: Six Essays.* London: Methuen, 1898.

———. "Introduction." In *Essays on the Teaching of History,* by F.W. Maitland, et al., pp. ix–xx. Cambridge: Cambridge University Press, 1901.

———. "William Stubbs, Bishop of Oxford." *English Historical Review* 16 (1901): 417–26.

Oman, Charles. *Memories of Victorian Oxford and of Some Early Years.* London: Methuen, 1941.

Petit-Dutaillis, Charles and Georges Lefebvre. *Studies and Notes Supplementary to Stubbs' Constitutional History.* Translated from *Notes et études historiques,* a section of *Histoire constitutionnelle de l'Angleterre,* the French edition of Stubbs's *Constitutional History,* by W.E. Rhodes (Vol. 1), W.T. Waugh (Vol. 2), M.I.E. Robertson and R.F. Treharne (Vol. 3). 3 vols. Manchester: Manchester University Press, 1908–29.

Pronay, Nicholas, and John Taylor. *Parliamentary Texts of the Later Middle Ages.* Oxford: Oxford University Press, 1980.

Richardson, Henry Gerald and George Osborne Sayles. *The Governance of Mediaeval England from the Conquest to Magna Carta.* Edinburgh: Edinburgh University Press, 1963.

Sayles, George Osborne. "The Changed Concept of History: Stubbs and Renan." *Aberdeen University Journal* 35 (1953–54): 235–47.

Shaw, William Arthur, ed. *A Bibliography of the Historical Works of Dr. Creighton, late Bishop of London; Dr. Stubbs, late Bishop of Oxford; Dr. S.R. Gardiner; and the late Lord Acton*, pp. 15–23. London: Royal Historical Society, 1903.

Slee, Peter R.H. *Learning and a Liberal Education: The Study of Modern History in the Universities of Oxford, Cambridge and Manchester, 1800–1914*. Manchester: Manchester University Press, 1986.

Stephen, Leslie, ed. *Letters of John Richard Green*. New York: Macmillan, 1902.

Stephens, William Richard Wood. *The Life and Letters of Edward A. Freeman, D.C.L., LL.D.* 2 vols. London: Macmillan, 1895.

Tanner, J.R. "The Teaching of Constitutional History." In *Essays on the Teaching of History*, by F.W. Maitland, et al., pp. 51–68. [See above under Maitland.]

Tout, Thomas Frederick. "William Stubbs." *Dictionary of National Biography*. 2nd supp. Vol. 3, pp. 445–51. London: Milford, 1912.

Trevelyan, George Macaulay. *An Autobiography and Other Essays*. London: Longmans, Green, 1949.

Waitz, Georg. *Deutsche Verfassungsgeschichte*. 8 vols. Vols. 1–2, Kiel: Schwers. Vols. 3–8, Homann, 1844–78.

Williams, N.J. "Stubbs's Appointment as Regius Professor, 1866." *Bulletin of the Institute of Historical Research* 33 (1960): 121–25.

Woodward, [Ernest] Llewellyn. "The Rise of the Professional Historian in England." In *Studies in International History: Essays Presented to W. Norton Medlicott*, edited by Donald Cameron Watt and Kenneth Bourne, pp. 16–34. London: Longmans, 1967.

HENRY CHARLES LEA

(1825–1909)

Edward Peters

Henry Charles Lea, the greatest historian in nineteenth-century America and the most accomplished American historian of medieval Europe before Charles Homer Haskins, was born in Philadelphia on 19 September 1825. His mother, Frances Carey Lea, was a skilled linguist and botanist, the daughter of the Philadelphia publisher Mathew Carey and the sister of the political economist and publisher Henry Charles Carey, after whom Lea was named. Lea's father, Isaac Lea, one of the leading conchologists in North America, was admitted into the Carey publishing house upon his marriage to Frances Carey. The firm passed then to Henry Charles Lea, who converted it to medical and scientific publishing and operated it until his formal retirement in 1880.

The Lea-Carey household was prosperous, intellectually active, and Quaker-Catholic in religion. Isaac Lea was a Quaker who had been read out of meeting for joining a volunteer rifle company during the War of 1812 and later became an Episcopalian, along with his wife, who was originally a Roman Catholic. Henry Charles Lea, raised as an Episcopalian, eventually joined the Unitarian church, of which he remained a member for the rest of his life. Lea and his older brother, Matthew Carey Lea, later a lawyer and internationally recognized research chemist, were tutored privately at home until 1843, when Matthew went to read law with William Meredith and Henry joined the family publishing firm as a junior employee. The eleven years of private tutoring, with additional education from their parents, gave the Lea brothers a remarkable foundation in languages and literature, mathematics, and science, and they shared their parents' interests in botany and conchology.

Henry Charles Lea's own first interests lay in research science and literary criticism. His first published articles, appearing in 1841, dealt respectively with a new species of fossil shell and with an original examination of the peroxide of manganese, and his third article of 1841—he was sixteen years old—was a review of Brougham's *Miscellanies*. Between 1841 and 1850 Lea published ten original articles of scientific research, twenty-one of literary criticism, and original poetry. His entry into the publishing firm in 1843 proved too demanding in addition to this scientific and literary work, and he suffered a breakdown in 1847, after which he was prohibited by his physician from sustaining his rigorous program of work and study. Lea then devoted his energies to his business career and domestic life. He married his cousin Anna Jaudon in 1850.

Intellectually restless Lea turned to the reading of history, first in the court memoirs of seventeenth- and eighteenth-century France, a taste for which he had earlier evinced in his article on the poet Gilles Menage, published in the *Southern Literary Messenger* in 1846. The memoirs of court life in the seventeenth and eighteenth centuries soon led Lea back to the sixteenth century and then to the narrative histories of medieval France, those of Froissart, Joinville, Villehardouin, and the chronicles of Saint-Denis, and back to the Carolingians. This interest was sparked by his acquisition of the chronicle of Richer, discovered by the German medievalist G.H. Pertz and first published in 1845. The result of Lea's new interest was a forty-page, still unpublished manuscript account of the rise of the house of Capet until it ascended the throne of France in 987. Lea's remarkable mind and breadth of reading are evident in his first published essay on medieval history in 1856, a learned review of Francis Palgrave's *History of Normandy* in the *North American Review*.

Lea might have been expected to continue on in the history of medieval France and England, conventional historical subjects in the early-national period of the United States. But his interests soon shifted from the high road of political history to the then novel problems of analyzing and describing what he later came to call the "inner life" or "interior history" of medieval society. He turned to the study of the history of law, since he thought that the legal culture of peoples in the past was a far more reliable key to their mentality than the actions of leading political figures. Lea's new interest led to the series of review essays that he collected in 1866 and published under the title *Superstition and Force*. Also in 1866 Lea discovered W.E.H. Lecky's *History of the Rise and Influence of the Spirit of Rationalism in Europe*, an original work in the field now called cultural history. Both his study of legal history and the influence of Lecky confronted Lea with the problem of the medieval church. From 1866 he became in one way or another a historian of the church in society.

Lea was well informed about the contemporary Roman Catholic church, both in Europe, where the liberalizing movements of the 1850s and 1860s had produced a reaction from conservative Catholics, and in the United States, where the growth of Roman Catholicism had made the question of the civil power of ecclesiastical institutions a burning issue. In 1867 he published *An Historical Sketch of Sacerdotal Celibacy in the Christian Church*, which concluded with a review of the question as it stood in the mid-nineteenth century, and in 1869 he published *Studies in Church History*, essays whose real theme is the rise of political authority within the church and the history of the relations between the spiritual and temporal powers. During these years and later Lea also addressed problems of contemporary Catholicism, notably in several articles on the church and free thought, such as "The Religious Reform Movement in Italy" and "Monks and Nuns in France."

In contemporary criticism and in historical writing Lea strove to separate dogma and devotion from institutional history, and his criticism fell heaviest upon institutional ecclesiasticism. He identified the institutional history of the church with what he called "sacerdotalism"—both the separation of the clergy from the rest of society (by celibacy) and the authority of prelates in civil affairs. Disliking prelates of all faiths, Lea pilloried the Episcopal Bishop Hopkins of Vermont, who had cited scriptural texts to defend the institution of slavery in a book that Lea parodied by using the same method, *A Bible View of Polygamy* (1863). Lea's fascination with the power of prelates in civil affairs was sharpened by contemporary papal policy, including the bull *Qui Pluribus* in 1846, the condemnation of modernism in *Lamentabili Sane Exitu* of 1907, the appearance of *Quanta Cura* with the Syllabus of Errors in 1864, the canonization of the inquisitor Pedro Arbues in 1867, and the events of the First Vatican Council of 1870. Lea's own political and religious interests, as well as events in his own time and world, confirmed the direction that his historical work had taken since the mid-1850s.

Although by 1866 Lea had found the field in which he was to spend the rest of his scholarly life, he could work at history only intermittently during a public life that was otherwise active and full; much of his early historical writing was done on family vacations. His full-time work was managing the publishing house. He conducted pioneering research which led to the copyright law of 1891, many of whose most important points were his contribution, and participated in movements for civic reform. Throughout his life Lea remained an active reformer, publishing hundreds of political pamphlets on behalf of civic causes.

Upon the outbreak of the Civil War Lea turned his energies to support of the Union. He paid for and equipped two soldiers to substitute for himself and threw himself into organizing Union sympathizers in Philadelphia. As one of the founders of the Union League Club in Philadelphia and a member of its board of publications, Lea wrote many influential pamphlets advocating the Union cause. He was a member of the Supervisory Committee on Colored Enlistments, responsible for recruiting and equipping several regiments of African-American troops for the Union army, and of the Association for the Relief of Refugees from Rebel Armies, an organization that supported Confederate deserters. He served on the Bounty Fund Commission, the organization established in 1863 to recruit Union soldiers by offering bounties for local enlistment. Lea's time between 1861 and 1865 was almost entirely taken up with war service, which was acknowledged with gratitude by a number of political and military figures, Abraham Lincoln among them.

In the wake of the Civil War and the political turmoil in Philadelphia Lea worked unreservedly for a series of reform movements whose targets were Philadelphia machine politics and which focused upon the infamous Gas Trust, the financing of public buildings, passenger railway franchises, and the city waterworks. From the end of the war to the end of his life local political affairs occupied a substantial part of Lea's time. On the national level Lea campaigned vigorously for economic protectionism and civil-service reform, opposed the income tax, and labored to pass the legislation concerning international copyright, which finally emerged in the Chace Bill of 1891. During this period Lea drew materials from his historical research to drive home present positions on public policy, frequently citing Spanish experience as examples for American people and legislators to avoid.

Lea was able to undertake these activities because of his energy, sense of civic responsibility, and wealth. His fortune, which had begun with the family publishing firm and had expanded into the third-largest real-estate fortune in Philadelphia history, allowed him a style of living that was comfortable but modest and abstemious. He collected art and books, assembling what was probably the most impressive personal scholarly library in the United States, and he poured funds into benevolent causes. Remaining well informed in scientific literature and the public role of the physical sciences, Lea paid for and equipped the first Laboratory of Public Hygiene at the University of Pennsylvania in 1891 but only after having made his donation conditional upon revising the curriculum of the university Medical School to make public-health study mandatory. He also funded libraries in Philadelphia, paying for a new building to house the venerable Library Company in 1898.

Lea's public and private work between 1869 and 1884 was carried out in the shadow of increasing ill health, which caused his resignation as a trustee of the University of Pennsylvania and which he hoped to cure by a voyage to England in 1873. A particularly difficult passage and news of his mother's death caused him to return to America after only three days in England. As recuperative strategy, in 1875 Lea spent four months of the winter in the West Indies and in 1878 two months in Florida. A brief trip to England in 1879 appears only to have delayed the most severe onset of his illness, which struck him with particular severity when he largely disposed of the ownership of his publishing firm and entered a life of retired scholarship. Instead of the research and writing he had hoped to do Lea found himself in a state of nervous collapse and near blindness. Two courses appear to have helped him overcome these problems. From 1881 to 1884 he cruised the Caribbean and the Atlantic coasts in his schooner the *Vega* (whose logs and visiting cards survive today), and during his intermittent returns to Philadelphia Lea placed himself under the care of his old friend the physician-novelist S. Weir Mitchell, whose friendship and therapeutic advice soon restored to Lea something of his old energy and capacity for work.

From 1884 until his death in 1909, Lea turned most of his energy to writing his great histories of the Inquisition of medieval Europe and early-modern Spain and to revising editions of his earlier works, writing book reviews, and producing monographs on aspects of his general research. He continued to be active in public affairs and politics, and his long life of scholarship and civic involvement brought him many honors, from learned societies in Europe to political, civic, and scholarly groups in the United States. He received honorary doctoral degrees from Pennsylvania, Princeton, and Harvard, corresponded with an international network of friends and scholarly helpers, saw his works acknowledged as masterpieces by an increasingly professionalized scholarly profession, was elected president of the American Historical Association in 1902, and was invited by Lord Acton to write the chapter "The Eve of the Reformation" for the first volume of *The Cambridge Modern History*.

Lea had begun work on the Inquisition in the late 1860s. He had moved away from the compact topics he had written on earlier and had settled on this ambitious enterprise that required nearly twenty years of preparatory research. His first historical works, *Superstition and Force* (1866), *An Historical Sketch of the History of Sacerdotal Celibacy* (1867), and *Studies in Church History* (1869), all shared characteristics that he had developed as a self-taught historian. The research was based upon original texts, with little attention to secondary scholarship; Lea did his research and writing with an eye to contemporary ecclesiastical, especially Roman Catholic, affairs in Europe and the United States; his work focused more and more upon the history of law and theories of law in shaping the lives of early Europeans. "The history of jurisprudence," Lea observed in the second edition of *Superstition and Force*, "is the history of civilization" (v). For the vast subject of the Inquisition Lea built a network of scholars, booksellers, librarians, archivists, and friendly nonscholars, managed by an unceasing flow of correspondence, in order to gain access to the original source materials, often including original manuscripts, that would be required by his high standards for any history of ecclesiastical coercion that was not to be simply another piece of confessional polemic.

As early as 1868 Lea wrote to a correspondent that he hoped, if leisure allowed, to write a history of the Inquisition. Previous European scholars had tried to do so, but their work had met with obstacles and severe criticism. One of them, Charles Molinier, had observed to Lord Acton that Lea's project was "simply a chimera" (Bradley, 257). On his side Lea had determination, energy, linguistic and technical competence—and luck. He corresponded with W.E.H. Lecky, whose *History of the Rise and Influence of the Spirit of Rationalism in Europe* (1865) seemed to be exactly the kind of historical work that Lea was attempting to do himself. Their correspondence put Lecky at Lea's service at crucial points in his acquisition of documents and transcripts of documents. In 1869 Lea began to correspond with G.B. de Lagrèze, whose *Histoire du droit dans les Pyrénées* Lea had reviewed in the *North American Review* in 1868. Interested in Lea's Inquisition project, Lagrèze observed to Lea that his relative the king of Sweden had shown him an Inquisition manuscript in Copenhagen the previous year. Through Lagrèze's chance hint Lea obtained from the Royal Library of Copenhagen the famous Moldenhower Codex, a virtual directory of the practices and laws of the Spanish Inquisition, whose acquisition this early in his research gave his work a direction and structure that would otherwise have taken years to develop. By the 1870s Lea was in correspondence with almost every European scholar who knew anything at all about Inquisition sources.

By that time Lea also knew precisely how large a project he had taken on. Realizing that some topics grew disproportionately, he developed the habit of dealing with them more fully in separate articles and monographs so as to keep his major work balanced and compact. Between 1888 and 1906 he published twenty-two articles about aspects of Spanish history touching on the Inquisition and the monographs *Chapters from the Religious History of Spain Connected with the Inquisition* (1890), *A Formulary of the Papal*

Penitentiary in the Thirteenth Century (1892), the three-volume *A History of Auricular Confession and Indulgences in the Latin Church* (1896), *The Dead Hand: A Brief Sketch of the Relations Between Church and State with Regard to Ecclesiastical Property and the Religious Orders* (1900), and *The Moriscos of Spain: Their Conversion and Expulsion* (1901). This work not only prepared Lea superbly to finish his immense Inquisition history, but made him the leading North American historian of Spain.

Although he had always thought of the Inquisition as a single institution, developed out of Latin Christian preeminence in medieval Europe and perfected in Spain after 1478, Lea now found that his material was far too extensive for a single study. He undertook first to write on the Inquisition of the Middle Ages. Collecting materials even through the physical and nervous collapse of 1873–84, Lea turned his renewed energies into four years of intense writing and produced the *History of the Inquisition of the Middle Ages* in three large volumes in 1888, a work that made Lea's reputation in Europe and was translated into French, German, and Italian.

A History of the Inquisition of Spain appeared in four volumes in 1906 and 1907, to the same acclaim that had welcomed the study of the Inquisitions of the Middle Ages. It was hailed as superior to the work of José Amador de los Rios, the leading Spanish historian of the subject, and it rivaled Ernst Schäfer's great study *Beiträge zur Geschichte des spanischen Protestantismus und der Inquisition im sechzehnten Jahrhundert*, which Lea had reviewed in the *American Historical Review* in 1903. Even in his extraordinarily detailed archival and other source work, however, Lea did not lose sight of his original reasons for undertaking his research. The sharp comments on Latin Christianity and its instruments and policies of religious coercion scattered throughout his Inquisition histories led to a wave of criticism from Catholic historians and polemicists that has continued to the present. Although such criticism troubled Lea, it did not halt his pace. Two further articles appeared in 1906, and Lea published *The Inquisition in the Spanish Dependencies: Sicily, Naples, Sardinia, Milan, the Canaries, Mexico, Peru, New Granada* in 1908.

His great Inquisition histories and monographs completed, Lea plunged into a new project in the early years of the twentieth century, one that he had begun even before the Inquisition research and that had fascinated him since he began working in medieval history—the nature of magic and witchcraft. He had compiled several thousand pages of reading notes and tentative conclusions when he was taken ill with what developed into pneumonia on 20 October 1909. Four days later he died. Some thirty years later Lea's work was edited and published posthumously by Arthur Howland in three volumes as *Materials Toward a History of Witchcraft* (1939). Howland also collected a number of Lea's earlier essays in a volume entitled *Minor Historical Writings and Other Essays* (1942).

When Lea began to write, historiography in the United States was generally informed by a combination of Protestant millennialism, civic republicanism, and a theory of divine immanence. Lea's immediate predecessors and contemporaries—William H. Prescott, George Bancroft, J. Lothrop Motley, and Francis Parkman—had focused either on the moral destiny of the United States or on those parts of European history that appeared to provide precursors of aspects of the North American experience. Lea was the first American historian to take the Middle Ages as his province, fully aware of the prevailing Enlightenment view that Europe had modernized only by escaping from the Middle Ages. Lea had encountered medieval Europe by accident, as he read history therapeutically from his collapse in 1847 into the early 1850s, and his first essay was generally straightforward political history. But his growing fascination with the history of law as a means of approaching what he called "the inner life" or "interior history" of past peoples, reinforced by his reading of Lecky in 1865, led him in a roundabout way back to a subject in which he had formed an independent interest long before, the nature and place of the Roman Catholic church in contemporary Europe and North America. Lea's dislike of "prelacy" and "sacerdotalism" was fed by research that revealed to him the importance of the church in transforming late Iron Age Europe and what he considered the dangers of its continuing civil influence and protected status.

The works on sacerdotal celibacy, ecclesiastical temporal power, and auricular confession all carry up to Lea's own day, and they were intended to be historical briefs against current practices. Politically and religiously a liberal, Lea believed, as did Prescott, in a form of ideal Christianity that consisted chiefly of a few elementary gospel truths, the first of which was to love one's fellow man, and then the inviolability of conscience, religious pluralism, the restriction of clerical authority in civil affairs, and in the idea that these represented not only the original purpose but also a higher historical stage of the Christian religious life. These views carried into the histories of the Inquisition and of magic and witchcraft as well.

But Lea's reading and dealings with archival materials also taught him a great deal about the historical circumstances of medieval Europe. In a number of places, notably his 1865 essay on slavery, Lea insisted upon the beneficial and humanitarian influence of the Latin church on European society. In this respect Lea differed sharply from the opinion of other Americans, without at the same time slipping into an ill-informed romantic nostalgia of the kind that characterized the later Henry Adams. Thus, although Lea became more and more skeptical about the value of moral judgments in history—the result of his familiarity with the inner workings of ecclesiastical thought and action in medieval and early-modern Europe—he often stated that his objective presentation of "the facts" would assist his readers in drawing the proper conclusions.

Lea's influence was thus tempered by his running argument with ecclesiastical authority in general and by his sensitivity to the instrumental use of law in the past to achieve the ends of power and orthodox belief and practice. Yet he had demonstrated that the early history of Europe lay open to scholars with the proper skills, time, and willingness to read documents. His recognition by the increasingly academically professionalized American Historical Association, and the respect he earned from such later scholars as Charles Homer Haskins and E.P. Cheney, meant that although many of his fields would be left for later scholars to cultivate, his work stood as a model for all American students of medieval history. Even his prose style, developed so as to remove the temptation to make rhetorical arguments and to emphasize the primacy of sources, is essentially that in which scholarly history is still written.

Lea opened the vast storehouse of medieval European documentation to American readers, and he argued that only through work on the original documents could history have any value at all. Lea was as good as his word: a number of American scholars at the end of the nineteenth and beginning of the twentieth century were welcomed to his library and its resources—at the time the finest library of medieval history in the United States.

Lea's subjects still engage scholars. The judicial ordeal, torture, excommunication, slavery, church history, ecclesiastical political theory, Inquisition history, magic and witchcraft, and European Christian treatment of non-Christians—all of these topics have been the subject of research in the past several decades. In a sense it took the American historical profession half a century to catch up with Lea. It is almost as if he had laid out a blueprint for research in medieval history that scholars have been following throughout much of the later twentieth century.

Lea introduced European historians and readers to American work at a level that could not be ignored or dismissed. His acknowledgment in Europe—membership in learned societies, regular correspondence with major European historians, inclusion among the contributors to *The Cambridge Modern History* under the editorship of Lord Acton, and the translations of his work into the major European languages (the history of the Spanish Inquisition appeared in Spanish for the first time in 1983)—meant that

American scholarship was now a fixture of the European scholarly scene, especially in a field that had been dominated by Europeans up until Lea's own day.

Lea is remembered in Philadelphia for both his civic life and his scholarly work. A public school is named after him in West Philadelphia, and his library and many of his papers and correspondence were given to the University of Pennsylvania in 1925 by his three surviving (out of four) children. His family endowed teaching chairs in history in Lea's name at the University of Pennsylvania, Princeton, and Harvard. A marble bust stands in the Library Company. Most of his own scholarly works remain in print and in use at the end of the twentieth century. Although scholarship in Lea's fields has continued and has revised many of his judgments, the body of his work retains the admiration of all scholars who know it. No single scholar in Lea's fields has since rivaled his range and comprehensiveness.

Selected Bibliography

A bibliography of Lea's work appears in Bradley.

Works

Books

Superstition and Force: Essays on the Wager of Law, the Wager of Battle, the Ordeal, and Torture. Philadelphia: Lea, 1866. Rev. and enlarged ed., 1892.

An Historical Sketch of Sacerdotal Celibacy in the Christian Church. Philadelphia: Lippincott, 1867. Rev. and enlarged ed., Boston: Houghton Mifflin, 1884. Rev. ed. 2 vols. New York: Macmillan, 1907.

Studies in Church History: The Rise of the Temporal Power, Benefit of Clergy, Excommunication. Philadelphia: Lea, 1869. Rev. as *Studies in Church History: The Rise of the Temporal Power, Benefit of Clergy, Excommunication, the Early Church and Slavery,* 1883.

A History of the Inquisition of the Middle Ages. 3 vols. New York: Harper, 1888. Rev. ed. 1906. Uniform edition with *The Inquisition in the Spanish Dependencies,* London and New York: Macmillan, 1908.

A Formulary of the Papal Penitentiary in the Thirteenth Century. Philadelphia: Lea, 1892.

A History of Auricular Confession and Indulgences in the Latin Church. 3 vols. Philadelphia: Lea, 1896.

The Dead Hand: A Brief Sketch of the Relations Between Church and State with Regard to Ecclesiastical Property and the Religious Orders. Philadelphia: Dornan, 1900.

The Moriscos of Spain: Their Conversion and Expulsion. Philadelphia: Lea, 1901.

A History of the Inquisition of Spain. 4 vols. New York: Macmillan, 1906–07.

The Inquisition in the Spanish Dependencies: Sicily, Naples, Sardinia, Milan, the Canaries, Mexico, Peru, New Granada. New York: Macmillan, 1908.

Materials Toward a History of Witchcraft. Edited by Arthur C. Howland. 3 vols. Philadelphia: University of Pennsylvania Press, 1939.

Minor Historical Writings and Other Essays. Edited by Arthur C. Howland. Philadelphia: University of Pennsylvania Press, 1942.

Most of Lea's scholarly books, letters, and papers are housed in The Henry Charles Lea Library at the University of Pennsylvania.

Sources

Bradley, Edward Sculley. *Henry Charles Lea: A Biography*. Philadelphia: University of Pennsylvania Press, 1931.

O'Brien, John M. "Henry Charles Lea: The Historian as Reformer." *American Quarterly* 19 (1967): 104–13.

Peters, Edward. "Henry Charles Lea and the 'Abode of Monsters'." In *The Spanish Inquisition and the Inquisitorial Mind*, edited by Angel Alcalá, pp. 577–608. Highland Lakes, N.J.: Atlantic Research and Publications, 1987.

———. "Ecclesiastical History in Nineteenth-Century Perspective: Henry Charles Lea's *Studies in Church History*." Introduction to reprint of Lea, *Studies in Church History*. New York: AMS, forthcoming.

Ryan, E.A. "The Religion of Henry Charles Lea." In *Mélanges Joseph de Ghellinck*, vol. 2, pp. 1043–51. Gembloux: Duculot, 1951.

LÉOPOLD DELISLE

(1826–1910)

David Bates

Léopold-Victor Delisle was born on 24 October 1826 at Valognes, twelve miles to the southeast of Cherbourg in western Normandy. He was the descendant of a family long native to that region, and the son of a doctor, Victor-Amédée Delisle, who, although he returned to Valognes to practice, had been educated in Paris. Léopold Delisle attended local schools, where he received, as far as was possible in a small provincial town, the good formal training typical of the nineteenth-century French educational system. His early acquaintance with Greek, English, and German nonetheless appears to have been slight. Although Léopold Delisle rose to great eminence from origins that were not exactly propitious, it would be considerable exaggeration to say that his social and educational background did not provide him with opportunities.

Delisle's future career was decisively shaped by the encouragement and patronage of Charles Duhérissier de Gerville (1769–1853), whom the young Delisle first encountered in about the year 1840. A former aristocrat and a monarchist who had lived in exile in England during the French Revolution, Gerville, a distinguished antiquarian, made it one of his concerns to copy and preserve the manuscripts that came into his possession. According to Delisle, Gerville introduced him to Latin palaeography by lending him the thirteenth-century cartulary of the abbey of Saint-Sauveur-le-Vicomte to transcribe during the summer holidays; Delisle's first achievement was supposedly the transcription of a charter of Henry II. Gerville was also important to Delisle's development because he possessed the contacts required to foster his protégé's talents. It was with Gerville's support, and that of another distinguished nineteenth-century Norman antiquarian, Auguste Le Prévost, that Delisle entered the École des Chartes in 1846.

Delisle's years at the École were interrupted by the events of the 1848 Revolution and by a disruptive reorganization. He used the considerable time at his disposal to research the history of medieval Normandy, and after graduating from the École in 1849 he appears to have become effectively a full-time researcher, spending his days in the local Archives Départementales of Normandy, being given free access to the records by the archivists and copying a prodigious amount of material. At this stage Delisle's sole ambition was to become the archivist of one of the Norman *départements*. He was diverted from his goal by the intervention of his former master at the École des Chartes, Benjamin Guérard. In 1851, when Delisle was about to be offered the post of archivist of Seine-Inférieure (now Seine-Maritime), the largest of the Norman departmental archives, based in Rouen, Guérard told him not to accept because his future lay at the Bibliothèque Nationale, where Guérard had been appointed Conservateur in the Département des Manuscrits. Delisle was appointed to the Département des Manuscrits on 1 November 1852 and rose through the posts of Bibliothécaire (1866) and Conservateur des Manuscrits (1871) until he became Administrator General of the entire Bibliothèque Nationale in 1874. He remained Administrator General until his enforced retirement at seventy-nine in 1905, an event he first became aware of when he read the name of his successor in the *Journal officiel*.

Although Léopold Delisle's most profound long-term contribution arguably lies in the fields of palaeography and diplomatics, his extraordinary productivity—Paul Lacombe's bibliography of his published writings contains 2,102 items—includes a remarkable range of contributions and displays of technical brilliance whose results frequently remain the foundation from which all modern scholarship has to proceed. In everything he undertook Delisle made accessible the previously inaccessible, applying an outstanding clarity of mind that can truly be appreciated only by following him through an intellectual problem. His precocity is astounding. By thirty his output included a fundamental contribution to an edition of Orderic Vitalis's *Historia ecclesiastica*, a catalog of the *acta* of Philip Augustus and the over 700–page *La classe agricole*. Its modern editor has called the former work "one of the finest achievements of nineteenth-century scholarship" (Chibnall, 2: vi). The latter was praised as "L'ouvrage capital . . . sur la diplomatique des Capétiens" in the *Livre du centenaire* of the École des Chartes.

In assessing the direction that Delisle's creative life took, it is important to recognize that for over fifty years he was a librarian and that for over thirty of these years he was responsible for running one of the great libraries of the world. Delisle began his career intending to devote himself to the history of Normandy and to the end retained an unshakable personal and intellectual commitment to his *pays natal*. However, from 1852, as he himself said in his important "Souvenirs de Jeunesse," he committed his life to the Bibliothèque Nationale ("Résolu à consacrer ma vie à la Bibliothèque . . ." [xxiv]), a task whose scale can be appreciated only when it is grasped that much of its vast collection of manuscripts was simply not catalogued when Delisle took up his post. At the end of his life Delisle several times expressed regret about the turn his career had taken, even—perhaps with heavy irony—that he had always wished to be an archivist: "Quinze jours à peine avant sa mort, il me disait encore en souriant: 'J'ai manqué ma vocation, j'aurais dû être archiviste'" (Le Cacheux, 11). His enforced career change has prompted some reflection over the years about what might have been. Although Delisle was spoken of as "le grand bibliothécaire" during his lifetime, one of the many tributes published after his death saw him as a historian by temperament and a librarian by vocation.

On 10 June 1857 Delisle married Louise-Laure Burnouf, daughter of the orientalist Eugène Burnouf and a member of a family that also came from the vicinity of Valognes. Laure Delisle's own great abilities were entirely absorbed into her husband's work and career. The marriage was childless, a matter of regret to both of them. Delisle's own testimony and letters suggest an affectionate marriage that was also a professional partnership. Laure acquired skill as a Latin palaeographer and worked with her husband on many of his projects. In a letter written after her death to Ulysse Chevalier, Delisle goes as far as to identify her as the author of some of the articles that appeared under his name. This same letter also paints a touching picture of them studying together manuscripts that Delisle had brought home to the flat in the Rue des Petits-Champs, which went with Delisle's post at the Bibliothèque. A specific contribution to her husband's work in all probability derived from her knowledge of several languages, which may well have compensated for his weakness in this area. Laure Delisle's health became fragile in the last years of her life, and she died on 11 March 1905, shortly after she and her husband had learned of his tactless and brutal removal from his post.

Neither Delisle's publications nor his published letters contain much in the way of reflection on the purpose and nature of historical studies or signs of rapport with any of the intellectual debates of the later nineteenth century. They contain no mention of the turbulent politics of those years, except for references to the siege of Paris of 1870 as a terrible event. Delisle's only direct contact with politics was his courageous refusal to leave his post in 1871 in favor of an unqualified appointee nominated by the Commune. His patriotism (both French and Norman) and his Christianity are well attested. He was also profoundly influenced by personal and second-hand memories—some of them deriving from his time with Gerville—of the destruction of medieval manuscripts and buildings that followed the Revolution. For him that had been a time of vandalism, against which the future must be protected; the publication of texts was, he believed, necessary not just for the preservation of the past but for the maintenance of civilization itself. The tributes written after his death speak of a reserved, deliberate man, thinking before speaking, a formidable presence, but shy and courteous. His letters are for the most part concerned with manuscript scholarship, publication, and the often complex maneuvers of contemporary academic politics. They suggest a consummate man-of-affairs, skillful with people as well as manuscripts. Personal pleasantries abound, but they are mostly the courtesies of domestic enquiries and reports on health. They show Delisle, when required, as capable of expressing emotion powerfully and appropriately and as a loyal and supportive friend. However, an early letter to his lifelong friend Charles Robillard de Beaurepaire shows Delisle as capable of devastating personal assessment (Nortier, "Lettres": 10–14); he was an incisive judge of character and abilities.

Delisle possessed a highly developed sense of responsibility. It goes without saying that he worked hard—he once famously described a visit to a library in Ravenna as a day of debauchery. His health was excellent and he continued to write and correspond up until the day of his death. His affability and kindness to others were frequently remarked on; Charles Homer Haskins's moving tribute to "rare afternoons" spent with the elderly Delisle at Chantilly can speak for all the others. In any controversy he was invariably courteous, acknowledging what he believed to be just criticisms and setting out fully his reasons when he wished to justify the position he had adopted. He was an active member of many learned societies and took a special interest in the École des Chartes; the assistance he gave to the École's students was legendary and—despite his eminence—he was still correcting palaeographical exercises for the École in the weeks prior to his death.

Delisle's first article, a study of mortuary rolls, was published in 1847 while he was still a student at the École des Chartes. It is remarkable for the range of the literature on which it is based and for Delisle's determination to place his chief text, the roll of St. Vitalis of Savigny, in the context of other similar rolls. The main publications of these early years were "Des revenus publics," which consisted of the major part of his École des Chartes *thèse* on Norman ducal finance, and *La classe agricole*. Despite the undoubted originality of both, they basically suggest that the young Delisle was still following the path laid out by his early teachers, since they drew their inspiration respectively from Thomas Stapleton's edition of the Norman Pipe Rolls and Guérard's interest in rural history. The survival of some of Delisle's notes for *La classe agricole* gives an idea of his working methods (B.N., nouv. acq. fr. 21845). Sometimes entire documents were transcribed onto a single sheet of paper and notes made of their importance; sometimes a phrase or sentence, with its source, was written on a slip of paper, again with its significance clearly noted. This methodical way of working indicates that Delisle assembled his evidence within already defined categories, which, at its worst, meant that some chapters in the book were little more than lists.

Most of Delisle's main subsequent Norman publications were either editions of charters and administrative records, such as the *Cartulaire normand* of 1852 and the *Recueil de jugements de l'Échiquier* of 1864, or contributions to the editing of the great Norman historians of the eleventh and twelfth centuries. He himself published what remains the definitive edition of the chronicle of Robert of Torigni in 1872–73. Earlier he had finished Auguste Le Prévost's edition of the *Historia ecclesiastica* of Orderic Vitalis, contributing considerably to the text of Volumes 4 and 5 and writing an introduction that Orderic's modern editor has described as "remarkable." He also laid the foundations for the modern edition of the *Gesta Normannorum ducum*, identifying Orderic Vitalis's script in Rouen, Bibliothèque Municipale 1174 (Y14), and Robert of Torigni's contribution to Leiden, Universiteitsbibliotheek BPL 20. His deductions were eventually incorporated into a full edition of the *Gesta*, produced in 1913 by Jean Marx. After 1905 he returned with vigor and enthusiasm to a project of his youth, an edition of the charters of Henry II, king of England, duke of Normandy, duke of Aquitaine, and count of the Angevins (r. 1154–1189). He produced a magisterial study of the formulae of the address-clauses, demonstrating that the *Dei gratia* formula was introduced at a precise moment sometime between May 1172 and early 1173, which, as Delisle appreciated, was an invaluable aid to dating the charters. He produced an extensive introduction in the year before he died; the project was brought to a conclusion on the basis of Delisle's notes by his pupil Élie Berger.

La classe agricole received great praise when it was published and earned its author the first of his many academic distinctions, the Prix Gobert of the Institut de France. The book's lasting importance rests in the mass of material that Delisle assembled. His approach was generally descriptive—as he himself admitted. His conclusion that the Norman countryside had changed little between the thirteenth century and the nineteenth betrays a conservative approach, and for this reason alone it is unsurprising that *La classe agricole* received little attention in Marc Bloch's seminal *Les caractères originaux de l'histoire rurale française* (1931). For a much more modern commentator, Guy Bois, who is the only scholar subsequently to have covered some of the same archival ground as Delisle, *La classe agricole* remains definitive on such matters as agricultural techniques; the book has "stood the test of time" (Bois, 187–89). At its worst *La classe agricole* is a catalog of facts, but at its best it is a work of imagination and excitement, engaging fruitfully with such subjects as lordship and credit and trying to bring the peasantry alive.

While Delisle's work on Norman finance was to a large extent superseded by Charles Homer Haskins's *Norman Institutions* (1918) and by Sir Maurice Powicke's *The Loss of Normandy* (1913), his capacity to unravel difficult topics makes "Des revenus publics" a still indispensable source for some aspects of its subject. It was Delisle, for example, who first tackled the matter of exchange rates between Norman, Angevin, and sterling, and his conclusions, largely overlooked by Powicke, mostly still stand. Likewise it was Delisle who unraveled the structure of the Norman *bailliages* and set out clearly the revenue categories of ducal Normandy in a manner from which all have profited. Delisle's breadth of vision and his knowledge of the basic texts remain inspiring; he was, for example, clearly aware that the Norman Pipe Rolls had great potential for economic analysis, a topic that is only just coming alive.

Delisle's work on the great eleventh- and twelfth-century Norman historians is the foundation on which all modern work is based. His methodology built on the ideas of Mabillon but was a distinct advance in the context of his time, founded as it was a detailed comparative inspection of all manuscripts of a particular text. Although Delisle's work on Orderic Vitalis has been superseded by Marjorie Chibnall's edition, Chibnall's (excessively modest) statement that it was only the inaccessibility of Le Prévost's and Delisle's edition and the progress of historical knowledge that justified its replacement is a remarkable one (Chibnall, 2: vi); Delisle's discussion of the composition of the *Historia ecclesiastica* and the literary and intellectual background against which Orderic worked is masterly. Elisabeth van Houts's new edition of the *Gesta Normannorum ducum* convincingly arranges the earliest recensions of this difficult source in an order different from Delisle's, along lines also suggested by the late R.H.C. Davis in 1980. Van Houts's new edition does, however, confirm the fundamental correctness of Delisle's deductions about the interpolations made by Orderic Vitalis and Robert of Torigni, and his palaeographical deductions about the additions made on Torigni's orders remain in place. Delisle's work in this field has also laid the basis for other editions of chronicles, such as that of Adémar of Chabannes.

The *Recueil des actes de Henri II* is manifestly incomplete, even on its own terms since the full title includes the phrase "concernant les provinces françaises." Its strength is in its collection of texts from Normandy and, to a lesser extent, Anjou. Despite Delisle's attempts in his last years to come to terms with the English charters with the aid of H.E. Salter, we must await the completion of Sir James Holt's current project for anything like a full record of Henry's *acta*. Alongside the *Recueil*'s incompleteness Delisle's treatment of the chancery has not stood the test of time. The basic problem lay in his assumption that the Angevins possessed a well-regulated chancery with fixed rules. He therefore set out to analyze the formulae of the *acta* in the belief that they would allow them to be classified. This notion has been invalidated by T.A.M. Bishop's remarkable collection and analysis of the hands of the scribes of all Henry II's charters, an achievement that has demonstrated great variations within the work even of an individual scribe. Bishop's conclusions have been reinforced by Richard Mortimer's analysis of the criteria of authenticity to be applied to Henry's charters. To be fair to Delisle, whose chief published works on Henry II's charters are the efforts of an octogenarian relying on notes made over half a century earlier, it must be said that the intellectual framework for an approach to charters that put the accent on production by the beneficiaries did not exist in his day; the development of this framework did not truly start to come into being until the end of his life with the production of Maurice Prou's edition of the *acta* of Philip I and the editing of many more charters from the eleventh century.

In the *Recueil des actes de Henri II* Delisle was basically using the methods that he had followed in his earlier and greater work on charters, the *Catalogue des actes de Philippe Auguste*, published in 1856. Delisle's interest in Philip Augustus's charters went back to around 1848, and he produced an edition of some of the king's Norman charters in 1852. In the context of what was being accomplished in the 1850s Delisle's *Catalogue* is a startlingly original work. His achievement lay in the comparative analysis of the charters' formulae, which enabled him to understand both chronology and chancery diplomatics; his introduction is a masterpiece that succeeded precisely because Philip's chancery was a well-regulated organization. The twentieth-century edition of Philip's *acta*, which has taken most of the century to produce, and is still incomplete, has added some material unknown to Delisle, although not a dramatically larger quantity. Delisle also succeeded in producing the first systematic study of Philip's Registers, an analysis that in its general outlines has stood the test of time. Aspects of the compilation of the Registers have provoked controversy since Delisle wrote; his belief, for example, that Register A is founded on an earlier lost register has not been universally accepted, nor has his argument that the copies of the *acta* on the Registers were equivalent to minutes, rather than haphazard copies, with modern opinion still divided. John Baldwin's recent work on the government of Philip Augustus represents a leap forward in our understanding of the reign, but a clear assessment of the main documentation will not be achieved until the modern edition of the Registers is finished and the introductory fifth volume to the *Recueil des actes de Philippe-Auguste* is published. The publication of the *Catalogue* was followed shortly afterward by Delisle's election as a Membre de l'Institut.

As a side-result of the *Catalogue* Delisle produced a study of Innocent III's chancery in 1857, a consequence of having to read so many papal documents in order to analyze Philip's. The scholarship of this too has endured. In 1967, for example, Christopher and Mary Cheney wrote that "by far the most readable account of the chancery and its products is Léopold Delisle's 'Mémoire,' still not superseded, though at various points corrected, by later work" (Cheney and Cheney, xi, n. 3). The strength of Delisle's work again lay in the comparative analysis of formulae as the basis from which to understand the chancery's procedures. He set out here his frequently reiterated guiding principles of diplomatic studies, namely Mabillon's rule that all the evidence should be taken into account and the statement that diplomatic analysis can only be based on the texts of the originals.

The Bibliothèque Nationale absorbed Delisle's energies from the start. He records that immediately after his appointment, Guérard, who was to die shortly afterward, summoned him and announced that it was their responsibility to catalog the Bibliothèque's manuscripts. Even allowing for the fact that a nineteenth-century employee of the Bibliothèque would not have had to deal with the same amount of administration and readers as his late twentieth-century successors, Delisle's achievements were enormous. He produced the first list of over 10,000 of the Latin manuscripts, a catalog that, as Delisle acknowledged, does not measure up either to modern or to nineteenth-century critical standards (nor indeed to Delisle's own splendid catalog of the Fonds de Cluni), but that made the collection accessible and is still the finding aid on which we rely. One of Delisle's successors, Jules Cain, remarked in his preface to the catalog of the 1960 Delisle exhibition that "les inventaires et les catalogues établis par lui ou sous son impulsion demeurent des modèles" (Nortier [1960], Preface). As Administrator-General Delisle was also responsible for establishing the principles on which the massive *Catalogue général des livres imprimés* was based and for publishing the first twenty-one volumes. Delisle is universally regarded as one of the Bibliothèque's greatest administrators. There were complaints about his rule in the later years—his employees, for example, were notoriously ill paid, and neither electricity nor the telephone were installed in the building until after his retirement—but modern users of the Bibliothèque Nationale must quickly realize that it is only on the foundations laid personally by Delisle that they can explore its rich collections.

The three-volume *Le cabinet des manuscrits* was unquestionably Delisle's greatest publication during his time at the Bibliothèque; many regard it as his greatest work. He added a volume of lithographed plates; an index of the manuscripts cited therein was produced by Emmanuel Poulle in 1977. In *Le cabinet* Delisle set out to establish and describe the history of all the collections that had come into the Bibliothèque during its entire history. For patriotic reasons he was obliged to begin with Charlemagne, a duty that he discharged quickly before moving on to Charles V, the first king with serious claims to be a book collector. The work is at its greatest in its description of the acquisitions of the seventeenth and eighteenth centuries. The history of each collection is set out, and then each of its manuscripts that passed to the Bibliothèque Nationale is described, with its salient features identified. Often reference is made to manuscripts from the collection held in other libraries. The book discusses over 7,000 manuscripts, and the accompanying volume of plates is effectively a history of script throughout the medieval centuries. The 1977 index illustrates a methodological problem that appears not to have been apparent to Delisle, namely that researchers might wish to work back from the manuscript to Delisle's commentary; his book was conceived not as a work of reference, which it has become, but as a history of the Bibliothèque's collections.

Delisle himself came to believe that the whole book needed to be redone and said as much when he published in 1907 a second, much enlarged, analysis of the manuscripts surviving from Charles V's library. Delisle had come to appreciate that a full assessment of a manuscript's significance requires not just a grasp of the history of the collection in which it survives but a knowledge of its history from the moment of writing to its entry into its modern repository. This principle guided many of the most important publications of his later years.

Delisle's methodical treatment of manuscripts and his powerful visual memory, which enabled him to identify characteristics of script in a way given only to the gifted, produced a range of studies in his later years whose significance must nowadays be regarded as multidisciplinary. An example is his study of the calligraphy of the ninth-century school of Tours, published in

1885. Here Delisle analyzed twenty-five manuscripts surviving in a large number of libraries, but, as he showed, all demonstrably products of the school of Tours in the ninth century. He proceeded from a reconstruction of the library to analyze the characteristic features of the Tours scriptorium and establish principles that would enable other manuscripts to be identified. He was able to apply the same approach to other Carolingian scriptoria. His general views on the origins of Caroline minuscule as a sharp break with the past based on a decision to copy Roman script are no longer acceptable, but his methodology is fundamental to modern discussions of the writing and circulation of Carolingian manuscripts and the evolution of their script. The same approach enabled him to tackle liturgical, theological, and illuminated manuscripts in a way that established a clear chronological sequence, thereby creating a basis on which secure deductions have been made about, for example, sacramentaries, representations of the Apocalypse and Books of Hours. While Delisle was in no sense either a liturgist or an art historian, his application of the basic techniques of palaeography and diplomatics was seminal to the chronological and stylistic organization of a large number of manuscripts. His contribution is acknowledged by scholars working in many distinct fields.

It is both fascinating and futile to speculate on what Delisle might have achieved if he had not been employed at the Bibliothèque Nationale and had not devoted himself so wholeheartedly to its welfare. Across the spectrum there were gains and losses. His earliest works display an interest in social history and a capacity to unravel technical problems that could have led to great achievements. A major study of the reign of Philip Augustus was certainly abandoned. The documentation for the history of medieval Normandy would have been in much better order at a much earlier date if Delisle had devoted his life to it, as he once planned. Against this there is no doubt that the great benefit for posterity that resulted from the combination of Léopold Delisle and the Bibliothèque Nationale was that it made him feel and act as if he were responsible for all the manuscripts of France. A second level of patriotism overlaid his first loyalty to Normandy. At a given moment in, for example, the 1880s Delisle could be found producing seminal monographs on manuscripts of the entire medieval period, successfully regaining from England the Ashburnham manuscripts that had been fraudulently removed from French libraries and instructing the students of the École des Chartes in the basics of palaeography and diplomatics. The Norman Delisle would have been an important historian, but his impact would not have assumed the national and international proportions that followed from his work on behalf of the Bibliothèque Nationale.

The sharpest criticism that can be made of Delisle as a historian is one of intellectual incompleteness, that ideas were not always taken to their logical conclusion—the charge was made by Edélestand du Méril in a contemporary review of *La classe agricole* (B.N. nouv. acq. fr. 21845), and it has been repeated in a recent review of Delisle's achievements commissioned by the Institut de France (Anon.: 436). Delisle was no great narrative historian, and he showed little interest in theory. He belonged firmly in the midst of the positivist second half of the nineteenth century, and he seems firmly to have believed that his contributions were part of human progress. All these points are valid. Reduced to the lowest common denominator, Delisle's publications and career show him as essentially a problem solver; his intellect was of the sort that can define a topic with razor-sharp clarity and produce persuasive solutions.

Yet such an assessment is inadequate. The scope and quantity of the problems to which Delisle produced solutions are what create his greatness, above all as a master of palaeography and diplomatics but also as a librarian and administrator. And although he never wrote extensively in conceptual terms, his contribution to the study of palaeography, manuscripts, charters, and historical writing represents a major theoretical contribution to historical method. The combination of energy, vision, and technical brilliance places Delisle among the most important and influential of the individuals who have contributed to the study of the western European Middle Ages.

SELECTED BIBLIOGRAPHY
For a full bibliography on Delisle, see Lacombe.

Works

BOOKS AND ARTICLES

"Des revenus publics en Normandie au XIIe siècle." *Bibliothèque de l'école des chartes* 10 (1848–49): 173–210, 257–89; 11 (1849–50): 400–51; 13 (1852): 97–135.

Études sur la condition de la classe agricole et l'état de l'agriculture en Normandie au moyen âge. Évreux: Hérissey, 1851.

Ed. *Cartulaire normand de Philippe-Auguste, Louis VIII, Saint Louis et Philippe-le-Hardi.* Caen: Hardel, 1852.

Ed. with A. Le Prévost. *Orderici Vitalis angligenae, coenobii Uticensis monachi, Historiae ecclesiasticae libri tredecim.* 5 vols. Paris: Renouard, 1838–55.

Ed. *Catalogue des actes de Philippe-Auguste.* Paris: Durand, 1856.

Mémoire sur les actes d'Innocent III, suivi de l'itinéraire de ce pontife. Paris: Durand, 1857.

Ed. *Recueil de jugements de l'échiquier de Normandie au XIIIe siècle (1207–1270) suivi d'un mémoire sur les anciennes collections de ces jugements.* Paris: Imprimerie impériale, 1864.

Ed. *Rouleaux des morts du IXe au XVe siècle.* Paris: Renouard, 1866.

Histoire du château et des sires de Saint-Sauveur-le-Vicomte suivie de pièces justificatives. Valognes: Martin, etc., 1867.

Le cabinet des manuscrits de la Bibliothèque impériale [nationale]. 3 vols + album. Paris: Imprimerie impériale, 1868–81.

Ed. *Chronique de Robert de Torigni, abbé du Mont-Saint-Michel: suivie de divers opuscules historiques de cet auteur et de plusieurs religieux de la même abbaye.* 2 vols. Rouen: Le Brument, 1872–73.

Mémoire sur l'école calligraphique de Tours au IXe siècle. Paris: Imprimerie nationale, 1885.

Mémoire sur d'anciens sacramentaires. Paris: Imprimerie nationale, 1886.

Livres d'images destinés à l'instruction religieuse et aux exercices de piété des laïques. Paris: Imprimerie nationale, 1890.

With P. Meyer. *L'Apocalypse en francais au XIIIe siècle (Bibl. nat. fr. 403).* Paris: Firmin-Didot, 1901.

"Hommage à l'Académie des Inscriptions et Belles-Lettres, 1857–1907: Souvenirs de Jeunesse." In his *Recherches sur la librairie de Charles V.* 2 vols., 1, pp. xi–xxvii. Paris: Champion, 1907.

Ed. with Élie Berger. *Recueil des actes de Henri II, roi d'Angleterre et duc de Normandie, concernant les provinces francaises et les affaires de France.* 4 vols. Paris: Imprimerie nationale, 1909–27.

LETTERS AND PAPERS

Delisle's letters to his closest and lifelong friend Charles Robillard de Beaurepaire remain almost entirely unedited. See B.N. nouv. acq. fr. 23912. Delisle destroyed all the letters he had received on his abrupt ejection from the rue des Petits-Champs in 1905. They had up until that point been splendidly preserved.

Delisle presented his personal library and his collection of transcripts to the Bibliothèque Nationale. The latter are preserved in sixty-eight volumes, B.N. nouv. acq. fr. 21806–73. See Nortier, Michel. "Les sources de l'histoire de la Normandie à la Bibliothèque Nationale de Paris." *Cahiers Léopold Delisle* 9 (1960): 19–33.

Lettres de Léopold Delisle à M. le chanoine Tougard, à M. Auguste Castan, à M. le chanoine Ulysse Chevalier, à M. Léon de La Sicotière, à M. Louis Blancard, à Henry d'Arbois de Jubainville, edited by Xavier Delisle. Saint-Lô, etc. (1911–13).

Sauvage, René-Norbert. "Lettres de Léopold Delisle à Antoine Charma, secrétaire de la Société des Antiquaires de Normandie (1849–68)." *Bulletin de la société des antiquaires de Normandie* 37 (1926–27): 351–89.

Nortier, Michel. "Lettres inédites de Léopold Delisle." *Cahiers Léopold Delisle* 9 (1960): 1–18.

Sources

Anon. "L'érudition et l'édition des documents médiévaux à l'Académie: Léopold Delisle (1826–1910)." In *L'Institut de France dans le monde actuel: catalogue de l'exibition, Musée Jacquemart-André,* pp. 436–38. Paris: Institut de France, 1986.

Baldwin, John W. *The Government of Philip Augustus: Foundations of French Royal Power in the Middle Ages.* Berkeley: University of California Press, 1986.

Bishop, Terrance Aean Martyn, ed. *Scriptores regis: Facsimiles to Identify and Illustrate the Hands of Royal Scribes in Original Charters of Henry I, Stephen, and Henry II.* Oxford: Clarendon, 1961.

Bloch, Marc. *Les caractères originaux de l'histoire rurale française.* Oslo: Ascheoug; Cambridge, Mass.: Harvard University Press, 1931.

Bois, Guy. *The Crisis of Feudalism: Economy and Society in Eastern Normandy, c. 1300–1550.* Cambridge: Cambridge University Press; Paris: Éditions de la Maison des Sciences de l'Homme, 1984.

Cheney, Christopher Robert and Mary G. Cheney, eds. *The Letters of Pope Innocent III (1198–1216) concerning England and Wales: A Calendar with an Appendix of Texts.* Oxford: Clarendon, 1967.

Chibnall, Marjorie, ed. *The Ecclesiastical History of Orderic Vitalis.* 6 vols. Oxford: Clarendon, 1969–80.

École Nationale des Chartes. *Livre du centenaire (1821–1921).* 2 vols. Paris: École des Chartes, 1921.

Espinas, Georges. "Léopold Delisle: 1826–1910," pp. 121–75. Paris: Bulletin et mémoires de la société nationale des antiquaires de France, 1911.

Huard, Georges. "Léopold Delisle et la Normandie." *Cahiers Léopold Delisle* 1 (1947): 5–29.

Lacombe, Paul. *Bibliographie des travaux de M. Léopold Delisle, membre de l'Institut, administateur général de la Bibliothèque nationale.* Paris: Imprimerie nationale, 1902. *Supplément, (1902–10).* Paris: Leclerc, 1911.

Le Cacheux, Paul. *Léopold Delisle et le pays de Valognes.* Cherbourg: Imprimerie de la Dépêche de Cherbourg, 1910.

Mortimer, Richard. "The Charters of Henry II: What Are the Criteria of Authenticity?" *Anglo-Norman Studies* 12 (1990): 119–34.

Nortier, Michel. *Léopold Delisle: Exposition organisé pour le cinquantenaire de sa mort.* Paris: Bibliothèque Nationale, 1960.

———. "Les actes de Philippe Auguste: notes critiques sur les sources diplomatiques du règne." In *La France de Philippe Auguste: le temps des mutations,* edited by Robert-Henri Bautier, pp. 429–51. Paris: Centre nationale recherche scientifique, 1982.

Poole, Reginald L. "Léopold Delisle, 1826–1910." *Proceedings of the British Academy* 5 (1911–12): 203–21.

Van Houts, Elisabeth, ed. and trans. *The "Gesta Normannorum Ducum" of William of Jumièges, Orderic Vitalis, and Robert of Torigni.* 2 vols. Oxford: Clarendon, 1992–.

Varry, Dominique, ed. *Les bibliothèques de la Révolution et du XIXe siècle: 1789–1914.* Volume 3 of *Histoire des bibliothèques françaises,* edited by André Vernet. Paris: Cercle de la Libraire-Promodis, 1991.

This essay has benefited from the assistance of and conversations with many scholars knowledgeable about the enormous range of Léopold Delisle's writings. I am particularly grateful to M. Michel Nortier, Conservateur-en-Chef Honoraire at the Bibliothèque Nationale, for a valuable discussion and for practical assistance. I have received valuable photocopies from Mme. Mireille Pastoureau of the Bibliothèque de l'Institut de France and Mlle. Béatrice Poulle of the Archives du Calvados. I must also thank Marjorie Chibnall, Giles Constable, Lindy Grant, Sir James Holt, Rosamond McKitterick, Vincent Moss, Nigel Ramsay, Nora Temple, and Elisabeth van Houts for their assistance.

Henry Adams

(1838–1918)

Karl F. Morrison

Henry Brooks Adams, an American historian whose claim to the attention of medievalists depends on one improbable book, was born in Boston on 16 February 1838 and died in Washington, D.C., on 27 March 1918. Except for some passages in *The Education of Henry Adams*, which was written as a companion volume in 1906, and an earlier essay on "The Anglo-Saxon Courts of Law" (1876), *Mont-Saint-Michel and Chartres* (1904) stands alone in his oeuvre as holding a significant place in medieval studies. It engaged the imagination of a wide public. Continuously in print for nearly a hundred years, it is still widely used for teaching in North America. Adams undertook the book in secrecy in 1897 and treated even its printing in 1904 as a private matter, paying for 150 copies, which he distributed to his closest friends. A second private printing of five hundred copies (1912) contained some emendations. Soon thereafter, with an elaborate show of reluctance, Adams allowed the book to be released to the public in 1913.

The reasons for this esoteric behavior lay in Adams's temperament and general way of life. The book marked a departure from his main scholarly ventures, as exotic in its way as his *Memoirs of Marau Taaroa, Last Queen of Tahiti*, which was also printed in a small, private edition (1893; reprinted as *Memoirs of Arii Taimai*, 1901). The strangeness of *Mont-Saint-Michel and Chartres* lies in its antihistorical disregard for facts and in its defiance of the "scientific method" that as a young man Adams had learned in Germany and introduced, with the graduate seminar, into the curriculum at Harvard. Although he recognized the difference between professional historians' need for precision of detail and his own aim for architectonic correctness of "the ensemble" (*Letters*, 5: 628), Adams considered his study of the Middle Ages part of a broad attempt to demonstrate that the course of history had followed natural laws of development known through physics. His evocation of the eleventh and twelfth centuries is so idiosyncratic and his manipulation of data so sovereign that *Mont-Saint-Michel and Chartres* must be considered as belles lettres, or poetry, rather than as history, a book little regarded among medievalists outside the United States.

The great-grandson and grandson of United States presidents, Adams was one of five children born to Charles Francis Adams, who held elective and appointive offices in Massachusetts and in the federal government, and to Abigail Brooks Adams, who brought to the marriage a network of dynastic associations and wealth. Educated privately, Henry gained proficiency as a child in Greek, Latin, and French and limited competence in German. He attended Harvard College, where he excelled in composition and rhetoric.

Adams's education at Harvard added other striations to his habits of thought. As an undergraduate he was swept up into the ever-expanding controversy between advocates of received religious doctrines about creation and human destiny and proponents of new scientific ideas. Much taken by what he learned about botany and geology, he gained a lasting conviction that natural law underlay the course of history, a version, he thought, of Darwinism. By a philosophical positivism derived from Auguste Comte he was won over to the search for an organic unity of culture, nationalistically conceived. James Russell Lowell, one of his professors, introduced him to German methods of research and instilled in him a fascination with historical literary analysis. His later, gloomy assessment that Harvard had been the ruin of him fell short of the mark.

After graduation he traveled extensively in Europe (1858–60) to study civil law, first in Berlin and later, with flagging enthusiasm, in Dresden and in Italy. His attention to legal history evolved from pride in the distinction that his father and many of his forebears had won as attorneys. He himself at first intended to follow in their footsteps, and although he eventually gave up his plans to become a lawyer, his studies of law and legal history in Germany had unexpected results. He learned new methods of textual criticism that he applied in his brief teaching career, especially when he instituted both graduate instruction (leading to the Ph.D. degree) and the graduate seminar at Harvard.

On his return from Germany in 1860 Adams found the United States at the threshold of civil war. Just appointed minister to England, Charles Francis Adams engaged his son as private secretary, and the ambassadorial perspective in London (1861–68) deepened Henry's knowledge of parliamentary institutions and their histories and established personal ties, some of them with historians, that long continued.

When Charles Francis Adams's appointment ended, father and son returned to the United States together. Adams worked as a journalist in Boston and in Washington before accepting an invitation to teach medieval history at Harvard, a task for which, he noted, he was entirely unqualified. More than modesty prompted this appraisal. In the mid- and late nineteenth century specialized professional qualifications were commonly regarded as skills that could be acquired on the job. Adams had little expert knowledge to commend him. Ephraim Whitney Gurney, later Adams's brother-in-law, was professor of ancient history at Harvard and head of the history department. He was seeking a young colleague who could assist him in advancing the reorganization of the curriculum in history. He knew Adams's family and had social obligations to them; he knew Adams as a contributor to his journal, the *North American Review*. He recommended the appointment to President Eliot, who also had longstanding ties with the Adamses and who was able to prevail over Henry Adams's initial reluctance. As a measure of Adams's lack of specialist knowledge one of his students, J. Lawrence Laughlin, recalled many years later that while teaching at Harvard Adams had been asked to define transubstantiation. "Good Heavens!" he answered. "How should I know? Look it up!" (Stevenson, 117).

His years on the Harvard faculty (1870–77) were notable. He introduced new methods of both undergraduate and graduate teaching. In a collaborative venture he published the landmark *Essays in Anglo-Saxon Law* (1876), comprising a monograph by Adams and doctoral dissertations by three of his graduate students on courts, land law, family law, and legal procedure. Adams set a common tone by denying that Anglo-Saxon legal institutions had sprung from a distinctive historical experience and followed an unparalleled line of development. Popular assemblies and their customary practices, he wrote, were the source of law among all Germanic peoples. But as the eighty pages of select cases indicate, the contributions were highly positivistic. No effort was made to give the four studies a single, thematic harmony.

Adams's seminar did not prove a nursery of medieval studies in the United States. Of the three students who contributed to *Essays in Anglo-Saxon Law* none continued as a medievalist. Ernest Young (1852–1888) died early. J. Lawrence Laughlin (1850–1933), turning to banking and to political economy, established that subject with great distinction at the University of Chicago (1892–1916). Henry Cabot Lodge (1850–1924) became a dominant figure in national politics. Lodge, however, made one further contribution to literature on the Middle Ages: he planted in Adams's mind the seeds of *Mont-Saint-Michel and Chartres*.

Two other companions of the Harvard years did a great deal to shape medieval history as an academic field. Ephraim Emerton (1851–1935) was

Adams's younger colleague at Harvard, an instructor in history and German (1876–78) and later Winn Professor of Ecclesiastical History. A more assiduous student than Adams had been in Germany, Emerton studied in Berlin and earned a doctorate at Leipzig. Like Adams he imported German methods of historical analysis to North America. Although Emerton's research concerned primarily the Renaissance and Reformation, his widely used textbooks on medieval history established a national standard of knowledge and instruction. The other companion was Henry Osborn Taylor (1856–1941), who studied in Adams's classes on United States history. Adams's influence may have entered into Taylor's decision to study law, first at Columbia and afterward at Leipzig, as it may also have colored his later fascination with the transformations of "sensibility" on which he centered his *The Medieval Mind* and his celebrated books on the transmission of classical tradition to the Middle Ages. The correspondence between Adams and Taylor establishes that both men recognized their fundamentally discrepant objectives, motives, and methods, a discrepancy also evident in Taylor's respectful but uncommending review of *Mont-Saint-Michel and Chartres*.

Adams's attention at Harvard soon wandered. He had not yet abandoned hopes of entering politics by way of journalism. Succeeding Gurney as editor of the *North American Review*, he made every effort to pull levers as an arbiter of political and literary judgment. At the same time he moved the subjects of his courses away from the Middle Ages toward the constitutional history of England and finally to that of the United States.

It is hard to appraise Adams's achievement at Harvard. Although he attracted a wide following in his undergraduate lectures and inaugurated graduate studies in medieval history according to the German seminar method, these were personal accomplishments, lacking the institutional continuity of programs. They did not ramify through the careers of his students, and Adams himself abandoned them. He gradually left aside responsibilities that ceased to interest him, including courses in medieval history, and in time he confined graduate teaching to repetitive exercises. When with the jaundiced eye of his later years Adams himself took stock of his academic career in *The Education of Henry Adams*, he found little rewarding to mention, least of all his experiments in medieval history, jettisoned as he wandered into the constitutional history of the United States.

While at Harvard Adams added a further dynastic alliance to his family's inventory through his marriage in 1872 to Marian Hooper (known as "Clover"). Apart from eminence in lineage and wealth Clover brought to the union intellect and a keen aesthetic judgment. Her brother, Edward Hooper, treasurer of Harvard and a distinguished connoisseur and collector of art, became one of Adams's closest friends and introduced him into a circle of men who through the years powerfully educated his aesthetic judgment; the circle included the painter John La Farge and the architect H.H. Richardson. During their honeymoon Adams and his wife found life on the high seas of a world capital, London, more invigorating than life in an academic backwater. Increasingly repelled in the next years by what he considered the "idiocies" of university education, he resigned his position in 1877.

Moving to Washington, Adams completed his major scholarly ventures, all dedicated to the history of the United States: the *Life of Albert Gallatin*, accompanied by an edition of Gallatin's writings (1879); *John Randolph* (1882); and, most distinguished of all, his *History of the United States from 1801 to 1817* (9 volumes, 1885–91). More and more scornful of ways of thinking employed, taught, and rewarded by professional historians, he never resumed teaching. His vice-presidencies and presidency of the American Historical Association (1891–94) were characterized chiefly by his absences from the country. His political ambitions failed. His sense of isolation and distaste for the new social order evolving around him became increasingly bitter, especially after the suicide of his wife in 1885.

Chronic restlessness beset him; he traveled frequently and widely, to Japan and Ceylon, to Polynesia, to Cuba, and annually to Europe. An abiding need for power drew him into intrigues that contributed to the Cuban revolt against Spain and thus to the Spanish-American War (Samuels [1989], 323–24). He undertook his two most celebrated works, *Mont-Saint-Michel and Chartres* and *The Education of Henry Adams*, late in life, as diversions from the cynic's greatest enemy, boredom.

Adams once confided to William James that the last chapter in *Mont-Saint-Michel and Chartres*, on Thomas Aquinas, was "the only thing" that he had ever written that he "almost" thought good (Mane, 218). Convinced that his own epoch had degenerated into chaos, even as the Gothic synthesis had been overtaken by disintegration, Adams characterized Aquinas as he characterized himself—an architect of thought, building according to meticulous design, "stone by stone," a structure of equilibrium that concealed its own instability. What Thomas and Gothic architects achieved by "the power of broad and lofty generalization" were analogs of those accomplished through application of modern theories of energy, including Adams's own applications of the laws of physics to the broad sweep of history. They all proclaimed their aspirations through magnificent unity of plan; but they buried in their foundations, "as [their] last secret," "self-distrust and anguish of doubt." And, Adams concluded, "to me, this is all" (Adams [1936], 377).

The conception of unity, of "the ensemble," expressed in *Mont-Saint-Michel and Chartres* also concealed anguish and self-doubt. Dramatizing *Mont-Saint-Michel and Chartres* as private intellectual "travels," Adams recast Thomas Aquinas as a persona of himself, just as, indeed, he made the road from Mont-Saint-Michel to Chartres sketched in the book a topography of Adams's mind, rather than one of France or its history. Through the book as self-portrayal there also ran a fascination with power, or energy, released in a calculated play of visible structure against secret faults. Adams regarded *Mont-Saint-Michel and Chartres: A Study of Thirteenth-Century Unity* and *The Education of Henry Adams: A Study of Twentieth-Century Multiplicity* as coordinates in his reflections on the loss of unity, not least in the study of his own mind (Adams [1931], 431–35). *Mont-Saint-Michel and Chartres*, like *The Education*, is novelesque, if not a novel, and all the characters, including both Abelard and the Blessed Virgin, are masks of Henry Adams (Samuels [1964], 353). As self-portrayal *Mont-Saint-Michel and Chartres* partakes of Adams's sense in later life that he had long since died, and that he survived in an unreal, "posthumous" existence.

While the book may initially have been prompted by boredom, the great puzzle is what kept Adams writing *Mont-Saint-Michel and Chartres* and writing in a way that, as he recognized, had little to do with the methods of professional historians. There is no evidence, for instance, that Adams had even read Aquinas's own writings. In general his discussion of medieval intellectual history was drawn from intermediate, scholarly analyses, some of them outdated. Likewise, Adams visited Mont-Saint-Michel only once and Chartres twice. His on-site observations were cursory, and even though he consulted architectural photographs extensively while writing the book, his comments indicate incomplete, and in some regards mistaken knowledge.

Adams had begun collecting materials for his book as early as 1897, but its configuration of ideas took shape in 1893–95. Visiting the World's Columbian Exposition at Chicago in 1893, he encountered a "Babel" in the industrial and historical exhibits and technical advances that both fascinated and terrified him. The human ability to create unbounded energy, represented by the dynamo, aroused his love of power, but the inhumanity of the dynamo and its applications marked the end of the ordered eighteenth-century world into which, he judged, he had been born and fragments of which he had wrapped around himself as a cocoonlike insulation from reality.

His forebodings appeared justified by the financial panic of 1893. Through astute management he was able to rescue his personal wealth and his family's trusts from jeopardy. However, danger of sudden impoverishment compounded his sense that his loyalties belonged to a social order whose time had passed, an order morally superior to its enemies and subverters. Longstanding prejudice taught him that bankers, personified in his mind as Jews, were the most treacherous. His brother Brooks Adams, in *The Law of Civilization and Decay*, argued that the present crisis replicated earlier circumstances, when the growth and dominance of financial institutions, especially those designed for the manipulation of credit, had destroyed the most splendid of all civilizations, that of thirteenth-century Europe. Henry Adams regarded *The Law of Civilization and Decay* as one of the greatest historical studies. He labored over it exhaustively as editor and saw to its publication and later to its translation and publication in French. He easily assimilated its pessimism, its idealization of an aristocratic society brought to ruin by usurers, and its use of art as a barometer of cultural splendor and decay.

The lessons of 1893 were compounded when Adams returned to Paris for the Exposition of 1900. Awestruck to the point of prayer in the hall of dynamos, he recognized that "forty-five years of study had proved to be quite futile for the pursuit of power" (Adams [1931], 389). Disoriented, he found that he did not know how to look at the exhibits of contemporary art. The vicissitudes of life had gradually convinced him that art, in its durability, was more real than human life, in its transience. Adams's fascination with art came to him primarily from his wife, her family, and a small circle of friends gathered around them. His brother Brooks disclosed that art was a barometer of culture; cherishing a residue from the vanished happiness of his marriage, Adams reached farther. In 1900 he again proclaimed that art was a vernacular in which the laws of physics were made intelligible, a vernacular that had governed the dynamics of western culture down to his own age. By those same laws, he thought, the West had become exhausted, fearful, engulfed by ignorance, and chaotic in the disintegration of its mind.

As he traveled in Europe from 1895 onward, Adams discovered, or invented, his ancestral origins in eleventh-century Normandy. His companion and guide there was his former student Henry Cabot Lodge, who as United States Senator raised his own racist convictions to the level of public policy. In 1895 Lodge introduced Adams to Mont-Saint-Michel, Chartres, and other cathedrals and churches. He also reinforced in Adams a sense of ethnic identity, with its associated hatreds. Adams said that although he had visited Amiens, he had "never thoroughly felt it before" (*Letters*, 4: 311).

Adams identified himself with Norman rather than Anglo-Saxon ancestry. As the senior collaborator on *Essays in Anglo-Saxon Law* he had argued that in England Teutonic institutions were the source of popular, democratic, and free principles of government. The feudal and manorial systems, imported through conquest, temporarily effaced them; but they revived as the alien systems withered. Although divided over whether Anglo-Saxons or Normans were the authentic founders of the English nation, historians agreed that the Norman Conquest, with the introduction of feudalism, supplanted Anglo-Saxon values and institutions. In 1876 Adams's scholarship placed him on the side of the democratic conquered, overwhelmed for a time yet eventually reaffirmed. Twenty-five years later he identified himself with the aristocratic conqueror, whose ultimate failure brought the *Götterdämmerung* of all European history in its wake. Significantly, the Normans had an ambiguous character, neither French nor English, but assimilating characteristics from, and for a time dominating, each.

Adams's feelings of Norman identity, which had been drawn out by architecture, were heightened when he and Lodge visited Norman buildings in Sicily (1899). Their tour was decisive; for Adams's thoughts then so coalesced that he began to write *Mont-Saint-Michel and Chartres* almost immediately after his return to Paris. However, he ostentatiously avoided consulting any medievalists or architectural historians, including Gabriel Monod, with whom Adams had had cordial dealings for thirty years. He had come to despise Monod as his "idiot friend" for what Adams considered philo-Semitism in the Dreyfus case (1894–1906). He was, as he wrote on another occasion, used "to audiences of one" (Adams [1931], 339).

Although experiences between 1893 and 1895 were decisive for the general conception of *Mont-Saint-Michel and Chartres*, the ideas that they refined had long been present. Chief among them was the sense of being called to a glorious destiny by inheritance, the inheritance that at the same time prevented him from achieving it, relegating him to the estrangement and powerlessness of a "posthumous" existence. When Adams composed *The Education*, he recalled how he had been "branded" by his dynastic legacy and "handicapped in the races of the coming century." He learned, he said—equally in the rustic simplicity of the Adamses at Quincy and in the opulence of his maternal grandfather Brooks at Boston—how "a cruel universe combined to crush a child" (Adams [1931], 3, 12). His artful reconstruction of the past combined these metaphors of hurt and helplessness with others of estrangement, all emotions that Adams significantly attached to a woman, his paternal grandmother.

Adams found his own sense of estrangement paralleled in the life of Mrs. John Quincy Adams (born Louisa Catherine Johnson), who was kept on the margins of the Adams family circle. Born in London in 1775, the daughter of an Englishwoman and a merchant from Maryland, she spent her childhood as an alien in England and France. After her marriage in 1797 she accompanied John Quincy Adams on his diplomatic postings in other alien environments, in Berlin, and, after an interlude in the United States, in Russia and London. Subsequently her husband's duties as secretary of state, president, and member of Congress kept her in Washington. Her mother-in-law, Abigail Adams, considered Louisa not up to the standards of New England womanhood; Adams recalled that her "primal sin"—not being "of pure New England stock"—had passed also to her son, Henry Adams's father, who had entered old age "before he quite accepted Boston, or Boston quite accepted him" (Adams [1931], 19). Henry portrayed the lives of Louisa and her son as studies in how wives could be made strangers in their husbands' houses and how children could be kept on the margin of the society into which their mothers had married.

Yet ambivalence of gender prevailed in his own marriage; he found himself among both excluders and excluded. Convinced that he had been kept on the periphery of Brahmin society as his mother's child, Charles Francis Adams used his own household to form a hollow square against outsiders. Among those kept at a distance was his daughter-in-law Clover Adams, whom he made to feel an outsider within the gates, even though she was a Boston Brahmin of the highest order and brought a considerable fortune to her marriage. Henry was in turn excluded from the agnatic circle of his wife. He had no part in the intense affection between Clover and her father, whose last sickness and death was a prelude to her suicide. During the depression of her last weeks Clover anticipated being buried near her father at Mount Auburn Cemetery in Cambridge. Adams associated the agnatic marginalism that both he and Clover experienced with wives and female descent. His decision to provide a common burialplace for her and himself at Rock Creek Cemetery in Washington asserted the priority of his marginalism over hers and placed them both beneath a gynandrous monument that carried no name.

When he came to write *The Education*, Adams held that his family's tendency to "doubts and self-questionings" had originated in the "severe stress and little pure satisfaction" that the ambivalence of a woman, Louisa Adams, had imprinted on her lineage. Diminutive as an adult, Adams had been as a child conscious of physical inferiority to his brothers and of "a certain delicacy of mind and bone" (Adams [1931], 19). Adams assimilated characteristics that a biographer identified as "almost feminine ambiguities," traits of character by which Adams "insulated [himself] from the free give and take of the masculine world" (Samuels [1958], 284; [1964], 455, 549). Convinced of his own helplessness and admonished to uphold his family's masculine tradition of public service, Adams from childhood displayed a gender ambivalence: he was later to write two novels about women, issuing one (*Esther*, 1884) under a feminine *nom de plume*, and eventually to identify himself with the Blessed Virgin, as the supreme embodiment of energy, "the greatest force the Western world ever felt" (Adams [1931], 388–89). The childlessness of his marriage reinforced these feelings.

Mont-Saint-Michel and Chartres is an excursion through three centuries (from the eleventh through the thirteenth), "not," as Adams wrote, to get "anything that can possibly be useful or instructive; but only a sense of what those centuries had to say, and a sympathy with their ways of saying it" (Adams [1936], 60). The journey begins with the sheer power and genius for warfare and government wielded by the Normans. It continues, and reaches its goal, in the intellectual and spiritual glories of the Île de France, above all in mysticism and scholastic philosophy. The Archangel Michael stood for power; the Blessed Virgin, for grace. And Adams made the different architectural vernaculars of those two great shrines, the abbey of Mont-Saint-Michel in Normandy and the cathedral of Chartres ("the court of the Queen of Heaven"), the symbolic brackets of his journey. But the journey was through Adams's mind as much as it was through one vast segment of European civilization.

Mont-Saint-Michel and Chartres took shape in a mind preoccupied with the disintegration of European culture. Brooks Adams's *The Law of Civilization and Decay* was urgently in Henry Adams's mind as he experienced his illumination in Normandy, looking, as he thought, at the grandeur in which the decadence of his own time had originated. Characteristically Adams resolved ambivalences in irony, elucidated in metaphors of gender. For there was, he saw, a worm at the heart of the Virgin's rose. Her reign was a brief, illusory interlude. In the end the cult of the Virgin and the glories ramifying from it were disclosed to be a "fausse route" by the nightmares that they concealed (Adams [1936], 247–48). Worship gave way to satire; hope, to despair; unity, to disintegration genetically akin to the dissonance that repelled Adams from his own culture.

Nurtured by readings in oriental philosophies, his youthful observations also planted in his mind the idea that history itself was the dialectical opposition between a male principle, codified in the theology of a masculine Trinity, and a female principle. Exalted and glorified in the Virgin's cult between the eleventh and thirteenth centuries, the female principle was eventually driven into a covert and ambiguous existence, just as non-New Englanders were marginalized in Boston and as wives and their offspring could be, among the Adamses, "exotic" like his grandmother or "half-exotic" like his father. He left unspoken the ambivalences of his own marriage. Using this grand theme, the decline of the feminine principle, as a key to the decline of the West, Adams found in the degradation of the feminine into exoticism an allegory and an explanation of his own disappointed hopes, perhaps even of his childless marriage.

Although Adams considered the "French solution" to architectural problems in the cathedral dedicated at Chartres to the Virgin the most successful of all, yet he found the transition from the "masculinity" of Romanesque to the "femininity" of Gothic had already been made in Normandy in an architectural movement beginning at the abbey of Mont-Saint-Michel and ending at the cathedral of Coutances. At Coutances Adams noted the contrast between the masculinity of the façade, united and animated throughout by "the Norman nature," and the femininity of its Gothic interior, revealing "the passionate outbreak of religious devotion to the ideal of feminine grace, charity, and love . . . among the most hard-hearted and hard-headed races in Europe" (Adams [1936], 50). He stressed the hiddenness of this femininity as a trait of character: "The Normans, as they slowly reveal themselves, disclose most unexpected qualities; one seems to sound subterranean caverns of feeling hidden behind their iron nasals" (Adams [1936], 49–50).

Adams recalled his visit to Coutances at sunset on 23 August 1895 as a moment of emotional intensity. Suddenly, he thought, he laid hold on the faith that gave Gothic architecture its energy, daring, and grace. By a leap of imagination he conceived that his Norman soul was built into the cathedral of Coutances, with its masculine façade and slowly revealed feminine interior. The composition of *Mont-Saint-Michel and Chartres* was a sequel to this profound realization. By the time he wrote the book, Adams had identified the repressed energies in himself with a characteristic that he considered distinctly feminine: its concealment, its nuanced many-sidedness. And he had also identified two facets that he considered feminine: the first, the experience of being "exotic" or "half-exotic," as in marriage; the second, an esoteric turning inward, as Louisa Adams of whose "interior life" nothing was known, had turned inward and as the architects of Coutances had done in concealing a feminine sanctuary behind a masculine front. Gender ambivalence inherent in those traits was expressed in Adams's tactic of placing himself in the company of women with whom he could not broach the possibility of remarriage and so demonstrating again his procreative incapacity. He visualized this ambivalence not only in his dramatic pose of having died simultaneously with Clover Adams but also in the androgynous image that he commissioned Augustus Saint-Gaudens to make for the grave where he intended to be buried with her.

The misogyny in Adams's gender ambivalence accompanied an aristocratic contempt for the unprivileged orders of society and a hatred of Jews. His correspondence during the summer of 1895 is full of revulsion at the sightseers crowding his cherished buildings. He esteemed the Norman austerity of Coutances over more elaborate ornamentation in later churches, including Chartres, because the Gothic visual richness testified to the exploitative zeal of moneylenders, "infernal Jews." "In spite of her own origin," Adams wrote, the Virgin, one of Adam's personas, "disliked Jews and rarely neglected a chance to maltreat them" (Mane, 82–87; Adams [1936], 263).

Contrasting strands of pride and impotence parallel those of gyniolatry and misogyny in Adam's self-portrayal. Self-analysis and representation engaged both discordant sides of his gynandrous temperament. In a telling passage of *The Education* Adams observed that women were known chiefly through historical documents written by men. "The woman who is known only through a man is known wrong, and excepting one or two like Mme. de Sévigné, no woman has pictured herself. The American woman of the nineteenth century will live only as the man saw her . . ." (Adams [1931], 353). The masculine in Adams determined what of himself, masculine and feminine, would be disclosed. The general scale of omission is indicated by Adams's decision to obliterate his wife and their marriage entirely from his memoirs. With equally total concealment he passed over in silence the twenty years between his appointment at Harvard in 1871 and the complete publication of his *History of the United States* in 1892. To secure the omissions he made in *The Education* he had (1888, 1890, 1898) destroyed diaries, segments of correspondence, and other papers that could have been used as corrective evidence (Samuels [1948], ix).

Much of himself celebrated in the gyniolatry of *Mont-Saint-Michel and Chartres* was consigned to this narrative void. In *The Education* Adams omitted any account of how he gained his knowledge of medieval history and his journalist's skill in clarifying by metaphor; his aestheticism; his sense of isolation from and hostility toward overriding currents in contemporary society; and thus also his delight in a covert existence and in writing for his own amusement without a wider audience. By such omissions he deliberately failed to elucidate characteristics that made him virtually alone, exotic, esoteric, characteristics that he considered feminine.

His exaltation of what he took to be archaic feminine power entered into his *Memoirs of Arii Taimai*, in which he assumed the narrative persona of the "chiefess," and most notably in *Mont-Saint-Michel and Chartres*, where he followed the pattern that he ascribed to women who "for thousands of years," in their consistent rebellion against degradation, "had made a fortress of religion"—though in his case the fortress, the cult of the Virgin, was one built by and for his own imagination (Adams, [1931], 446). "His disgust with the male" (Decker, 249) was balanced by his assertion of masculinity, not least in his creation of a fictive but historical self-portrait; his idealization of women was balanced by what passes for misogyny, closely entwined with Adams's sense of failure and impotence.

Adams associated religion with femininity. The prominence of religion in *Mont-Saint-Michel and Chartres* is one of its greatest improbabilities; for Adams himself disclaimed religious sensibility. Although he recalled in passing an "aching consciousness of religious void" about 1895, the "religious instinct" possible in the "mild deism" of his youth had long since "vanished and could not be revived, although one made in later life many efforts to recover it" (Adams [1931], 34, 352). He had forbidden the cross that Clover, in the end, installed on the façade of the house designed for them by H.H. Richardson. And yet after his wife's death, perhaps attempting to recapture some of her unfocused spirituality, Adams's own exoticism prompted him to inquire into Buddhism.

The quest for Nirvana was one reason for his opulent voyage to Japan and Ceylon in the spring of 1886, on which his friend the painter John La Farge trained his eye with lessons in watercolor painting. (On a visit to France La Farge introduced him to the history and aesthetic possibilities of stained glass, instruction later put to use in *Mont-Saint-Michel and Chartres*.) Under the influence of the visit to the Far East Adams composed a poem entitled "Buddha and Brahma," a work that is instructive as an opening on Adams's conception of civic life, including his own. Although he admired the Buddha, Adams portrayed the Buddha's way to wisdom as a renunciation of life, one that by its very self-contained incommunicability caused perplexities even to the Buddha's most faithful disciples. If they followed him, shutting the world out as they withdrew into the most inward contemplation, rulers and benefactors of the human race would induce a frenzy of mutual slaughter by removing their restraint on collective, selfish greed. Those who were wise and yet remained in the world, tolerating what they could not change, lived two divided lives: an active outward life in the practical world, a jungle where wisdom had no place, and another life, contemplative and covert, a flight from universal corruption to the pure truth of inward silence. The poem, Adams characteristically noted, was written in boredom, perhaps with "the great calm of Buddha" (Adams [1916]: 82).

Still, in Japan he conceived what became the famous Saint-Gaudens monument and later refined his ideas of it as a variation on Buddhist iconography, although, as he observed, the execution of the memorial by Saint-

Gaudens and the architect Stanford White departed from his orientalized ideal. Engaged by the exoticism of Buddhist art, Adams was also attracted by the antimetaphysical nature of the Buddha's teachings, by his opposition to dogma, and by his teachings on the illusory character of the world and enlightenment of the wise through annihilation of personhood.

Adams's associations with femininity entered into this search in so far as it was religious; but its emphasis on the illusory character of life as a passage into nothingness gave it at least two morbid corollaries. The first was by direct personal experience. To one convinced that autobiography was a way to "murder" one's own life (*Letters*, 2: 532) the twin works of *Mont-Saint-Michel and Chartres* and *The Education* opened a passage into that void and became ironic analogs to Clover Adams's suicide. The second corollary was abstract. To a convinced agnostic, given to urbane impieties, the power exercised over nations by the Buddha's tenderness, love, simplicity of heart, and inward power had only one analog: the consummate feminine, the Virgin. But here too the feminine persona was to be annihilated by forces of disintegration (Adams [1936], 255).

The pieces began to fit together in 1895; the puzzle known as *Mont-Saint-Michel and Chartres* was complete in 1904. An essential part of that puzzle was the dialectic of bleak anguish that, in *The Education*, Adams reported feeling as he found himself between the unbounded energy of the dynamo and the "boundless sympathy" of the Virgin (Adams [1936], 182).

We return to the fact that Adams presented his self-portrayals, with their dialectic, as a private amusement, a flight from the anguish of powerlessness. Even after the architect Ralph Adams Cram published *Mont-Saint-Michel and Chartres* in an effort to popularize his own neo-Gothic enthusiasm, Adams withheld *The Education* for posthumous publication. As public documents the books gained functions quite different from those intended by Adams, and audiences alien alike to his frames of reference and to his easy, mannered, and condescending ironies.

Enough has been said to indicate how various were the strands in Adams's temperament, intellect, and experience and how fortuitous was their convergence in *Mont-Saint-Michel and Chartres*. Specialists seeking legitimation for new fields of inquiry in medieval studies, particularly in branches of literature and linguistics, welcomed Adams's sanction and delighted in the recognition, and the public, that his book gave them beyond the academic pale. Yet medievalists on the whole took exception to Adams's idiosyncratic principles of selection, omission, and emphasis. Though finding few technical errors, they considered the concepts through which the whole was refracted to be a distorting mirror. Nevertheless, the book brought Adams the public eminence that his works in United States history had not gained. It would be wrong to overstress the dearth of translations into other languages, but this is a symptom of its character as a work of North American, or even national literature, rather than a historical inquiry. As a personal evocation the book was almost universally acclaimed.

There is no need to describe the last stages of Adams's life, when his preoccupation with applying laws of physics to historical change, generally with outdated theories and logically inconsistent arguments, only increased his disdain for professional historians and deepened his scornful isolation of mind. Before the 1913 publication of *Mont-Saint-Michel and Chartres* Adams had recovered, with some residual impairment, from a stroke (1912). As his sight gradually deteriorated into blindness, he turned from visual to auditory arts, beginning inquiries into twelfth- and thirteenth-century music. His annual excursions to Europe continued until World War I intervened. He remained until his death an adept and respected figure in fashionable Washington society. His delight in ironies, particularly in the disjuncture between the transience of life and the permanence of art, life's mimic, would have been compounded many times over had he anticipated that he would die and be buried in Passiontide beneath Saint-Gaudens's gynandrous adaptation of a Buddha.

SELECTED BIBLIOGRAPHY

Works

BOOKS AND ARTICLES

"The Anglo-Saxon Courts of Law." In *Essays in Anglo-Saxon Law*. Boston: Little, Brown; London: Macmillan, 1876.

Mont-Saint-Michel and Chartres. Washington, D.C.: Privately printed, 1904. Modern edition, with an introduction by Ralph Adams Cram, Boston and New York: Houghton Mifflin, 1936.

The Education of Henry Adams. Washington, D.C.: Privately printed, 1907. Modern edition, New York: Modern Library, 1931.

"Buddha and Brahma." *Yale Review*, n.s. 5 (1916): 82 [letter to John Hay, 26 April 1895.

LETTERS AND PAPERS

At several moments in his life Adams systematically and selectively destroyed diaries, letters, and other personal papers. The bulk of what survives has been deposited in the Houghton Library at Harvard University and above all in the Adams Papers, which the Adams Manuscript Trust has given into the keeping of the Massachusetts Historical Society.

The Letters of Henry Adams. 6 vols. Edited by J.C. Levenson et al. Cambridge, Mass.: Belknap Press of Harvard University Press, 1982–88.

Sources

Adams, James Truslow. *Henry Adams*. New York: Boni, 1933.

Conder, J. *A Formula of His Own: Henry Adams's Literary Experiment*. Chicago: University of Chicago Press, 1970.

Decker, William Merrill. *The Literary Vocation of Henry Adams*. Chapel Hill: University of North Carolina Press, 1990.

Levenson, J.C. *The Mind and Art of Henry Adams*. Boston: Houghton Mifflin, 1957.

Mane, Robert. *Henry Adams on the Road to Chartres*. Cambridge, Mass.: Belknap Press of Harvard University Press, 1971.

O'Toole, Patricia. *The Five of Hearts: An Intimate Portrait of Henry Adams and His Friends, 1880–1918*. New York: Potter, 1990.

Pick, Daniel. *Faces of Degeneration: A European Disorder, c. 1848–c. 1918*. Cambridge: Cambridge University Press, 1989.

Samuels, Ernest. *The Young Henry Adams*. Cambridge, Mass.: Harvard University Press, 1948.

———. *Henry Adams: The Middle Years*. Cambridge, Mass.: Belknap Press of Harvard University Press, 1958.

———. *Henry Adams: The Major Phase*. Cambridge, Mass.: Belknap Press of Harvard University Press, 1964.

———. *Henry Adams*. Cambridge, Mass.: Belknap Press of Harvard University Press, 1989.

Stevenson, Elizabeth. *Henry Adams: A Biography*. New York: Macmillan, 1955.

FREDERIC WILLIAM MAITLAND

(1850–1906)

Robert Brentano

> *"How to describe anybody! I can only shovel evidence into heaps and chuck it at the public"* [Maitland to Henry Jackson, 30 July 1905: Letters, 45, no. 444].

Frederic William Maitland, medievalist and legal historian, was born on 28 May 1850 and died on 20 December 1906. He was, it is worth remembering, a slightly younger contemporary of Gerard Manley Hopkins, who himself lived from 1844 to 1899. The two men had no visible personal connection, although Robert Bridges certainly knew them both, but they performed significantly similar services to the arts they espoused.

Maitland's life was, by the standards applied to Victorian historians, quiet, "uneventful" as his biographer and brother-in-law H.A.L. Fisher wrote. Maitland's story "tells itself," according to Fisher, "not in outward details of perils endured, places visited, appointments held, but in the revelation of the scholar's mind given in his work" (Fisher, 1). Fisher knew Maitland well; he himself was an exact historian. His words suggest a tone that is true. But they are also odd words about a man who fought death in the Canary Islands, who with his appointments changed the history of law and the face of history and took part in Cambridge's "Revolution of the Dons," a man who fought that university degrees might be given to women and fought to make the past nonsectarian.

Maitland did not appear a placid man, with (in his daughter Ermengard's words) his "bird bright eye," "listening ear," and "sensitive apprehensions," "his light, quick steps like those of a mountain creature," or with his clothes: "He dressed as one who had seen himself, disliking his necessary blacks, choosing rather to wear brown tweeds, low collars when others wore high, and plain, warm-coloured ties when convention said dots and stripes" (Ermengard Maitland, 6–7). Fisher's just words in fact provoke a realization of Maitland's complexity, as they did in Ermengard Maitland; when Fisher wrote of Maitland's avoiding picture galleries and poetry in his later life, Ermengard Maitland responded: "I am sure that this was how my father wished it to seem, and largely how it had to be, and yet—" (Ermengard Maitland, 5).

Ermengard, in her own quite complex reminiscence, produces a Maitland acutely responsive to sensory stimulus, "woods, streams, hills, the craters and caves, the geranium hedges and prickly pears . . . seen and enjoyed in relationship to each other" (a scene from Cézanne), and tulips, a rose "dark velvety red shading to black" (Ermengard Maitland, 6). But Fisher is surely right, too, in practically beginning his "biographical sketch" with a more purely intellectual Maitland, who remembered, after a thirty-year interval, Henry Sidgwick's teaching at Cambridge:

> However small the class might be, Sidgwick always gave us his very best; not what might be good enough for undergraduates, or what might serve for temporary purposes, but the complex truth just as he saw it, with all those reservations and qualifications, exceptions and distinctions which suggested themselves to a mind that was indeed marvellously subtle but was showing us its wonderful power simply because, even in a lecture room, it could be content with nothing less than the maximum of attainable and communicable truth [Fisher, 8].

With this memory Maitland shaped the memory of his own thought, and thus his life, through thirty years of first growth and then intensifying productivity, of writing and of his reaction to writing, as can be seen in his remarkable collection of letters. Through his broken syntax and a related, coaxing informality, he had tried to break the disguising surface of prose and lead his reader-listener to a new reality. He had sought the same thing in the exposure of documents—what really had been written in the past—and, so far as was possible, he sought through what had been written for what had really existed. He had not sought, at least consciously, for curiosities: "the history of law is not a collection of curiosities" (Select Pleas, xxiv). He had believed that documents revealed continuing significance: "the rapid development of the common law is mirrored on the surface of the rolls" (Select Pleas, x). But he had, through his rolls, seen man, woman, and life. He had tried not to be "flat or tawdry" (Letters, 339).

When Maitland published his first Selden Society volume, Select Pleas of the Crown in 1888, he had achieved what, in this sense, he wanted: the display through example of the value of the early thirteenth-century plea roll, with a powerful and incisive introduction. With the introduction to his edition of the *Memoranda de Parliamento, 1305*, published as a volume in the Rolls Series in 1893, he showed that his method, used by him, could both reform our understanding of an institution as central to English history as Parliament and teach us how to think history. With his publication with Frederick Pollock of the *History of English Law* in 1895 he demonstrated his power in extended analytical and descriptive narrative; and with his obituary for William Stubbs in the *English Historical Review* for 1901, he showed his self-conscious mastery of the nature of historical enquiry and thought. If Maitland had written nothing more than these four works much, and much that is very stimulating, would not exist, but Maitland would have established himself as an incomparable historian.

Maitland was born in London. Although he quite clearly became a Cambridge man, he also was and remained in a very special sense a Londoner, a point that is emphasized rather than denied by his intense affection for Gloucestershire and perhaps the Grand Canary. He was born to a family of intellectual note. His father, John Gorham Maitland, was the son of Samuel Roffey Maitland, the historian of heretics and at one time Lambeth historian, who wrote, in Ermengard's words "learned and peculiar books . . . astringent, contentious, and amusing" (Ermengard Maitland, 7). Maitland wrote in 1891 that Samuel Roffey, of whose books he admired *Facts and Documents* most, had done "what was wanted just at the moment when it was wanted and so has a distinct place in the history of history in England." And in a letter to his sister Selina, Maitland noted, "One still has to do for legal history something like the work that S.R.M. did for ecclesiastical history—to teach them, e.g., that some statement about the 13th century does not become truer because it has been constantly repeated . . . . It is the 'method' that I admire in S.R.M. more even than the style or the matter . . ." (*Letters*, 98). Frederic William's mother was Emma Daniell, the daughter of John Frederic Daniell, a physicist, who at twenty-three had been elected a fellow of the Royal Society, who became professor of Chemistry at King's College, who is said to have invented the hygrometer, and who wrote a once well-known *Introduction to Chemical Philosophy* (Fisher, 2).

Maitland's mother died the year after he was born, in 1851, and his father died twelve years later in 1863. Samuel Roffey Maitland died in 1866, and from him Frederic William inherited land and a house in Gloucestershire. Frederic William and his two sisters, Selina Caroline and Emma Katherine, were raised by his mother's sister, Charlotte Louisa Daniell, and by, among others, German governesses. In 1863, soon after his father's death, Maitland left a Brighton preparatory school for Eton. At Eton, he was undistinguished.

"He failed," Fisher wrote, "to become prominent either in work or play." Remembering Eton much later, in a debate about compulsory Greek in the Cambridge Senate, Maitland talked of a "boy at school not more than forty years ago who was taught Greek for eight years and never learnt it . . . who if he never learnt Greek, did learn one thing, namely to hate Greek and its alphabet and its accents and its accidence and its syntax and its prosody, and all its appurtenances . . . to vow that if ever he got rid of that accursed thing never, never again would he open a Greek book or write a Greek word." He was supposedly "brought out by Chaucer," loved music, and had, a schoolmate remembered, a "jolly, curiously-lined face" (Fisher, 5–6). His Eton letters to his sister Selina seem rather stiff, a little facetious, products perhaps of a rather frozen childhood.

In the autumn of 1869 Maitland, like his father and grandfather before him, went up to Trinity College, Cambridge, and there his life changed. He ran, and got a blue as a three-miler, and he rowed. He listened to Sidgwick, and he turned to philosophy. He won a Trinity scholarship, and he was bracketed at the head of the Firsts in the Moral and Mental Science Tripos in 1872. With a fellowship dissertation entitled "A Historical Sketch of Liberty and Equality as Ideals of English Political Philosophy from the Time of Hobbes to the Time of Coleridge" he competed, admired but unsuccessful, for the Trinity Fellowship in Moral and Mental Science. His dissertation contained pieces of live Maitland: "I am inclined to think (though there is great risk of such speculations being wrong) that Hobbes was led to exaggerate his account of man's naturally unsocial character by a desire to bring the state of nature into discredit" (Fisher, 11; Maitland [1911], 1: 31–32). An intellectual success, with intellectual friends, Maitland was discovered to have charm and finally became a social success. He was chosen a member of Cambridge's precious, select group the Apostles, and he was elected first secretary, then president of the Union.

In 1872 Maitland left Cambridge for London and the law and Lincoln's Inn. In 1876 he was called to the bar, again as his father and grandfather had been after leaving Trinity (and he would, as they did, later leave the practice of law for other interests and callings). Maitland read with B.B. Rogers (himself a translator of Aristophanes), and when Rogers's health was in "a precarious state," as he later wrote, Maitland superintended Rogers's law business. Working partly for Rogers, Maitland became interested in and understanding of the art and skill of conveyancing, which art and skill Fisher convincingly argues, helped form Maitland's historical interests and abilities.

This lawyer Maitland was attracted by the writings of two historians, William Stubbs and Friedrich Savigny, one very English and one very continental, a combination that would characterize Maitland's later work. In 1879 he published an essay in the *Westminster Review*, "The Law of Real Property," which began: "It may be hoped that the reform of our land laws will at some not distant day come within the sphere of practical politics" (Maitland [1911], 1: 162). In 1883 he published in *Mind* an amusingly destructive essay called "Mr. Herbert Spencer's View of Society." He walked and climbed in Austria, Switzerland, and Germany. He went alone to Munich to hear opera and with his sisters to Bonn to a Schumann commemoration. He gave lectures on political economy and political philosophy in and out of London. Frederick Pollock, a prominent lawyer interested in history, made Maitland his friend. In 1880 Maitland became a part of "the godly company, fellowship or brotherhood of the Sunday Tramps" (Maitland [1906], 357–58), of which Pollock formed another part as did George Croom Robertson, the editor of *Mind*. The group had been organized during the previous year by Leslie Stephen, whom Maitland had gotten to know in London and who remained a dominant figure in Maitland's life even after Stephen's death in February 1904. The Sunday Tramps lasted until March 1895, and they were a force both in forming and in explaining the intellectual as well as the social Maitland—these little English, train-aided trips of people who had climbed and would climb Swiss mountains and who were not bound in their friendships by anything so narrow as profession or academic discipline. In a way they were the extension of the mind of Leslie Stephen, who thought and wrote and talked about everything, and from which mind sprang, it is reasonable to say, the actual *Dictionary of National Biography* as well as much that was long accepted about the nature of eighteenth-century thought. Maitland, remembering the Tramps after Stephen's death, wrote a greeting to the "Sons of the Tramps" who were reviving the institution: *Beati omnes qui ambulant.*

The Tramps included Robert Bridges and W.P. Ker. They were on occasion "hospitably entertained" by George Meredith and Charles Darwin, men important to both Stephen and Maitland. And one day, 20 January 1884, on one of the tramps Maitland met a guest from Russia, Paul Vinogradoff. Vinogradoff was younger than Maitland—he had been born in 1854—but he had been trained in Theodor Mommsen's seminar in Berlin and knew a kind of historical professionalism that Maitland in England could hardly have known. Vinogradoff, just in that year about to begin his professorship at Moscow, although not to publish his first major work in English, *Villainage in England*, until 1892, was himself a model for Maitland, an inspiration, a trusted, critical, corresponding friend. It was a friendship that developed quickly: "The day [Sunday, 11 May 1884, at Oxford] was fine and the two scholars strolled into the Parks, and lying full length on the grass took up the thread of their historical discourse" (Fisher, 24). "On the following day," according to Fisher, Maitland "returned to London, drove to the Record Office," and, with his Gloucestershire connections, asked for the earliest plea roll from that county. He was given a roll for 1221. Before the end of the year Maitland had published the roll, "a picture," as he said, "or rather, since little imaginative art went into its making, a photograph of English life as it was early in the thirteenth century, and a photograph taken from a point of view at which chroniclers too seldom place themselves" (Fisher, 25). Maitland dedicated the little book to Vinogradoff.

Maitland's friendship with Stephen brought him at times into the quite brilliant circle of the family and connections of Stephen's second wife, Julia Prinsep Jackson Duckworth, a woman of extraordinary beauty who had posed for G.F. Watts, Edward Coley Burne-Jones, and her own aunt, the photographer Julia Cameron (and for her own daughter Virginia Woolf, as Mrs. Ramsay in *To the Lighthouse*). Maitland described, or perhaps parodied, his position in the circle, as it met at Little Holland House, the house of Henry Thoby Prinsep, Mrs. Stephen's uncle by marriage, "a grand specimen of the Indian official of the days of the Company." Maitland wrote:

> The house had a character of its own. People used to go there on Sunday afternoons; they had strawberries and cream, and played croquet, and strolled about the old fashioned garden, or were allowed to go to Watts' studio [then in the house] and admire his pictures. I went there pretty often, and used, I must confess, to feel very shy. It was silly enough, but I have always been shy with artistic people, who inhabit a world unfamiliar to me. And there used to be Leighton, now Sir Frederick, in all his glory, and Val Prinsep and his friends, who looked terribly smart to me.

Then Maitland turns a little:

> I was, I say, silly, for the parties were really far less alarming than those at the Leweses, where one had to be ready to discuss metaphysics or the principles of aesthetic philosophy, and to be presented to George Eliot, and offer an acceptable worship [Maitland (1906), 316–17].

In the Prinsep, not the Lewes, circle Maitland found a wife, Florence Henrietta Fisher, Mrs. Stephen's niece. It was in the Stephen drawing room,

Maitland remembered twenty years later, "that I asked a (to me) important question" (*Letters*, 472).

Florence Henrietta Fisher and Frederic William Maitland were married in a village church in Hampshire in 1886. Their two daughters, Ermengard (named, according to Ermengard herself, for a woman in *Bracton's Note Book*) and Fredegond, were born in 1887 and 1889. Florence was fourteen years Maitland's junior. Maitland, the writer of the *Life and Letters of Leslie Stephen*, could not himself have been expected to reveal much that was intimate about their marriage. Ermengard wrote: "In those days a child took its parents' happiness together for granted, but I had a good nose for trouble and I never smelt even a whiff of fire save over miracles and the Boer War and he for Dickens she for Thackeray" (Ermengard Maitland, 10). The marriage which Ermengard and the letters reveal is characterized by playful positions and lightly ironic attitudes, her collection of animals, his sometimes tiresome or pompous houseguests, her photography and seeming tolerance of unreason. To the outsider's eye the two assigned themselves casual roles not unconventional to the sex of each. Their skit was given structure by financial caution apparent in kitchen and housekeeping, which Florence was seen to have managed with humor, grace, and disguised efficiency; by a related grimmer structure, similarly handled by both, the felt necessity of difficult travel to the islands; and most of all by Maitland's long illness and approaching death. Maitland's last letters to Florence, in the winter of 1906, when she and Ermengard had sailed before him (particularly when they are seen against the playful pattern of his normal sequence and with his generally very careful selection of words in mind) are moving: "Beloved, . . . Now good-bye and a happy voyage to you. [This letter was written from Cambridge to a hotel in London.] I shall soon be with you. . . . So with many kisses good-bye. Your own F." (*Letters*, 491–92). In a world of last names, these two did not use them for each other.

In a letter of 1906 to Melville Bigelow, a professor of law at Boston University, Maitland wrote, "Those two little girls that you used to know are young women now and all that I could wish" (*Letters*, 472). No reader would suspect that growth could be, and Ermengard Maitland's reminiscences assure us that it was not, quite so smooth. Maitland's combination of humor and seriousness, his ideas about education and freedom, made him a complex father:

> Spanish grammar, French, Norman-French, any grammar but English. We were not to learn that, we were to read, and read, and then write. All the rules of grammar had been broken by great writers. . . . One

would not have expected a conventional sense of education from one who felt that Eton had wasted so much of his time but, considering his labours on behalf of degrees for women, it seems to me a little odd that we were allowed to drift so pleasantly [Ermengard Maitland, 9].

In 1883 Maitland applied for but was not appointed to the Readership in English Law at Oxford. A readership was being proposed at Cambridge, but it did not materialize until it had been pushed into being by a subsidy from Henry Sidgwick. Maitland was elected to the Cambridge readership in November 1884, and he gave his first course of lectures, on contracts, in the Lent term of 1885 (Fisher, 30). In 1888 the Downing Chair of the Laws of England fell vacant, and Maitland was elected. The chair came with a house at Downing, and the Maitlands moved into it. Later, in 1902, Prime Minister Balfour would ask Maitland to succeed Lord Acton to the Chair of Modern History at Cambridge, but by then he would be too physically weakened and would feel that there was still too much else to do for him to accept (Fisher, 168–69). In these Cambridge years Maitland was a good citizen not only to the scholarly historical world in general, but most particularly to Downing and Cambridge. Fisher described the variety of Maitland's college and university activities, including his service after election to the Council of the Senate in 1894. Fisher also wrote of the nature and effectiveness of Maitland's participation in debates in the Senate. Maitland seems to have brought to them the tone of non-dogmatic, wry, agnostic, Liberal liberalism that informed his view of external politics; but he was also an effective speaker. His speaking was, Fisher reports from others' accounts, unlike the speaking of others: "The whole man seemed quick with fire" (Fisher, 66–68). The power of Maitland's teaching was well remembered when Fisher wrote; it is still in some part available in his published lectures, in the lucidity of *Forms of Action* and in the imaginative structure of *The Constitutional History*.

It was in these Cambridge years, from 1886 to 1906, that Maitland with remarkable speed (Elton, 57) wrote, edited, and published the works that define him as a medieval and legal historian. In 1888, for the Selden Society which he helped form, he published the Society's first volume, his *Select Pleas of the Crown*. In the same year he published an article, "The Suitors of the County Court," and a review in the third volume of the *English Historical Review*, a new and, for England, different kind of historical periodical, which had first appeared in 1886. Both the Selden Society and the *English Historical Review* offered Maitland forums for his particular kind of historical expression. He encouraged them, and they at times encouraged him, trellis and vine almost indistinguishable. The Selden Society, for which Maitland edited eight of the first twenty-one volumes, is his own particular monument. It embodies his purpose in history; for him, it made available the actual (although difficult) words of the actual (although difficult) past; and it offered a series of edited documents that could better compete with continental editions than could the Rolls Series, partly because of the Selden Society's date and sponsorship, partly because it opened to the viewer a kind of document specific to England and specifically susceptible to a kind of English learning formed from a continuing English fascination with and use of common law and now finally subject to a new historicism. This was the historicism that Maitland himself had preached in his inaugural lecture "Why the History of Law Is Not Written," in which he had attacked "the traditional isolation of English Law from every other study" (Maitland [1911], 1: 487; Fisher, 35). The Selden editions led to Maitland's publications in 1903, 1904, and 1905 of those Year Books of Edward II in which Maitland could read the language and hear the voices of his past judges and lawyers. He found a special kind of satisfaction in the difficult, close, methodical work of the preparation of the Year Books, and (he and those who have studied him would argue) in his dying years—a kind of protection, perhaps. But the Selden Society was not without pain. A very painful letter to Melville Bigelow, written from Cambridge in November 1894 begins:

> I had assigned to-day for a long letter to you—it is a Sunday—and now there is but one thing I can write about, the sad disaster. Dove has destroyed himself, and there can I fear be no doubt that the cause of his act is to be found in the affairs of the Selden Society [*Letters*, 139–40].

Edward Dove had been the secretary and treasurer of the Selden Society, and its funds seemed to have totally disappeared. Maitland explained: "I fear that one need not say *cherchez la femme*—she is apparent. Poor Dove! I did not like some of his ways but I never suspected this." The horror, like something from a sensational Victorian novel, breaks the usual tone of Maitland's letters. But sufficient funds returned to the society and equanimity to Maitland's prose.

The importance to Maitland of the *English Historical Review* is obvious. The essays of *Domesday Book and Beyond* were first published in it; so were the most important essays in *Roman Canon Law in the Church of England*. The *Review* became in the 1890s a kind of glasshouse for him. Before he sent the *Review* the first of the canon-law essays, he had written in September 1895 to Reginald Lane Poole, who had been associated with the *Review* from the beginning and who was by then one of its editors: "When I send you my stuff you and S.R.G. [S.R. Gardiner, the other and senior editor] can say whether you will open your pages" (*Letters*, 171). But to Maitland and to the other serious historians wakening around him the *Review* was much more in those years. It was a place where intelligence, wit, and learning met, and met professionally. In the *Review*'s reviews capable historians spoke to each other eagerly. It gave, as its issues still can, real pleasure. Maitland wrote back to Poole from the Grand Canary in January 1899: "I thank you for sending the E.H.R. You can hardly guess how pleasant its cover was in my eyes. The inside I shall take by small doses, trying to spread my enjoyment over a week" (*Letters*, 238).

But as much as the *Review*, perhaps more, it was Poole himself. In this Oxford historian, whose own work makes him seem in many ways different from Maitland, Maitland found the person to whom he could write. Together they bridged that Oxford-Cambridge distance of which Maitland was conscious: "My own very strong opinion is that within a few years A. [Lord Acton] did more than any one else could have done to elevate the study of history here towards the position that it has at Oxford. If we had had him here ten years earlier we might by this time be within measurable distance of you." So he wrote, perhaps not quite candidly, to Poole in 1902, when Poole was hesitant about writing in an obituary notice of Acton's Cambridge life as Maitland had been about Stubbs's Oxford life the year before (*Letters*, 332, 283). Not only did the two historians bridge distance and difference, but the distance seems to have been a benefit to them or at least to Maitland; he was forced to, allowed to, put his most exactly chosen words about historians and history into letters that could be read and exactly understood on the other side of Bletchley. In Poole, it became increasingly clear as time went on, Maitland thought he could count on understanding—frankness, as complete a lack of condescension as he himself offered. Few recorded medievalists have found such a satisfactory audience. Maitland could in February 1897, the year of his Ford Lectures, perhaps about them, write a letter with this single line: "Did'st ever feel like a bubble that was going to be pricked?" (*Letters*, 191). When in 1900 Maitland had stirred the crazily difficult J. Horace Round to animosity by disagreeing with him, he wrote to Poole, "I see that I shall now have J.H.R. as an assailant until the end of our joint lives. . . . Have you any advice to give? You know how I value your counsel" (*Letters*, 214). But even more valuable than counsel perhaps was Poole the reader, to whom he could talk plainly of his judgments about history and sentiments toward other historians, like Hubert Hall, one of Round's victims, with his "curious fluffy mind," or toward the able but endlessly dilatory editor G.J. Turner, of whom in the month of his death Maitland wrote to Poole, "—but I need not say more to you for I saw that you love the little man. I love him very much" (*Letters*, 225, 389). Life, among other things, was for Maitland and Poole a scholarly joke, and for them the battle of Hastings or Senlac, over which Round and Edward Augustus Freeman fought, was "that infernal palisade" (*Letters*, 203).

In fact Maitland's first essay for Poole's *English Historical Review*, although brief and less weightily potent than some of his later essays would be, offered clear indications of what could be called the Maitland method. The essay opened with—its first sentence was—a direct question: "Who were the suitors at the county court?" Maitland quickly stated the "generally accepted answer"—"all the freeholders of the county"—but immediately went on to argue that for the thirteenth century the documentary evidence did not support this answer; rather it indicated that suit of court was a burden that fell on specific lands and that, when subinfeudation increased the number of tenants, the number of those who owed suit of court did not increase correspondingly. Maitland based his response primarily but not entirely on evidence drawn from a reading of the Hundred Rolls of 1279. Moving forward into the little essay, he asked further direct questions, some with rather specific Maitland turns of phrase and thought: "How could this somewhat capricious distribution of the burden, to which the Hundred Rolls bear witness, have been effected?" It provoked the reader to explore thirteenth-century thought and understanding: "The words in the writ of summons directing all freeholders to come may well have been understood to mean all freeholders who owed suit." It mocked the notion of the freeholder's right to attend: "But would such a right have been conceivable by a man of the thirteenth century? If we asked him of the existence of such a right, might he not reply by asking us whether those modern Englishmen who are not bound to pay income tax, enjoy the right of paying it if they please?" Finally Maitland led the essay and its reader to a more overtly political-historical problem, "a big question," that of the county franchise. Maitland, with a characteristic disingenuous dodging feint at the future, wrote, "We may someday have to confess that the original 'county franchise'. . . so far from being settled by the simple rule that all freeholders have votes, was really distributed through an intricate network of private charters and prescriptive liabilities" (Maitland [1911], 1: 458–66; originally *English Historical Review*, July 1888). "The Suitors of the County Court" has a characteristic Maitland plot line; it starts with a question and ends in a web.

In 1893 Maitland published, quite unpretentiously, what G.R. Elton has understandably called his "most explosive contribution to English history" (Elton, 57), *Records of the Parliament Holden at Westminster*, his edition for the Rolls Series of a Parliament roll for 1305. The explosion was in the introduction: "It is hard to think away out of our heads a history which has long lain in a remote past but which once lay in the future; . . . it is hard to look at the thirteenth century save by looking at it through the distorting medium of the fourteenth" (Cam [1957], 91). Trying to recover the past, as it had existed, without the gloss of its own future, was a normal intention for Maitland, as it was and is for many historians. But in this case he was thinking away the political gloss on England's taxing and legislating institutional hero, Parliament.

Maitland looked at his roll, and he found that "by far the greater part of our parliament roll is occupied by entries which concern the audience of petitions" (*ibid.*, 68). Although he did not deny that "the germ of the house of commons already existed," Maitland found that "we may believe that the council often gives audience, advice, instructions to particular knights and burgesses" (*ibid.*, 85). He found that the line between judicial business and the hearing of petitions was "not very sharp" (*ibid.*, 85). He had found that many of the "doings that are recorded on our roll were done after the estates had been sent home" (*ibid.*, 53), when the king remained at Westminster surrounded by his councilors, including his "kinsfolk" (*ibid.*, 61), and he saw the importance of the "ill-defined" council; and he admitted that, looking back through the fourteenth century, he found it hard to imagine there not being "jealous dislike of the council, an aristocratic jealousy on the part of the nobles, a professional jealousy on the part of the judges and common lawyers. But," he asked, "do we really see this?" (*ibid.*, 93). Maitland looks at his roll; and he makes his reader see what he sees.

What we see through Maitland has been quickly described by Helen Cam in her very fine introduction to her very fine collection of Maitland's writings: "Maitland suggested, only too cautiously, that parliament was in essence royal, not popular, a court of justice before it was a legislature; an expansion of an aristocratic and a bureaucratic council before it had any representative character" (*ibid.*, xviii). Maitland adjusted a balance, as many of his modern commentators have noted, so that his readers were forced to notice the judicial, the high court, the royal-court aspect of Parliament. He made his reader see that "in these parliaments the whole governmental force of England is brought into focus" (*ibid.*, 82). Most strikingly, most revolutionarily, he argued, "A parliament is rather an act than a body of persons. One cannot present a petition to a colloquy, to a debate" (*ibid.*,

78). In showing the course of petitions, he exploded an institution, exploded a definition, and made all future historians think, if they would, differently about this and many other institutions. As Cam wrote, "Parliament was not an institution, but an event. Things were done *in* parliament, not *by* parliament. 'Parliament' cannot, at this stage, be the subject of a verb, nor the object" (*ibid.*, xviii). This may well be Maitland's greatest substantive revision of history. It is worth noting that it was done by looking at original sources and by questioning with words and with grammar.

It has been repeatedly noted by modern commentators that the importance of Maitland's introduction was not fully appreciated before the appearance of Charles McIlwain's less nuanced *The High Court of Parliament and Its Supremacy* in 1910, and then A.F. Pollard's *The Evolution of Parliament* in 1920; the reaction against Maitland's work is in fact a reaction against his exploiters. But it is only fair to notice that Fisher, although he wrote little about Maitland's introduction among his personal recollections (published in 1910), was exact in his description, remarking that "the word *Parliamentum* is never found in the nominative" (Fisher, 74–75). All of Maitland's work asked for addition and revision; H.E. Bell showed the sort of addition and revision that had occurred by 1965, when his *Maitland* was published (Bell, 91–95). Cam, moreover, pointed out that "much of what he [Maitland] says is to be found in his magnificent but ambiguous master, Stubbs" but that "it is the light of law that Maitland turns on his history" (Cam, xviii).

Two years after the publication of the parliament roll, Maitland published his most grandly powerful work, the two volumes of *The History of English Law before the Time of Edward I*—which would be published in a second edition in 1898. Maitland was not the sole author of the *History*; he wrote with Sir Frederick Pollock, who had succeeded to his baronetcy in 1888 and had been Corpus Professor of Jurisprudence at Oxford since 1883—and who would live until 1937. It was not an easy writing relationship, although the two men were friends, and Pollock, five years Maitland's senior, was and felt himself to be a patron to Maitland. As the book moved from planning to writing, Maitland became increasingly aware of the difficulty. In May 1892 he wrote to Vinogradoff:

F.P., who is now in the West Indies and may go to India in the winter, has written an Anglo-Saxon chapter. *Between ourselves* I do not like it very much, partly because it will make it very difficult for me to say anything about A-S law in any later part of the book. My effort now is to shove on with the general sketch of the Norman and

Angevin periods so that my collaborator may have little to do before we reach the Year Book period—if we ever reach it [*Letters*, 110].

Maitland succeeded. Pollock wrote only the Anglo-Saxon chapter. They never reached the Year Book period. Maitland could write, in his own chapter on "The Dark Age in Legal History," of the complexity of early beginnings, or nonbeginnings: "Such is the unity of all history that any one who endeavours to tell a piece of it must feel that his first sentence tears a seamless web" (Pollock and Maitland [1898], 2: 1). His general sketch of the Norman and Angevin periods was so successful that it practically became the history of those periods. Henry II had been written by Stubbs; now he was rewritten as the director of "The Age of Glanvill" by Maitland.

The History of English Law is in content very big. Its second volume offers a great variety of descriptions and analyses of how the law worked, of the structure it formed, as Maitland leads his readers through subjects like seisin, conveyance, contract, inheritance, marriage, trespass, pleading, and proof. When readers are puzzled by snags in their own sources, they are irresistibly drawn to Maitland's lucid, comprehensive explanations. Maitland has drawn a map of the whole system; perhaps he has replaced life (whatever that was) with his drawing. S.F.C. Milsom, in many ways Maitland's most helpful and most helpfully learned critic, has said it best: "Maitland's indestructible memorial is that the great outlines he drew of the history of the common law, for which so much material survives, have so long seemed obvious. New or unnoticed detail at last begins to obtrude: but you cannot usefully erase an outline, only propose what seems a better fit" (Milsom, [1976], 1). But it would be a mistake to think of this work of Maitland's as a massive expression of power in the normal language of power or even the high language of the seamless web. The chapter on contract begins: "The law of contract holds anything but a conspicuous place among the institutions of English law before the Norman Conquest. In fact it is rudimentary" (Pollock and Maitland [1898], 2: 184).

Modern readers generally find Maitland's Henry II a little too alone with his law, a little too much in control, a little too hesitant in exposing what Milsom called "the feudal component in the framework of English society" (Milsom, [1976], 1), perhaps a little too legal and too little social. But it is always wise to look with new learning and wisdom at the cautious and rich quality of Maitland's actual statements. Their wary depth is frequently surprising. But in Maitland's (and everyone else's) city of thirteenth-century history there has been one major collapse that really has brought greater change than the unexpected revision that ordinarily occurs as new records are examined. Bracton has fallen. Samuel Thorne's intensely intelligent and perceptive reading of "Bracton" has unraveled the text, so that "Bracton" in the old sense is no longer seen to exist, and so neither is Maitland's "Age of Bracton." The explosive effect of this invention is wonderfully caught in the preface to Paul Hyams's *King, Lords and Peasants* (1980), parts of which had had to be "completely rewritten" after Hyams had read Thorne's "Translator's Introduction" to Volume 3, which convinced Hyams that "the new understanding of the treatise and its context carried the ring of truth" (Thorne, 3: xxxiii-lii). Hyams was willing to concede "that this was a blessing in disguise," but he said, "I merely note that authors do not need many such blessings at so late a stage" (Hyams, ix). Hyams's humor speaks for all historians of the thirteenth century and all readers of Maitland. Beyond the great reshaping that the new Bracton must give Maitland's thirteenth century, those who like Hyams continue to use and admire his great work find in it misdirected perceptions that are not dependent upon the unavailability to Maitland of more recently discovered material. In Hyams's reexamination of the definition of villeinage in "Bracton," for example, he found that Maitland, like Vinogradoff, "apparently did not notice the specific context of the uncertainty principle" (Hyams, 195). It is crucial in understanding later historians' almost incredibly high evaluation of Maitland that it does not depend upon the absence of this kind of misdirection in his work.

Neither does it depend upon the compellingness of his answers. *Domesday Book and Beyond*, published as an assembled book in 1897, offered an interpretation of burghal origins and existence that the wise and sharp critic James Tait rejected immediately; Maitland quickly expressed his gratitude. Like much Anglo-Saxon work from the nineteenth century *Domesday Book* seems insufficiently informed. But it lacks that air of repulsive dullness that often marks seemingly wrong work (like the Anglo-Saxon parts of Stubbs) and that Maitland himself disliked. Its structure, approach, and line-by-line brilliance make it instead intensely exciting. An extravaganza of mobile question asking, phrase making, definition evading, it pushes from relative simplicity to relative complexity to almost unintelligible complexity, as is evident from the beginning of the first sentence, "At midwinter in the year 1085 William the Conqueror wore his crown at Gloucester . . ." to the last two sentences, "Above all, by slow degrees the thoughts of our forefathers, their common thoughts about common things, will have become thinkable once more. There are discoveries to be made; but also there are habits to be formed" (Maitland [1897], 23, 596). For Maitland the difficult Domesday was, like the ordnance map, a "marvellous palimpsest" (*ibid.*, 38); through "misty regions," observing "tangled skeins," if the "right questions" were asked, one could probe more deeply into more distant Anglo-Saxon law and land and behavior—a course that could not be "straightforward"; and "sometimes we shall be compelled to leave a question but partially answered while we are endeavouring to find a partial answer for some yet more difficult question" (*ibid.*, 398, 98, 25, 50). Maitland did ask questions—the "dreary old question"— "What was the hide?" (*ibid.*, 416)—but also: what were the ploughstrip, the manor, the folkland; what were *imperium* and *dominium*; what did "soke" mean; what does "feudalism" mean? All the time he believed that "as we go backwards the familiar outlines become blurred; the ideas become fluid, and instead of the simple we find the indefinite" and that "simplicity is the outcome of technical subtlety; it is the goal not the starting point" (*ibid.*, 31). One answer he thought he found, that Domesday was a geld book: "One great purpose seems to mould its form and its substance: it is a geld-book" (*ibid.*, 25). That answer drove V.H. Galbraith, a man in some ways of very different mind, wild; in the way Galbraith understood the phrase, Domesday could not be a geld book: it did not permit the assessment of the geld and its collection.

In his 1897 Ford Lectures, only the second in that prestigious Oxford series in which much of the best work in medieval English history has been stated and then published, Maitland displayed further flamboyance in both his use of evidence and his making of phrases. The lectures, published in 1898, were both oral and Cambridge-local, and they were unwontedly visual. They attacked the problems of corporation with the "certain uncertainty" that gave Maitland pleasure (*Township and Borough*, 10). Then in his *Roman Canon Law*, the essays of which were assembled and published in 1898, Maitland moved into a somewhat alien world. He was not always exact in his control of the detail of decretal formation, but, in delightful prose even a little more open than usual, he completely disestablished Stubbs's position that the church of England was *de jure* canonically independent before the Reformation—although *de facto* independence Maitland did not really consider.

In "On F.W. Maitland's Death" (*Law Quarterly Review*, 1907), Oliver Wendell Holmes wrote, "His last work, the *Life of Sir Leslie Stephen*, was a no less successful excursion into new fields, and showed the same gifts, coupled with unconscious spirituality, which did not surprise, but which found freer scope for expression there" (Holmes, 283–84). Elton has made light of this "American" view (Elton, 2), and much has been written about Maitland's interruption of his work on his beloved Year Books in order to perform his quasifilial duty to Stephen, who had thought that only Maitland could properly perform the task. But Holmes seems right. *The Life and Letters of Leslie Stephen* depends a great deal on personal letters. Clementine Oliver, in an unpublished paper, has written of the book: "In short, just as law reveals the logic of the community, so too do letters reveal the logic of the man." Within the bounds of discretion that he had set himself, after a great search for primary evidence—noticeably among the New England friends to whom Stephen was attached—Maitland pieced together in good part from Stephen's own words the life of a man whom he had known well. Maitland's design and proposed use of evidence is as carefully stated in his introduction as it would have been in the introduction to any thirteenth-century history. His stalking is similar when, for example, he examines the nature of Stephen's leaving the Anglican faith and the Anglican clergy: "It is true that late in life he had a way of saying that he 'never believed' some of the legends that are to be found in the Old Testament. But this phrase, so far as I am aware, always occurs in connection with a discovery that he makes, namely the discovery that he has never believed" and, on his mood on his leaving of clergy and Cambridge: "The answer is not quite simple" (Maitland [1906], 133, 145). The stakes were high in *Leslie Stephen*; Stephen and the people around him were real in a way that Henry II and his court and the pseudo-Bracton and his courts could never quite be. And occasionally in *Leslie Stephen* Maitland's dominant comic muse allows the entry of more serious muses, as quite startlingly, in Maitland's description of Julia Prinsep Jackson Duckworth, Stephen's second wife: "Her friends Watts and Burne-Jones did their best; Mrs. Cameron her best; Leslie himself said a little in the 'Forgotten Benefactors'; eyes that saw and ears that heard can never be satisfied" (Maitland [1906], 312)—and Maitland produced Julia Margaret Cameron's haunting photograph of Julia Duckworth in the book. His description caught the historian's eye of Helen Cam (Cam [1957], xxix). Surely even Maitland would have come close to being satisfied by Julia's portrait as Mrs. Ramsay in her daughter Virginia's *To the Lighthouse*, a book that played according to very different rules but that in some ways confirms Maitland's family portrait. Maitland himself used another novelist's portrait in thinking of Stephen, George Meredith's Vernon Whitford in *The Egoist* (Maitland [1906], 423). And the tone of Meredith surely binds the biographer, Maitland, and his subject, Stephen, together.

Historians whom Maitland has influenced he has influenced completely. He seems never to have left Sir Maurice Powicke's mind. He haunts Helen Cam's *The Hundred and the Hundred Rolls*. Naomi Hurnard fought him in lecture after lecture. T.F.T. Plucknett and Donald Sutherland followed him and adjusted him. Milsom has been seen. Hyams speaks of Maitland's "farseeing shrewdness" (Hyams, viii). Barbara Harvey can seem very like him. In the 1940s Mary Albertson, superb teacher of English medieval history at Swarthmore College, advised her undergraduates to read a little Maitland before taking examinations because it would raise the level of their thought and prose. Miss Albertson was right.

Maitland's heritage is not primarily a redefinition of Domesday, the borough, Henry II's assizes, suitors, English canon law, or even Parliament. His heritage is primarily a deepening and broadening of historical thought, of perceiving, of using evidence, a refining of prose and wit, a realization of the value of creative doubt, an opposition to dogmatism and narrowing convention, in life as well as art. As he wrote in 1906 of the engagement of Vanessa Stephen to Clive Bell, and their approaching marriage, "Well, it [the timing] isn't conventional but it seems to me all natural and right and beautiful" (*Letters*, 494). He was free—but never completely free of the idea of progress nor of an attachment to England that did not propel him into support of the African war certainly but may have encouraged his Unionist position.

Maitland was a lawyer who remembered Robert Browning's *The Ring and the Book*, a historian who thought of Honoré de Balzac as he recreated the French of the Year Books. He thought of the sort of thing "Brer Fox might say if he talked Latin" (*Letters*, 298). His work is full of noise; he hears "blaspheming while crockery crashed" (*Letters*, 138, 280, 269). Sometimes "tawdry," he is almost Brechtian. The last paper he read to the Eranus Society in May 1906 was either "Do Birds Sing?"—according to Fisher— or "Do Poets Sing?"—according to the minutes of the Society (Fifoot, 275).

The *English Historical Review* for 1907 printed a perceptive if clumsy obituary of Maitland by Vinogradoff but also a more pungent memorial, a note in the long appreciative obituary that Poole wrote of Mary Bateson, Maitland's most personal student, who had been like Maitland's own daughters a Cambridge child. Poole had asked Maitland to write the obituary, but he was already writing elsewhere. Poole began the note, "While these sheets are passing through the press I learn the grievous news that Dr. Maitland also is lost to us. Of what this loss means something will be said in our next number . . ." (*English Historical Review*, 22 (1907): 66–67, note 1). Florence would survive until 1920, after having married Sir Francis Darwin in 1913. For Maitland himself "during his last illness, the mosquito nets round his bed were translated into Blake's angels" (Ermengard Maitland, 6). This master of words died in a painting. He had joked with the language, sprung its sentences, and in his joking tried to show "the complex truth just as he saw it"—as he the trained lawyer saw it. Passion was not his normal mode, although he wrote his dying letters to Florence, he loved Turner, and his eyes had seen Julia Duckworth. He could occasionally gnaw off a nose, at least Round's nose (Cam, 259). He approached truth, coruscating, to use a Vinogradoff word, with ironic detachment. He knew that "of all the people in the world lovers are the least likely to distinguish precisely between the present and the future senses" (Delany, 114; Pollock and Maitland [1898], 2: 368–69). And the ironic muse, Meredith's not Hardy's, was capable of catching this meticulous man. Maitland wrote the short biography of his own father, "civil servant," for Leslie Stephen's *Dictionary of National Biography*. In it the position of "sources" is filled by the phrase "Personal knowledge." The printed page in the 1921–22 printing says, above the initials "F.W.M.": "His [John Gorham Maitland's] wife Emma, daughter of John Frederic Daniell [q.v.], survived him with a son and two daughters" (*Dictionary of National Biography*, 12: 811).

SELECTED BIBLIOGRAPHY

Works

BOOKS AND ARTICLES

Ed. *Pleas of the Crown for the County of Gloucester Before the Abbot of Reading and His Fellow Justices Itinerant: In the Fifth Year of the Reign of King Henry the Third and the Year of Grace, 1221.* London: Macmillan, 1884.

Ed. *Bracton's Note Book: A Collection of Cases Decided in the King's Courts During the Reign of Henry the Third: Annotated by a Lawyer of That Time, Seemingly by Henry of Bratton.* 3 vols. London: Clay, 1887.

Ed. *Select Pleas of the Crown. Vol. 1, A.D. 1200–1225.* London: Quaritch, 1888.

"The Suitors of the County Court." *English Historical Review* 3 (1888): 417–21. Reprinted in *Collected Papers*, vol. 1, pp. 458–66.

Ed. with William Paley Baildon. *The Court Baron: Being Precedents for Use in Seignorial and Other Local Courts, together with Select Pleas from the Bishop of Ely's Court of Littleport.* London: Quaritch, 1891.

Ed. *Three Rolls of the King's Court in the Reign of King Richard the First A.D. 1194–95.* London: Wyman, 1891.

Ed. *Records of the Parliament Holden at Westminster on the 28th Day of February in the Thirty-third Year of the Reign of King Edward the First (A.D. 1305).* Rolls Series, 98. London: Eyre and Spottiswoode, 1893.

"John Gorham Maitland." In *The Dictionary of National Biography: From the Earliest Times to 1900*, edited by Sir Leslie Stephen and Sir Sidney Lee, vol. 12, p. 811. London: Oxford University Press, 1921–22 (originally 1893).

With Frederick Pollock. *The History of English Law before the Time of Edward I.* 2 vols. Cambridge: Cambridge University Press, 1895. 2nd ed., 1898.

Domesday Book and Beyond: Three Essays in the Early History of England. Cambridge: Cambridge University Press, 1897. [Pagination in the text is from the edition with introduction by Edward Miller. London and Glasgow: Collins-Fontana Library, 1960.]

Roman Canon Law in the Church of England: Six Essays. London: Methuen, 1898.

Township and Borough: Being the Ford Lectures Delivered in the University of Oxford in the October Term of 1897. Cambridge: Cambridge University Press, 1898.

Trans. and Intro. *Political Theories of the Middle Age,* by Otto Friedrich von Gierke. Cambridge: Cambridge University Press, 1900.

Ed. with Mary Bateson. *The Charters of the Borough of Cambridge: Edited for the Council of the Borough of Cambridge and the Cambridge Antiquarian Society.* Cambridge: Cambridge University Press, 1901.

English Law and the Renaissance. Cambridge: Cambridge University Press, 1901.

"William Stubbs, Bishop of Oxford." *English Historical Review* 16 (1901): 417–26. Reprinted in *Collected Papers,* vol. 3, pp. 495–511.

Ed. *Year Books of Edward II, 1307–1310.* 3 vols. London: Quaritch, 1903–05.

Life and Letters of Leslie Stephen. London: Duckworth, 1906.

The Constitutional History of England: A Course of Lectures. Edited by H.A.L. Fisher. Cambridge: Cambridge University Press, 1908.

The Forms of Action at Common Law: A Course of Lectures. Edited by A.H. Chaytor and W.J. Whittaker. Cambridge: Cambridge University Press, 1936.

The Frederic William Maitland Reader. Edited by V.T.H. Delany. New York: Oceana, 1957.

Selected Historical Essays of F. W. Maitland. Edited by Helen Cam. Cambridge: Cambridge University Press, 1957.

Frederic William Maitland Historian: Selections from His Writings. Edited by Robert Livingston Schuyler. Berkeley: University of California Press, 1960.

LETTERS AND PAPERS

Maitland's letters and papers are housed in a number of collections, among which are Cambridge University Library; Harvard Law School Library; Houghton Library at Harvard University; Girton College, Cambridge University; Trinity College, Cambridge University; Bodleian, Oxford University; Public Records Office.

The Collected Papers of Frederic William Maitland. Edited by H.A.L. Fisher. 3 vols. Cambridge: Cambridge University Press, 1911.

The Letters of Frederic William Maitland. Edited by C.H.S. Fifoot. Cambridge, Mass.: Harvard University Press with the Selden Society, 1965.

Sources

Bell, Henry Esmond. *Maitland: A Critical Examination and Assessment.* London: Black, 1965.

Brentano, Robert. "The Sound of Stubbs." *Journal of British Studies* 6 (1967): 1–14.

Cam, Helen M. *The Hundred and the Hundred Rolls: An Outline of Local Government in Medieval England.* London: Methuen, 1930.

Cameron, James Reese. *Frederic William Maitland and the History of English Law.* Norman: University of Oklahoma Press, 1961.

Elton, G.R. *F. W. Maitland.* London: Weidenfeld and Nicolson; New Haven: Yale University Press, 1985.

Fifoot, C.H.S. *Frederic William Maitland.* Cambridge, Mass.: Harvard University Press, 1971.

Fisher, H.A.L. *Frederic William Maitland, Downing Professor of the Laws of England: A Biographical Sketch.* Cambridge: Cambridge University Press, 1910.

Galbraith, V.H. *The Making of Domesday Book.* Oxford: Clarendon, 1961.

Harvey, Barbara. *Westminster Abbey and Its Estates in the Middle Ages.* Oxford: Clarendon, 1977.

Holmes, Oliver Wendell. *Collected Legal Papers.* Edited by Harold Laski. New York: Harcourt, Brace, 1920.

Hyams, Paul R. *King, Lords and Peasants in Medieval England: The Common Law of Villeinage in the Twelfth and Thirteenth Centuries.* Oxford: Clarendon, 1980.

Maitland, Ermengard. *F. W. Maitland: A Child's-Eye View*. London: Quaritch, 1957.

Milsom, S.F.C. *The Legal Framework of English Feudalism: The Maitland Lectures Given in 1972*. Cambridge: Cambridge University Press, 1976.

———. "F.W. Maitland." *Proceedings from the British Academy* 66 (1982 for 1980): 265–81.

Plucknett, T.F.T. *Legislation of Edward I*. Oxford: Clarendon, 1949.

Powicke, F.M. *Modern Historians and the Study of History: Essays and Papers*. London: Odhams, 1956.

Rothblatt, Sheldon. *The Revolution of the Dons: Cambridge and Society in Victorian England*. London: Faber, 1968.

Sutherland, Donald W. *The Assize of Novel Disseisin*. Oxford: Clarendon, 1973.

Tait, James. Review of *Township and Borough*. *English Historical Review* 14 (1899): 344–46.

Thorne, Samuel E., trans. *Bracton de Legibus et Consuetudinibus regni Angliae*, edited by George E. Woodbine. 4 vols. Cambridge, Mass.: Harvard University Press, 1968–77.

HENRI PIRENNE

(1862–1935)

Bryce Lyon

Jean Henri Otto Lucien Marie Pirenne, preeminent historian of medieval urban structures and economy, was born on 23 December 1862 in Verviers, an industrial town in eastern Belgium not far from Liège and but a few miles from the German border. His father and mother were from two leading Verviétois families with ties cemented by a partnership in the largest wool industry in Verviers. Pirenne's father, Lucien Henri Joseph Pirenne, was a well-known denizen, widely traveled and read, an energetic bourgeois entrepreneur who took little interest in religion, staunchly supported the Liberal Party, and served as an *échevin* (alderman) of Verviers. His mother, Virginie Duesberg, was a devout Catholic who daily attended early mass throughout her long life, worried about the spiritual health of her offspring, and presided over a strict regimen for her household. Henri, the eldest of six children, grew up in a spacious house in the shadow of his father's factory with the sounds of an industrial enterprise clearly audible. That as a boy he frequently visited the factory and talked with the workers undoubtedly influenced him to specialize in economic and social history.

Henri Pirenne began his formal education at age seven in the communal school of Verviers, whose tenets were predominantly French in philosophy and methodology. He excelled in history, geography, French grammar and literature, Latin, Greek, and German, which he spoke fluently. He early demonstrated a phenomenal capacity for memorization and effortlessly quoted prodigious numbers of lines from the French classics, especially Victor Hugo. To his father's chagrin he never excelled in the natural sciences or in mathematics. Endowed with a facility for the spoken word, Pirenne at age fifteen was selected to deliver the welcoming address of the school's students to King Leopold II when he made a visit to Verviers. In 1879 Pirenne was certified to have completed his studies with great profit (Lyon [1974], 5–25).

In the autumn of 1879, when Pirenne made preparations for matriculation at the University of Liège, his father, although hoping that he would take a degree in engineering, realized that his son's talents were not in this field and counseled him to take a degree in law as good training for entering the family business. Pirenne began his studies in law but soon fell under the spell of Godefroid Kurth's lectures on medieval history and determined to become a medieval historian (*ibid.*, 27–46; for Kurth see Pirenne [1924]: 193–261). He was fortunate in his choice of Liège. Kurth, a specialist in early-medieval cultural and religious history, was offering for the first time in Belgium seminars and courses on *explication des textes*, training (already de rigueur in Germany and France) that was producing the first truly professional historians. Both Kurth and his colleague Paul Fredericq, a specialist in the history of the Inquisition, had visited German and French universities, attended seminars and courses, and then introduced these forms of German and French instruction to Liège (Pirenne [1924], 311–74). Under the guidance of Kurth and Fredericq, Pirenne learned to read primary sources critically and to assess historical methodologies. By the summer of 1883, having completed the requirements for the doctorate, he was advised by Kurth and Fredericq to pursue further study in France and Germany.

In Paris during 1883–84 Pirenne took courses at the École Pratique des Hautes Études and the École des Chartes and attended lectures at the Sorbonne. He studied with such scholars as Gabriel Monod, founder of the *Revue historique*, and Arthur Giry, the specialist in medieval economic history and diplomatics. The lectures of Fustel de Coulanges that synthesized, clarified, and related the particular to the general enthralled him (Lyon [1974], 47–58). In late summer a walking trip in the Black Forest was the prelude to a year's study at German universities. After studying Latin paleography in Leipzig with Wilhelm Arndt, he went to Berlin and took the seminars of Harry Bresslau on diplomatics and the courses of Gustav Schmoller on economic history, courses that fortified his resolve to specialize in economic and social history. He also met Georg Waitz, the learned president of the Monumenta Germaniae Historica, and Leopold von Ranke, the renowned innovator of objective history, then in his ninetieth year. Most important, however, was his acquaintance with Karl Lamprecht, whose polemics against the *Rankianer* and whose pleas for a new collective history minimizing political, diplomatic, military, and biographical history, were to have a paramount influence on Pirenne's methodology (*ibid.*, 59–65; Pirenne [1897]: 50–57; Lyon [1966]: 161–231). Pirenne's social talents made him a favorite in the student Akademischer Historischer Verein, where he mingled with many of Germany's future historians.

Before Pirenne's return to Belgium in the summer of 1885 he had already obtained an appointment as a *chargé de cours* at the University of Liège. He began by teaching a *cours pratique* and one on palaeography and diplomatics. After one year at Liège he accepted a position at the University of Ghent, where he remained until his retirement in 1930. At Ghent he met and married Jenny Vanderhaegen, had four sons, and established himself as one of Europe's foremost medieval historians. He resumed association with Paul Fredericq, who had also left Liège for Ghent, and became a friend of such distinguished scholars as Franz Cumont, much respected for his studies in classical history. During his years at Ghent Pirenne founded the "Ghent School of History," training many able Belgian students, such as François L. Ganshof, Hans Van Werveke, and Charles Verlinden, as well as others from all over Europe and the United States (Lyon [1974], 66–89; Ganshof [1959]: 671–723), [1960]: 38–49). As his prestige grew, so too did his association with the foremost Belgian and European cultural and professional organizations. Secretary of the Commission Royale d'Histoire for twenty-eight years, he became its heart and soul and was responsible for the excellence of its editions and publications (Pirenne [1934]).

With the onset of World War I in 1914 Pirenne saw three of his sons depart for military service and never stopped grieving for the youngest, who was killed in battle near the Yser River. Ghent was soon occupied by the Germans and the university closed. When the German authorities tried to reopen the university under their auspices, Pirenne and Fredericq led the fight to keep it closed. Their resistance put them under arrest in March 1916 and sent them as prisoners to Germany, where they remained until after the Armistice. Imprisoned first in a camp for officers and then moved to a civilian camp, Pirenne was finally sent to solitary captivity in the little village of Creuzburg an der Werra, where to sustain his intellectual vigor he began writing what became his *Histoire de l'Europe des invasions au XVIe siècle* (Lyon [1974], 197–276; Pirenne [1920]: 539–60, 829–58).

After World War I Pirenne served as rector of the University of Ghent and received dozens of honorary degrees and membership in numerous learned organizations and academies. In great demand, he spent part of 1922 lecturing at American universities from coast to coast (Lyon [1974], 298–301; Pirenne [1923]: 151–76). He also became an unofficial intellectual adviser to King Albert I. Shortly after World War I Lucien Febvre and Marc Bloch, young historians at the University of Strasbourg, sought Pirenne's support for founding a new journal of social and economic history, a gesture that began a long friendship and ultimately resulted in *Annales d'histoire économique et sociale* (Lyon [1980]: 69–84). In 1930, when a law mandated that all instruction at the University of Ghent be given in Dutch (Flemish), Pirenne retired because he disagreed with this decision, even though he himself was fluent in Flemish. He accepted an appointment at the University of Brussels, where he offered courses until his death on 24 October 1935.

Under Kurth's guidance Pirenne had written a monograph on the ninth-century Latin poet Sedulius of Liège, which was published when he was but nineteen (*Sedulius de Liège*, 1882). Although he subsequently wrote on a broad range of subjects, particularly those connected with Belgian history, he concentrated upon medieval economic and social history. Soon after arriving at Ghent he reworked his doctoral thesis on Dinant into a book dealing with the town's origins, economic function in the Meuse Valley, guilds of copper beaters, and preeminence as a center for the fabrication of copper ware. This work initiated the research on medieval urban history that continued to the end of his career. Belgian towns had been the leading commercial, industrial, and financial centers of northern Europe in the Middle Ages; Pirenne recognized their pivotal importance for the Belgian past and sought to integrate their development within the context of western European urban history. This led him to explore the origins and functions of medieval towns in a series of fundamental articles in the *Revue historique* and other journals, articles that initiated the investigation of medieval urban history from an economic and social perspective (Pirenne [1893]: 53–83; [1895]: 57–98, 293–327; [1898]: 59–70; [1903]: 9–32). By 1900 Pirenne had become one of the three or four leading authorities on the subject.

Convinced that too much history had been written from chronicles and from badly edited texts, Pirenne began to focus on the edition of key social and economic records. His first notable edition was the account by Galbert de Bruges of the murder of Count Charles the Good of Flanders in 1127–28, an edition that has never been superseded and has remained valuable not only for its information about twelfth-century urban history in Flanders but also for the light it sheds on the medieval mentality of clerics, feudal aristocrats, and bourgeoisie (1891). Most of Pirenne's editions stemmed from research on specific problems: wanting to learn more about thirteenth-century agrarian history and incomes, he edited the *polyptique* of the abbey of Saint-Trond; his study of the bitter urban and agrarian uprisings and conflicts in the fourteenth century led him to edit a chronicle that described this discontent in Flanders just before it came under the rule of the dukes of Burgundy. He edited another group of records concerned with the peasant revolt in Maritime Flanders in 1323–28. An ambitious project was his collaboration with Georges Espinas on the edition of records dealing with the wool industry in medieval Flanders, an undertaking that produced four large volumes between 1906 and 1924 and that has been continued by Belgian medievalists to the present.

While setting new standards for editing texts, Pirenne also drew up exacting guidelines to govern the edition of texts by the Commission Royale d'Histoire with the aim of emulating the high quality of the editions of the Monumenta Germaniae Historica and the French Receuils and Documents Inédits. He instituted other efforts to improve the education of persons who would staff the Belgian state, communal, and religious archives (Lyon [1974], 113–15). For students of palaeography and diplomatics he drew upon the advice of Arthur Giry and his friend Maurice Prou, the future director of the École des Chartes, and collected representative examples of records, reproduced and accompanied by a manual of instruction, which appeared in 1908 as the *Album belge de diplomatique* (Lyon and Lyon [1965]: 71–107). Finally, to fill a longstanding need, he prepared a comprehensive bibliography for Belgian history, which appeared in 1893, and oversaw two revised editions.

As was normal for young historians in the late nineteenth century, Pirenne concentrated upon research, editorial projects, and monographs and articles during the first decade of his career. His first synthetic work, "Les Pays-Bas de 1280 à 1477," appeared in 1894 as a long section in the well-known *Histoire générale* directed by Ernest Lavisse and Alfred Rambaud. Although his first such effort, this essay clearly displayed his talent for focusing on essential historical developments and problems and for unifying them into a cogent whole. Here was collective history at its best. His next opportunity to do historical synthesis came from his friend Paul Fredericq. In 1894 Fredericq had been invited by Karl Lamprecht to write a volume on the Burgundian dukes for the Heeren-Uckert *Geschichte der europäischen Staaten*, of which Lamprecht was the director. Unable to accept this invitation, Fredericq recommended Pirenne, drawing Lamprecht's attention to Pirenne's contribution to the *Histoire générale*. That same year Lamprecht invited Pirenne to contribute to his series, and after some negotiation (which enabled Pirenne to publish a French version as well) Pirenne consented to write a multivolume *Histoire de Belgique* (Lyon [1966]: 161–231). Although medievalists are concerned only with the first two volumes, which took the history of what became Belgium down to the death of Charles the Bold (1477), it should be noted that the *Histoire de Belgique* henceforth occupied much of Pirenne's time: Volume 1 appeared in 1900; Volume 7, the last (which brought the history of Belgium to 1914), in 1932, with most of the volumes being issued in revised editions. Published first in German, then in French, and finally in Dutch (Flemish), this work was certainly Pirenne's most ambitious and successful synthetic effort and, as a number of reviewers emphasized, provided Belgians for the first time with a comprehensive, understandable, and scholarly history of their country.

The success of the *Histoire de Belgique* brought Pirenne invitations to write other such works. In 1910 he published *Les anciennes démocraties des Pays-Bas*. Drawing from his lectures in the United States in 1922, he wrote what many medievalists consider one of his finest syntheses, *Medieval Cities: Their Origins and the Revival of Trade* (1925). In 1927 it appeared in a more fully annotated French version as *Les villes du moyen âge: essai d'histoire économique et sociale*. In 1929 Volume 6 of the *Cambridge Medieval History* contained Pirenne's masterly "Northern Towns and Their Commerce," and in 1936 Volume 8 encompassed his history of the Low Countries under the Burgundian dukes. Ranking with his *Histoire de Belgique* and *Villes du moyen âge* as an enduring synthesis was "Le mouvement économique et sociale au moyen âge du XIe au milieu du XVe siècle," contributed in 1933 to Volume 8 of the *Histoire générale* edited by Gustave Glotz. For many years the best summary of medieval economic and social history, it was translated into English and published as a separate book in 1936, and in 1963 Hans Van Werveke brought out the first separate French edition, with an updated bibliography.

There was scarcely a subject in medieval economic and social history that Pirenne did not investigate. He wrote seminal articles on the wine and wool trades, the literacy of medieval merchants, the craft and merchant guilds, urban demography, social conflict, and the origins of capitalism (Pirenne [1903]: 1–32; [1901]: 189–96; [1929]: 13–28; [1933]: 225–43). As original and influential as were his articles on the medieval towns was his 1914 essay on "Les étapes de l'histoire sociale du capitalisme." Here he not only demonstrated the existence of capitalistic enterprise as early as the eleventh and twelfth centuries but also constructed a model for the stages of capitalistic endeavor in trade, industry, and finance. He also showed how old capitalistic families were replaced by new ones, which in turn gave way to others. And he argued that periods of strict economic regulation and of laissez-faire occurred in cycles. Although noted for pioneering new historical perspectives, Pirenne wrote only two articles on methodology. The first, "De la méthode comparative en histoire," which resulted from his presidential and welcoming address to the Fifth International Congress of Historical Sciences held at Brussels in 1923, was a plea for horizontal and vertical historical comparison to counteract the pernicious nationalistic and racial interpretation that had dominated history in the nineteenth century. The second article, "What Are Historians Trying to Do?" (1931), with its French version, "La tâche de l'historien," emphasized the provisional nature of historical conclusions and theses and contrasted the differences between the methodology of the historian and that of the sociologist.

Pirenne's interest after World War I in eastern European history, Byzantium, and the domination of the Mediterranean by Islam sprang from his association with Russian prisoners of war in a German camp. Through this association he became aware of the Byzantine influence on Russian culture and language and began to learn the Russian language (Lyon [1974], 232–33). He realized for the first time the effect of the Islamic domination of the Mediterranean and its impact on Byzantium and the Latin West. No longer did he consider satisfactory the traditional explanations for the end of the ancient world and the beginning of the Middle Ages. His first revisionist statement on this classic problem appeared in his manuscript on the *Histoire de l'Europe des invasions au XVIe siècle*, where he suggested that the ancient world ended only in the late seventh and early eighth centuries, when the *mare nostrum* of the Romans became the *mare nostrum* of the Arabs, the economic cohesion of the Mediterranean basin disintegrated, and the contact between East and West disappeared. Soon after World War I, probing into the impact of the Arabs on the decline of the ancient world and the origins of the Middle Ages, he published a series of articles from 1922 to 1934 concerned with this problem. At his death in 1935 the first draft of *Mahomet et Charlemagne* lay on his desk. It became his best-known and probably his most original, stimulating, and debatable book.

Pirenne died leaving a corpus of work remarkable for both its quality and its quantity. In a period noted for its medievalists and esprit for research, Pirenne had few equals—William Stubbs, Frederic W. Maitland, Georg Waitz, Fustel de Coulanges, and Ferdinand Lot. During this period Pirenne wrote thirty books (some translated into five or six languages), 265 articles, and nearly two hundred book reviews. These figures, moreover, are exclusive of his printed notes, memoirs, communications, lectures, and discourses (*Hommages et souvenirs*, vol. 1).

What influence did Pirenne's research and writing have upon traditional modes of thought among medieval historians? Though an excellent editor of texts, he did not make editing his principal preoccupation, as did Wilhelm Arndt and Maurice Prou, for example. His editing was not an end in itself but a means to make available reliable sources of research on problems and questions that concerned him. Gifted as a teacher and endowed with a charismatic personality, he attracted and trained many students who in their careers and through their own students widely disseminated Pirenne's ideas (*Hommages et souvenirs*, 1: 593–639). His ability to write clearly and simply, to synthesize, and to concentrate on the salient problems and developments in history appealed to students as well as to scholars. For years in the United States his books on medieval towns, his survey of medieval economic and social history, his history of Europe, and his *Mahomet et Charlemagne* were standard reading for courses on the Middle Ages. Perhaps only the works of Johan Huizinga and Marc Bloch attained equal recognition in the United States.

According to Ganshof, the most illustrious of Pirenne's students, the four contributions to medieval history that put Pirenne in the pantheon of historians are his *Histoire de Belgique*; his research on the medieval town; his writing on medieval economic and social history, in which he emphasized and discerned basic developments, trends, and junctures; and his famous thesis on the end of the ancient world and the beginning of the medieval, summed up in *Mahomet et Charlemagne* (Ganshof [1959]: 671–723). There is yet another major contribution. The model of Pirenne's methodology—his interest in allied fields of knowledge that he felt enriched history, his emphasis upon comparative history, and the priority he gave to social and economic phenomena over political, military, and diplomatic events—greatly influenced other historians and caused Febvre and Bloch to look to him for leadership in their quest for a "new" history and a journal in which to publish it. Because of Pirenne's influence and support he should stand with Febvre and Bloch as a founder of *Annales* history.

Let us look more closely at Pirenne's major contributions. Before his *Histoire de Belgique*—our concern is with its medieval parts—little had been written about Belgium that was professional and scholarly. Political histories of the seven provinces that comprised modern Belgium, such as Flanders, Brabant, and Liège, were particularistic and lacked scope. The few histories of Belgium either suffered from the romanticism that pervaded much of nineteenth-century Europe or rested upon linguistic and racial arguments. Pirenne found none of this satisfactory or historical because it ignored the unifying forces that ultimately glued these provinces together. Correctly he saw no racial or linguistic unity and few common cultural tendencies until the Burgundian period (1384–1477); but he did perceive common urban, economic, social, and class developments in all these medieval states as a molding and unifying force, and upon these collective tendencies he constructed his history.

In a letter of 1894 to Lamprecht Pirenne stated his intention of focusing upon the social development of these states; political events should receive attention only as manifestations of social and economic developments. So he wrote his history, concentrating on urban history from the North Sea to the Ardennes and on the common commercial, industrial, financial, social, institutional, religious, and cultural tendencies. But he did even more, and it was this that made his history a classic. He recalled that Lamprecht in his *Deutsche Geschichte* had referred to medieval Flanders and Brabant as "ein Mikrokosmos gleichsam des gesamten Landes zwischen Rhein und Seine" (Lamprecht, 3: 190). Paraphrasing Lamprecht in the preface to Volume 1 of the *Histoire de Belgique*, Pirenne referred to Belgium "comme un 'microcosme' de l'Europe occidentale" (Pirenne [1900], 1: xii). This recognition made his history European. He related every historical development in Belgium to those of medieval Europe, be they seignorialism, feudalism, faith and theology, the Crusades, economic revival, economic and social crisis in the fourteenth century, or Romanesque and Gothic architecture. Bloch called the *Histoire de Belgique* "histoire totale" and expressed the hope that someday France would have a similar history (Lyon and Lyon [1990], 139–40, letter 63).

The end of Pirenne's account of medieval Belgium leaves one in a mood of disappointment and frustration. Showing that by the fifteenth century the Burgundian dukes had finally unified those provinces that today make up the Netherlands and Belgium and that they ruled over a strong middle state more powerful than the conglomeration of states to the east in Germany and richer economically than France to the west, Pirenne then poignantly recounts how all was lost with the adventures of Charles the Bold and his death at Nancy in 1477. The Low Countries fell to the Hapsburgs and were subsequently fought over and divided for centuries.

Searching for the origins of the medieval town, Pirenne found most of the explanations unsatisfactory because they usually ignored the town as an economic and social fact. German historians had done the best research, yet for Pirenne their explanations were too legalistic, too military, too political, or too wedded to the famous *Markgenossenschaft* theory, which derived German towns from early free communities of German peasants. The arguments of French and Italian historians for a linkage between Roman *civitates*, *castra*, and *castella* made little sense to Pirenne because he was convinced that there had been a rupture in urban continuity in the early Middle Ages and that for centuries few real towns, in terms of economic and social functions, existed in the Latin West. Even the few historians who looked for economic explanations seemed to have garbled their evidence, deriving, for example, the town from the guild merchant, when, as Pirenne observed, guilds could come into existence only after there were towns enabling them to function.

From a reading of the pertinent literature and his research in the primary sources Pirenne concluded that the town was a new economic and social phenomenon that arose in the late tenth and early eleventh centuries. Before then there could be no real towns because at least since the seventh century the medieval West had become agrarian, and commerce and industry, the sine qua non for towns, were enterprises of the past. Exchange was by barter or by a few silver pennies, the only coins in circulation. This was the age of seignorialism and feudalism. Only with a change in this economic environment could there be towns. Pirenne saw this change coming in the tenth century, when he detected a demographic rise, a clearing of land for the production of more food, a gradual growth in agrarian production that resulted in some surpluses, and the restoration of political stability and order in some of the better-governed feudal states. These developments allowed trade to resume and goods to be fabricated. The first traders or merchants were itinerant, going from one fortified point to another, whether a castle, cathedral site, or monastery, all located strategically on rivers or highways and all affording protection. Eventually these merchants settled at various fortified sites. If these were small *Burgen* or *châteaux*, the merchants lived just outside the walls; if old Roman *civitates* or camps, they took advantage of the old fortifications that survived and lived within them. Settling then in suburbs (*faubourgs*) next to fortified points (*Burgen, bourgs,* boroughs), they came to be called *burgenses*, that is, bourgeoisie. Here was the genesis of the medieval town. Living first under the rule and protection of a feudal prince, abbot, or bishop, the bourgeoisie soon began seeking from these rulers, by bargaining or force, elementary privileges essential for their way of life that benefited them socially, economically, and legally and separated them from the peasants. As they acquired means and experience, they organized themselves into guilds and pressed for and gained political rights that made them self-governing. Many of these self-governing towns were called "communes." In states with strong rulers these towns remained under their territorial power, but in much of Germany and Italy, where central authority did not exist, the towns became politically independent, as, for example, the free cities of Germany and the Italian city-states.

These are the main features of Pirenne's so-called mercantile-settlement theory, which was generally accepted from the late nineteenth century into the 1940s. Since World War II, however, it has been criticized, revised, or regarded as insufficient. That Pirenne generalized too much from evidence mostly from the Low Countries and northern Europe; that he did not take into account local patterns of urban development; that he failed to recognize the continuity of urban life in southern Europe, particularly along the shores of the Mediterranean; that he dated urban revival too late; that he painted too black a picture of the Carolingian economy—these are the principal points of dispute. Few British medievalists have accepted Pirenne's explanation (Lyon [1960]: 437–93; Dhondt [1966]: 81–129; Nicholas [1969]: 53–114; Despy and Verhulst [1986], 28: 1ff.). Even if much of this criticism is just, it is indisputable that Pirenne was the first to insist that the medieval town was a development that could be understood only in terms of its economic and social environment. His thesis, more than any other, has energized research and debate from which emerged a clearer and richer picture of the medieval town. Believing that the task of a good historian was to question assumptions and to ask the right questions, Pirenne surely expected that his thesis would be debated and revised.

His research and writing on medieval urban development gave Pirenne much of the framework for his account of medieval economic and social history. Some major themes emerge. The ancient world continued to exist until the Arab conquests of the seventh and eighth centuries destroyed the economic unity of the Mediterranean. Deprived of economic relations with the East, the West became an agrarian economy exploited by seignorialism. The Carolingian period saw the western economy at its nadir. Gradual recovery came in the tenth century, a recovery first seen in Italy and southern France, from which came those attacks that loosened the Muslim grip on the western Mediterranean. By the late eleventh century Europe was strong enough politically and economically to mount the First Crusade, which not only symbolized recovery but resulted in western domination of the Mediterranean. The next two centuries witnessed a long-term economic renaissance that expedited social and economic freedom of the peasantry, long-distance commerce, specialized industries, population growth with larger and more urban centers, capitalistic enterprises, new financial techniques, and the increased circulation of more valuable silver and gold coins. By the late thirteenth century this flurry of activity began to falter, and according to Pirenne the fourteenth century saw economic retrenchment and general stagnation exacerbated by a multitude of setbacks and catastrophes: the Babylonian Captivity and the Great Schism, the Hundred Years' War and civil wars, the incapacity of rulers, social and economic strife between the privileged bourgeoisie and the growing proletariat beset with spreading unemployment, long periods of inclement weather bringing famine and disease, and the Black Death. Pirenne was the first historian to take the pulse of the economic and social crisis of the fourteenth century and, in his way, account for the waning of the Middle Ages much as Huizinga had done with his cultural, religious, artistic, and psychological approach. Much of Pirenne's account has been superseded by studies utilizing sophisticated techniques unknown to him. And yet most current research and revision, except for the generic and family research, wrestles with the themes and problems that occupied Pirenne. How truly Hans Van Werveke wrote, "It [*Histoire économique*] is, one can say, a work of which the reading continues to impose itself upon succeeding generations despite the increase in our knowledge of economic history and the revision it has brought" (Pirenne [1963], vi).

Until Pirenne proposed his explanation for the end of the ancient world and the origins of the Middle Ages, all previous explanations—whether political, military, economic, social, religious, cultural, psychological, physical, or racial—lay under the shadow of Edward Gibbon's classic work. Many corrected and revised Gibbon, but none seriously questioned his chronology. Whatever their reasons for the end of the Roman Empire, all historians agreed that the end came sometime in the fourth century or, at the latest, in the late fifth. Pirenne was to shatter this spell of Gibbon and to force ancient and medieval historians to view the late-imperial period and the early Middle Ages from an entirely different perspective.

Pirenne was convinced that the ancient world ended only after the Arab invasions of the seventh and eighth centuries had swept around the perimeter of the Mediterranean and had converted it into a Muslim lake, upon which, as one Arab writer graphically said, the Christians could no longer "float a plank" (Pirenne [1937]; Miall trans., 166). This Arab sweep destroyed the essential characteristic and lifeblood of the Roman Empire—its unity and coherence, resting upon control of the Mediterranean from the Bosphorus to the Strait of Gibraltar. For centuries the *mare nostrum* had sustained the empire. Over its waters had passed commerce, the Roman naval and military might, and the ideology of antiquity. The German tribes that had occupied the western empire had not destroyed this unity. They had in fact admired the superior Roman civilization and worked to continue it. Though the new German kingdoms had no effective political ties with the eastern empire, they still partook of the Mediterranean unity and enjoyed unbroken economic exchange with the East. With the Arab conquest of three sides of the Mediterranean, political, economic, and cultural exchange ended. Except for the most tenuous ties between Constantinople and a few Italian ports, the Arabs had rolled down an iron curtain between East and West that remained until the late tenth century. Henceforth it was the Crescent versus the Cross. In Pirenne's words Muhammad had made possible Charlemagne. The Carolingian empire of the eighth and ninth centuries was pushed away from the southern sea and became landlocked. It reverted to an agrarian economy, what Pirenne called "an economy of no outlets." Political organization disintegrated, urban life disappeared, and culture sank to abysmal depths. These centuries were indeed the Dark Ages.

From the moment that Pirenne proposed his unorthodox thesis it has been debated and criticized. Ancient historians never accepted it, and medievalists for many reasons have shown that evidence is inadequate to sustain various of its elements (Lyon [1971]; [1987], 135–45; *Moyen âge* [1960], 437–93; Lopez [1943]: 14–38; Riising [1952]: 87–130; Havighurst [1974]). Nevertheless, it has generated a huge corpus of writing comparable with that over the meaning of the Renaissance, the coming of the Reformation, and the causes of World War I. As yet, however, no more satisfactory explanation for the end of the ancient world has been proposed. Whatever will ultimately be the conclusion on this challenging thesis, historians will never regard these centuries from the fourth to the eighth in the same way. Pirenne turned their world upside down.

Pirenne takes his place with Febvre and Bloch as a founder of *Annales* history. The affinity of these three historians emerges from their writing, which shows how close they were in methodology and the objectives of history. Proof beyond doubt of the debt of Febvre and Bloch to Pirenne is found in the many letters they wrote to him between 1921 and 1935 (Lyon and Lyon [1990]). Here they acknowledged him as their master and as the historian most responsible for whetting their appetites for a new economic and social history. What could be a finer tribute to Pirenne and to his standing as a historian?

SELECTED BIBLIOGRAPHY
Works

BOOKS AND ARTICLES

Sedulius de Liège. Brussels: Mémoires de l'Académie Royale de Belgique, 1882.
Histoire de la constitution de la ville de Dinant au moyen âge. Ghent: Clemm (H. Engelcke), 1889.
Ed. and Intro. *Histoire du meurtre de Charles le Bon, comte de Flandre (1127–1128) par Galbert de Bruges*. Paris: Picard, 1891.
"L'origine des constitutions urbaines au moyen âge." *Revue historique* 53 (1893): 53–83; 57 (1895): 57–98, 293–327.
"Les Pays-Bas de 1280–1477." In *Histoire générale*, edited by E. Lavisse and A. Rambaud, vol. 3, pp. 416–62. Paris: Colin, 1894.
Ed. *Le livre de l'abbé Guillaume de Ryckel (1249–1272): polyptyque et comptes de l'abbaye de Saint-Trond au milieu de XIIIe siècle*. Brussels: Hayez, Imprimeur de l'Académie Royale de Belgique, 1896.
"Une polémique historique en Allemagne." *Revue historique* 64 (1897): 50–57.
"Villes, marchés et marchands au moyen âge." *Revue historique* 67 (1898): 59–70.
Ed. *Le soulèvement de la Flandre maritime de 1323–1328*. Brussels: Kiessling, 1900.
"Les coutumes de la gilde marchande de Saint-Omer." *Moyen âge* 14 (1901): 189–96.
Ed. *Chronique rimée des troubles de Flandre en 1379–1380*. Ghent: Vuylsteke, 1902.

"Les dénombrements de la population d'Ypres au XVe siècle. 1412–1506." *Vierteljahrschrift für Sozial und Wirtschaftsgeschichte* 1 (1903): 1–32.

"Les villes flamands avant le XIIe siècle." *Annales de l'Est et du Nord* 1 (1903): 9–32.

Ed. with Georges Espinas. *Recueil de documents relatifs à l'histoire de l'industrie drapière en Flandre.* Vols. 1–4. Brussels: Imbreghts, 1906–24.

Album belge de diplomatique: recueil de fac-similés pour servir à l'étude de la diplomatique des provinces belges au moyen âge. Brussels: Vandamme and Rossignol, 1909.

Les anciennes démocraties des Pays-Bas. Paris: Flammarion, 1910. Translated as *Belgian Democracy: Its Early History* by J. V. Saunders. Manchester: Manchester University Press, 1915.

"Les étapes de l'histoire sociale du capitalisme." *Bulletin de l'Académie Royale de Belgique, Classe des Lettres* (1914): 258–99. Translated as "Stages in the Social History of Capitalism." *American Historical Review* 19 (1914): 494–515.

"Souvenirs de captivité en Allemagne (mars 1916–novembre 1918)." *Revue de deux mondes* 55 (1920): 539–60, 829–58.

"De la méthode comparative en histoire." In *Compte rendu du Cinquième Congrès International des Sciences Historiques.* Brussels: Weissenbruch, 1923.

"Les universités américains." *Flambeau* (1923): 151–76.

"Notice sur Paul Fredericq." *Annuaire de l'Académie Royale de Belgique* (1924): 311–74.

Les villes du moyen âge: essai d'histoire économique et sociale. Brussels: Lamertin, 1927. Translated as *Medieval Cities: Their Origins and the Revival of Trade* by Frank D. Halsey. Princeton, N.J.: Princeton University Press, 1925.

"L'instruction des marchands au moyen âge." *Annales d'histoire économique et sociale* 1 (1929): 13–28.

Bibliographie de l'histoire de Belgique, catalogue méthodique et chronologique des sources et des ouvrages principaux relatifs à l'histoire de tous les Pays-Bas jusqu'en 1598 et à l'histoire de Belgique jusqu'en 1914. 3rd ed. Brussels: Lamertin, 1931.

"La tâche de l'historien." *Flambeau* 14 (1931): 5–22. Translated as "What Are Historians Trying to Do?" by Martha Anderson. In *Methods in Social Science*, edited by Stuart A. Rice, pp. 435–45. Chicago: University of Chicago Press, 1931.

"Un grand commerce d'exportation au moyen âge: les vins de France." *Annales d'histoire économique et sociale* 5 (1933): 225–43.

"La Commission Royale d'Histoire depuis sa fondation (1834–1934)." In *La Commission Royale d'Histoire: livre jubilaire.* Brussels: Académie Royale de Belgique, 1934.

Histoire de l'Europe des invasions au XVIe siècle. Paris: Alcan, 1936. Translated as *A History of Europe from the End of the Roman World in the West to the Beginnings of the Western States* by Bernard Miall. London: Allen and Unwin, 1939.

Mahomet et Charlemagne. 7th ed. Paris: Alcan; Brussels: Nouvelle Société d'Éditions, 1937. Translated as *Mohammed and Charlemagne* by Bernard Miall. London: Allen and Unwin, 1939.

Les villes et les institutions urbaines. 2 vols. Brussels: Nouvelle Société d'Éditions; Paris: Alcan, 1939.

Histoire économique de l'occident médiéval. Preface by E. Coornaert. Bruges: Desclée de Brouwer, 1951.

Histoire de Belgique. 4 vols. Brussels: Renaissance du Livre, 1952. [These four large volumes comprise the latest editions of the seven volumes of the *Histoire de Belgique* plus *La Belgique et la guerre mondiale*.]

Histoire économique et sociale du moyen âge. Edited by Hans Van Werveke. Originally in vol. 8 of *Histoire du moyen âge* by Henri Pirenne, Gustave Cohen, and Henri Focillon, 1933; Paris: Presses Universitaires de France, 1963.

LETTERS AND PAPERS

Pirenne's letters and papers are housed in the archives of the Université Libre de Bruxelles.

Sources

Bierlaire, Franz, and Jean-Louis Kupper, eds. *Henri Pirenne: de la cité de Liège à la ville de Gand.* Liège: University of Liège, 1987.

Caenegem, R.C. Van. "Henri Pirenne: Naar Aanleiding van de Honderdste Verjaardag van Zijn Benoeming te Gent." *Mededelingen van de Koninklijke Academie voor Wetenschappen, Letteren en Schone Kunsten van Belgi, Klasse der Letteren* 1 (1987): 87–105.

Despy, G., and A.E. Verhulst. *La fortune historiographique des thèses d'Henri Pirenne.* In *Archives et bibliothèques de Belgique,* vol. 28. Brussels: Archives et bibliothèques, 1986.

Dhondt, Jan. "Henri Pirenne: historien des institutions urbaines." *Annali della Fondazione Italiana per la Storia Amministrativa* 3 (1966): 81–129.

Ganshof, François L. "Pirenne (Henri)." *Biographie nationale publiée par l'Académie Royale des Sciences, des Lettres et des Beaux-Arts* 30 (1959): 671–723.

———. "Henri Pirenne (1862–1935)." In *Liber Memorialis (1913–1960: Rijksuniversiteit te Gent,* pp. 38–49. Ghent: Faculteit der Letteren en Wijsbegeerte, 1960.

Gérardy, Georges. *Henri Pirenne, sa vie et son oeuvre.* Brussels: Ministère de l'Éducation Nationale et de la Culture, 1962.

Havighurst, A.F., ed. *The Pirenne Thesis: Analysis, Criticism, and Revision.* 3rd ed. Lexington, Mass.: Heath, 1976.

Henri Pirenne: hommages et souvenirs. 2 vols. Brussels: Nouvelle Societé d'Éditions, 1938.

Lamprecht, Karl. *Deutsche Geschichte.* Vol. 3. Berlin: Weidmann, 1895.

Lopez, Robert S. "Mohammed and Charlemagne: A Revision." *Speculum* 18 (1943): 14–38.

Lyon, Bryce. "L'oeuvre de Henri Pirenne après vingt-cinq ans." *Moyen âge* 66 (1960): 437–93.

———. "The Letters of Henri Pirenne to Karl Lamprecht (1894–1915)." *Bulletin de la Commission Royale d'Histoire* 132 (1966): 161–231.

———. *The Origins of the Middle Ages: Pirenne's Challenge to Gibbon.* New York: Norton, 1972.

———. *Henri Pirenne: A Biographical and Intellectual Study.* Ghent: Story-Scientia, 1974.

———. "Henri Pirenne and the Origins of Annales History." *Annals of Scholarship: Metastudies of the Humanities and Social Sciences* 1 (1980): 69–84.

———. "Le débat historique sur la fin du monde antique et le début du moyen âge." In *La naissance de l'Europe,* pp. 135–45. Milan: Jaca Book, 1987.

———, and Mary Lyon. "Maurice Prou, ami de Henri Pirenne." *Moyen âge* 71 (1965): 71–107.

———, and ———. *The Journal de Guerre of Henri Pirenne.* Amsterdam: North-Holland, 1976.

———, and ———, eds. *The Birth of Annales History: The Letters of Lucien Febvre and Marc Bloch to Henri Pirenne (1921–1935).* Brussels: Commission Royale d'Histoire, 1990.

Nicholas, David. "Medieval Urban Origins in Northern Continental Europe: State of Research and Some Tentative Conclusions." *Studies in Medieval and Renaissance History* 6 (1969): 53–114.

Pirenne, Jacques. "Henri Pirenne, mon père." *Revue générale belge* (1962): 21–35.

Riising, Anne. "The Fate of Henri Pirenne's Theses on the Consequences of the Islamic Expansion." *Classica et Mediaevalia* 13 (1952): 87–130.

CHARLES HOMER HASKINS

(1870–1937)

Sally Vaughn

Charles Homer Haskins, one of the founders of medieval studies in the United States, was born on 21 December 1870 to Rachel A. McClintock Haskins and George Washington Haskins in Meadville, Pennsylvania. His father was a schoolteacher descended from eighteenth-century English immigrants; Rachel Haskins was of Scotch-Irish descent. The Haskins family had settled in Meadville after living first in Massachusetts or Connecticut, and then in Ticonderoga, New York. Charles was the first of three children. He early evidenced intelligence and energy for scholarship. As a boy of five Charles learned Greek and Latin from his father. The elder Haskins, while serving as superintendent of the Meadville schools, had been earning his degree in classics at Allegheny College in Meadville during the first five years of Charles's life. Shortly thereafter he became classics professor at Allegheny College, where he taught Greek and Latin from 1875 to 1886. Evidently the elder Haskins was possessed of both boundless energy and driving ambition, or at least a tremendous thirst for knowledge of a great variety, for he seems to have continued his studies, now taking on law and earning a degree that enabled him to practice as an attorney in addition to his university teaching during Charles's boyhood.

The son of such an intelligent, ambitious, and hardworking father also proved to be a high achiever. Charles himself entered Allegheny College as a student at the age of thirteen, perhaps with the encouragement or help of his father, who was still on the Allegheny faculty at Charles's admission in 1883. Charles quickly exhausted Allegheny's resources; probably in 1885 he decided to transfer elsewhere to finish his degree and applied to Harvard. Rejected for his youth (he was fifteen), Charles entered Johns Hopkins in 1886 and received his A.B. there in 1887, at the age of sixteen. After some study in Berlin and Paris under Charles Victor Langlois and Ferdinand Lot at the École des Chartes in Paris, Charles chose to return to Johns Hopkins to take his Ph.D. in history, which he received in 1890 at the age of nineteen. Although it is not clear how long he studied in Europe, only three or four years elapsed between his receipt of the A.B. and the Ph.D.

Haskins's study at Johns Hopkins centered on the famous "seminary" of Herbert Baxter Adams, who had been steeped in the new "scientific" methods of historical study current on the Continent in his graduate years at the universities of Göttingen, Berlin, and Heidelberg—at the latter of which Adams received his Ph.D. with highest honors in 1876. In that year Johns Hopkins University opened its doors. Focusing on postgraduate education, it especially sought European-trained faculty in history who could bring to American shores the new methodologies. In Europe the study and writing of history were changing dramatically in the midst of nineteenth-century nationalism. Impelled largely by the French Revolution, French historians divided into two opposing schools. The "Romantic School" was marked by an emotional, idealistic, moralistic, and sometimes imaginative reinterpretation of the past, often influenced by contemporary politics, often relying primarily on literary sources, and often resulting in impassioned histories of artistic and literary merit. The other school of thought, centered on the École des Chartes (founded 1821), concentrated on the collection, critical editing, and interpretation of documents rather than literary sources. But both focused on the French past, and this meant the Middle Ages. The German school of romantic nationalism, focused on the German Middle Ages, provoked a reaction led by Leopold von Ranke, whose rejection of romantic interpretations and (for the most part) of literary sources inaugurated "a new spirit [in] the theory and practice of history." The "scientific" study of history through analysis of legal documents, diplomatics, correspondence and official records began with Ranke, who developed his new methodologies in a new teaching environment. Rejecting the lecture room, he invented the "seminar" in 1833 in his own study at the University of Berlin. It was this new system of historical investigation and teaching that Johns Hopkins sought to install in its new university.

Before the experimental program initiated at Johns Hopkins in 1876 American graduate education largely had lacked plan and organization. Historical studies in the United States were still dominated by a romantic, literary, patriotic history infused with religious and moral ideals that had become out-of-date in Europe by the 1870s. Only at Harvard had the new scientific approach been introduced, and that only a few years before. In the early 1870s Henry Adams, who had studied only one year in Europe, was persuaded to join the Harvard faculty in history. He was soon joined by

Ephraim Emerton, educated at the University of Leipzig, and Charles Gross, with a degree from the University of Göttingen. Henry Adams had introduced strict new standards for graduate study in history at Harvard, including rigorous entrance requirements, the use of original sources in narrow fields of inquiry, and the use of the Harvard library (access to which had been strictly limited but was now open to all thanks to Adams). It may possibly have been this program at Harvard, which predated that at Johns Hopkins by a few years, that had motivated Haskins's initial application to Harvard. But his second choice, Johns Hopkins, served him well.

Herbert Baxter Adams used the new European method of meeting in small, intimate groups to train his students—who included Charles M. Andrews, Woodrow Wilson, and Frederick Jackson Turner, as well as Haskins—to apply principles derived from the scientific method and especially the model supplied by Ranke, rather than the literary model previously current in the United States. The literary paradigm saw history as blended with literature and philology, a continual unfolding of religious ideals and morals, with freedom and democracy for all as the ultimate utopia. The new "scientific" paradigm, on the other hand, saw documents as more valid than literary evidence for reconstructing the past and looked for Darwinian evolutions of such "goods" as freedom, democracy, and utilitarian moral values through the pragmatic day-to-day events discernible in court records, land transactions, treaties, legal documents, and other such evidence. These new educational techniques and new investigative and analytical methodologies, then dominant throughout Europe, evolved in the hands of Haskins, Turner, and their later Harvard colleagues into a coherent system of graduate education throughout the United States and largely through Haskins's role as dean of the Harvard Graduate School became the model for the study of history in most American universities until the present, when paradigms are shifting away from the scientific model.

In Adams's seminars (or "seminaries," as they were called), Haskins first applied these scientific methods to American history. His dissertation, still the definitive work on the Yazoo Land Companies of Mississippi and the dispute that led to the Supreme Court case of *Fletcher v. Peck*, is still regarded as a classic in American constitutional law and history. The dissertation reflects Haskins's own legal training: he completed all the requirements for a law degree at Allegheny College before entering Johns Hopkins but abandoned law when refused permission to take the bar exam because of his age (sixteen). By age twenty-one, when he would have been eligible, he apparently had lost interest in the field of law, although its influence would emerge markedly in his later researches into medieval documents.

Haskins taught at Johns Hopkins as a graduate student, but his first full-time position was at the University of Wisconsin (1892) as professor of medieval history. Frederick Jackson Turner already had been hired to teach American history, so it was circumstance rather than choice that led Haskins to turn his teaching and research toward Europe. Aged nineteen or twenty, he was little older than his students; whether he set out at first to investigate medieval students at the behest of his first mentors Langlois and Lot, or whether the topic had a natural appeal for the young man, he began with an exploration of the Vatican archives, producing an article on the archives themselves for the fledgling *American Historical Review* in 1896 and following it two years later with "The Life of Medieval Students as Illustrated by Their Letters" in the same journal.

Frederick Jackson Turner remained his fast friend, and the two colleagues seem to have enjoyed a fascinating intellectual dialog evident in their work and shaped against the background of their Johns Hopkins experience. Where Herbert Baxter Adams and his generation looked at the admired development of American democracy and freedom as almost genetically transmitted from the forests of Germany through the villages of England to the New England townships, Haskins and Turner appear to have looked for environmental causes. Turner emerged from the dialog with his famous Frontier Thesis and Haskins with his ground-breaking definition of the twelfth century as a true renaissance, the birth of Europe, at the same time blazing new trails in the study of medieval science and culture. His other field of interest was the Normans and the Norman Conquest, to which he applied the new "scientific" methodologies. His work with documents produced important breakthroughs in understanding, not least because Haskins could stand back from the Conquest as neither the French nor the English historians could at that time to produce a different perspective on this event that was crucial not only for England but for medieval European history in general.

While at Wisconsin Haskins appears to have lived a lonely life in a boardinghouse. He dabbled in land investments in the West, losing on the gamble to such an extent that he appears never to have tried such investments again. He corresponded with the new Stanford University, which was eager to hire him. Whether or not the disastrous land investments had discouraged him from seeking his future in the West, he eventually turned down the Stanford offers and returned to the East Coast.

By 1902 Haskins had moved to Harvard and later persuaded Turner to join him there. At Wisconsin Haskins had begun working in medieval history with his study of medieval students and had first visited Vatican archives for his research. In 1905 he began to focus on

Normandy, journeying to Norman archives and the Bibliothèque Nationale in Paris yearly until 1913, when World War I began to threaten. In these years he acquired a thorough knowledge of the European archives, which culminated in his most famous works: *The Normans in European History* (1915), *Norman Institutions* (1918), *The Rise of Universities* (1923), *Studies in the History of Mediaeval Science* (1924), *The Renaissance of the Twelfth Century* (1927), and *Studies in Mediaeval Culture* (1929). Haskins has been praised by such English scholars as Sir Frederick Maurice Powicke, who commented, "He knows his way about the manuscript collections, great and small, of Europe," and compared him to the English John Horace Round for his meticulous workmanship (Powicke [1925]: 421, 422).

In the years 1902–29 Haskins founded or aided many of the American institutions and journals fundamental to historical and medieval studies. He helped establish the History of Science Society and its journal *Isis*; the Medieval Academy of America and its journal *Speculum*, holding the post of president in 1926–27; and the American Council of Learned Societies, which he chaired 1920–26. He served as one of the first presidents of the American Historical Association (1922). He sat for many years on the selection committee for John Simon Guggenheim Fellowships and was one of the architects in the remodeling of American secondary and undergraduate education; his two earliest books were *A History of Higher Education in Pennsylvania* (1902, co-authored with William I. Hull) and *The Historical Curriculum in Colleges* (1904). As dean of the Harvard Graduate School he set the pattern for American graduate education throughout the country, on the model of his Johns Hopkins training and his own research and writing. His interest in undergraduate education was reflected in his teaching of one of the first Western Civilization courses in the United States—which he conceived and taught largely as medieval history. His students recall his diatribes against American cheese—"rat cheese"—as opposed to the European delicacies. Secretly they called him "The Duke," and although he is remembered largely with affection, some students knew him as a hard taskmaster who once required a student to turn in a late paper at his home on Christmas Eve.

A few years before World War I made European archives inaccessible, Haskins's life entered a new phase. He married Clare Allen. At the time of their marriage on 11 July 1912 Clare taught French at the May School in Boston. A 1903 Vassar graduate, she had traveled and lived in Europe, studied voice and literature in Paris, and taught in Wisconsin, New York, and Boston. She later joined the faculty of Radcliffe while heading a Boston girls' school. Clearly she was as energetic, ambitious, hardworking, and accomplished as her future husband. Haskins may well have married so late in life (at forty-two) because of family constraints: he had helped his brother through M.I.T. and financed his sister's education at Smith. His historical research necessitated expensive yearly trips to Europe (once taking his father, who had never been abroad). After many years of sharing a two-room apartment with his brother in Cambridge Haskins changed his style of life dramatically with his marriage.

The Haskinses reared three children—George Lee, Charles Allen, and Clare Elisabeth—while entertaining a constant stream of American and European scholars. These visitors included the French medievalists Léopold Delisle, Charles Victor Langlois, Henri Pirenne, André Morize, and Charles Bémont. Others to whom they extended hospitality were Sir Frederick Maurice Powicke, E.K. Rand, R.P. Blake, G.R. Coffman, George Sarton, G.M. Trevelyan (nephew of Lord Macaulay), and the Byzantine historian Charles Diehl. The household had a European flavor, as French and English alternated naturally in the Haskinses' daily routine, carefully overseen by the paterfamilias, who gave attention to every detail.

The Haskinses had honeymooned in Europe in 1912, and Haskins returned to London in 1913 to attend the International Congress of Historical Sciences. Thereafter the birth of the children and the storm clouds of war in Europe curtailed his research trips abroad. Nevertheless, Haskins had to be absent from Cambridge often, for the war years found him called to Washington as part of President Woodrow Wilson's advisory group, "The Inquiry." During these years Charles and Clare maintained the family unity, remaining in close touch with each other during his weekly absences through a devoted correspondence in French. Clare's letters to Haskins survive.

The Haskinses often spent summers in Maine and autumns in New Hampshire, where the family enjoyed hiking, or "tramping," as they called it, and canoeing. Friends like Frederick Jackson Turner and the classicists Francis G. Allinson and Moses S. Slaughter would join them in joint family picnics. Caravans of canoes, following carefully planned routes, would paddle to prepared campsites, there to picnic and tramp in the woods. A man of vast energy, Haskins had enjoyed hiking and climbing for two weeks each summer in the Alps before his marriage. Clare joined him there the two summers after their marriage. Wherever he was Haskins enjoyed walking, whether to and from his classes, which he did twice a day during the semesters, or in Maine, Paris, or Normandy. Haskins often visited his friend Theodore Roosevelt at his Long Island home and enjoyed "tramping" with him there.

Roosevelt and William Howard Taft were fellow members of the Century Association in New York, where Haskins often enjoyed long conversations with them and others. In Boston he belonged to the prestigious Saturday Club, and in Cambridge he joined fellow Harvard colleagues at two dining clubs. He numbered among his friends the eminent Bostonians of the day and numerous Harvard faculty outside the history department— Roscoe Pound and Joseph Warren of the law school, the biochemist Lawrence Henderson, and the theologian George F. Moore.

At home in Cambridge Haskins welcomed his graduate students with kind hospitality. With his German-educated medievalist colleagues Ephraim Emerton and Charles Gross, he instituted the European method of graduate education at Harvard. A stream of exchange professors and guest lecturers from Europe flowed into the Harvard graduate school from 1910 to 1930, many because of personal friendships with Haskins. Haskins seems to have taught as many as three graduate seminars per semester, along with the famous History I—the model for Western Civilization courses instituted throughout the country during World War I—with enrollments sometimes as high as a thousand. The Wilsonian effort to make the world "safe for democracy," it was thought, could not be accomplished unless young Americans knew their western heritage. Haskins also took upper-division classes, such as French Institutional History and Medieval Intellectual History, which he would teach in the morning at Harvard and in the afternoon at Radcliffe for an additional stipend.

Haskins's graduate classes seem to have been the most sought after, not only by students of medieval history but by classicists, students of modern Europe, and Americanists. They were drawn especially to his diplomatics and palaeography seminars, which Emerton and Samuel Eliot Morison later described as equal to the training a student could receive at the École des Chartes or a German university. Indeed these historians of Harvard describe Haskins's graduate program as attracting European students to study under him at the American Cambridge. Emerton and Morison regard the Harvard program in medieval history as equal to those of the finest European universities. From 1901 to 1928 the vast majority of Harvard history Ph.D.s were in medieval history, outnumbering every other field, even American. In this period, fourteen degrees in medieval history and twenty-three in English history, sixteen of whom were Haskins students after Charles Gross's death in 1920, were awarded. In these same years only five degrees were awarded in ancient history and five in Latin American history.

Haskins may well have been the first American educator to encourage interdisciplinary studies, such as history and literature, creating a program that was later emulated by colleges and universities throughout the United States. He also emphasized both independent study for graduate students and a close working relationship between them and their guiding professor. To encourage this style of education the rules he instituted for graduate degrees emphasized mastery of the subject and omitted time limits for completion. Rules were minimal, leaving the major guidance of a student's instruction in the hands of the professor responsible for it. Haskins also set up and encouraged a foreign-exchange program for graduate students and postdoctoral fellows, enabling them to visit libraries, museums, and archives for extended periods, much on the model of his own earlier research in Europe. At the same time he worked with Harvard librarians Justin Winsor, Archibald C. Coolidge, and Robert P. Blake to make the Harvard collection equal to those of the finest European universities. And while building the history and graduate program at Harvard, he was at the core of the group of scholars gathered by President Woodrow Wilson to structure a monumental peace for Europe.

"The Inquiry," a Harvard-dominated think tank, had as its mission the reordering of Europe at the end of World War I based on Wilsonian visions of a peace to end all wars. Even as victory seemed far removed, these political scientists and historians constructed a peace plan that they hoped would endure. In Washington and New York Haskins directed the work of the committee relating to the settlement along the northwestern frontiers of Germany—Belgium, Denmark, Alsace-Lorraine, the Rhine, and the Saar— probably the most sensitive of the negotiation issues. The victory gained, Haskins traveled in 1918–19 to the Paris Peace Conference at Versailles where he served as Wilson's interpreter in his meetings with the French prime minister, Georges Clemenceau, and as his personal adviser and sometimes spokesman.

The Inquiry's solutions were neither effective nor lasting, and the Wilsonian settlement now seems hopelessly idealistic. Yet a great deal of hard and practical work preceded these arrangements, as Haskins and his Harvard colleague Robert Howard Lord demonstrated in their account of the negotiations, *Some Problems of the Peace Conference* (1920). Curiously the book contains little information about Haskins himself and his role in the negotiations.

In Paris Haskins faced the first stirrings of the Parkinson's disease that was to cloud the final years of his life. He rejected a European diplomatic post to return to Harvard, where he produced in quick order the culmination of his life's work—his books on medieval universities, the twelfth-century renaissance, and medieval science and culture.

In these works of the 1920s Haskins epitomized the debate central to his scholarship: is history a literary art or a scrupulous science? He wrote his books in pairs; for example, *The Normans in European History* (1915), a graceful, eloquent exposition, mirrors for a general audience the scholarly *Norman Institutions* (1918), a rigorous and meticulous textual analysis and technical discussion with voluminous Latin footnotes. While the latter significantly advanced knowledge of the pre-Conquest institutions of Normandy and distinguished them from neighboring French institutions, the more general *Normans in European History* put the Norman Conquest into a broader vision of the thousand-year history of the European Middle Ages and speculated upon the impact of the Normans, as a distinct people, on European history in general.

Haskins worked a revolution not only in American medieval studies and graduate education but in the current European scholarship, French and English, on the Norman Conquest. Free of both British insularity and French exclusivity, Haskins could take a more balanced view of the currents and crosscurrents of the whole European medieval scene. It was Haskins who first saw the Normans as a distinctive people spreading their influence throughout Europe, not just a subgroup of Frenchmen conquering England. Haskins was the first to see Normandy and England as a cross-Channel empire and the Norman realms in Italy and Sicily as both connected to their Norman relatives to the north and a conduit for the intellectual and material riches of the East into the mainstream of Europe.

Haskins also was the first to see and interpret the explosion of medieval culture in the twelfth century as a watershed and foundation for Europe at least comparable to, perhaps more significant than, the self-proclaimed Petrarchan Italian Renaissance. Like Turner's influential Frontier Thesis in American history Haskins's theories opened new vistas for research in a chain of interpretation that is still working itself out.

Haskins paired *The Rise of Universities* (1923) with *Studies in the History of Mediaeval Science* (1924). The former is a delightful snapshot of the generation of universities out of student and teacher guilds, a wry, witty, and sometimes tongue-in-cheek depiction of student highjinks that can touch chords among students even today. This work may well reflect Haskins's own joy in his earliest research into his peers of eight hundred years before. Its gleeful quotes from students' purchased form letters home asking for money and ribald student drinking songs and parodies of church liturgy, its portraits of the student "nations" taunting each other in the streets and gambling dens, and the agonies of the rigorous disputations required before students could receive degrees still conjure up the lively scenes for modern students. He seems to have thoroughly enjoyed writing it.

Much of this material on medieval scholarship appears in a more serious vein in both *Mediaeval Science* and *Studies in Mediaeval Culture* (1929), where it is broadened to include the intellectual movements of European scholars and students and the sources of their knowledge. These two books contain hard data on the transmission of manuscripts from the Muslim to the European world, emphasizing the Norman role in this spread of information. It was not only through Italy during the Crusades that lost knowledge was transmitted to Europe, Haskins argues, but also through the fall of Toledo in Spain (1086) and the fall of Palermo in Sicily (1091), which predated the First Crusade (1096–99). Normans were involved in the former and controlled these events, thus reinforcing Haskins's earlier thesis on the impact of the Normans on medieval Europe.

Out of these studies Haskins's most influential work, *The Renaissance of the Twelfth Century* (1927), seems to have grown. Like *The Rise of Universities* and *The Normans in European History* the book is an exposition on a grand theoretical level. It posits that in the twelfth century all the elements normally attributed to the Italian Renaissance existed and flourished, creating a vibrant and exciting intellectual, artistic, and political world. Though published two years before *Studies in Mediaeval Culture* (1929), *The Renaissance* clearly relied on its research. Indeed Haskins's introduction to *The Renaissance* states that it is based on his investigations set forth in *Mediaeval Science* and on the technical studies he was preparing for *Mediaeval Culture*.

Haskins chose to focus on "the revival of learning in the broadest sense—the Latin classics and their influence, the new jurisprudence and the more varied historiography, the new knowledge of the Greeks and Arabs and its effects upon Western science and philosophy, and the new institutions of learning" (*The Renaissance*, vi-vii). This work created a new paradigm for the medieval world. No longer could it be viewed as the world of monkish dullness and darkness, with all eyes turned to the hereafter, blind to the beauty, joy, and knowledge of the world. As Haskins opened new questions and new areas of scholarship with his *Normans in European History*, so with his description of the medieval renaissance he opened discussion that is still working itself out among late-twentieth-century scholars.

The Rise of Universities likewise generated numerous new studies seeking to elaborate upon Haskins's discussion, to turn up scores of documents hitherto unexamined. The body of evidence now includes sermons, letters, legal documents and proclamations, and literary works like poetry and songs. Whereas previous scholarship had stressed government, war, and politics, Haskins opened the door to broader institutional studies.

A more expansive scholarly approach was set forth in *The Normans in European History*, which pointed both English and French historians toward a broader view of the Norman Conquest. It generated research on such topics as a cross-Channel empire as against an insular English history, Norman self-concept and mythology, Viking influence on the putatively French Normans, and the existence of a distinct Norman people. These questions arising from Haskins's European-wide view of Normandy and England inspired scholars on both sides of the Channel to reassess their native history to encompass a larger conceptual framework for both English and French history.

Haskins also pointed out that in 1166, a century after William's conquest of England, the Norman king Roger the Great of Sicily ruled an empire equal to that of Anglo-Norman England in its organization, rationality, order, and extent. New studies of these other Norman states, especially Norman Italy and Sicily, slower to attract scholars, were just in the 1980s and 1990s beginning to proliferate. Nearly all owe their existence to questions raised by Haskins. A consortium of scholars throughout Europe now cooperates to structure an integrated portrait of Norman activities, often including the influence of their Viking forebears. Historians from England, the United States, France, Italy, Denmark, Sweden, Belgium, the Netherlands, Scotland, Ireland, Wales, Israel—all areas affected by Norman activities—now can be found joining together to further the investigations Haskins began.

Two societies have been founded in tribute to Haskins's investigations on the Normans. In England the Battle Conference under the leadership of R. Allen Brown and continued by Marjorie Chibnall, began meeting annually in 1978 at Battle Abbey, the site of the Battle of Hastings. Here British, French, Italian, American, and other scholars have continued to spin out the implications of Haskins's work on the Normans and their impact on Europe. Its yearly publication, now called *Anglo-Norman Studies*, disseminates this research. In the United States the Haskins Society was founded in 1982 to study Viking, Anglo-Saxon, Anglo-Norman, and Angevin history in their connectedness and broader implications on the model of Haskins's scholarship. Its annual conference at the University of Houston brings together European and American scholars. The society works closely with the Battle Conference. Its annual publication *Haskins Society Journal* complements its British sister journal.

The most influential of Haskins's works was his identification of the twelfth-century renaissance. This new paradigm totally changed the view of twentieth-century medieval scholars. The new vistas Haskins opened almost defy enumeration. In the last half of the twentieth century studies on medieval humanism, art, literature, scholarship, historiography, architecture, political development, aristocratic women, and warfare primarily seem to be based on Haskins's identification of a kind of golden age of rebirth and creativity in the twelfth century. The concept of renaissances other than that of the Quattrocento has generated the identification of other periods of renaissance—Carolingian and Northumbrian, for example, before the twelfth century and English and French after the Quattrocento—to the point that the concept of "renaissance" itself is sometimes questioned. On the other hand the Quattrocento as *the* Renaissance has not yet lost its grip on the popular mind, at least in the United States.

Colleagues on both sides of the Atlantic praised Haskins for his innovative work, his style and grace, his technical precision, and his vision as he drew together a coherent schema of the European medieval world. He received honorary degrees from Harvard (1908, 1924), Allegheny College (1915), and the universities of Wisconsin (1910), Strasbourg (1919), Padua (1922), Manchester (1922), Paris (1926), Louvain (1927), and Caen (1932). He was named an officer of the French Legion of Honor and commander of the Order of the Crown of Belgium.

Haskins's work structured the questions, problems, and debates for the next two generations of scholars on both sides of the Atlantic. Many of the best-known American historians of medieval history in the last half of the twentieth century have been his students: Joseph Strayer, Charles H. Taylor, John L. LaMonte, L.J. Paetow, Jean Birdsall, C.W. David, Edgar B. Graves, William E. Lunt, Gaines Post, Carl Stephenson, and Lynn White, Jr., to name but a few. And their own students continue his work. From 1902 to 1928 about 75 percent of the Harvard Faculty of Arts and Sciences Ph.D.s were Haskins's students. Most of them became teachers. By 1929 the Harvard graduate school was awarding 332 degrees per year, up from 159 on Haskins's arrival in 1902. In 1929 one hundred members of the Faculty of Arts and Sciences at Harvard had Harvard degrees. Other Haskins graduate students went on to become clergymen, university presidents (fifteen), editors, librarians, diplomats, physicians, and members of Congress. One became a prime minister of Canada.

Haskins survived the early 1930s with difficulty, as his Parkinson's disease progressed toward its end. Clare and the children devoted themselves to him as his physical deterioration worsened, yet his mind remained sharp. At his death on 14 May 1937 tributes poured from his American and European students and colleagues across the western world. The French historian Longrais called him "the soul of the renascence of medieval studies in the United States" (cited in Vaughn, 124); the German scholar Theodor Mommsen, grandson of the great classicist of the same name, cited him as the rare case of "a man who combined the qualities of the efficient organizer, the original scholar, and the great teacher" (*ibid.*); Powicke ranked him next to the great English scholars R.L. Poole and John Horace Round, the former for methodology, the latter for the use of new materials to elucidate old problems: "A pupil of Langlois, he would probably regard the French as his masters, but his best work is as massive as that of the great German scholars" (Powicke [1925]: 422). "As an American, he is free from our tradition of insularity . . . yet his mind and outlook are English in the best sense of the word" (*ibid.*). With Haskins American scholarship in medieval studies came of age in European eyes. In America he virtually created the program of graduate education in history at Harvard that became the model for most American universities to this day, trained many of the scholars who implemented graduate and undergraduate teaching of history, and inspired the next two generations of medieval historians on both sides of the Atlantic to take up his work in medieval history with vigor and enthusiasm. His career spanned a significant era in which historical studies and methodologies were "modernized" and transformed: historical scholarship was placed on a professional footing; medieval history developed as a distinct, recognized field of study in America; and the professionalism and expertise developed in these processes were applied directly to the practical governance of the United States and the world arena. Haskins played a major role in all these developments.

SELECTED BIBLIOGRAPHY

Works

BOOKS AND ARTICLES

"The Yazoo Land Companies." *Papers of the American Historical Association* 5 (1891): 59–103.

"The Vatican Archives." *American Historical Review* 2 (1896): 40–58.

"The Vatican Archives." *Catholic University Bulletin* 3 (1897): 177–96.

"The Life of Medieval Students as Illustrated by Their Letters." *American Historical Review* 3 (1898): 203–29.

"Opportunities for American Students of History at Paris." *American Historical Review* 3 (1898): 418–30.

With others. "The Study of History in Schools, Being the Report to the American Historical Association by the Committee of Seven." In *Annual Report of the American Historical Association for the Year 1898*, pp. 474–564. Washington, D.C.: Government Printing Office, 1899.

"Robert le Bougre and the Beginnings of the Inquisition in Northern France." *American Historical Review* 7 (1902): 437–57, 631–52.

With William I. Hull. *A History of Higher Education in Pennsylvania*. Washington,

D.C.: Government Printing Office, 1902.

"The Early Norman Jury." *American Historical Review* 8 (1903): 613–40.

"The University of Paris in the Sermons of the Thirteenth Century." *American Historical Review* 10 (1904): 1–27.

The Historical Curriculum in Colleges. New York: Knickerbocker, 1904.

"The Sources for the History of the Papal Penitentiary." *American Journal of Theology* 9 (1905): 421–50.

"Report of the Conference on the First Year of College Work in History." In *Annual Report of the American Historical Association for the Year 1905*, pp. 147–74. Washington, D.C.: Government Printing Office, 1906.

"Knight-Service in Normandy in the Eleventh Century." *English Historical Review* 22 (1907): 636–49.

"The Norman 'Consuetudines et Iusticie' of William the Conqueror." *English Historical Review* 23 (1908): 502–08.

"Normandy Under William the Conqueror." *American Historical Review* 14 (1909): 453–76.

"The Administration of Normandy Under Henry I." *English Historical Review* 24 (1909): 209–31.

"A List of Text-Books from the Close of the Twelfth Century." *Harvard Studies in Classical Philology* 20 (1909): 75–94.

"A Canterbury Monk at Constantinople, c. 1090." *English Historical Review* 25 (1910): 293–95.

"Adelard of Bath." *English Historical Review* 26 (1911): 491–98.

"England and Sicily in the Twelfth Century." *English Historical Review* 26 (1911): 433–47, 641–65.

With others. "The Study of History in Secondary Schools: Report of the Committee of Five." In *Annual Report of the American Historical Association for the Year 1910*, pp. 209–42. New York: Macmillan, 1911.

"History—As a College and University Study." In *A Cyclopedia of Education*, edited by Paul Monroe, vol. 3, pp. 282–88. New York: Macmillan, 1911–13.

"The Abacus and the King's Curia." *English Historical Review* 27 (1912): 101–06.

"Normandy Under Geoffrey Plantagenet." *English Historical Review* 27 (1912): 417–44.

"Quelques problèmes de l'histoire des institutions anglo-normandes." *Compte rendu des travaux du Congrès du Millénaire de la Normandie* 1 (1912): 562–70.

"The Manor of Portswood Under Henry I." In *Mélanges d'histoire offerts à M. Charles Bémont*, pp. 78–83. Paris: Alcan, 1913.

"Nimrod the Astronomer." *Romanic Review* 5 (1914): 203–12.

"Moses of Bergamo." *Byzantinische Zeitschrift* 23 (1914): 133–42.

"The Government of Normandy Under Henry II." *American Historical Review* 20 (1914–15): 24–42, 277–91.

"Mediaeval Versions of the *Posterior Analytics*." *Harvard Studies in Classical Philology* 25 (1914): 87–105.

"The Reception of Arabic Science in England." *English Historical Review* 30 (1915): 56–69.

"The Place of the Newer Humanities in the College Curriculum." In *The American College*, pp. 41–57. New York: Holt, 1915.

The Normans in European History. Boston: Houghton Mifflin, 1915.

"The Materials for the Reign of Robert I of Normandy." *English Historical Review* 31 (1916): 257–68.

Norman Institutions. Cambridge, Mass.: Harvard University Press, 1918.

"L'histoire de France aux États-Unis." *Revue de Paris* 27 (1920): 654–72.

"The Greek Element in the Renaissance of the Twelfth Century." *American Historical Review* 25 (1920): 603–15.

With Robert Howard Lord. *Some Problems of the Peace Conference.* Cambridge,

Mass.: Harvard University Press, 1920.

"The 'De Arte Venandi cum Avibus' of Emperor Frederick II." *English Historical Review* 36 (1921): 334–55.

"Michael Scot and Frederick II." *Isis* 4 (1921): 250–75.

"Science at the Court of Emperor Frederick II." *American Historical Review* 27 (1922): 669–94.

"King Harald's Books." *English Historical Review* 37 (1922): 398–400.

The Rise of Universities. New York: Holt, 1923.

Studies in the History of Mediaeval Science. Cambridge, Mass.: Harvard University Press, 1924.

"Arabic Science in Western Europe." *Isis* 7 (1925): 478–85.

"Pascalis Romanus: Petrus Chrysolanus." *Byzantion* 2 (1925): 231–36.

"Magister Gualterius Esculanus." In *Mélanges d'histoire du moyen âge offerts à M. Ferdinand Lot,* pp. 245–57. Paris: Champion, 1925.

"Henry II as Patron of Literature." In *Essays in Medieval History Presented to Thomas Frederick Tout,* edited by A.G. Little and F.M. Powicke, pp. 71–77. Manchester: Privately printed, 1925.

"The Spread of Ideas in the Middle Ages." *Speculum* 1 (1926): 19–30.

"An Early Bolognese Formulary." In *Mélanges d'histoire offerts à Henri Pirenne,* pp. 201–10. Brussels: Vromant, 1926.

"An Italian Master Bernard." In *Essays in History Presented to Reginald Lane Poole,* edited by H.W.C. Davis, pp. 221–26. Oxford: Clarendon, 1926.

"The Latin Literature of Sport." *Speculum* 2 (1927): 235–52.

The Renaissance of the Twelfth Century. Cambridge, Mass.: Harvard University Press, 1927.

"The *Alchemy* Ascribed to Michael Scot." *Isis* 10 (1928): 350–59.

"Latin Literature under Frederick II." *Speculum* 3 (1928): 129–51.

"Formularies of the Officialite of Rouen." In *Mélanges Paul Fournier,* pp. 359–62. Paris: Sirey, 1929.

Studies in Mediaeval Culture. Oxford: Clarendon, 1929.

"The Graduate School of Arts and Sciences." In *The Development of Harvard University Since the Inauguration of President Eliot, 1869–1929,* edited by Samuel Eliot Morison, pp. 451–62. Cambridge, Mass.: Harvard University Press, 1930.

LETTERS AND PAPERS

Haskins's papers are collected at the Mudd Library, Princeton University. Other unpublished papers may be found in the collections of the Massachusetts Historical Society; in the Frederick Jackson Turner papers collected at the Huntington Library; and in the Woodrow Wilson Correspondence.

Sources

Blake, R.P., G.R. Coffman, and E.K. Rand. "Charles Homer Haskins." *Speculum* 14 (1939): 413–15.

Gooch, George Peabody. *History and Historians in the Nineteenth Century.* Boston: Beacon, 1959.

House, Edward M., and Charles Seymour, eds. *What Really Happened at Paris: The Story of the Peace Conference, 1918–1919.* New York: Scribner, 1921.

Lingelbach, William E. "Charles Homer Haskins." In *The American Philosophical Society Year Book, 1937,* pp. 356–57. Philadelphia: American Philosophical Society, 1938.

Morison, Samuel Eliot, ed. *The Development of Harvard University Since the Inauguration of President Eliot, 1869–1929.* Cambridge, Mass.: Harvard University Press, 1930.

Powicke, F.M. A Review of *Studies in the History of Mediaeval Science. English Historical Review* 40 (1925): 421–23.

———. "Charles Homer Haskins." *English Historical Review* 52 (1937): 649–56.

Taylor, Charles H., and John H. LaMonte, eds. *Anniversary Essays in Mediaeval History, by Students of Charles Homer Haskins, Presented on His Completion of Forty Years of Teaching*, pp. 389–98. Boston: Houghton Mifflin, 1929.

Vaughn, Sally N. "Charles Homer Haskins." In *Dictionary of Literary Biography*, vol. 47, pp. 122–44. Detroit: Gale, 1985.

LYNN THORNDIKE

(1882–1965)

Michael H. Shank

Lynn Thorndike, the pioneering historian of the occult sciences, came from a modest family with deep New England roots. His paternal ancestors had first settled in Salem, Massachusetts (ca. 1629), and later moved to Maine. His father, Edward Robert Thorndike, a Republican lawyer who became a Methodist minister, married Abbie Brewster Ladd, also from Maine (Jonçich, 11–12; *National Cyclopedia*, 51: 208). It was this "extraordinarily intelligent and capable person, of marked artistic ability, deeply religious and of shy, gentle manner but with a will of steel" (Woodworth, 209) who gave birth to Everett Lynn Thorndike on 24 July 1882 in Lynn, Massachusetts. Named for the towns of his father's favorite pastorates, he later dropped the "Everett." He and his two older brothers, Ashley Horace (1871–1933) and Edward Lee (1874–1949), were later joined by a sister, Mildred. Since the Methodists transferred their pastors frequently, the household moved often, thereby perhaps exacerbating the shyness of the three youngest children. Lynn in particular was "known in the family as one who prefers his own company and wants most to be left alone, who reads and plays chess and 'is no trouble as he hates to be talked to'" (Jonçich, 21). All four children made their mark in education, the daughter in the New York public schools, the sons on the faculty of Columbia University. Edward has been called the "father of American learning psychology"; Ashley was a leading scholar of Elizabethan literature and the benevolent dictator who ran the Columbia English department from 1906 until his death in 1933.

Like his brothers Lynn earned his undergraduate degree with honors at Wesleyan University, at the time a Methodist school. After graduation in 1902 Lynn immediately went on to graduate school in history at Columbia University (M.A., 1903; Ph.D., 1905); he was the first Columbia student to complete a doctorate under the leading spokesman for the "New History," James Harvey Robinson, with whom he took eight courses (Thorndike, review of Robinson, 367). At about this time Thorndike expressed to his father serious reservations about his religious faith (Columbia University, Lynn Thorndike Papers, Letter from E.R. Thorndike, n.d., File "Letters to 1907 or so").

It was in the Midwest that Thorndike rose through the academic ranks and established his reputation as a teacher and researcher. After a frustrating year (1906–07) as master of the University School in Cleveland Thorndike moved to Northwestern University as an instructor (1907–09), only to return to Cleveland as instructor in the fall of 1909 at Western Reserve University, where his brothers had preceded him on the faculty. His teaching at Western Reserve for fifteen years inspired and shaped his two textbooks, *The History of Medieval Europe* (1917) and *A Short History of Civilization* (1926), both of which proved successful commercially.

Thorndike first traveled to Europe in the summer of 1909. His exposure to manuscript sources marked him for life: his scholarship and his writing rarely strayed far from these texts. Diaries and correspondence for the next fifty years detail peregrinations through the manuscript collections of Great Britain and the Continent. He was to devote years to the lonely work of reading, transcribing, and collating manuscripts. In August 1914 he made it out of Germany on the last train to Belgium. He spent several months in Europe every other year during the 1920s and almost every year throughout the 1930s. He was in Europe again when World War II broke out (Diaries; Jonçich, 356, 496, 583–84).

The 1920s were years of professional ascent and institutional growth. When the American Historical Association met in Cleveland in 1919, "Thorndike organized and took part in the earliest meeting devoted to the history of science" (Guerlac, 108; Thorndike, [1920]). The 1920 Washington meeting of the AHA and the joint 1921 Cambridge, Massachusetts session of the AHA and the American Association for the Advancement of Science (which had organized its History of Science section the previous year) laid the groundwork for the creation of the History of Science Society in January 1924 (Thorndike, [1921] and "Historical Background," 488; Clagett, 89). During these years he became a charter fellow of the new Medieval Academy of America (1925) and served as first vice-president (1927) and then as fifth president (1928–29) of the History of Science Society. In 1929 he published his *Science and Thought in the Fifteenth Century*.

In 1923–24, his last academic year at Western Reserve, Thorndike published the first two volumes of *A History of Magic and Experimental Science in the First Thirteen Centuries of Our Era*, a project that would eventually encompass eight volumes and most of his career (1923–58). In the spring of 1924 he answered "the call" to Columbia University, joining Edward and Ashley, who had been on the faculty since 1900 and 1906, respectively. The move may have cost him personally. A wistful poem ("Oh Peggy mia! . . .") in his diary for 1926 hints that a romantic involvement with the daughter of a Western Reserve colleague was coming to an end. He never married.

As a classroom teacher Thorndike was more successful with graduate students than with undergraduates. His student Marshall Clagett remembers his lectures as "mines of detailed fact and novel judgment . . . presented in a somewhat dry and matter-of-fact way"; by contrast his public lectures were "far more lively" (Clagett, 86); "but he sparkled with dry wit and ideas in the informal atmosphere of discussion groups" ("Lynn Thorndike").

Many of Thorndike's graduate students became productive scholars in their own right, some of them making monumental contributions of their own: Marshall Clagett, Kenneth Setton, Charles Trinkhaus, Pearl Kibre, George B. Fowler, C. Doris Hellman, Francis Benjamin, Jr. (who did much of the work on Thorndike's edition of *The Herbal of Rufinus*), and Richard Lemay. The appointment of Clagett to one of two new positions at the University of Wisconsin in the nation's first department of the history of science proved decisive both for the history of science in general and for its subfield of medieval science (Hilts, 63ff.). Thorndike's students remember him as a shy, almost reclusive man whose gruff appearance belied his kindness. "With his stocky 5-foot-10-inch figure, his bald head, his square, rugged face and his pince-nez eyeglasses, Professor Thorndike was clearly distinguishable among his fellow savants. His neckties, which were broad, loosely knotted and often loudly striped, contrasted oddly with his usual conservative attire" ("Lynn Thorndike"). Thorndike was partial to dark beer and was "no mean gourmet" (Clagett, 87). He enjoyed playing tennis (his diaries record the scores) and throughout his life was an avid if mediocre golfer. Thorndike had begun to show signs of deafness in the late 1940s (Jonçich, 587). Though he retired from teaching at Columbia in 1950, he actively pursued his scholarship during the last fifteen years of his life.

In 1952 Thorndike's seventieth birthday was honored with a 500–page Festschrift, edited by George Sarton, that appeared as Volume 11 of *Osiris*. In 1954–55 Thorndike served as president of the American Historical Association, and in 1957 the History of Science Society awarded him its highest honor, the Sarton Medal. Volumes 7 and 8 of *A History of Magic* appeared the following year. He received honorary degrees from Wesleyan, Northwestern, Columbia, and the Case Institute of Technology. Other honors included his election as member of the American Philosophical Society, *membre effectif* of the Comité de l'Académie Internationale d'Histoire des Sciences (1928–), and *membre correspondent* of the Académie des Inscriptions et Belles Lettres (1946–). In 1958 he became a charter member of the new Society for the History of Technology (Thorndike [1957], 331; Kibre, [1967], 287; Boyer and Boyer, 391).

Though Thorndike's scholarly writing is sometimes pedantic, he did not hesitate to make his ethical and moral views known in his public addresses and often commented on current events. The first edition of his *A Short History of Civilization* reveals glimpses of a passionate antimilitarism (527; see also Thorndike, "Historical Background," 492) and a pragmatic openness to the "Soviet experiment." Another talk comments on the Scopes trial, attacks the quasimagical reliance on "mental illusions and delusions" by the advertising industry, and bemoans the universities' pandering "to this popular immoral and unscientific demand from the business world" ("Historical Background," 492–93). He retained a strong view of the autonomy of learning, which properly should serve no ideology. In the Foreword to *Science and Civilization* (1949) he resisted Cold War pressures in this direction:

> Some recent university presidents seem to believe that a main function and chief concern of an institution of higher education is defense of democracy and of our American mode of life. But some of us still cling to the old-fashioned notion that an institution of higher learning should attend to its own objective, which is—higher learning. . . . I certainly would not tie up learning with tyranny. But neither would I tie it up with Roman or with any other form of government. I would not mingle it with superstition—or with any other ideology, or anti-ideology. Learning, pure and undefiled—that is all!" [xii-xiii].

Thorndike's target here was almost certainly James B. Conant, president of Harvard, whose lectures at Columbia in 1945 (published in 1948) sought to enlist the universities in the Cold War effort (Conant, 1–37).

Thorndike remained active to the end. His last book, *Michael Scot*, appeared a month before he died of a stroke, at the age of eighty-three, on 28 December 1965. He is buried in the family plot in Riverside Cemetery, New Port, Maine. Clagett's eulogy in *Isis* (1966) precedes a posthumous Thorndike article. "A Daily Weather Record from the Years 1399 to 1401" was culled from a Basel manuscript and tentatively linked to the Besançon region thanks to data from the U.S. Weather Bureau. Nothing better illustrates Thorndike's passion for the sources, defense of marginalized topics, attitude toward research, or attention to detail.

Thorndike's writings run the gamut from commercially successful textbooks and popular articles through useful reference works and dry manuscript descriptions (his *Catalogue of Incipits* and many articles) to editions of texts and his eight-volume *A History of Magic and Experimental Science*. Since the corpus is too vast to be treated in brief compass, the following overview concentrates on the books, which are representative of his scholarship. About his articles suffice it to say that he published in a remarkable range of journals, from specialized notes in *Speculum* and *Isis* to articles in wide circulation magazines like *The Popular Science Monthly*.

Thorndike's early career shows the strong influence of his teacher James Harvey Robinson. An Illinois boy with early interests in biology, Robinson had earned his Ph.D. in history at Freiburg and became a quintessential "Progressive Era" historian at Columbia (1895–1919), before helping to found the New School of Social Research (Hofstadter, 221ff.). He urged his fellow historians to pay more attention to the methods and results of the natural and social sciences, the advances in which he admired. An advocate of the New History, he attacked the misplaced emphasis of historical writing on politics, chronology, and the melodramatic—to the neglect "of the lucid intervals during which the greater part of human progress has taken place" (Robinson, 12–13). Robinson stressed the impact of "creative ideas" on historical development and became an advocate for "intellectual history," first using the expression in a course title in 1904 (Skotheim, 79–83; Hofstadter, 223). In his seminars—a pedagogical medium recently pioneered in the United States by Henry Adams—he emphasized the close reading of primary sources, a trait associated with the new scientific history's "exhilarating sense of direct contact with a living past" (Shotwell, viii). Far from being self-serving internal professional developments, these approaches sought to improve society: "We must develop historical-mindedness upon a far more generous scale than hitherto, for this . . . will promote rational progress as nothing else can do" (Robinson, 24). Similar emphases characterize the work of his first doctoral student.

Robinson suggested the topic for Thorndike's first contribution to scholarship, his dissertation, *The Place of Magic in the Intellectual History of Europe*, which was an expansion of his M.A. thesis topic. Still in print in 1994, this slim work provides insight into the key assumptions that motivated and guided Thorndike's later investigations. Dissatisfied with earlier work, such as Alfred Maury's *La magie et l'astrologie dans l'antiquité et au moyen âge* (1860), Thorndike drew upon J.G. Frazer's *The Golden Bough* to argue that natural magic permeated the ancients' view of the natural world, antedating even their religions. "Magic" referred not to the supernatural (miracles or direct divine intervention) but to the preternatural—the marvelous in nature—and to the broad range of activities, thoughts, and worldviews associated with human control over it, including astrology, witchcraft, divination, necromancy, and alchemy. Attitudes toward magic were not static: "Men first regarded magic as natural, then as marvelous, then as impossible and absurd" (Thorndike [1905], 34). Although science eventually replaced magic and subsumed its methods, the two had lived side by side not only in the Middle Ages and early-modern period but in antiquity. Thorndike illustrated the point by surveying attitudes toward magic from Cicero and Pliny to Ptolemy (who wrote on astrology and astronomy). This continuity between antiquity and the Middle Ages belied the false impression that magic was a medieval aberration from which classical antiquity was immune (108–10). The social critic in Thorndike enjoyed pointing to manifestations of magical thinking in the political and social customs of his contemporaries (*History of Magic*, 2: 980–81). In striking contrast to his later work the dissertation used only printed sources. But Thorndike's interest in long-range issues, assumptions about continuity, and propensity to defend the Middle Ages would remain lifelong characteristics.

Thorndike's early insights into historical method are shown in "The Scientific Presentation of History" (1910), which is at once a piece of advocacy and a homage to James Harvey Robinson. Especially intriguing is the way in which Thorndike's discussion of historiography parallels his thinking about magic and science: history too must become more scientific in its outlook and presentation. Surveying recent manifestos on historical method, he rejects as inadequate such approaches to history as the intuitive ("a feeling-it-in-one's-bones method . . . more like a feat of magic than a work of science," 172); the narrative (history as literature, advocated in G.B. Adams's 1908 AHA presidential address); the excessive empiricism that encourages the indiscriminate collection of "facts"; and the single-hypothesis schemes, such as the Marxist economic interpretation of history. Instead a scientific historian should follow up the sources if they suggest a hypothesis and aggressively take the initiative if they do not. They will "look askance also at periods, movements and institutions" and be leery of "unjustifiable historical conglomerates" (178). Despite the problems involved scientific history should seek to measure its evidence: anecdotes are unsatisfactory without a sense both of how representative they are in relation to the available evidence and of how reliable the witness is. More positively "the method of presentation will probably somewhat resemble that employed by mathematics and the sciences. . . ." "Presentation will follow investigation step by step" (181). While this outlook seriously underestimates the wiliness of scientific rhetoric, it goes a long way toward explaining Thorndike's idiosyncratic style of historical writing.

Thorndike saw modern science as a standard for the presentation of history, not as a standard of historical judgment. Later he would point out the danger in writing the history of medieval science, in light of current science, as the history of error: when current science eventually goes out of date, so will the history. Instead he advocated attention to medieval goals, to "trace their own progress according to their own lights . . . . Historically, therefore, the simpler view would seem to be simply to reproduce the medieval view" (Thorndike [1929], 9). That Thorndike often, but not always, took his own advice seriously helps to account for the tone of his *History of Magic*: a descriptive contribution would be more accurate and enduring.

His second book, *The History of Medieval Europe* (1917), emerged from a decade of teaching history to freshmen at Western Reserve. This "first standard textbook on the subject in the United States" (Clagett, Kibre, and Post, 598) ranged from the Roman Empire to the beginning of the sixteenth century, with an eye on current events and social trends. Thorndike's purview as a sensitive New Historian included "the states and racial groups of central and eastern Europe" in deference to the many immigrants from those areas in the population he served. In passing he spit in the eye of royalty: "In these days of tottering thrones I have even ventured to lay the axe at the root of absolutism and to dispense with genealogical tables" (vi). The text diffused widely Thorndike's notion of the "Renaissance" as a misnomer coined by persons ignorant and contemptuous of medieval civilization. His text devoted two chapters to the "so-called" Italian Renaissance, which was memorable in the history of art but coincided with political regress— the loss of communal institutions and the rise of absolutism. Multiple printings and two revisions (1929, 1949) kept the book in print for almost forty years.

Soon after his move to Columbia and in the same year in which Robinson published *The Ordeal of Civilization*, Thorndike published his second textbook, *A Short History of Civilization* (1926; 2nd ed. 1948). "When the world war broke out in 1914, I determined to do what little I could to keep civilization alive" (v), first with a new course on the subject at Western Reserve, eventually with the book. He argued in the preface (v) that the text was on the one hand a move away from the past as the history of destruction and on the other the kind of book and course that premedical and science students should take if they took no other history course. The work surveyed prehistoric and primitive civilizations, the ancient Near East, classical Greece and Rome and their decline, the Far East, medieval Near Eastern civilization, and the medieval revival. A Chinese translation of the book appeared in 1967. These early textbooks, together with Thorndike's talks and articles in popular journals, reveal well-developed powers of synthesis, which are less obvious in his narrower field of expertise.

In 1923 Thorndike published in two volumes *A History of Magic and Experimental Science During the First Thirteen Centuries of Our Era*. While focused on the twelfth and thirteenth centuries, it devoted much space to late antiquity, for Thorndike was interested in the relation of magic and science to Christian thought. As in his dissertation he construed magic broadly, to include "all the occult arts and sciences, superstitions, and folk-lore" (*History of Magic*, 1: 2). But unlike his dissertation this work relied heavily on unpublished manuscripts. The second volume ended in 1327, by which time the revival of medieval learning was over (2: 969). The heroic language of Thorndike's conclusion sounds like the end of a magnum opus: at the time not even he suspected that this was the tip of an eight-volume, 6,500–page iceberg.

From the outset these two volumes proved both useful and controversial. They were the most frequently cited secondary source in Charles Homer Haskins's *Studies in the History of Mediaeval Science* (1924). Lewis Mumford's *Technics and Civilization* (1934) picked up some of Thorndike's conclusions, giving them perhaps wider currency than did Thorndike's own books. George Sarton, however, gave the books an unprecedented sixteen-page negative review in *Isis* (Sarton, [1924]). Sarton conceded the scholarly importance of the work as a history of the occult sciences, but he was incensed by the title (which promised a history of experimental science that the book never delivered) and even more so by the notion that progressive, rational science could grow out of irrational magic. He allowed that astrology and alchemy belonged squarely within the history of science, but magic proper had no place in such a history.

The review must have been difficult for both men, for it appeared in the very issue of *Isis* that announced the birth of the History of Science Society and made *Isis* its official journal. Until then *Isis* had been Sarton's personal journal—founded in Belgium in 1912, exiled by the war, revived at Harvard, and subsidized by Sarton's and his wife's salaries. The new History of Science Society, which Thorndike had helped to establish, now explicitly pledged itself to support the journal. In this issue of *Isis* Thorndike's name appeared not only in the review but on lists of charter members of the society and of financial contributors to the journal. Sarton might have asked someone else to review Thorndike's book, but he evidently cared too deeply about the issues it raised. Since he believed that a true historian of science should be trained first as a scientist, adding linguistic competence and historical skills later, he no doubt considered a historian like Thorndike underprepared for his career. *A History of Magic* and its author's failure to understand the nature of experimental science seemed to confirm Sarton's worst fears about the havoc that historians would wreak in the field.

These intellectual tensions are colored by institutional factors. During the 1920s, when Thorndike's two primary fields of interest, history of science and medieval studies, were creating their own professional societies, Columbia and Harvard were the leading universities in both areas (Courtenay, 12ff.; Cohen, 19). At Columbia Thorndike's colleagues with interests in these areas included Austin P. Evans, James T. Shotwell, Carlton J.H. Hayes (whose departmental report in 1923 was probably responsible for the hiring of Thorndike), and in the philosophy department John Herman Randall, Jr., Richard P. McKeon, Ernest A. Moody in the 1920s and 1930s, and later (since 1939) Paul Oskar Kristeller (Hofstadter, 230–41; Randall, 130ff.). At Harvard, apart from Sarton (who held no formal faculty position until 1940), Charles Homer Haskins was the leading force. He had come to Harvard from the University of Wisconsin in 1912 and joined Sarton's effort as associate editor of the revived *Isis*. He became one of the founders of the Medieval Academy of America (1925) and its organ, *Speculum* (Wenger, 23). Thorndike's relations with Haskins were, and remained, formal and tense. Thorndike had reviewed *Studies in the History of Mediaeval Science* in the *American Historical Review*, on the whole positively, but the few criticisms had stung. The two men sparred with a flurry of notes in the first volume of *Speculum* (1926), while the tone of their private correspondence in the 1920s is downright testy.

Thorndike's relations with Sarton were already standoffish and critical by around 1921. The review did not improve matters. By the late 1920s, however, the interaction between the two men had grown more cordial, and eventually, they became friendly: their correspondence extends to a few months before Sarton's death in March 1956 (Thorndike [1957]). The tide had turned by 1929, when Thorndike published his *Science and Thought in the Fifteenth Century*. This collection of essays and Latin texts sought to poke holes in "sweeping generalizations" about the period derived from the "humanistic bias which has prevailed ever since the fifteenth century" (vii). More than a hundred pages of appendixes, consisting primarily of transcriptions from manuscripts, portend the emergence and growth of Thorndike's textual phase. Although some of the essays were revised versions of articles published in *Isis*, Sarton again gave the book a lengthy review, this time more friendly than critical.

In 1934 Thorndike published Volumes 3 and 4 of *A History of Magic*, devoted to the fourteenth and fifteenth centuries, this time with Columbia University Press. Since he had changed publishers, he had an opportunity either to take a new angle or to modify his title. He did neither. Instead he doggedly cast his new work as a sequel of the old and in the preface continued to press his strong claim for "the outgrowth of scientific experimental method from the experimentation of magic" (3: vii). Some of his views did change, however. Although he also treated other topics, he now focused on astrology, alchemy, and the magical aspects of medicine (4: 611)—the fields that Sarton had endorsed. Whereas Volume 2 had concluded that medieval learning seemed to be waning by the early fourteenth century, Thorndike was now much more sanguine about the significance of this period. He continued, however, to see the fifteenth century as "distinctly inferior to the fourteenth" (4: 612, 614). He also pointed to his growing reliance on manuscripts with each passing volume (3: vii). The many summaries of material that is still accessible only in manuscript remain one of the most valuable aspects of *A History of Magic*. During his many years of work in manuscript libraries, Thorndike accumulated a wealth of information about the texts he had consulted. His personal research notes became the basis for one of the fundamental research tools in medieval studies. In 1937, with the help of his former student Pearl Kibre, he co-authored *A Catalogue of Incipits of Mediaeval Scientific Manuscripts in Latin*.

Volumes 5 and 6, devoted to the sixteenth century, appeared in 1941. Learning had now become more superficial, turning from the medieval "works of a refined learning designed for advanced and specialized . . . students" toward elementary summaries. The tendency to write compendia and epitomes, a symptom of decline, received a boost from printing, which made it possible to spread "a little learning thin" (6: 3–6). But the sixteenth century gave magic more positive connotations than had earlier centuries (6: 13), seemingly a substantiation of Thorndike's claims for the congruence of magic and experiment. P.O. Kristeller's review of these volumes praised Thorndike for "a high standard of scholarship . . . and unusual wealth, variety, and accuracy of information" (Kristeller, 690). But he took issue with Thorndike's narrow view of experimental science, particularly the exclusion from his purview of not only philosophy and theology but also mathematics and logic. He implicitly criticized Thorndike's factual approach and reluctance to paint a large picture. In the end he saw the work as a useful "chronicle" (692).

The following year Dana B. Durand published in *Isis* an admiring full-length article reviewing Thorndike's six-volume accomplishment. He no doubt believed that he had seen the end of the project. Thorndike himself thought so, for he drew up a grand cumulative index to all six volumes. Although *A History of Magic* reveals a remarkable consistency of purpose, Durand shrewdly noticed significant alterations in Thorndike's definitions of magic and of science. In his early volumes Thorndike had left science undefined and had treated magic in Frazeresque anthropological terms. In his latest volumes he defined science as a "systematized and ordered knowledge, a consistent body of truth attained . . . independently of faith, emotion, prejudice . . ." and magic as a "systematized and ordered marvel-believing and marvel-working, a consistent body of error . . . influenced by faith, emotion . . ." (5: 12–13). Over the years Thorndike had evidently reached accommodation with Sarton's views, almost to the point of undermining his title, a point that tact may have prevented Durand from making. Durand did, however, object to Thorndike's "debunking" of Nicholas of Cusa, Georg Peurbach, Johannes Regiomontanus, Leonardo, Copernicus, and Vesalius, an attitude that Durand explained by pointing to a distrust of generalizations and "hagiographophobia" (Durand, 707).

Thorndike's other books during the 1940s moved away from magic in the narrow sense. In 1944 he published *University Records and Life in the Middle Ages*, an important collection of university documents in a sometimes flawed English translation that ranged from the twelfth century through the seventeenth. Between 1946 and 1950 Thorndike brought out three important book-length editions of Latin texts. World War II had motivated his edition of *The Herbal of Rufinus* (from a rotograph transcribed by his student Francis S. Benjamin, Jr.): Thorndike feared that the unique manuscript (in the Biblioteca Laurenziana, Florence) might disappear forever. Although the publication was delayed until 1946, Thorndike curiously did not check the text against the original. The text was important evidence against the notion that little of value had happened in botany during the Middle Ages. Thorndike argued that Rufinus made original observations and reached a higher level of specificity and discrimination in his descriptions of some plants "than any previous author, ancient or medieval." The work also evinced contacts between a literate monk and herbalists and care in dealing with multiple nomenclatures (xvi-xvii, xxiv). In contrast to the unique Rufinus manuscript the edition of Sacrobosco's *On the Sphere* (1949) made available the most heavily copied astronomical textbook of the Middle Ages and several commentaries on it. *The Latin Treatises on Comets* (1950, although first completed in August 1945) brought out thirteenth- and fourteenth-century texts that combined astrological and astronomical significance.

In 1958 Thorndike published the last two volumes (7–8) of *A History of Magic*, devoted to the seventeenth century. He took an undisguised pleasure in listing the ways in which such paragons of scientific rationality as Johannes Kepler and Isaac Newton thought and wrote about astrology or alchemy. Especially striking in these volumes is Thorndike's relatively rare interaction with recent secondary literature on the subject (e.g., Alexandre Koyré on Galileo). Equally noteworthy is his attention to the neglected contemporaries of the great names (7: ch. 3), whom he often brings to light to show how "useless" their compilations were and how many errors they made. To his credit he also includes such marginalized topics as magic in Portugal and Spain, the occult in German universities, popular science, divination, natural history, and botany.

Much of Thorndike's work is descriptive rather than analytical, oriented to breadth rather than depth or problem solving. And although he held strong views on many topics, his scholarship interacts little with existing historiography. His goals, subject matter, and approach to history all help to explain these traits. His goal of "scientific presentation of history" valued the descriptive mode highly, an approach well suited to dealing with little-known, marginalized, or new material that required a summary. Not least, however, he wanted this material to speak on its own terms, without interference from the criteria of twentieth-century science, which in his view would itself become passé. Even though he did not always reach it, Thorndike's ideal of accurate summary and careful reporting, together with his attempts to uncouple his writing from "presentist" science, has contributed mightily to the unusual longevity and enduring usefulness of his work.

Thorndike's reputation rests primarily on the massive *History of Magic*, which has sold in several thousand sets and is still in print at this writing (1994). A pioneering effort in the history of the occult sciences, it remains a crucial resource in the field. Thorndike explored, read, and synthesized an enormous number of primary sources, providing unprecedented access to seventeen centuries of material. The uniform binding and sequential numbering of the eight volumes convey a strong impression of single-mindedness and continuity. The common title, however, masks notable changes in Thorndike's approaches, purposes, and sensibilities, not only as his scholarly career evolved but as he responded to the centuries he covered and, less obviously, to his critics.

His project grew out of a broadly based vision of the history of civilization: magic represented an early stage of thinking about nature, a stage that had been dominant in most early cultures and remained significant, although underrated, in many later ones. Representing a later stage of such thinking, science must somehow have developed out of magic. The missing premise was supplied by Thorndike's belief in the continuity of thought about nature. "As anthropologists have shown, magic plays a great part in the life and thought of primitive peoples. . . . But science did not come down from above nor invade from without. It grew up in the very midst of superstition and mental anarchy, just as the states of modern Europe had their beginnings in feudal society" (Thorndike [1915], 290). Phrased in this way, the thesis sounds almost self-evident: the problem then lay in discovering where "magic" turned into "science." Clearly the place to look for the transformation was between antiquity and modernity, namely, in the medieval period.

In the first two volumes of *A History of Magic* Thorndike defined magic broadly and science not at all. Working with loose notions during the neglected "first thirteen centuries of our era," he stressed the terminology of *experimentum* or *scientia experimentalis* as he found it in such figures as Pliny, Albertus Magnus, and Roger Bacon. Indeed, even though Bacon shied away from the word "magic," Thorndike seems to have viewed him as the very type of the connection sought: "It is not fair merely to call Bacon's science superstitious; we must also note that he tried to make his magic scientific" (2: 667). Admittedly connected with magical elements, Bacon's notion of experimental science nevertheless stood at a considerable remove from modern notions.

Thorndike's demonstration of a continuity between magical thinking in late antiquity and in the Middle Ages advanced two of his goals. Magic represented not a medieval aberration but the heritage of antiquity. There was no need to despise magic, for it had developed an experimental strain that fed the beginnings of experimental science. This case for a genetic connection between magical and scientific experimentation might be termed the "strong" version of Thorndike's thesis, which is most characteristic of his early years. In his later work Thorndike seemed satisfied with a "weaker" version: that magic and science coexisted and interacted in the intervening period, in the minds and in the practices of leading and minor figures. An important component of modern science had grown out of environments and ways of thinking that now appear alien to it.

In the second pair of volumes, on the fourteenth and fifteenth centuries, the "magic" of the title gained in specificity, more and more coming to mean astrology and to a lesser extent alchemy and medicine. To his surprise Thorndike also discovered the fourteenth century to be a period worthy of study, sometimes for reasons that had little to do with "magic" (e.g., the mathematical natural philosophy of Richard Swineshead). He continued, however, to see the fifteenth century as overrated. In each case he tried to avoid drawing inappropriate ties to modernity in what he considered a "chapter in the history of human thought. Read it and smile or read it and weep, as you please. We would not credit it with the least particle of modern science that does not belong to it, nor would we deprive it of any of that magic which constitutes in no small measure its peculiar charm" (4: 615).

With his third pair of volumes (1941), devoted to the sixteenth century, Thorndike moved beyond his usual chronological boundaries. But he also encountered problems for his grand schema. Whereas the term "magic" had had negative connotations for authors like Roger Bacon, the late fifteenth and sixteenth centuries distinguished two species of magic, one natural and benign, the other demonic and forbidden, and evinced a heightened interest in both, at the very time when one might expect a decline of magic associated with the growth of science. Concluding his introduction, he noted: "Like Moses we have brought the reader through the wilderness to within sight of the promised land of modern science" (5: 15).

Unlike Moses, though, Thorndike reached his goal, almost two decades later. When his fourth pair of volumes, on the seventeenth century, appeared in 1958, the problems presented by his title were acute. Specialists in a period viewed as experimental *par excellence* criticized him for failing to give due attention to leading experimentalists, like Blaise Pascal, in what he still professed to be a "history of experimental science." Thorndike nevertheless saw these volumes as the culmination of his efforts. Both the conclusion to his last volume and his other work during this period show that he saw Isaac Newton as marking the Jordan. Thorndike argued that before Newton science had operated under a universal astrological law, according to which the celestial bodies governed the realm of nature. Newton had now replaced this law with the law of universal gravitation (Thorndike [1955], 273ff.). Newton marked the major watershed in the history of science. If his alchemical studies demonstrated that he was not innocent of "magic" in the broad sense, he differed from many of his predecessors in formally separating his alchemy from his mathematical natural philosophy.

Despite the problems with its conceptualization Thorndike's magic-to-science schema found resonance in book titles from Charles Singer's *From Magic to Science: Essays on the Scientific Twilight* (1928) to Paolo Rossi's *Francis Bacon: From Magic to Science* (1957/68) and in classics on the experimental tradition, such as A.C. Crombie's *Robert Grosseteste and the Origins of Experimental Science* (1953, 19). But its attention to the occult sciences also prepared the ground for the stimulating controversies that followed the publication and reception of Frances Yates's *Giordano Bruno and the Hermetic Tradition* (1964).

Whatever one might think of Thorndike's search for a genetic connection between magic and experimental science, the sheer quantity of the material he surveyed and brought together made it impossible to dismiss the occult sciences as cultural aberrations or their practitioners as cranks. An indefatigable bibliographer and manuscript hound, Thorndike demonstrated the longevity and pervasiveness of the occult tradition and its close association with both the most revered names in the history of science and several thousand minor figures. In the last four volumes alone he surveyed more than twenty-eight hundred authors on the basis of manuscripts, incunabula, and early printed works (8: 635). For this reason medievalists and early-modernists will long use *A History of Magic* as an invaluable research and reference tool.

Thorndike's manuscript work in particular contributed signally to medieval scholarship. His many years in European manuscript libraries, some of which still have inadequate catalogs, gave him the privileged knowledge of a scout. With the help of Pearl Kibre he made this hard-won knowledge available to the wider scholarly community in his *Catalogue of Incipits of Mediaeval Scientific Manuscripts in Latin* (1937). The revised edition (1963) is still in print and in heavy use as a reference. A committed medievalist, he also served time as an editor of texts—a slow, demanding, and tedious activity that garners few professional rewards and little recognition outside a small circle of colleagues. Alone, his contribution of more than a thousand pages of editions and transcriptions earns him a place of honor in medieval scholarship.

From a historiographical point of view a notable, indeed notorious, aspect of Thorndike's reputation is his stance on the problem of the Renaissance. In 1948 Wallace K. Ferguson pointed to the tendency of some scholars to dissolve Jacob Burckhardt's notion of the Italian Renaissance by annexing the period to the Middle Ages. He saw this "Revolt of the Medievalists" clearly instantiated in Haskins's *The Renaissance of the Twelfth Century* (1927), which restored to the classics a crucial role in the culture of this era, and in George Sarton's claim that the period of the Renaissance coincided with a decline in science. But Ferguson was surely right to see in Thorndike the culmination of the revolt against Burckhardt (Ferguson, 384–85). Of Burckhardt's *The Civilization of the Renaissance in Italy* (1860), Thorndike thought that only Part 3 ("The Revival of Antiquity") was "scholarly and just" (Thorndike [1943], 69).

Thorndike differed from both Haskins and Sarton, however, in rejecting not only the signified but also the signifier: the term "Renaissance" itself was symptomatic of a deeply flawed philosophy of history. Since history was unidirectional, the very notion of a renaissance was inconceivable: the past cannot be recaptured; nothing is ever reborn; nothing ever repeats itself (Thorndike [1943], 65). Even under another name the period would have remained for Thorndike a "classical reaction" that had spread its valuation of form over substance and superficiality over depth, from literature and related areas in the fifteenth century to the sciences in the sixteenth (*History of Magic*, 5: 3ff.). Thorndike did use the term "humanism," but neither limited it to the fourteenth and fifteenth centuries nor associated it with enlightenment (Thorndike [1944], xv; *History of Magic*, 4: 386ff.). The problems in Thorndike's reaction to Renaissance historiography appear at their starkest with respect to the fifteenth and later centuries. To the end of his life he associated the fifteenth century with scientific decline, an assessment that does not square easily with his view that fifteenth-century science was still beyond the reach of a synthesis. If he did not know enough to write a synthesis, did he know enough to judge the period to be in scientific decline?

Foremost among the factors that shaped Thorndike's estimation of the Renaissance was his conviction that historians had maligned the Middle Ages out of ignorance. His skepticism about periodization notwithstanding, he defended the notion of a diverse but distinctive medieval civilization. It had received much from antiquity but also had developed original institutions and points of view and passed on to posterity crucial elements of this originality. One such development was the university. Despite his dim view of the category "institutions" as a form of generalization Thorndike helped bring the medieval university to life with documents varying from the informative and often entertaining pieces in his *University Records and Life* to his edition of Sacrobosco's *Sphere*.

Thorndike's pronouncements on the Renaissance reflected a larger concern for historical balance and fairness, which led him at once to focus on marginalized topics and individuals and to cut down to size those who had been praised to excess. Thorndike was profoundly interested in marginality *avant la lettre*: he went out of his way, both in his texts and in his scholarly work, to deal with neglected topics, subject areas, geographical regions, and individuals. Nor was his concern for redress limited to the Middle Ages and Renaissance: it emerges clearly in his discussion of antiquity. He argued that the rationality of Greek antiquity had received too much attention, to the neglect of Greek fascination with magic, for example. He criticized German scholarship for its emphasis on the Hellenistic period, with its allied tendencies to neglect Babylonian and Egyptian contributions on the one hand and to berate the science of the Roman Empire on the other (*History of Magic*, 1: 30–32). Conversely the Renaissance and early-modern periods had been glorified beyond their just deserts: their debts to the Middle Ages had been obscured, their sense of novelty though strong was misplaced, and what was representative of these eras had been squelched for the sake of hagiography. What others have sometimes seen as Thorndike's animus against the Renaissance was in his eyes a more judicious assessment of its place in the history of civilization as a whole.

Not all of Thorndike's work has withstood the test of time—most notably perhaps his own implicit large-scale generalization. He sought, however, to present his research in a form that as much as possible let his sources speak for themselves. These descriptive passages constitute by far the bulk of Thorndike's contribution, and they have retained much of their utility. Thorndike noticeably broadened his discipline's conception of the sources relevant to the history of science. His significance is more apparent to recent generations of historians, who see the demarcation between the rational and the irrational less clearly than did their predecessors seventy-five years ago and are less ashamed by the occult bedfellows of natural philosophy.

From an institutional point of view Thorndike played an important role as well. During the first generation of the History of Science Society, which he helped to establish, Thorndike's voice was that of a historian often arguing with scientists about approaches to the history of science. He paid little heed to modern disciplinary boundaries, which the scientifically trained historians of science among his contemporaries unconsciously imposed upon earlier times. His students cultivated a variety of interests— Charles Trinkhaus even wrote a dissertation on Renaissance humanism at Thorndike's suggestion—and advanced medieval scholarship in such diverse areas as mathematics, university history, Byzantium, and Arabic science.

If Thorndike erred in constructing his categories, it was on the side of inclusiveness rather than on that of analytical clarity. His research and writing display a daunting breadth of interest. He was willing to explore all evidence for the history of thought, wherever it might occur, including medicine, botany, magic, astrology, technology, meteorology, necromancy, and divination. If he erred in his judgments, it was more often by emphasizing the otherness of past thought than by slipping into anachronistic evaluations. In each case these attitudes placed Thorndike at odds with the trends in his field and cast him in the role of gadfly with respect to the interpretive frameworks of his colleagues. There is every reason to believe that Thorndike enjoyed this role; he certainly played the part superbly.

SELECTED BIBLIOGRAPHY

This bibliography includes all of Thorndike's published books and monographs and a small sample of his other writings. For a complete list of his works through 1952 see Kibre (1954).

Works

BOOKS AND ARTICLES

The Place of Magic in the Intellectual History of Europe. New York: Columbia University Press, 1905.

"The Scientific Presentation of History." *Popular Science Monthly* 76 (1910): 170–81.

"Natural Science in the Middle Ages." *Popular Science Monthly* 87 (1915): 271–91.

The History of Medieval Europe. Boston: Houghton Mifflin, 1917. Rev. eds., 1928, 1949.

"The Conference at Cleveland on the History of Science." *Science*, n.s., 51 (1920): 193–94.

"The Washington Conference on the History of Science." *Science*, n.s., 53 (1921): 122.

"The Historical Background of Modern Science." *Scientific Monthly* 16 (1923): 488–97.

A History of Magic and Experimental Science During the First Thirteen Centuries of Our Era. 2 vols. New York: Macmillan, 1923. *A History of Magic and Experimental Science.* Vols. 3 and 4, *The Fourteenth and Fifteenth Centuries.* New York: Columbia University Press, 1934; vols. 5 and 6, *The Sixteenth Century,* 1941; vols. 7 and 8, *The Seventeenth Century,* 1958.

Review of *Studies in the History of Mediaeval Science* by Charles Homer Haskins. *American Historical Review* 30 (1924–25): 344–46.

A Short History of Civilization. New York: Crofts, 1926. Rev. ed., 1948.

Science and Thought in the Fifteenth Century: Studies in the History of Medicine and Surgery, Natural and Mathematical Science, Philosophy and Politics. New York: Columbia University Press, 1929.

Review of *The Human Comedy* by James Harvey Robinson. *Journal of Modern History* 9 (1937): 367–69.

With Pearl Kibre. *A Catalogue of Incipits of Mediaeval Scientific Writings in Latin.* Cambridge, Mass.: Mediaeval Academy of America, 1937. Rev. ed., 1963.

"Invention of the Mechanical Clock About 1271 A.D." *Speculum* 16 (1941): 242–43.

"Renaissance or Prenaissance?" *Journal of the History of Ideas* 4 (1943): 65–74.

Ed. *University Records and Life in the Middle Ages.* New York: Columbia University Press, 1944.

Ed. with Francis S. Benjamin, Jr. *The Herbal of Rufinus, Edited from the Unique Manuscript.* Chicago: University of Chicago Press, 1946.

Ed. and trans. *The Sphere of Sacrobosco and Its Commentators.* Chicago: University of Chicago Press, 1949.

"Foreword" and "Some Unfamiliar Aspects of Medieval Science." In *Science and Civilization,* edited by Robert C. Stauffer, pp. xi–xiii, 33–64. Madison: University of Wisconsin Press, 1949.

Ed. *Latin Treatises on Comets Between 1238 and 1368 A.D.* Chicago: University of Chicago Press, 1950.

"The True Place of Astrology in the History of Science." *Isis* 46 (1955): 273–78.

"Whatever Was, *Was* Right." [Presidential address to the American Historical Association, 29 December 1955.] *American Historical Review* 61 (1956): 265–83.

"Some Letters of George Sarton (1922–1955)." *Isis* 48 (1957): 323–34.

Michael Scot. London: Nelson, 1965.

LETTERS AND PAPERS
	The rare-book collection of the Columbia University library holds the major collection of Lynn Thorndike's letters and papers (ca. 30,000 items), including a set of diaries that spans the years 1902–63.

Sources

Barnes, Harry Elmer. "James Harvey Robinson." In *American Masters of Social Science*, edited by Howard W. Odum, pp. 319–408. New York: Holt, 1927.

Boyer, Carl B., and Marjorie N. Boyer. "Memorial: Lynn Thorndike (1882–1965)." *Technology and Culture* 7 (1966): 391–94.

Clagett, Marshall. "Lynn Thorndike (1882–1965)." *Isis* 57 (1966): 85–89.

Clagett, Marshall, Pearl Kibre, and Gaines Post. "Lynn Thorndike." *Speculum* 41 (1966): 598–99.

Cohen, I. Bernard. "A Harvard Education." *Isis* 75 (1984): 13–20.

Conant, James Bryant. *Education in a Divided World: The Function of the Public Schools in Our Unique Society*. Cambridge, Mass.: Harvard University Press, 1948.

Courtenay, William. "The Virgin and the Dynamo: The Growth of Medieval Studies in America, 1870–1930." In *Medieval Studies in North America: Past, Present, and Future*, edited by Francis G. Gentry and Christopher Kleinhenz, pp. 5–22. Kalamazoo, Mich.: Medieval Institute, 1982.

Durand, Dana B. "Magic and Experimental Science: The Achievement of Lynn Thorndike." *Isis* 33 (1942): 691–712.

Guerlac, Henry. "Award of the George Sarton Medal to Lynn Thorndike." *Isis* 49 (1958): 107–08.

Hilts, Victor L. "History of Science at the University of Wisconsin." *Isis* 75 (1984): 63–94.

Hofstadter, Richard. "The Department of History." In *A History of the Faculty of Political Science, Columbia University*, edited by R. Gordon Hoxie et al., pp. 207–49. New York: Columbia University Press, 1955.

Jonçich, Geraldine. *The Sane Positivist: A Biography of Edward L. Thorndike*. Middletown, Conn.: Wesleyan University Press, 1968.

Kibre, Pearl. "A Bibliography of the Published Writings of Lynn Thorndike." *Osiris* 11 (1954): 8–22.

———. "In Memoriam: Lynn Thorndike (1882–1965)." *Archives internationales d'histoire des sciences* 20 (1967): 285–88.

Kristeller, Paul Oskar. Review of *A History of Magic and Experimental Science*, vols. 5–6, by Lynn Thorndike. *Journal of Philosophy* 38 (1941): 690–92.

"Lynn Thorndike." *New York Times* (29 December 1965), 29.

National Cyclopedia of American Biography. Vol. 51, pp. 208–10, 214–15. New York: White, 1969.

Randall, John Herman, Jr. "The Department of Philosophy." In *A History of the Faculty of Philosophy, Columbia University* [edited by Jacques Barzun], pp. 102–45. New York: Columbia University Press, 1957.

Robinson, James Harvey. *The New History: Essays Illustrating the Modern Historical Outlook*. New York: Macmillan, 1912.

Sarton, George. Review of *A History of Magic and Experimental Science During the First Thirteen Centuries of Our Era* by Lynn Thorndike. *Isis* 6 (1924): 74–89.

———. Review of *Science and Thought in the Fifteenth Century* by Lynn Thorndike. *Isis* 14 (1930): 235–40.

Shotwell, James T. *The History of History*. Rev. ed. New York: Columbia University Press, 1939.

Skotheim, Robert Allen. *American Intellectual Histories and Historians*. Princeton, N.J.: Princeton University Press, 1966.

Wenger, Luke. "The Medieval Academy and Medieval Studies in North America." In *Medieval Studies in North America: Past, Present, and Future*, edited by Francis G. Gentry and Christopher Kleinhenz, pp. 23–40. Kalamazoo, Mich.: Medieval Institute, 1982.

Woodworth, Robert S. "Edward Lee Thorndike, 1874–1949." In *Biographical Memoirs, National Academy of Sciences of the United States of America* 27 (1952): 209–37.

MARC BLOCH

(1886–1944)

Carole Fink

Marc Bloch, one of the twentieth century's most sophisticated, innovative, and critical scholars and teachers, was born on 6 July 1886 in Lyon, France. He was the descendant of a family of Alsatian Jews who after the Revolution entered the mainstream of French life. His great-grandfather fought against the Prussian army in 1793; his grandfather was a teacher and primary-school administrator in Strasbourg; and his father, Gustave Bloch, became an eminent historian of ancient Rome at the University of Lyon and at the Sorbonne. Bloch's mother, Sarah Ebstein, born in Lyon to an Alsatian-Jewish family and married at nineteen, lent order and vitality to the academic household. Marc Bloch was raised in Paris, the glittering capital of the Third Republic, where he experienced France's scientific and cultural achievements and imbibed a strong sense of patriotism.

Between ages eight and twenty Bloch also witnessed the great drama of the Dreyfus affair, which split France in two. Like many assimilated Jews he emerged from the affair with a heightened confidence in his homeland, which had ultimately acquitted and reintegrated the falsely accused captain. As an aspiring historian Bloch developed his lifelong skepticism toward the press and the army and his fascination with the production and dissemination of rumors, lies, and falsification. In joining his generation's search for the medieval origins of the modern world Bloch conceived his own set of critical principles, which reflected his strongly democratic beliefs: his France, the bestower of freedom and justice, was an amalgam of disparate groups and peoples, a nation with both a royal and a revolutionary heritage in which he ardently shared.

Bloch was educated at the elite lycée Louis-le-Grand and at the École Normale Supérieure at a time of intellectual ferment. His teachers Charles Seignobos and Charles-Victor Langlois were struggling against popular, romanticized history as well as the excesses of "scientific" history. New strands of social, economic, and cultural history were emerging, and the social sciences, especially the school led by another of Bloch's teachers, the sociologist Émile Durkheim, contended for intellectual dominance.

Bloch, who studied for a few months in Berlin and Leipzig, became a scholar who was resolutely opposed to closed methodological and ideological systems and deeply committed to openness and to comparison. Aware of the gaps in his sources, the imperfection of human testimony, and the fallibility of even the best analysts, he developed a rigorous research procedure that was bolstered by a mastery of languages and literature, the social and physical sciences, law and custom, religion and philosophy.

Twenty-eight when World War I erupted, Bloch served bravely for four years and rose from sergeant to captain. He fought at the Marne, in the trenches in the Argonne Forest, and at the Somme and did brief duty in the desert of Algeria. Self-confident and courageous, he walked to the rear after suffering a head wound ("If I'm not dead in two minutes, I'll be all right" [Bloch (1969), 39]) and a year later returned immediately to the front after an attack of typhoid fever. In 1918 his unit withstood Ludendorff's final offensive against Paris and then marched over the Vosges to liberate Alsace.

Already mature, Bloch was nevertheless affected by World War I. His four years of grueling combat reinforced his prejudice against army officialdom, his esteem for the ordinary soldier, and his fascination with the birth and spread of falsehood. Faced with fresh and abundant evidence of geographical illusions, technical breakdowns, and failed plans, the historian-soldier rejected all determinacy and upheld the human dimension of history's continuum within chance.

Shortly after his demobilization Bloch was appointed to the University of Strasbourg, which was refounded by the French after almost five decades of German control. Here for seventeen years he established himself as one of Europe's outstanding medievalists. Supported by an excellent library and distinguished colleagues, and driven by a hunger to "take up the tools left to rust upon the benches" (Bloch [1946], 215–16), Bloch plunged into a career of teaching, research, and writing with extraordinary energy and enthusiasm. His marriage in 1919 to Simonne Vidal provided him with an intelligent, supportive companion. With their six children and his aged mother, as well as the wife and children of his deceased brother and Simonne Bloch's family, the Blochs had a large, closely knit circle of relatives. In 1930 they purchased a country home in the village of Fougères in the Creuse, where they gathered during summers and holidays.

In January 1929 Bloch and his Strasbourg colleague Lucien Febvre founded a journal, the *Annales d'histoire économique et sociale*. Febvre, eight years Bloch's senior and a specialist in the sixteenth century, shared Bloch's commitment to a "new" history. Inspired by the cosmopolitan values of Henri Pirenne and chastened by World War I and its bleak aftermath, Bloch and Febvre embarked on a pioneering editorial venture to break down national, disciplinary, and temporal barriers and to create a journal devoted to contemporary as well as historical problems. During its legendary first decade the *Annales* promoted international collaboration, produced lively (occasionally acerbic) book reviews, offered abundant information on research and archives, and stressed a problem-oriented history that extended to the non-European world. This was a history that eschewed narrative and leaned heavily on the social sciences; that concentrated on case studies to reveal significant social and economic forces; that strove to generalize with tact and precision about its human subjects and avoided the nationalism and "metaphysics" common to journals across the Rhine.

With Bloch's expanding list of publications and growing reputation Paris beckoned. In 1932 Febvre was appointed to the Collège de France, and Bloch tried to follow. But when his candidacy for the elite Collège was blocked by academic politics, economic constraints, and anti-Semitism, Bloch accepted in 1936 a more demanding chair in economic history at the Sorbonne. The Paris to which he returned was seething with controversy over the policies of the Popular Front and the leadership of its Jewish prime minister. ("Better Hitler than Léon Blum!" cried the right). At fifty Bloch had reached the height of his career, but he had only three years to enjoy his new position and complete his scholarly projects before taking up arms once more for France.

At the outbreak of World War II he was first assigned to Strasbourg. While Poland succumbed to the Nazi blitzkrieg, Bloch rapidly became disgruntled at his, and France's, inactivity. Rescued by his official connections, he was sent to First Army Headquarters in Picardy, near the Belgian border, where he was placed in charge of fuel supplies. For seven months the fifty-three-year-old Bloch ("the oldest captain in the French army") suffered through the *drôle de guerre*, the phoney war; then in May 1940 the German onslaught caught the French and their allies and drove them back to the Channel. Bloch ordered the burning of fuel tanks and took part in the frenzied evacuation at Dunkirk, returning to the coast of Normandy the same day to take part in more dismal retreats. When the Germans caught up with him at Rennes just days before the armistice, he decided neither to flee to England nor be taken prisoner but donned civilian clothes and spent almost two weeks under Nazi occupation before returning to Fougères. In a "white heat of rage" he wrote *L'étrange défaite*, his stunning testimony to France's greatest debacle, sparing himself and the nation no pain and assigning responsibility to every quarter of French society.

With France's defeat and partition Bloch, in danger because of his Jewish heritage, pursued a teaching position in the United States, but his effort was frustrated by the difficulty of securing visas for his mother and two older children and tinged by his ambivalence about deserting France. When Bloch hesitated too long, his offer from the New School for Social Research was withdrawn. Due to his eminence and professional connections Bloch secured an exemption from the Vichy government's racial laws and was allowed to teach for two years in the unoccupied zone, at the University of Strasbourg-in-exile in Clermont Ferrand and at the University of Montpellier.

During this time of fear and privation Bloch faced a series of personal crises. These included the death of his beloved mother and the illness of his wife; the loss of the *Annales*, which Febvre insisted on saving by removing the non-Aryan Bloch from the editorship; the theft of his library and his private papers by the Nazi rulers in Paris; and the daily danger of surveillance and harassment. Continuing stoically with his teaching and research, Bloch composed in 1941 his moving testament (read long after his heroic death) that avowed his loyalty to France.

When the Germans crossed the demarcation line in November 1942, Bloch weighed his obligations and made the fateful decision, at age fifty-six, to join the French underground. After securing safe places for his family he journeyed to his birthplace, Lyon, in the spring of 1943 and devoted the last year of his life to the liberation of France.

Bloch's duties in the underground were varied and significant. He wrote for the Resistance press and organized personnel and material for the liberation of southern France. He became a regional chief of the organization Franc-Tireur, joined the directorate of the Mouvements Unis de Résistance, and was one of the editors of the *Cahiers politiques*, which was put out by the Comité Général d'Études in Paris. In his new life, with the pseudonyms "Arpajon," "Chevreuse," and "Narbonne," the small, bespectacled professor became a revered underground chief, who traveled to Paris and the provinces and planned the future Fourth Republic, in which he no doubt would have been a leader.

On 8 March 1944 Bloch was arrested in a major roundup by the Vichy Militia and was turned over to the Gestapo of Klaus Barbie. The Vichy and Nazi press trumpeted the "decapitation" of Lyon's "Communist-Jewish-terrorist" leadership. Incarcerated in the dreaded Montluc prison, near the center of Lyon, Bloch was tortured and fell seriously ill; but he refused to give information to his captors. While imprisoned, he reportedly taught French history to one of the young inmates.

In anticipation of the Allied invasion the Nazis began disposing of their mounting number of captives by deporting them to the Reich. Between May and August 1944 some seven hundred prisoners were also shot in scattered, isolated locations to avoid detection and reprisals. On the night of 16 June 1944, ten days after the landings at Normandy, Bloch and twenty-six other Montluc inmates were taken by truck to a field near Saint-Didier de Formans, where they were shot by German soldiers. Moments before his death, Bloch reportedly reassured a young fellow victim that the bullets would not hurt. His last words reputedly were "Vive la France!"

A brilliant and prolific writer, Marc Bloch produced an oeuvre that extended over thirty-three years; some of his unfinished works were published after his death. As a young student his research centered on the emancipation of the serfs during the twelfth and thirteenth centuries in the rural regions around Paris. From these pre-World War I investigations emerged many of Bloch's lifelong interests: slavery and serfdom, feudalism and the practices of feudal justice, the development of urban society, and the economic transformation of medieval Europe.

Bloch's first publication, *L'Île-de-France (les pays autour de Paris)*, appeared separately in Henri Berr's *Revue de synthèse* in 1912–13 and as the ninth and final volume in Berr's series Les Régions de la France (1913). In this short monograph the twenty-seven-year-old Bloch produced a light, readable human geography extending up to his own time, based on impressive scholarly research and peppered with interesting observations on the region's language and architecture as well as on its lack of historical and geographic unity.

After World War I Bloch completed his thesis, *Rois et serfs* (1920), a greatly reduced version of his original design. He limited his scope to an examination of two emancipation ordinances by Louis X (1315) and Philip V (1318), about which several historical fables had developed. This brief monograph not only punctured the myths but delineated some patterns of serfdom; traced a tentative pattern of royal, ecclesiastical, and seignorial emancipation in the cities and countryside around Paris; and contributed to the history of the Capetian monarchs.

Four years later came Bloch's first masterwork, *Les rois thaumaturges* (1924), an examination of the healing powers of the kings of France and England from the eleventh century to the nineteenth. Searching through both conventional and unusual sources, Bloch amassed an immense amount of detail on how the miracle illuminated the rise and fall of royal power in the two western monarchies. A pioneering work in the history of *mentalités*, *Les rois thaumaturges* drew on Bloch's earlier interest in the collective consciousness as a mirror of deeper realities of the epochs in which the royal healing power appeared, survived, and ultimately disappeared.

Moving on to other terrain, Bloch now produced his most innovative and thought-provoking work, *Les caractères originaux de l'histoire rurale française* (1931). Originally a series of lectures delivered at the Institute for the Comparative Study of Civilizations in Oslo in 1929, *Les caractères* displayed Bloch's virtuosity in analyzing French agrarian civilization, its diversity and continuity from ancient times to the present. Rejecting all determinist theories, Bloch explained similarities and variations in terms of a host of human and physical factors; having reached a tentative synthesis, he continued to work on the evolution of rural life until his last days.

La société féodale (2 volumes, 1939–40), completed on the eve of World War II, was written for the broad audience of Berr's series L'Évolution de l'Humanité. Combining his skills in languages, law, literature, iconography, toponymy, geography, and psychology, Bloch produced a brilliant representation of the social structure of western and central Europe between the middle of the ninth century and the beginning of the thirteenth. Employing the investigatory approach of the *Annales*, Bloch postulated two feudal periods and proceeded to analyze and compare similar and diverse feudal and nonfeudal systems in Europe. He also attempted to define the fundamental characteristics of European feudalism over a long period of four centuries.

Bloch presented his ideas in scores of articles and hundreds of reviews in the *Annales* and in other journals; the shorter scholarly format was ideal for setting out his hypotheses and critical inquiries. Even before World War I Bloch manifested his keen interest in economic and monetary history, which remained a favorite subject throughout his life. He studied price history and the mutations of currency, looking at long trends between the medieval world and the present. Bloch insisted on sound data analysis and a flexible interpretative framework over the straitjackets of economic theory and historicism. Absorbed by technology, Bloch produced an inventive history of the watermill; but he also warned against mechanical explanations for complex changes. He was fascinated with agrarian field patterns, with variations in, and absence of, feudal practices, and with the problem of servitude; he patiently examined a variety of texts, hunted for error and misinterpretation, and displayed his own erudition modestly.

As a reviewer Bloch entered several areas of controversy, including the debates over the legacies of Latin and Germanic, Anglo-Saxon and Norman civilizations and also over the Pirenne thesis of Islamic expansion. Bloch abhorred the "idol of origins," which had plagued and politicized his profession. He tended to follow a balanced and moderate course between racial theories and nationalist claimants of "who had arrived first."

Bloch, who in his failed application to the Collège de France had termed himself a historian of "comparative European societies," never restricted himself to the medieval period. His comparative approach enabled him to enter the modern and contemporary period with conviction and confidence. His last two books, written during World War II and published posthumously, demonstrated another kind of scholarship; they were two masterly, highly personal apologia that linked the man and his times.

In *L'étrange défaite* Bloch gave testimony to the human causes of France's defeat by Germany. As historian and citizen he interpreted it as the result of a gigantic misreading by France's leaders of the people, the enemy, and history itself. Two years later, before joining the Resistance, Bloch completed the draft for his final book, *Apologie pour l'histoire*. Like *L'étrange défaite* the *Apologie* was a memoir; before the new forces of barbarism Bloch bravely and candidly examined the historian's *raison d'être*. In four completed chapters and one fragment he attacked old demons, such as the artificial barriers between the past and present, and preached "historical sensitivity" (Bloch [1949], 96). Ranging broadly over space and time, he outlined his sense of the craft: the search for evidence as a pursuit of "tracks," the relentless critique of sources, the striving for an appropriate vocabulary, and above all the need not to judge but to understand.

During the dark times Bloch contributed a stack of reviews on a variety of subjects to the renamed *Annales*, and he prepared a study of the barbarian invasions. In the underground press he published a series of political articles on the debacle of 1940, Nazi propaganda, racism and elitism in the French academy, the prospects for economic cooperation in the postwar world, and the need for a sweeping *épuration* after the liberation. After his death Bloch's oldest son in conjunction with Lucien Febvre and Fernand Braudel published some of his unedited lectures and articles; a second volume of *Les caractères originaux* based on Bloch's notes appeared in 1956. A collection of his major articles appeared in *Mélanges historiques* in 1963, and his unfinished memoir of World War I, *Souvenirs de guerre: 1914–1915*, was published in 1969.

Marc Bloch's legacy resides in the enduring quality of his work and his teaching, his contribution to the historical profession and to posterity.

Although a good deal of his writing has been corrected and superseded by other scholars, Bloch's spirit remains vital and his quest unfinished.

One of Bloch's main contributions to medieval scholarship was his analysis of rural life, in the clarity and precision of his work on field patterns and field systems and on regional variations. He needed, and used, long periods of time to draw his slow-moving panorama of rural history. "Human time will never conform to the intractable uniformity or fixed divisions of clock time" (Bloch [1949], 185). Bloch was at his best in tracing the development of technology, laws, customs, and institutions, which he placed in a perpetual balance with human adaptation and ingenuity. Yet no homely anonymous peasant "Bodo" occupies Bloch's historical landscape; his peasants, lords, clerics, monarchs, and townspeople were composite creations and thus largely abstract figures.

Bloch was skilled in depicting in his lucid, concrete prose the intellectual and emotional climate of feudal society: its violence, its religiosity, its complex loyalties, its continuities with the past, its similarities and differences with the "modern" mind. Others have corrected his intuitions, broadened his canvas, and refined his periodization. But Bloch's investigations of medieval legends and popular beliefs remain model efforts at synthesis.

Bloch's work on sacred medieval kingship expanded the study of medieval politics and power. He well understood how the cultivation and management of a powerful "illusion" helped to create a new model, the Christian monarch, which rivaled the clergy for popular support. Rather than exclude politics from his vista Bloch contributed to enlarging the notion of authority. Bloch's name is closely associated with comparison, a technique he freely borrowed from the linguist Antoine Meillet and from Pirenne. Comparison was his prized antidote for the parochialism and anachronism that plagued most history. Subjects for Bloch existed in the round, not in narrow isolation of time and place; he crossed decades and centuries as well as mountains and seas to examine ideas, institutions, and societies. Comparison was a technique for understanding uniqueness and difference, marginality and variations, change and endurance, in solid, specific terms.

Out of his belief in comparison developed Bloch's commitment to collective research. Aware that no scholar could master all essential details, Bloch became an ardent advocate of collaboration. He was an indefatigable correspondent. He initiated the *Annales'* collaborative investigations (its "Inquiries"), drew up the "questionnaires" on field plans and on the evolution of the European nobility, and compiled the results. Thus Bloch was the forerunner of much of the collaborative research in postwar France and elsewhere, of team investigations of historical phenomena.

An innate cosmopolitan, Bloch after World War I was a strong supporter of the revival of the International Congress of Historical Sciences, in which he worked to reestablish the broken ties among European scholars. He journeyed to Norway, Spain, England, Italy, and Germany. During the interwar years Bloch, France's main authority on medieval Germany, took up Pirenne's mission of forging a dialog between scholars across the Rhine.

His great creation, the *Annales*, well fitted Bloch's internationalist mission. Although it was based in France, he and Febvre aimed at creating a universal forum for a broadly conceived social and economic history. Even if that goal was not entirely achieved, Bloch succeeded in shaping the medieval sections of the journal to reflect his critical, comparative perspective. He prodded his colleagues to refine their methods, ask better questions, and cast an eye across regional boundaries and borders. Under Febvre, Braudel, and their successors the *Annales* after World War II became one of the most admired and emulated of all history journals, celebrating its half-century in 1979 and still continuing with its original founders on the masthead.

A devoted pedagogue, Bloch was resolute in initiating reforms in French education, especially in the teaching of history. He left an impressive legacy in the students he trained. These included such medievalists as William Mendel Newman, André Déleage, Robert Boutruche, Michel Mollat, Robert Folz, and those who entered other fields, such as Henri Brunschwig, Pierre Goubert, and François Chevalier. Among his students and disciples (Charles Morazé, Philippe Wolff) and their students and their disciples (the German Karl Ferdinand Werner, the Russian Aron Gurevich, the Czech Ferdinand Graus, the Pole Bronisław Geremek, and the American Natalie Zemon Davis), there are unmistakable aspects of Marc Bloch's heritage: his probing questions and nondogmatic answers, his boldness and creativity, his sense of fairness and zest for knowledge, his receptiveness to new ideas and methodologies, and his keen critical sense.

Few scholars have so estimably integrated their life, work, and ideas. Bloch's years coincided with an era of significant historical events: the revolutionary works of Freud and Einstein; the eruption of fascism and Bolshevism; the pinnacle and decline of European imperialism; the two world wars and the Holocaust. A brilliant, energetic researcher and a vital citizen of his age, Bloch transcended his early training as a medievalist to become a broad seeker of historical understanding. In Marc Bloch's legacy the ancient craft of history is a noble *jeu d'esprit*. Rather than subordinate itself to theoretical constraints or political purposes, it pursues the "smell of human flesh," seeking out "the solid and the concrete behind the empty and the abstract" (Bloch [1946], 51).

SELECTED BIBLIOGRAPHY

Works

BOOKS AND ARTICLES

"Blanche de Castille et les serfs du chapître de Paris." *Mémoires de la Société de l'Histoire de Paris et de l'Île-de-France* 38 (1911): 224–72.

"Les formes de la rupture de l'hommage dans l'ancien droit féodal." *Nouvelle revue historique de droit français et étranger* 36 (1912): 141–77.

L'Île-de-France (les pays autour de Paris). Paris: Cerf, 1913.

Rois et serfs: un chapître d'histoire capétienne. Paris: Champion, 1920.

"Serf de la glèbe: histoire d'une expression toute faite." *Revue historique* 136 (1921): 220–42.

"Réflexions d'un historien sur les fausses nouvelles de la guerre." *Revue de synthèse historique* 33 (1921): 41–57.

"La vie de saint Edouard le Confesseur, par Osbert de Clare avec introduction sur Osbert et les premières vies de saint Edouard." *Annalecta bollandiana* 41 (1923): 5–131.

Les rois thaumaturges: étude sur le caractère surnaturel attribué à la puissance royale particulièrement en France et en Angleterre. Strasbourg: Publications de la Faculté des Lettres de l'Université de Strasbourg, 1924.

"La vie d'outre-tombe du roi Salomon." *Revue belge de philologie et d'histoire* 4 (1925): 349–77.

"La société du haut moyen âge et ses origines." *Journal des savants* (1926): 403–20.

"La organización de los dominios reales Carolingios y las teorias de Dopsch." *Anuario de historia del derecho español* 3 (1926): 89–119.

"Les 'colliberti': étude sur la formation de la classe servile." *Revue historique* 157 (1928): 1–48, 225–63.

"Un problème d'histoire comparée: la ministérialité en France et en Allemagne." *Revue historique de droit français et étranger* (1928): 46–91.

"Pour une histoire comparée des sociétés européennes." *Revue de synthèse historique* 46 (1928): 15–50.

With Lucien Febvre. "À nos lecteurs." *Annales d'histoire économique et sociale* 1 (1929): 1–2.

"Les plans parcellaires." *Annales d'histoire économique et sociale* 1 (1929): 60–70, 225–31, 562–75.

"L'empire et l'idée d'empire sous les Hohenstaufen." *Revue des cours et conférences* 30 (1929): 481–94, 577–89, 759–68.

"La lutte pour l'individualisme agraire dans la France du XVIIIe siècle." *Annales d'histoire économique et sociale* 2 (1930): 329–83, 511–56.

"Comparaison." *Bulletin du Centre International de Synthèse: Section de Synthèse Historique* 9 (1930): 31–39.

Les caractères originaux de l'histoire rurale française. Oslo: Ascheoug, 1931.

"European Feudalism." In *Encyclopedia of the Social Sciences*, vol. 4, edited by Edwin R.A. Seligman, pp. 203–10. New York: Macmillan, 1931.

Projet d'un enseignement d'histoire comparée des sociétés européennes. Strasbourg: Dernières Nouvelles, 1933.

"Le problème de l'or au moyen âge." *Annales d'histoire économique et sociale* 5 (1933): 1–34.

"Liberté et servitude personnelles au moyen âge, particulièrement en France." *Anuario de historia del derecho español* 10 (1933): 19–115.

"Christian Pfister, 1857–1933: sa vie, ses oeuvres." *Revue historique* 172 (1933): 548–70.

"Le salaire et les fluctuations économiques à longue période." *Revue historique* 173 (1934): 1–31.

"Avènement et conquêtes du moulin à eau." *Annales d'histoire économique et sociale* 7 (1935): 538–63.

"Les 'inventions' médiévales.'" *Annales d'histoire économique et sociale* 7 (1935): 634–43.

With Lucien Febvre. "Pour le renouveau de l'enseignement historique: le problème de l'agrégation." *Annales d'histoire économique et sociale* 9 (1937): 113–29.

"Que demander à l'histoire?" *Centre Polytechnicien d'Études Économiques* 34 (1937): 15–22.

"Technique et évolution sociale: réflexions d'un historien." *Europe* 47 (1938): 23–32.

"Économie-nature ou économie-argent, un pseudo-dilemme." *Annales d'histoire sociale* 1 (1939): 7–16.

Aspects économiques du règne de Louis XIV. Paris: Cours de Sorbonne, 1939.

La société féodale: la formation des liens de dépendence. Paris: Michel, 1939.

La société féodale: les classes et le gouvernement des hommes. Paris: Michel, 1940.

"The Rise of Dependent Cultivation and Seignorial Institutions." In *The Cambridge Economic History of Europe.* Vol. 1, edited by J.H. Clapham and Eileen Power, pp. 224–77. Cambridge: Cambridge University Press, 1941.

"Les plans cadastraux de l'ancien régime." *Mélanges d'histoire sociale* 3 (1943): 55–70.

"Notes pour une révolution de l'enseignement." *Cahiers politiques* 3 (1943): 17–24.

"Le Dr. Goebbels analyse la psychologie du peuple allemand." *Cahiers politiques* 4 (1943): 26–27.

"La vraie saison des juges." *Cahiers politiques* 4 (1943): 28–30.

"L'alimentation humaine et les échanges internationaux d'après des débats de Hot Springs." *Cahiers politiques* 4 (1943): 20–25.

"Sur les grandes invasions: quelques positions de problèmes." *Revue de synthèse historique* 60 (1945): 55–81.

"Reliquiae: les invasions: deux structures économiques." *Annales d'histoire sociale* 1 (1945): 33–46.

"Reliquiae: les invasions: occupation du sol et peuplement." *Annales d'histoire sociale* 2 (1945): 13–28.

L'étrange défaite: témoignage écrit en 1940. Paris: Société des Éditions "Franc-Tireur," 1946.

"Les transformations des techniques comme problème de psychologie collective." *Journal de psychologie normale et pathologique* 41 (1948): 104–15.

Apologie pour l'histoire ou métier d'historien. Paris: Colin, 1949. Critical ed., Paris: Colin, 1993.

Esquisse d'une histoire monétaire de l'Europe. Paris: Colin, 1954.

La France sous les derniers Capétiens (1223–1328). Paris: Colin, 1958.

Seigneurie française et manoir anglais. Paris: Colin, 1960.

Mélanges historiques. 2 vols. Paris: Service d'Édition et de Vente des Publications de l'Éducation Nationale, 1963.

Souvenirs de guerre, 1914–1915. Paris: Colin, 1969.

Letters and Papers

The major collection of Marc Bloch's papers and letters is held in the Archives Nationales in Paris. Other letters can be found in private collections in the Bibliothèque Nationale and the library of the Institut de France.

Bédarida, François, and Denis Peschanski, eds. *Marc Bloch à Etienne Bloch: lettres de* la *"drôle de guerre."* Paris: Institut d'histoire de temps présent, 1991.

Febvre, Lucien. "Marc Bloch: témoignages sur la période 1939–1940: extraits d'une correspondance intime." *Annales d'histoire sociale* 1 (1945): 15–32.

Pluet-Despatin, Jacqueline, ed. *Ecrire la société: lettres à Henri Berr, 1924–1943.* Paris: Institut Memoires de l'édition contemporaine, 1992.

Rutkoff, Peter, and William Scott. "Letters to America: The Correspondence of Marc Bloch, 1940–41." *French Historical Studies* 12 (1981): 277–303.

Sources

Atsma, Hartmut, and André Burguière. *Marc Bloch aujourd'hui: histoire comparée et sciences sociales.* Paris: Éditions de l'École des Hautes Études en Sciences Sociales, 1990.

Baulig, Henri. "Marc Bloch: géographe." *Annales d'histoire sociale* (1945): 5–12.

Bloch, Étienne. *Marc Bloch: Father, Patriot, and Teacher.* Poughkeepsie, N.Y.: Vassar College, 1987.

Boutruche, Robert. "Marc Bloch vu par ses élèves." In *Mémorial des années 1939–1945,* pp. 195–207. Paris: Belles Lettres, 1947.

Brâtianu, G.I. "Un savant et un soldat: Marc Bloch (1886–1944)." *Revue historique de sud-est européen* 23 (1946): 5–20.

Braudel, Fernand. "Marc Bloch." In *International Encyclopedia of the Social Sciences,* vol. 2, edited by David L. Sills, pp. 92–95. New York: Macmillan and Free Press, 1968.

Brunschwig, Henri. "Vingt ans après (1964): souvenirs sur Marc Bloch." In *Études africaines: offertes à Henri Brunschwig,* edited by Jan Vansina, et al., pp. xv–xvii. Paris: Éditions de l'École des Hautes Études en Sciences Sociales, 1982.

Burguière, André. "La notion de 'mentalités' chez Marc Bloch et Lucien Febvre: deux conceptions, deux filiations." *Revue de synthèse* (1983): 333–48.

Cannon, John. "Marc Bloch." In *The Historian at Work,* edited by John Cannon, pp. 121–35. London: Allen and Unwin, 1980.

Chirot, Daniel. "The Social and Historical Landscape of Marc Bloch." In *Vision and Method in Historical Sociology,* edited by Theda Skocpol, pp. 22–46. Cambridge: Cambridge University Press, 1984.

Davies, R.R. "Marc Bloch." *History* 52 (1967): 265–82.

Davis, Natalie Zemon. "History's Two Bodies." *American Historical Review* 93 (1988): 1–30.

Day, John. "The History of Money in the Writings of Marc Bloch." In *Problems of Medieval Coinage in the Iberian Area,* edited by Mario Gomes Marques and M. Crusfont i Sabater, vol. 2, pp. 15–27. Aviles, 1986.

Dollinger, Philippe. "Notre maître Marc Bloch: l'historien et sa méthode." *Revue d'histoire économique et sociale* 27 (1948–49): 109–26.

Febvre, Lucien. "De l'histoire au martyre: Marc Bloch, 1886–1944." *Annales d'histoire sociale* 1 (1945): 1–10.

———. "Marc Bloch et Strasbourg: souvenirs d'une grande histoire," pp. 171–93. Paris: Publications de la Faculté des Lettres de l'Université de Strasbourg, 1947.

Fink, Carole. "Marc Bloch: The Life and Ideas of a French Patriot." *Canadian Review of Studies in Nationalism* 10 (1983): 235–52.

———. *Marc Bloch: A Life in History.* Cambridge: Cambridge University Press, 1989.

Friedmann, Georges. "Au dela de 'l'engagement': Marc Bloch, Jean Cavaillès." *Europe* 10 (1946): 24–43.

Geremek, Bronisław. "Marc Bloch, historien et résistant." *Annales: économies, sociétés, civilisations* 41 (1986): 1091–105.

Ginzburg, Carlo. "A proposito della raccolta dei saggi storici di Marc Bloch." *Studi medievali* (1965): 335–53.

Gurevich, Aron. "Marc Bloch i 'Apologija istorii.'" Postface to *Apologija istorii ili remeslo istorika.* Moscow: Nauka, 1986.

Lyon, Bryce. "The Feudalism of Marc Bloch." *Tijdschrift voor Geschiedenis* 76 (1963): 275–83.

———. "Marc Bloch: Did He Repudiate *Annales* History?" *Journal of Medieval History* 11 (1985): 181–91.

Mastrogregori, Massimo. "Nota sul testo dell' 'Apologie pour l'histoire' di Marc Bloch." *Rivista di storia della storiografia moderna* 7 (1986): 5–32.

Perrin, Charles-Edmond. "L'oeuvre historique de Marc Bloch." *Revue historique* 199 (1948): 161–88.

Raftis, J.A. "Marc Bloch's Comparative Method and the Rural History of Mediaeval England." *Mediaeval Studies* 24 (1962): 349–68.

Sewell, William H., Jr. "Marc Bloch and the Logic of Comparative History." *History and Theory* 6 (1967): 208–18.

Weber, Eugen. "About Marc Bloch." *American Scholar* 51 (1981–82): 73–82.

EILEEN POWER

(1889–1940)

Ellen Jacobs

Eileen Edna le Poer Power, a pioneer in the field of economic and social history and one of the first to develop the study of women's history, was born in Altrincham, Cheshire, on 9 January 1889, the eldest of three daughters of Mabel Grindley Clegg and Philip Ernest le Poer Power, a London stockbroker. She was among the first in Britain to hold a chair in economic history, having succeeded Lilian Knowles as professor of economic history at the University of London in 1931, a position that she held until her sudden death at the age of fifty-one in August 1940. She was a vivid and ebullient personality, whose lucid prose commended her work to both academic and popular audiences. A tall and elegant figure, with a fine wit, inherited perhaps from her Anglo-Irish ancestors, and a love of dancing and travel, she was introduced to the chancellor of the University of Manchester upon the occasion of the award of an honorary doctorate as one who combined "the graces of the butterfly with the sober industry of the bee" (Tawney [1940]: 94).

Eileen Power spent the first twenty years of her life largely in the company of women. Following her mother's early death she and her two sisters were raised by unmarried aunts. The aunts, "vigourous, independent personalities," according to Power's London colleague and friend the historian Charles K. Webster, arranged for their education in the Oxford High School for Girls. Power went up to Girton College, Cambridge, as the Clothworkers Scholar in 1907, winning the Pioneers' Prize for History in 1908, 1909, and 1910 as well as a First in Parts 1 and 2 of her historical examinations. The climate of politics in the years surrounding World War I led to her support of pacificist efforts abroad and women's suffrage and social legislation at home.

For several years Power was secretary to the College Suffrage Society, which was associated with the reformist wing of the women's suffrage movement, the National Union of Women's Suffrage Societies. Suffrage activism was a sisterly affair; Beryl Millicent le Poer Power (1891–1974) went up to Girton as a student in 1910 and after college worked as an organizer and speaker on behalf of the National Union of Women's Suffrage Societies. Together the three Power sisters fulfilled the promise of the women's movement. Beryl Power became a permanent civil servant in the Ministry of Labor, serving as a member of the Royal Commission on Labor in India (1929–31). Rhoda Delores le Poer Power (1890–1957) traveled widely, witnessing at first hand the 1917 Bolshevik revolution in Russia. She was a pioneer of radio broadcasts to schoolchildren for the British Broadcasting Corporation, co-authoring with Eileen Power several children's books on world history that resulted from their broadcasts in the late 1920s and 1930s.

Power was sustained in her career by the support of her sisters, biological and collegial. She retained a lifelong devotion to her college, dedicating to her colleagues and students at Girton, 1913–20, her popular collection of historical essays, *Medieval People*. Among the many Girton friends and colleagues were M.G. Jones, historian of eighteenth-century charity-school movements and biographer of Hannah More, and medievalists H.M. Murray and Helen Maud Cam. Bonds of friendship and solidarity sustained numerous female scholars in the historical profession in the early years. Power was the sole to marry among her sisters and close Girton colleagues, and she did so at the age of forty-eight, to a former student and colleague at the London School of Economics, the medieval economic historian Michael Moissey Postan. She also differed from her colleagues in calling herself Eileen Power on her title pages, rather than conforming to the English practice of using only initials. After her marriage she retained her own name, declaring that "two medieval economic historians named Postan" would be "too much of a strain for future bibliographers."

Power's success in her historical examinations in 1910 led to the award of the Gilchrist scholarship, which enabled her to pursue advanced studies for a year in Paris with Charles-Victor Langlois at the Sorbonne and the École des Chartes. Although her vision of the historians' territory was more populist than that of Langlois, she later dedicated to him the text of a fourteenth-century manual on female deportment that she edited and translated, *Le ménagier de Paris*. She gathered materials for a biographical study of Isabella of France, Edward II's queen; this sadly went unfinished.

Upon return to London in 1911 Power was awarded a research scholarship at the London School of Economics, sponsored by Charlotte Shaw (George Bernard's wife). The award, open only to women, required them "to perfect themselves in the methods of investigation and research" and to "study their subjects at first hand, with a view to the preparation of short monographs." Her successor as Shaw scholar was Alice Clark, author of *The Working Lives of Women in the Seventeenth Century* (1919), suggesting that the award of the scholarship in those years was directed toward deserving women scholars sympathetic to the aims of the women's movement. Collaboration in the effort to make visible the working lives of women, past and present, was already underway among numerous activist historians, including Alice Clark; B.L. Hutchins, author of *Women in Modern Industry* and co-author of *A History of Factory Legislation*; Olive Schreiner, author of *Woman and Labour*; and others who applied their craft to contemporary feminist, socialist, and pacifist concerns. Clark acknowledged Power in her book, thanking her for providing information concerning the working lives of medieval women.

Power embarked upon a similar project for the medieval period—the investigation of the social and economic position of women in the thirteenth and fourteenth centuries, narrowing her topic to focus upon the history of pre-Reformation English nunneries. She remained at the London School of Economics until 1913, returning to Girton as lecturer and director of historical studies until 1920.

Power was the first woman to receive the award of an Albert Khan Travelling Fellowship, which enabled her to embark on a *tour du monde* from September 1920 to September 1921. The fellowship gave scholars the opportunity to travel for at least one year in foreign countries with the hope that by drawing comparisons "of national manners and customs and of the political, social, religious and economic institutions of other countries," they would become better qualified to instruct and to educate their countrymen.

Traveling in India, Burma, China, and Java, Power used her knowledge of medieval civilization as a point of reference, drawing analogies between medieval merchants, fairs, and pilgrimages and the peddlers, markets, and holy men she encountered in her travels. India impressed her not so much for the difference between East and West as for that of "a difference between modern and medieval." Of all the countries she encountered in her travels she preferred China and the "reasonableness" of its people; she returned several years later to lecture in the National University in Beijing on the importance of teaching politics and world history as a means of promoting the "solidarity of mankind." Contemporary developments in the politics of empire were also observed. She interviewed Gandhi on several occasions, attending the Nagpur Congress in 1921. Learning that women were denied passage up the Khyber Pass, she disguised herself as a man, traversing the boundaries of geography and sex.

Power's world tour had a significant effect upon her, enlarging her understanding of civilizations and societies, moving her toward a comparative approach to the studies of peoples and their histories, cultures, and civilizations. "The Albert Khan fellowship has been my ruin," she wrote to G.G. Coulton, fellow of St. John's College, Cambridge, and social historian of medieval life, religion, and custom. "My heart will stray outside its clime and period. I think I shall have to compromise by working at the trade between Europe and the East in the middle ages. . . ."

The tour also marked her departure from Girton; while traveling she received the offer of a joint appointment as lecturer in medieval economic history at the London School of Economics and in economic history at Kings College, University of London. Reluctant to leave Girton, she took the counsel of her friend and colleague M.G. Jones and of the mistress of Girton, Katherine Jex-Blake, who advised that the experience gained elsewhere would allow her to return one day as head of one of the women's colleges. She had also been discouraged by the vote in 1920 that continued to refuse women full rights of membership in Cambridge University. She grew accustomed to the "utilitarian" atmosphere of the London School of Economics and the "mixed, cosmopolitan" society of London. Some seventeen years later she refused to let her name go forth for nomination as successor to J.H. Clapham in the chair of economic history at Cambridge, declaring herself "a convinced Londoner."

Power flourished in London, serving as lecturer, reader, and professor in the university from 1921 to her death in August 1940. She taught many subjects to undergraduates, ranging from specialized courses in medieval and Tudor economic history—which resulted in the three volumes compiled with R.H. Tawney, *Tudor Economic Documents* (1924)—to modern subjects, including a history of the West in modern times and a two-year course, "The Economic Development of Great Powers," which she shared with her London School of Economics colleagues Tawney, H.L. Beales, and Evan Durbin.

At the center of Power's subject were her seminars in medieval economic history at the Institute of Historical Research beginning in 1924, from 1926 on taught jointly with Michael Postan. She took an immense interest in the work and career of many of her students, who continued to attend even after the award of the doctorate. Her significant contribution to the field of medieval social and economic history is evident in the roster of students attending the seminar, including Postan himself, Eleanora Carus-Wilson, Sylvia L. Thrupp (who dedicated to Power *The Merchant Class of Medieval London*), Marjorie Chibnall, R.A.L. Smith, Winifred Haward, Dorothea Oschinsky, and Philippe Wolff, a visiting student of Marc Bloch.

Marc Bloch, Elie Halévy, Henri Pirenne, and François L. Ganshof were among her scholar friends. She admired Bloch's work and his editorship, with Lucien Febvre, of the *Annales d'histoire économique et sociale*, which represented the sort of history that most appealed to her. She arranged for Bloch to contribute to the first volume in the new Cambridge series that she and Clapham planned, starting in 1934, *The Cambridge Economic History of Europe*.

Within the university Power had a wide circle of friends, including those responsible with her for the teaching of economic history at the London School of Economics, as well as the social theorist T.H. Marshall, political scientist Harold J. Laski, sociologist Karl Mannheim, and historians Charles K. Webster, F.M. Powicke, and A.V. Judges. Numerous political and literary figures who shared her Labor-socialist principles, including Ruth (Fox) Dalton and Hugh Dalton, friends from her early years as a research scholar at the London School of Economics, Hugh Gaitskell, Bertrand Russell, and H.G. Wells, met as guests in her home at 20 Mecklenburgh Square.

Power received numerous professional awards and honors, including an honorary doctorate (D.Litt.) from the University of Manchester in 1933 and another from Mount Holyoke College [Doctor of Letters] as part of that school's centenary celebration in 1937. She was elected fellow and later vice-president of the Royal Historical Society, and was a corresponding member of the Medieval Academy of America, a fellow and member of Girton's council, and the Ford Lecturer in Oxford in 1938–39. A lecturer of international reputation, she was invited to teach at Barnard College in New York in 1930 and lectured to audiences at the University of Wales, Aberystwyth, and at the National University in China. She helped to organize the first meeting of the economic-history section in the plenary of the Anglo-American Conference at the University of London in 1926, and joined Tawney, William Ashley, J.R. Scott, and others in the founding of the Economic History Society, which she served as secretary and as a member of the editorial board of its journal, the *Economic History Review*. Moving beyond the boundaries that confined women to narrow spaces and restricted lives in the academy and the profession, Power displayed a capacious vision of the historian's territory that was fittingly honored at the time of her death by colleagues, friends, and pupils with the creation of a memorial fund established in her name to enable historians to travel abroad and to pursue their studies in social and economic history.

Never the "student" of any particular school or person, Power was advised in her research on medieval conventual life by Coulton and aided in the study of visitation records of religious houses by A. Hamilton Thompson. The result of her research was the great monograph of economic and social history *Medieval English Nunneries c. 1275 to 1535*, which appeared in 1922 as a volume in Cambridge Studies in Medieval Life and Thought, the series edited by Coulton.

This was the first in a string of publications drawn from her research in which women and others of marginal status in traditional accounts figure prominently. They include the texts that appeared in the Routledge Broadway Medieval Library series, which she co-edited with Coulton, including her translated edition of *Le ménagier de Paris*, *The Goodman of Paris* (1928) and her introduction to Johannes Herolt's fifteenth-century *Miracles of the Blessed Virgin Mary* (1929); her study "Medieval Ideas About Women," which was revised at the request of the editors, E.F. Jacob and C.G. Crump, to include materials on women and work and which appeared as "The Position of Women" in *The Legacy of the Middle Ages* (1926); the essays on medieval women edited by Michael Postan, *Medieval Women* (1975), and her popular text *Medieval People* (1924), with its portraits of representative individuals, including Chaucer's Prioress and the *ménagier's* wife.

While at work on her study of medieval nunneries Power embarked on a second line of research into English rural life, which resulted in her first published book, *The Paycockes of Coggeshall* (1920). This short study (sixty-six pages) of an Essex clothier's family, their industry, and their house marked her first attempt to turn the study of rural history away from the traditional political accounts of lord, serf, and manor to an account that devoted space to the study of "ordinary people," of social classes and village life, agriculture and trade. In the two decades that followed she researched the history of the English wool trade, "working back and forward between the trade and the flocks that supplied it." "Her main interests," Clapham wrote, seem "to lie sometimes in the English countryside and sometimes among the merchants." Her studies of the wool trade and its people include the popular essays on merchant and clothier that appear in *Medieval People*; the essay "The English Wool Trade in the Reign of Edward IV," which appeared in the *Cambridge Historical Journal* (1926); her study "Peasant Life and Rural Conditions," which appeared in the *Cambridge Medieval History* (1932); and the essay on the English wool trade that appears in the volume she co-edited with Postan, *Studies in English Trade in the Fifteenth Century* (1933). The culmination of her research on the wool trade was evident in her Ford Lectures, delivered at Oxford in January and February 1939, where she skillfully portrayed the lives, work, and culture of those upon whose labors the prosperity of England was built.

Power's attempt to make history accessible to a popular audience is evident in the series she co-edited for Routledge in the 1920s and 1930s. They include the Broadway Travellers series, co-edited with the Oriental scholar Sir Edward Denison Ross, which produced twenty-six volumes from 1925 to 1938; the Broadway Diaries and Letters series, co-edited with E.A. Drew; and the Medieval Life and Letters series, co-edited with Coulton. She joined Tawney, Beales, and other London colleagues active in the Workers Educational Association, publishing essays on rural history in the journal of the association, the *Highway*. Her poetry and occasional reviews of women writers appeared in the early numbers of the feminist political weekly, *Time and Tide*, founded in 1920 by women who had battled for women's suffrage. And she joined modernist writers H.G. Wells, Rebecca West, Naomi Mitchison, and others on the editorial board of the short-lived journal of scientific humanism the *Realist*, which appeared for six months in 1929.

In 1924 she published *Medieval People*, an immensely popular history that invoked the style and tone of her many lectures on historical people and cities delivered to general audiences from the 1920s until her death. "Social history," she thought, called for "a personal treatment." The social historian, she told an audience in China, necessarily emphasizes the likenesses and debts of one civilization to another, asking, "what was the ordinary everyday life of [an] ordinary person like at this or that moment?"

The "personalized," individual approach to social history was also evident in her history lectures to schoolchildren in the late 1920s and 1930s on the BBC. The books that she co-authored with her sister Rhoda, *Boys and Girls of History*, *More Boys and Girls of History*, and *Cities and Their Stories*, followed from her broadcasts. Her engagement in popularizing history for a literate society was also evident in many reviews and essays for the *Nation*, *Athenaeum*, *New Leader*, *Times Literary Supplement*, *Weekly Westminster*, *Spectator*, and *New Statesman* from the early 1920s until the mid-1930s.

To academic audiences Power emphasized the integral relationship of social and economic history to the social sciences. "Social history is, of course, a wide subject . . .," she declared in her 1933 inaugural lecture as professor of economic history at the University of London. Attempting to create a bridge between history and the social sciences, she made an eloquent plea for "the use of a genuinely scientific method of abstraction and comparison."

Her remarks drew upon her participation in a group of University of London historians, economists, sociologists, and anthropologists that met from 1928 to 1934 to create interdisciplinary connections among their subjects. They planned a collective historical inquiry into the family, a subject familiar to anthropologist Bronisław Malinowski and others in the group but hitherto neglected by historians. The comparative study of social groups and social institutions, and familiarity with the economic theories of Werner Sombart and sociological theories of Max Weber, are evident in her Ford Lectures, *The Wool Trade in English Medieval History*, delivered in 1939, a year before her death. Her carefully written lecture notes were prepared for publication by Postan with the aid of M.G. Jones, Cam, Tawney, and Powicke and published by the Oxford University Press in 1941. Despite the exigencies of wartime Britain, which led to the omission of the scholarly apparatus of appendixes and footnotes, the work bore witness to the range and depth of her scholarship. Drawing upon a variety of sources, with historiographic references to Frederic Maitland, Frank Stenton, and William Stubbs, in particular, she analyzed the economic, social, and political effects of England's rise to prosperity with its commerce in wool. There were statistics pertaining to trade and finance, but it was in her discussion of the people—shepherds, sailors, merchants—that her narrative came to life.

Power's project was essentially modernist; she traversed the boundaries of her discipline, joining sociologists and anthropologists in the attempt to construct a bridge between their social studies. She was part of the generation of historians who shaped the "new history" of the 1930s—one that was concerned with new problems, particularly in relation to the study of people and society in the past. The "new" history marked a shift away from the study of political elites toward the expanding field of social history, with its study of social institutions and the "masses." Power's approach resonates today in the approach to cultural history evident in the work of Natalie Zemon Davis and Carolyn Walker Bynum.

Power believed that history should be taught not as a "dead subject" but as a way to elucidate the present as well as the past. In lecture hall, press, and radio broadcasts she made accessible to popular audiences the "obscure lives and activities" of the "great mass of humanity, upon whose slow toil was built up the prosperity of the world . . ." (*Medieval People* [1963], 18). Fond of quoting Lord Acton's remark, "The great historian now takes his meals in the kitchen," she went frequently "to the kitchen." The results were evident in her sympathetic portraits of individuals and their families, communities, industries, and worldviews. She invoked a narrative voice, "personifying" the past with accounts of representative individuals who figured in the landscape of medieval economic and social life. Although there were statistics and economic analysis in her later work on the wool trade, it was the social aspect, the study of people in social groups, that held her from the first.

Power's essays in which women figure prominently, including those that appear in her bestselling *Medieval People*, in the posthumous collection *Medieval Women*, and in her 1926 essay "The Position of Women" in *The Legacy of the Middle Ages*, remain essential to an understanding of the role of gender in medieval economy and society.

Medieval English Nunneries c. 1275 to 1535 (1922), Power's longest work, was held by a contemporary to be "incomparably better . . . than anything of the kind that has been done before or since in any European language" (Tawney [1949], 718). Her Cambridge colleague and friend, the economic historian J.H. Clapham, thought that it was in her chapters describing apostate nuns that the full range of her personality and scholarship came together: "Eileen Power set out to tell all that was worth telling about the English nunneries and their place in society. She did it so well, exploding old fallacies and uncovering fresh truth, that no one need try the theme again for a generation or two" (Clapman: 354).

Medieval English Nunneries remains a landmark of its genre, providing a history of institutions brought to life by her literary and narrative skills. Although her subject was seemingly austere, Power framed a portrait of irreverent, witty, and apostate nuns. They were "fish out of water," her title for a brilliant chapter that records the ways in which nuns roamed freely in the world, dressed gaily, kept pets and lovers, and traversed the boundaries of conventual enclosures. Another chapter describes how, engaging in "the olde daunce," sexual liaisons, nuns took lovers within and outside convent walls, gave birth, ran away, saved for dowries for their daughters, and performed numerous acts of disobedience. These were acts of willful women.

Matching her portrait of boisterous nuns, Power introduced readers to a Blessed Virgin Mary with a "predilection for the disreputable." In her 1928 introduction to Herolt's collection *Miracles of the Blessed Virgin Mary* Power directed attention to a Virgin who demanded love and faith rather than justice and obedience, befriending apostate nuns, poor and ignorant clerks, acrobats-turned-monks, and those like the thief who could not be hanged because she stood beneath the gallows and held his feet. Power presents a mother who disrupts her son's church, a woman in revolt against the rule of the sons, and a woman whose power is unbound by law.

Power placed women in the forefront of her medieval studies, drawing attention to the lives of discordant and disorderly women and others of "minority" status, including nuns, monks, pilgrims, vagabonds, and rogues who traversed the boundaries of cloistered lives. An active supporter of women's suffrage, she moved beyond the boundaries set by custom and tradition that greeted the first generations of women historians in the ancient universities and within the historical profession.

Power's dissonant portrait of medieval women and society did not go unchallenged by contemporaries. While applauding the wit and charm of *Medieval English Nunneries*, at least two reviewers, Bertha Haven Putnam and Hilda Johnstone, reminded readers of the "devout obedience" of nuns, which left a lighter imprint upon the historical record than the scandals caused by "gamblers, rebels, or sinners." Another reviewer challenged Power's depiction of the social status of women entering the convent, arguing that they were not likely to have been drawn from the aristocracy or the privileged classes, as she had suggested. This view has been recently sustained by feminist historians who have studied the relationship of aristocratic women to convents in the years 1450–1540.

The portraits that appear in Power's enormously popular *Medieval People*, and elsewhere, went largely unremarked in the learned historical journals. This was due perhaps to the relative "newcomer" status of social history as a field of study or more likely to the conflation of Power's subject matter, which included those hitherto left in the margins of history, with the popular format in which many of her discussions appeared. By her radio-broadcast lectures, journalism, and addresses to general audiences, as well as in her work as translator and editor of numerous publications, Power attempted to engage both popular and learned audiences in the excitement of the study of history. Her project of inclusiveness of subject and of audience has been left largely to subsequent generations of historians.

Power's legacy is marked by her attempt to place women at the center of the historical narrative, making the analysis of gender integral to the study of history. Numerous feminist historians of the generation that followed, including Alice Clark, Ivy Pinchbeck, Dorothy George, and Dorothy Marshall, acknowledged their debt to her. They "saw" women in their panorama of the past, "framing" them, so to speak, not as addenda to the traditional versions of the past but as subjects integral to understanding the past. Power was a leader among a pioneer generation of women historians and historians of women.

SELECTED BIBLIOGRAPHY
Works

BOOKS AND ARTICLES
"The Cult of the Virgin in the Middle Ages." *Cambridge Magazine* (28 April 1917): 534–36.
"The Cult of the Virgin in the Middle Ages. II. Miracles of the Virgin." *Cambridge Magazine* (5 May 1917): 558–59.

"The Cult of the Virgin in the Middle Ages. III. The Sinners' Advocate." *Cambridge Magazine* (12 May 1917): 594–96.

"The Cult of the Virgin: A Reply to Mgr. Moyes." *Cambridge Magazine* (9 June 1917): 710–12.

"Tittivillus." *Cambridge Magazine* (24 November 1917): 158–60.

"Historical Revisions. VII: The Effects of the Black Death on Rural Organisation in England." *History*, n.s., 3 (1918): 109–16.

"Medieval Ideas About Women." *Cambridge Magazine* (2 November and 9 November 1918): 109–12.

"Nunnery Pets in Literature." *Cambridge Magazine* (23 November 1918): 172–75.

Ed. *A Bibliography for Teachers of History*. London: Women's International League, 1919.

The "New World" History Series. Book One: Earliest Times to 1485. Edited by Bernard L. Manning. London: Collins, 1920.

"Historical Revisions. XII: English Craft Gilds in the Middle Ages." *History*, n.s., 4 (1920): 211–14.

The Paycockes of Coggeshall. London: Methuen, 1920.

Ed. and intro. *A Bibliography for School Teachers of History*. 2nd ed., rev. London: Methuen, 1921.

"A Plea for the Middle Ages." *Economica* 2 (1922): 173–80.

"Alien Immigrants and English Arts & Crafts." *Home-Reading Magazine* 1–8. (1922–23): 9–11, 39–41, 72–75, 104–07, 136–39, 168–70, 200–02, 232–34.

Medieval English Nunneries c. 1275 to 1535. Cambridge: Cambridge University Press, 1922.

Report to the Trustees of the Albert Kahn Travelling Fellowship. London: Privately printed, 1922.

"Pierre du Bois and the Domination of France." In *The Social and Political Ideas of Some Great Medieval Thinkers*, edited by F.J.C. Hearnshaw, pp. 139–66. New York: Holt, 1923; London: Harrap, 1923.

Medieval People. London: Methuen, 1924; New York: Barnes and Noble, 1963.

Ed. with R.H. Tawney. *Tudor Economic Documents*. 3 vols. London: Longmans, 1924.

"Pekin." *Time and Tide* (2 January 1925): 15.

"The English Wool Trade in the Reign of Edward IV." *Cambridge Historical Journal* 2 (1926): 17–35.

"The Opening of the Land Routes to Cathay." In *Travel and Travellers of the Middle Ages*, edited by A.P. Newton, pp. 124–58. London: Routledge, 1926.

"The Position of Women in the Middle Ages." In *The Legacy of the Middle Ages*, edited by C.G. Crump and E.F. Jacob, pp. 401–34. Oxford: Clarendon, 1926.

With Rhoda Power. *Boys and Girls of History*. Cambridge: Cambridge University Press, 1926.

With Rhoda Power. *Cities and Their Stories: An Introduction to the Study of European History*. Boston: Houghton Mifflin, 1927; London: Black, 1927.

The Industrial Revolution 1750–1850: A Select Bibliography. London: Economic History Society, 1927.

Trans. and intro. *Life and Work in Medieval Europe*, by Prosper Boissonnade. London: Routledge, 1927.

Trans. and intro. *The Goodman of Paris (Le ménagier de Paris): A Treatise on Moral and Domestic Economy by a Citizen of Paris (c. 1393)*. London: Routledge, 1928.

Intro. *Miracles of the Blessed Virgin Mary, by Johannes Herolt (1435–1440)*. Translated with Preface and Notes by C.C. Swinton Bland. London: Routledge, 1928.

With Rhoda Power. *More Boys and Girls of History*. Cambridge: Cambridge University Press, 1928.

With Norman H. Baynes. *Europe Throughout the Ages: From the Coming of the Greeks to the End of the Middle Ages.* London: Routledge, 1929.

"Peasant Life and Rural Conditions (c. 1100 to c. 1500)." In *The Cambridge Medieval History,* 8 vols. Edited by J.R. Tanner et al., vol. 7, pp. 716–50. Cambridge: Cambridge University Press, 1932.

"The Wool Trade in the Fifteenth Century." In *Studies in English Trade in the Fifteenth Century,* edited by Eileen Power and M.M. Postan, pp. 39–90. London: Routledge, 1933.

Ed. with M.M. Postan. *Studies in English Trade in the Fifteenth Century.* London: Routledge, 1933.

"Our Debt to the Past-XI-XIII: Political Life and Thought in the Middle Ages"; "Economic Ideas of the Middle Ages"; "The Achievement of Medieval Art." *Listener* (14 December 1932; 21 December 1932; 4 January 1933): 845–47; 904–05; 18–20.

"Wool-Gathering in the Cotswolds." *Highway* (October 1933): 7–10.

"On Medieval History as a Social Study." Inaugural Lecture, the London School of Economics and Political Science. *Economica,* n.s., 1 (1934): 13–29.

"On the Need for a New Edition of Walter of Henley." *Transactions of the Royal Historical Society* (London), 4th ser., 17 (1934): 101–16.

"Class: An Enquiry into Social Distinctions. I: What Feudalism Meant in England." *Listener* (20 October 1938): 817–18.

Ed. with J.H. Clapham. *The Cambridge Economic History of Europe from the Decline of the Roman Empire.* Vol. 1. Cambridge: Cambridge University Press, 1941.

The Wool Trade in English Medieval History, Being the Ford Lectures. London: Oxford University Press, 1941.

Medieval Women. Edited by M.M. Postan. Cambridge: Cambridge University Press, 1975.

LETTERS AND PAPERS

Cambridge University Library. Eileen Power papers. Uncataloged papers including syllabi, lecture notes, manuscript drafts of published works, and research notes.

Girton College Library. Archives. Eileen Power papers. Includes published works and correspondence with G.G. Coulton.

Girton College Library. Archives. Beryl M. Power and Rhoda D. Power papers. Includes manuscripts and papers pertaining to their careers.

Girton College Library. Archives. Helen Maud Cam papers. Includes correspondence between Helen Maud Cam and Eileen Power.

Nuffield College Library, Oxford. Archives. Economic History Society papers, 1926–40.

Sources

Barker, T.C. "The Beginnings of the Economic History Society." *Economic History Review,* 2nd ser., 30 (1977): 1–19.

Berg, Maxine. "The First Women Economic Historians." *Economic History Review,* 2nd ser., 45 (1992): 308–29.

Cantor, Norman. *Inventing the Middle Ages: The Lives, Works and Ideas of the Great Medievalists of the Twentieth Century,* pp. 381–95. New York: Morrow, 1991.

Clapham, J.H. "Eileen Power, 1889–1940." *Economica,* n.s., 7 (1940): 351–59.

Coleman, D.C. *History and the Economic Past: An Account of the Rise and Decline of Economic History in Britain.* Oxford: Clarendon; New York: Oxford University Press, 1987.

Coulton, G.G. "Memories of Eileen Power." *Cambridge Review* 62 (1940): 28–29.

Davis, Natalie Zemon. "History's Two Bodies." *American Historical Review* 93 (1988): 1–30.

Harris, Barbara J. "A New Look at the Reformation: Aristocratic Women and Nunneries, 1450–1540." *Journal of British Studies* 32 (1993): 89–113.

Jones, M[ary] G[wladys]. "Memories of Eileen Power." *Girton Review* (1940): 3–13.

Moyes, Rev. Mgr. J. "The Cult of the Blessed Virgin." *Cambridge Magazine* (2 June 1917): 677–79.

"Obituary. Dr. Eileen Power. Professor of Economic History." *Times* (London) (9, 13, 15, and 19 August 1940): 7 [for each].

"Power, Eileen." In *Who's Who*, pp. 2579. New York: Macmillan, 1939.

Smith, Bonnie G. "The Contribution of Women to Modern Historiography in Great Britain, France, and the United States, 1750–1940." *American Historical Review* 89 (1984): 709–32.

Stone, Lawrence. "History and the Social Sciences in the Twentieth Century." In *The Future of History*, edited by Charles Delzell, pp. 3–42. Nashville, Tenn.: Vanderbilt University Press, 1977.

Tawney, R.H. "Postan, Eileen Edna le Poer." In *Dictionary of National Biography*, 5th Supplement, 1931–40, pp. 718–19. London: Oxford University Press, 1949.

———. "Obituary." *Economic History Review* 10 (1940): 92–94.

Webster, Charles K. "Eileen Power (1889–1940)." *Economic Journal* 50 (1940): 561–72.

Wolff, Philippe. "Necrologie: Eileen Power." *Annales d'histoire sociale* 7 (1945): 127–28.

Claudio Sánchez-Albornoz y Menduiña

(1893–1984)

James F. Powers

Claudio Sánchez-Albornoz, member of an intellectual renaissance in Spain sometimes called the "Generation of '23," was born to Nicolás Sánchez-Albornoz and Teresa Menduiña Jové in Avila on 7 April 1893, on the same day that his father took the oath of office as delegate from Avila in the National Cortes (parliament). In some ways reminiscent of the historian-politicians of the nineteenth century, Don Claudio supplemented his scholarly endeavors by serving as a member of the Constituent Cortes, as ambassador of the Republic to Portugal, and finally for a time as head of the Spanish Republican government in exile. Sánchez-Albornoz's secondary education was completed in Madrid at the Escuelas Pias. He then enrolled in the Central University of Madrid to study both in the School of Law and that of Philosophy and Letters.

In 1911–12 Sánchez-Albornoz entered the class of Eduardo de Hinojosa, holder of the chair of medieval Spanish history at the Central University, an experience that caused the young scholar to abandon his legal studies and concentrate on medieval history. From the outset Sánchez-Albornoz's primary interest would be institutional history and the evolution of the Castilian monarchy during the early and central Middle Ages. Hinojosa soon brought Don Claudio into his ongoing seminar managed by the Centro de Estudios Históricos in the Biblioteca Nacional. Here Sánchez-Albornoz shared studies and ideas with other rising scholars, such as Galo Sánchez and José María Ramos Loscertales. When Hinojosa's illness curtailed the operation of the seminar in 1914, Sánchez-Albornoz nonetheless continued his remarkable progress by obtaining his doctorate in the same year at a precocious twenty-one years of age. Two years later he placed first in a grant competition sponsored by the national organization of archivists, librarians, and archaeologists, in whose journal part of his dissertation had been published. Assisted by this and a grant from the Biblioteca Nacional,

Don Claudio traveled to Portugal to study the Portuguese royal council during the twelfth and thirteenth centuries. This study became the subject of his first published book in 1920.

His professional career matched this remarkable pace. In 1918 he won the competition for the Spanish history chair at the University of Barcelona, and in 1919 he acquired another chair at the University of Valladolid. With the passing of Hinojosa, the chair of medieval history at the Central University in Madrid became vacant, and Sánchez-Albornoz, just twenty-seven years old, won this prestigious position in 1920. In that same year the National Legislature created the Premio Covadonga, a prize commemorating the twelve-hundredth anniversary of the Battle of Covadonga, the semilegendary "first battle of the Reconquest." The theme, ironic in light of the decline of King Alfonso XIII's rule destined to experience military disaster at the hands of the Moroccans at Annual in 1921, consisted of the origins and development of the Asturo-Leonese kingship. Spain's preeminent medieval scholar, Ramón Menéndez Pidal, strongly encouraged Don Claudio to enter the competition.

Newly married and accompanied by his bride, the young scholar departed for an extensive survey of the northern archives, seeking to transcribe many of the documents housed in their collections. Within the required two years Sánchez-Albornoz produced a massive study on the origins of the Asturian monarchy. Despite winning the Premio Covadonga, however, the multivolume work did not achieve final publication for a half-century. Don Claudio's health had been adversely affected by the chilly reading rooms of Cantabrian Iberia, and intervening events stalled the work's preparation for the publisher. But the text of this enormous work, laced with numerous transcriptions of previously unedited documents, nourished his classes and seminars in the following years. In memory of Hinojosa Sánchez-Albornoz founded in 1924 the *Anuario de historia del derecho español* (*Annual on the History of Spanish Law*), soon to be the major journal of Spanish institutional history. In the next year he was elected to membership in the Real Academia de la Historia, at thirty-two the youngest scholar ever to be so honored. His essay of induction, given on 28 February 1926, described conditions of life in the royal capital of León at the end of the first millennium, with Menéndez Pidal serving as official commentator.

Claudio Sánchez-Albornoz had thus reached an early peak in his rapidly developing career. He attracted some of the most able young scholars to his seminar, among them the promising Luis G. de Valdeavellano, who would become a major institutional historian in his own right. In 1928, after a year of study with Alfons Dopsch in Vienna, Don Claudio reinstituted

Hinojosa's former research seminar. This Seminario de Historia de las Instituciones met each Thursday afternoon in a room in the Centro de Estudios Históricos and included such future luminaries as Valdeavellano, José María Lacarra (the great historian of Navarre and Aragon), and Luis Vázquez de Parga. The group concentrated its attention on the midlevel aristocratic class known as the *infanzones*, which produced, among others, Rodrigo Díaz de Vivar, better known as El Cid. This seedbed of seminal ideas would bear a rich harvest in succeeding decades both in Spain and in Argentina.

The year 1931 brought dramatic changes to Spain and to Sánchez-Albornoz. A bloodless revolution gave birth to the Second Republic and opened up seemingly boundless political opportunities for intellectuals. Within months of the departure of the self-exiled Alfonso XIII, Don Claudio had been named counselor of public instruction and dean of the philosophy and letters faculty at the Central University. He was also elected to the Constituent Cortes as a member of Manuel Azaña's Acción Republicana party, holding his father's old seat from the city of Avila. He was especially active in the Cortes debates on agrarian reform, drawing upon his rich knowledge of aristocratic landholding practices. Sánchez-Albornoz became rector of the University of Madrid in 1932, then minister of state and vice-president of the Cortes in 1933. Despite these distractions Don Claudio maintained his scholarly endeavors. He undertook the major project of gathering a huge collection of Spanish historical sources, to be entitled Monumenta Hispaniae Histórica, for which his students made numerous visits to the archives of Iberia to photograph and transcribe thousands of documents. He also planned the creation of a map of Spain in A.D. 1000. Both projects would fall victim to the outbreak of the Spanish Civil War in 1936.

At the onset of the generals' revolt and the Nationalist counterrevolution Sánchez-Albornoz served as ambassador to Portugal. Frustration resulted for the scholar-politician when the Portuguese government declared its support for the Nationalist cause, leaving Don Claudio virtually isolated in the ambassador's residence. Inoperative in Lisbon, he made his way to France, where he was able to acquire a professorship at the University of Bordeaux with the help of the French Hispanist Georges Cirot. Sánchez-Albornoz managed to visit Republican Spain several times during the Civil War but remained in France after Spain's collapse in 1939. In 1940 France surrendered to Germany, leading him to flee in turn to Free France, Algiers, Portugal, and finally to Argentina. With great difficulty he was able to bring a large portion of his notes and transcriptions of archival sources with him, a cache that would sustain him and his future students for decades to come.

Based initially at the University of Cuyo in the Province of Mendoza, in 1941 Don Claudio published the famous work on feudalism that was to achieve for him an international reputation. One year later he moved to the University of Buenos Aires, where he was awarded a chair in Spanish history in the philosophy and letters faculty. Here the scholar spent the bulk of his forty-year self-imposed exile. It was anything but an isolated sulk in a scholarly monastic cell. Sánchez-Albornoz peppered the pages of *La prenza* and other Argentine newspapers and journals with his ongoing commentary upon events in Franco's Spain. From 1959 to 1970 he held the presidency of the Spanish Republican government in exile. When Franco placed a statute of limitations on Civil War "crimes" in 1969, he declared all exiles to be thereafter self-imposed. The historian-president would have none of this, refusing to return to a Spain ruled by a dictator. But this unflinching belief in a democratic Spain and commitment to argue its case from abroad would hardly have been sufficient by itself to occupy completely a historian of his stature at the zenith of his career. Rather he set about the task of recreating much of his old world in the fertile fields of the new.

Sánchez-Albornoz created the Instituto de Historia de España, later renamed the Instituto de Historia de la Cultura Español Medieval y Moderna, which drew some of the finest students in Latin America to study Peninsular history under his direction. Already in 1944 the Instituto began publication of a major historical journal, the *Cuadernos de historia de España*, possessing an orientation similar to that of his earlier *Anuario de historia del derecho español*. Through its pages he and his students renewed and expanded the directions of his mature historical thought. The *Cuadernos* also served as a vehicle to attack alternative views of Iberian history, which met with Sánchez-Albornoz's often scathing disapproval. The journal welcomed the essays of scholars, many of them his former students, who had survived the Civil War and continued to pursue careers in Spain.

Between 1941 and 1966 Sánchez-Albornoz concentrated on systematizing his ideas in extended articles and books that drew his earlier concepts into larger theoretical formulations, indicating the main directions with a series of shorter articles in the *Cuadernos* and other journals. He also involved himself in a longstanding debate with a fellow exile and member of the "Generation of '23," Américo Castro. The evolution of this conflict is discussed below. After 1966 and well into his seventies Don Claudio focused little on new work, preferring to make minor emendations in his earlier writings and gathering his articles into accessible, large collections. His students in Argentina, especially the prolific writer Hilda Grassotti, have amplified and extended his arguments in their own work. His international reputation continued to grow, enhanced by his receipt of the Feltrinelli Prize from the Academia dei Lincei de Roma in 1971 and by his papers given at the Spoleto Conferences.

Finally there was triumph, however belated. Following the death of Franco in 1975 Sánchez-Albornoz returned briefly to his homeland in the spring of 1976 to a hero's welcome. With the change in political conditions Don Claudio brought his forty-year exile formally to an end and returned for good in 1983. The scholar was greeted warmly by the monarchy whose early history he had delineated, and he was deluged by prizes—the Gran Cruz de Alfonso el Sabio, the Medalla de Oro de la Universidad Complutense, the Gran Cruz de Carlos III, the Principe de Asturias Prize. Press tributes flowed unceasingly, some of them written, as Peter Linehan notes, "by aging ex-Francoist ideologues who in their youth had calumniated him with equal zest" (Linehan [1985], 1144). But soon his health declined, confining him to a clinic in his native Avila. Here death found him on 8 July 1984. Sánchez-Albornoz left a remarkable heritage of long life, scholarly productivity, tragic exile, and an example of devotion to the ideal of liberty. He also left two daughters, María Cruz and María Concepción, and a son, Nicolás, a well-known scholar in economic history. Nicolás himself endured two exiles, both his father's and subsequently his own from the military junta in Argentina. Like his father Nicolás also achieved success in two worlds, Argentina and the United States.

The main themes of Sánchez-Albornoz's explorations emerged early in his career (1914–22), starting with his doctoral work on the growth of royal power in early Asturias-León, progressing to his book on the royal council in Portugal, and finally maturing in his Covadonga Prize research dealing with institutions of the Asturo-Leonese monarchy from the eighth century to the eleventh. This research soon led Sánchez-Albornoz to his life-long hypothesis, signaled by his 1923 article in the *Revista de occidente*, that Spain had developed very differently from the rest of Europe, especially France. He devoted the remainder of his lengthy career to exploring this "difference."

His thinking, grounded in his examination of early Iberian kingship, led to the following postulations: an unusually free class of small peasant landholders developed in the depopulated Duero river valley before the year 1000; an arrested ("immature") form of feudalism resulted from the constraints provided by this peasant class combined with an open southern frontier; the continuing influence of that frontier in medieval Spain was sustained by the force of the Reconquest; Islamic culture and institutions exerted little influence on Hispanic formation; and frontier towns played a democratic role, both in their local councils (*concejos*) and in the evolving Castilian Cortes.

Sánchez-Albornoz first explored the free peasantry in his articles in the 1920s on the *behetrías*, peasant communities that negotiated their service obligations with their lords. His 1926 entry into the Royal Academy occasioned a book on the precocious urban development of the royal capital of León by 1000, suggesting the interesting and early evolution of Castilian municipalities. Don Claudio also explored the institutions of Visigothic Spain, seeking out the Germanic influences on later Castilian institutions. But he had just begun to journey down these several avenues when the politics of the Second Republic offered its distractions, soon followed by the terrible dislocations in his life engendered by the Civil War. These themes were destined to be more fully developed during his long Argentine exile.

En torno a los orígenes del feudalismo, a three-volume study of the origins of feudalism that in some minds is his greatest work, was written in Bordeaux and published in Argentina in 1942. Sánchez-Albornoz's close study of the chronicles and other Arabic evidence led him to challenge Heinrich Brunner's famous argument that Charles Martel had introduced horse warfare for his military retainers as a result of fighting the "mobile" Muslims at Tours in 733. Don Claudio demolished Brunner's thesis by demonstrating that (1) there were clear precedents for feudal practices in earlier Visigothic tradition; (2) the Iberian Arabs and Berbers utilized primarily camels as mounts in the period, not horses; and (3) the Muslim force that fought at Tours was infantry-centered, much the same as that of the Franks. These volumes on feudalism made him internationally famous. In the following year Sánchez-Albornoz published his study on the disintegration of the Roman towns in Iberia during the Germanic invasions, laying the framework for his hypothesis that the influence of Germanic tradition exceeded that of Roman civilization in Spanish institutional development. His studies on Muslim chronicles and Visigothic prefeudalism soon followed. The first harvests of Argentine exile were rich indeed.

A serious distraction for Sánchez-Albornoz was the publication of Américo Castro's *España en su historia* in 1948 (reworked several times thereafter, and published in English as *The Structure of Spanish History*). One might have expected Don Claudio to ignore it, since Castro's book concentrated on the late Middle Ages and was written by a philologist with a focus on cultural behaviorism, not fields in which Sánchez-Albornoz had either interest or expertise. However, Castro's conclusion that a close blending of Christian, Muslim, and Jewish cultures was the basic framework for

Spanish history ran counter to Sánchez-Albornoz's concept, informed by institutional documentation, of a Reconquest-centered Spain in which Muslim and Jewish influences were marginal. The debate tends to be more familiar to the English-speaking audience from Castro's side. Written primarily at Princeton University, Castro's works have rarely lacked an English translator. Moreover, literary historians have tended to support his literature-based arguments. Sánchez-Albornoz's enormous output has on the other hand rarely had the advantage of an English translation, and his lengthy two-volume rebuttal of Castro, *España, un enigma histórico* (1956), received only a belated and inadequate English translation. The two Spanish exiles largely talked past each other, and Sánchez-Albornoz's intense rejection of Muslim and Jewish influences seemed to many to border on anti-Semitism. The controversy did provoke him to extend his model for Spanish history across a vast canvas, an extension achieved more by theorizing than by the dense citation of sources to which his followers had become accustomed. The debate between the two models has continued down to the present, generating more heat than light.

The main thrust of Sánchez-Albornoz's work continued to be the elaboration and extension of his early institutional concepts. He remained hampered by the limits of the sources he had been able to bring to Argentina, and his nonperson status in Franco's Spain tended to cut him off from his natural audience, including some of his former colleagues at the *Anuario*, who often refused to review his work. Still he created, edited, reedited, restated, and continually revised his theses. Two of these, *Despoblación y repoblación del valle Duero* (1966), his documentation of the depopulation and subsequent repopulation of the Duero valley by the early Asturian kings, and "El ejército y la guerra en el reino asturleonés, 718–1037" (1968), his study of the Asturo-Leonese military establishment presented at Spoleto, are important summations and documentations of his earlier ideas. Thereafter Sánchez-Albornoz increasingly concentrated on collecting and republishing his past writings, sometimes with changes. When his visit to Spain allowed the completion of his volume in the Menéndez Pidal series La España Cristiana de los Siglos VIII al XI, he himself admitted that it was a synthesis of his earliest work that had won the Covadonga Prize of 1922 and a series of articles that had been published many years before his return. We can only conjecture how powerful a synthesis it might have been had he written it while still in full possession of his creative powers, in close proximity to the archives, in the company of his professional peers in Spain. The stress of exile took its greatest toll here, adding an occasional touch of stridency to his argument, an echo of isolation.

Sánchez-Albornoz's underlying assumptions were those of a Germanist who believed that German institutions had been more influential than Roman in the making of European civilization. He had been clearly influenced by the scientific approach of Leopold von Ranke, with its emphasis on documents, and by the socioeconomic ideas of Marc Bloch. His disciples in Spain (especially L.G. de Valdeavellano, J.M. Lacarra, L. Vázquez de Parga, and Carmen Pescador) and in Latin America (especially Hilda Grassotti and Carmen Carlé) would have these same aspects basic to their work. Affected by the linguistic studies of Ramón Menéndez Pidal, Don Claudio also accepted the centrality of Castile in Spanish history. Moreover, while it was no more than coincidence that he was born in the same year that Frederick Jackson Turner first propounded his Frontier Thesis, this conceptualization also found its way into his work. Sánchez-Albornoz synthesized these influences into his own distinctive view of pre-Roman, Roman, and Visigothic Iberia, as well as the Asturo-Leonese epoch he studied so closely.

Don Claudio's greatest overall contribution to the discipline of history consisted in the application of these extra-Peninsular approaches to Spain's past. Like the intellectuals of many other nations, Spaniards have tended to view their history as a unique experience, failing to notice that their challenges, struggles, triumphs, and failures, along with the forces that shaped them, often have close parallels in European and non-Western history. Spanish historians badly needed the historiographical jolt that Sánchez-Albornoz would apply to Peninsular history. However, it is ironic that the Albornozan methodology led the scholar to reformulate in yet a new way the older notion that Spain was unique. This theory of *unicidad nueva* has provoked a great deal of criticism. One can see this best by examining his major thematic interests and the support and controversy they subsequently met with.

Sánchez-Albornoz argued that a particular period shaped Spain, the early Middle Ages during which the Asturo-Leonese state first developed. Many of his critics have been Romanists who believed that he sold antiquity short. Others, like Castro, saw the formative period in the later Middle Ages, still others in the age of the Catholic Kings or the Hapsburg period. J.M. Pérez-Prendes and others question whether any one period can profoundly shape the distant ages to come. Suffice it to say that while all historians are inclined to see as especially important the period they have chosen to examine, Don Claudio made a strong case for the early Middle Ages. From the point of view of an institutional historian the period that formed, both inside and outside Iberia, the territorial monarchies that evolved into the Western nation-states has strong claims in this regard.

The support lent by Albornozan theory to Castilian dominance has provoked much negative response. Spanish scholars with cultural and research interests in the other regions recognize Castile's predominance in the Peninsula in population and territorial extent, as well as its role in absorbing and dominating (critics would argue imperializing) the remainder of Iberia. Nonetheless, Sánchez-Albornoz has been justifiably criticized for imposing a Castilian model on the evolution of the other Spanish cultures and regions. Probably J.N. Hillgarth has made the most pointed critique; he notes important elements in the evolution of Catalan history that do not fit the Castilian mold. Hillgarth has also made a persuasive case for Castro's contention that Muslims and Jews were vital to Spanish and Castilian culture, not just Catalan. While Hillgarth's view, like Castro's, is shaped by a rich background in literary history, it must be admitted that Don Claudio theorized under the influence of a strong Castilian bias that has a long history in Spain. This does not rule out the possibility that forces that shaped Castilian history also operated in other places, but that measured point was not the one that Sánchez-Albornoz intended to make. Hillgarth has also taken exception to the Albornozan assumption that Visigothic tradition has uniformly shaped all regions in the Peninsula, again a kind of Castilian perception imposed throughout the Peninsula. This is a view shared in varying aspects by the Spanish historians Antonio Ubieto Arteta, Torres López, Marcelo Vigil, and Abilio Barbero.

Another interesting and provocative concept pressed by Sánchez-Albornoz was his view regarding the depopulation of the Duero valley by King Alfonso I during the middle of the eighth century and its repopulation by Cantabrian, Castilian, and Basque settlers in the ninth and tenth centuries under the sponsorship of the growing Asturo-Leonese state. Don Claudio formed this conception from a close study of the early documents, which frequently offered the phraseology *eremavit, incultus atque desertus* ("barren, uncultivated and deserted") as a description of territories being absorbed. Whether true or not to the extent that he claimed, the *despoblado* theory has framed a major line of ensuing research. Here archaeology has provided a major addition to the arsenal of the historian, an approach from which Sánchez-Albornoz was blocked by his exile. Salvadore de Moxó has established important distinctions between the region north of the Duero and the zone to the south, and others have offered refinements east and west of the zone. Ramón Menéndez Pidal established a compromise position, to which others have adhered, that some small nuclei of residents remained in the area. This dispute has strong implications for the Albornozan position that independent small holders entered the empty lands south of Asturias as the first phase of Christian expansion. Given the dominance of pastoral activity in the region, it seems likely that numerous empty tracts of land existed to permit settlement by freeholders, and sparse settlement seems the only effective explanation for the rapid Asturo-Leonese expansion into the zone in the tenth century, a development that prepared the way for the ultimate domination of central Spain by León-Castile.

Closely tied to this theory, Sánchez-Albornoz postulated that an underdeveloped or immature form of the feudal system emerged in Spain during the tenth and eleventh centuries, a form lacking a fully developed feudal hierarchy, especially with regard to the inheritance and subinfeudation of fiefs. The open-land hypothesis combined this arrested-feudal-development thesis with the famous Albornozan dictum that Spain was an island of free peasants in the feudal sea of Europe. As García Cortázar has aptly noted, much of the debate rising from this view has centered on how one chooses to define "feudalism," "immaturity," and "Spain." Sánchez-Albornoz assumed the Bloch archetype of a fully developed feudal society, probably paying insufficient heed to the important adjustments in that definition made subsequently by those who followed Bloch. Here again Don Claudio fell victim to critics distressed by his imposition of a centrist, even Asturo-Leonese, experience on the entire Peninsula. Historians have had difficulty with the concept of "immature," since it assumes some kind of "mature" model that existed in the remainder of Europe for comparison. The essence of the criticism (voiced in Spain by Abilio Barbero, Marcelo Vigil, Reyna Pastor, Julio Valdeón Baruque, Luis G. de Valdeavellano, and P. Iradiel Murugarren and elsewhere by Pierre Bonnassie, Archibald Lewis, and Thomas Bisson, among others) is that feudalism took varying forms inside the Peninsula, and that these variances are not dissimilar to the varieties of feudal societies to be found north of the Pyrenees. Spain and even Castile share the European experience rather than being distinct from it. Nonetheless, while allowing for small compromises, Sánchez-Albornoz spared no ink in maintaining to the end his position on this question.

The issue of personal and political freedom in the history of Spain, so central to Don Claudio's own life, has also led to the creation of theories that have sparked controversy. He postulated a free peasantry, soon joined by the citizens of the frontier towns managed by a class of lower aristocrats, the *caballería popular* or *caballeros villanos*, whose ranks remained open to all who possessed and fought on a horse. These freemen and knightly classes gave Spaniards an unparalleled record of personal freedoms through the end of the Middle Ages. They functioned best by means of their municipal organizations (*concejos*), protected by their remarkably extensive law codes (*fueros*). Their representatives joined the Curia Regis of the kings to form parliamentary bodies, the Cortes in the late twelfth and early thirteenth centuries, well in advance of the other European monarchies. In Sánchez-Albornoz's view, as expressed in his 1956 *Enigma* study, their power to restrain monarchy was not overcome until the failed Communero revolt against Charles V in 1520 made them the victims of Hapsburg despotism. Other historians have called for modifications, pointing to a notable penetration of the Duero frontier in the late tenth century by great landlords and monastic settlements holding large estates. The Leonese kings sponsored this development to stabilize the frontier savaged by the raids of Al-Manzur, and these *ricos ombres* gained domination over many of the peasant settlers of the region. Critics also stress the ample evidence of the reduction of municipal independence by both kings and nobles in the fourteenth and fifteenth centuries, well before the outbreak of the Comunero uprising. However well either of these models explains Castilian developments, neither is useful for explaining Catalan evolution over the same epoch.

Most enduring of Sánchez-Albornoz's theories regarding the evolution of medieval Spain is that of the impact of the frontier on its history. For readers of English this view is best, if briefly, expressed in Don Claudio's "The Frontier and Castilian Liberties," a paper given in Austin, Texas, in 1959 and published in 1963. If one strips away the notion that the Reconquest means a formal reestablishment of the Visigothic monarchy in the Peninsula, and sees the period instead as more than seven hundred years of continuing territorial expansion, we have an influence that clearly affected all Peninsular monarchies, peoples, and institutions, although not always in the same way. The frontier application has always appealed more to American than to English and continental historians because the former are more acutely aware of the impact of this powerful force in the American West; thus the frontier concept intimately connects the Old World with the New. Charles Julian Bishko and Robert I. Burns are only two of the many Hispanic and American scholars who have mined this potentially rich vein.

Claudio Sánchez-Albornoz is remembered as a potent thinker who applied important twentieth-century theories and methodologies to the history of his native Spain, deriving conclusions that have meaning to historians well beyond his homeland. Not all of his conjectures have met with universal acceptance, and ambiguities and internal contradictions have confused his message, as with the question of the extent to which Spain is or is not "European." Peter Linehan has thus described him as "both the [John

Horace] Round and the [Edward Augustus] Freeman of medieval Spanish scholarship . . ." (Linehan [1985]: 1144). One might add the Bloch, the Turner, and the Pirenne, as well, inasmuch as Don Claudio compelled the generation that followed to come to terms with him, even if in disagreement. His not inconsiderable ego and the enforced isolation of his exile doubtless contributed to a sometimes disdainful tone that was often more apparent than real. His fondness for a good fight derived from his view that the resultant discussion advanced everyone's understanding. No historian more effectively evoked the concept of liberty in his life, words, and research than did this thoughtful and outspoken Abulense. Sánchez-Albornoz was a person to be reckoned with, as scholar, as thinker, and as a human being.

SELECTED BIBLIOGRAPHY
Works
BOOKS AND ARTICLES

"La potestad real y los señorios en Asturias, León y Castilla: los siglos VIII al XIII." *Revista de Archivos, Bibliotecas y Museos* 21 (Madrid, 1914): 263–90. Reprinted in his *Viejos y nuevos estudios sobre las instituciones medievales españolas.* 3 vols. Madrid: Espasa-Calpe, 1976, hereafter *VNE*.

La curia regia portuguesa en los siglos XII y XIII. Madrid: Junta para la Ampliación de Estudios e Investigaciones Científicas. Centro de Estudios Históricos, 1920.

"Las behetrías: la encomendación en Asturias, León y Castilla." *Anuario de Historia del Derecho Español* 1 (Madrid, 1924): 158–333, hereafter *AHDE*. Reprinted in his *VNE*.

Estampas de la vida en León durante el siglo X. Madrid: Revista de Archivos, 1926.

"Muchas páginas más sobre las behetrías." *AHDE* 4 (1927): 1–157. Reprinted in *VNE*.

"La primitiva organización monetaria de León y Castilla." *AHDE* 5 (1928): 301–24. Reprinted in his *VNE*.

"España y el Islam." *Revista de Occidente* 24 (Madrid, 1929): 1–30, hereafter *RO*. Reprinted in his *De la invasión islámica al Estado continental: Entre la creacion y el ensayo.* Sevilla: Universidad de Sevilla, 1974, hereafter *DI*.

En torno a los orígenes del feudalismo. 3 vols. Mendoza, Argentina: Universidad Nacional de Cuyo, 1942.

Ruina y extinción del municipio romano en España e instituciones que le reemplazan. Buenos Aires: Facultad de Filosofia y Letras, 1943.

"El precio de la vida en el reino asturleonés hace mil años." *Logos* 3 (1944): 225–64. Reprinted in his *VNE*.

"Dónde y cuándo murió Don Rodrigo, último rey de los godos." *Cuadernos de Historia de España* 3 (Buenos Aires, 1945): 1–105, hereafter *CHE*. Reprinted in his *Orígenes de la nación española: Estudio críticos sobre la Historia del reino de Asturias.* 3 vols. Oviedo: Instituto de Estudios Asturianos, 1972–75, hereafter *ON*.

La España musulmana: según los autores islamitas y cristianos medievales. 3 vols. Buenos Aires: El Ateneo, 1946.

"El culto al Emperador y la unificación de España." *Anales del Instituto de Literaturas Clásicas* 3 (1946): 1–120. Reprinted in his *Miscelanea de Estudios Históricos.* León: Centro de Estudios e Investigación "San Isidoro," 1970, hereafter *ME*.

"El aula regia y las asambleas políticas de los godos." *CHE* 3 (1946): 5–110.

"Asturias resiste: Alfonso el Casto salva a la España cristiana." *Logos* 5 (1946): 9–33.

El "Stipendium" hispano-godo y los orígenes del beneficio prefeudal. Buenos Aires: Facultad de Filosofia y Letras, 1947.

"La auténtica batalla de Clavijo." *CHE* 9 (1948): 94–136.

"Itinerario de la conquesta de España por los musulmanes." *CHE* 10 (1948): 21–74. Reprinted in his *ON; Orígenes del Reino de Pamplona: Su vinculación con el valle del Ebro.* Pamplona: Institución Principe de Viana, Diputación Foral de Navara, 1981, hereafter *OR; Vascos y navarros en su primera historia.* Madrid: Ediciones del Centro, 1974, hereafter *VNP.*

"Alfonso III y el particularismo castellano." *CHE* 13 (1950): 19–100. Reprinted in his *ON, VNP,* and *Investigaciones sobre Historiografía Hispana Medieval, Siglos VIII al XII <por> Claudio Sánchez-Albornoz.* Buenos Aires: Instituto de Historia de España, 1967.

"España y el feudalismo carolingio." In *Problemi della civiltà carolingia,* vol. 1, pp. 109–45. Spoleto: Panettoe Petrelli, 1954. Reprinted in his *VNE.*

España, un enigma histórico. 2 vols. Buenos Aires: Editorial Sudamericana, 1956. Translated as *Spain, a Historical Enigma* by Colette Joly Dees and David Sven Reher. 2 vols. Madrid: Fundación Universitaria Española, 1975.

"Problemas de la historia Navarra del siglo IX." *CHE* 25–26 (1957): 5–82. Reprinted in his *ME, OR, VNP,* and *Orígenes y destino de Navarra.* Barcelona: Planeta, 1984.

"El culto de Santiago no deriva del mito dioscórido." *CHE* 28 (1958): 5–42. Reprinted in his *ME* and *Del ayer de España: Tripticos históricos.* Madrid: Editorial Obras Selectas, 1973, hereafter *DE.*

"Tradición y derecho visigodos en León y Castilla." *CHE* 29–30 (1959): 244–65. Reprinted in his *Investigaciones y documentos sobre las instituciones hispanas.* Santiago de Chile: Editorial Juruidica de Chile, 1970, hereafter *ID.*

"Pervivencia y crisis de la tradición jurídica romana en la España goda." In *Il pasaggio dall'antichita al medioevo in Occidente,* pp. 128–99 and 221–32. Spoleto: Centro Italiano di studi sull'alto medioevo, 1962. Reprinted in his *VNE.*

"The Frontier and Castilian Liberties." In *The New World Looks at Its History,* edited by Archibald R. Lewis and Thomas F. McGann, pp. 27–46. Austin: University of Texas Press, 1963.

"¿Burgueses en la curia regia de Fernando II de León?" *Revista Portuguesa de Historia* 12 (1964, Lisbon): 1–35, hereafter *RPH.* Reprinted in his *ID.*

Despoblación y repoblación del valle Duero. Buenos Aires: Instituto de Historia de España, 1966.

"La pérdida de España I: el ejército visigodo: su proto-feudalización." *CHE* 43–44 (1967): 5–73. Reprinted in his *ID.*

"El ejército y la guerra en el reino asturleonés, 718–1037." In *Ordinamenti militari en Occidente nell'alto medioevo,* pp. 202–408. Spoleto: Centro italiano di studi sull'alto Medioeva, 1968. Reprinted in his *ID.*

"Repoblaciones del reino asturleonés: proceso, dinámica y proyecciones." *CHE* 53–54 (1971): 236–461. Reprinted in his *DE, VNE.*

"Homines mandationis y iuniores." *CHE* 53–54 (1973 for 1971): 1–235. Reprinted in his *VNE.*

"Commissa, comitatus, mandationes." In *Studi storici in onore di Ottorino Bertolini.* Vol. 2, pp. 169–655. Pisa: Pacini, 1972.

"El Fuero de León: su temprana redacción unitaria." In *León y su historia.* Vol. 2. León: Centro de Estudios e Investigación San Isidoro, 1972. Reprinted in his *VNE.*

"Sobre el acta de consagración de la iglesia de Compostela en 889." In *Festschrift in Honor of the Rev. Joseph M. F. Marique, S.J.,* edited by P. T. Brannon, pp. 275–92. Worcester, Mass.: Institute for Early Christian Iberian Studies, 1975.

"El palatium regis asturleonés." *CHE* 59–60 (1976): 5–104. Reprinted in his *VNE.*

"Los judios en el reino asturleonés." *CHE* 61–62 (1978 for 1977): 343–56. Reprinted in his *VNE.*

El régimen de la tierra en el reino asturleonés hace milaños. Buenos Aires: Instituto de Historia de España, 1978.

La España cristiana de los siglos VIII al XI: el Reino Astur-Leonés (722–1037). Vol. 7 of *Historia de España.* Edited by José María Jover Zamora. Madrid: Espasa-Calpe, 1980.

LETTERS AND PAPERS

The documents and papers of Claudio Sánchez-Albornoz are deposited in the Fundación Sánchez-Albornoz in Avila, Spain.

Sources

García de Cortázar, José Angel. "La inmadurez del feudalismo español." *RO* 50 (1985): 35–64.

Glick, Thomas F. *Islamic and Christian Spain in the Early Middle Ages.* Princeton, N.J.: Princeton University Press, 1979.

Hillgarth, J.N. "Spanish Historiography and Iberian Reality." *History and Theory* 24 (1985): 23–43.

Ladero Quesada, M.A. "Presentación." *En la España Medieval* 5 (1986, Madrid): 13–18, hereafter *EEM.*

Linehan, Peter. "A History of Isolation." *Times Literary Supplement* (11 October 1985): 1144.

———. *History and the Historians of Medieval Spain.* Oxford: Clarendon, 1993.

Pérez-Prendes, J.M. "Semblanza y obra de don Claudio Sánchez-Albornoz." *EEM* 5 (1986): 19–52.

Powers, James F. "Frontier Municipal Baths and Social Interaction in Thirteenth-Century Spain." *American Historical Review* 84 (1979): 649–67.

Valdeavellano, Luis G. de. "Don Claudio Sánchez-Albornoz y Menduiña." *Boletín de la Real Academia de la Historia* 181 (Madrid, 1984): 337–45.

———. "El tema y los temas de Sánchez-Albornoz." *RO* 50 (1985): 7–20.

Valdeón Baruque, Julio. "Castilla y España: de Sánchez-Albornoz a nuestros días." *RO* 50 (1985): 21–34.

PERCY ERNST SCHRAMM

(1894–1970)

János Bak

Percy Ernst Schramm, one of the major researchers of the medieval state and the founder of systematic research into the iconography of rulership, was born on 14 October 1894 in Hamburg. A scion of a prominent Hamburg burgher family, which could look back to at least nine generations of leading citizens in the Hanseatic city—Schramm's father, Max, was mayor—Schramm grew up in elegant, Anglophile (witness his first name) patrician wealth. That idyll was destroyed by World War I, a shock that perhaps made Schramm choose as a motto (now at the head of his unpublished memoirs) the words of T.S. Eliot: "Human kind cannot bear very much reality" (*Murder in the Cathedral*, Act II).

As a patriotic young *Rittmeister* (cavalry captain) in 1916, he soon realized the futility and tragedy of the war. Afterward he was shattered by the collapse of both the German empire and peaceful prosperity. In the interwar years, like many members of the professional middle classes, more frightened by the Bolshevik danger than the menace from the right, Schramm supported Field Marshal Hindenburg and briefly even the National Socialists, but these political escapades did not color his historical studies. He saw Germany embark on barbarian internal politics and on a war that he knew could not be won. Schramm spent the last third of his life explaining to the postwar generations of Germans what that war, in which he had served as diarist to the German High Command, meant and who Hitler was. In the late fifties medievalists were a small minority among the doctoral candidates at Schramm's weekly seminars. The others were all studying some aspect of World War II, the German documents of which Schramm was editing in those years. Another important, if smaller, group of writings—about Hamburg and the achievements of the German merchant (written mainly during the Nazi era and the war years, when the German bourgeoisie and urban values were attacked by Goebbels)—will not be treated here. The following biography and bibliography will cover at most two-thirds of its subject's scholarly output. There remains to be summarized, nonetheless, the rich scholarly life of a great teacher, one of the last of those grand-seignorial professors who used to characterize German academia but—maybe because of his burgher background, maybe under the influence of his American experience in 1933—lacking their proverbial haughtiness.

Percy Ernst Schramm's interest in history began early in his high-school years with the study of the past of his hometown and family in the Hanseatic city archives. It was enhanced and widened by his filial friendship with a fellow Hamburg patrician, the art historian Aby Warburg. After the war Schramm completed his studies in Heidelberg, where in 1922 he received his doctorate with a thesis on the age of Emperor Otto III. Two years later he became Dr. habil. (or *Privatdozent*, the advanced degree necessary to become professor) with a study of imperial ideas from the ninth century to the twelfth, which came to be the basis of his first important book, *Kaiser, Rom und Renovatio* (1929). Between 1923 and 1926 he worked with Harry Bresslau at the great workshop of medieval studies, the Monumenta Germaniae Historica, on the edition of the charters of Emperor Henry III and other projects. In 1929 Schramm was offered the chair of medieval history in Göttingen, recommended by the famous early-modern historian Karl Brandi, and for four decades he remained connected to the Universitas Georgia Augusta.

In 1925 Schramm married a fellow historian, daughter of a well-known Prussian family, Ehrengard (Eta) von Thadden (1900–1985), a student of modern Greek history. They had three sons. The oldest, Jost (b. 1926), remained true to the family's roots and became an architect in Hamburg. Gottfried (b. 1929) is professor of history in Freiburg im Breisgau. The youngest, Gebhard (b. 1932), is an engineer in Karlsruhe. Ehrengard Schramm-von Thadden was a dynamic partner. When family duties, which during the war years were formidable and included the care of many refugees, finally permitted, she completed her second book on modern Greece. She became active first in city politics, and finally sat as a Social Democratic member of the Lower Saxony State Legislature for several parliamentary periods. Her interest in Greece brought about the foundation of a German-Greek cooperative project helping thousands of youth from the Peloponnesus to study abroad. With her husband she hosted the famed Sunday dinners to which selected pupils were invited. For many decades the guests also had the pleasure of conversing with Percy's mother (born O'swald), a fine lady and critical reader of her son's books.

At the time of the Nazi takeover Schramm was Shreve Fellow at Princeton, where he tried to explain in positive terms German feelings regarding a national renewal. When he arrived home, however, he was faced with open attacks from National Socialist professors and local potentates for his international connections and open-mindedness. The subsequent atrocities against Jews and oppositionists cured him of any initial illusion he may have had about the new regime. During the war the Gestapo became ever more interested in him and his family, especially when his sister-in-law, Elisabeth von Thadden, was arrested and executed as a member of the Resistance. Friends of Schramm secured him a professionally suitable position in the Wehrmacht as keeper of the official diary of the High Command, where he could safely serve until the end of the war. When the front collapsed, he rescued, in truly adventurous ways, much of the official war diary, acting against explicit orders that called for its destruction—something his historian's heart could not accept. A POW of the United States Army, he volunteered to be a witness for the defense of General Jodl at the Nuremberg trials. His attention from then on was split between medievalist and modern studies. Both of them brought him national and international attention and fame, his modernist efforts attracting more controversy, to be sure, than his medievalist ones. The absurdity that his activities should qualify him to be a "war criminal" has been put forth, unjustly and inaccurately, only by Norman Cantor (92). An official chronicler of military operations, however highly placed, can hardly be compared to masters of slave laborers or commanders of troops committing atrocities.

A recipient of numerous honors, Schramm was perhaps most pleased to be a member of the papal commission that opened the Bernini tabernacle containing an ancient throne called the Cathedra Petri in St. Peter's in Rome, and established, as Schramm had demonstrated from written and pictorial evidence many years before, that the venerated treasure of the Roman church was in fact a gift to the pope by Charles the Bald. In 1958 Schramm became a member of the highly prestigious German order "Pour le Mérite" in Scholarship and Art, and in 1963 was named its chancellor. He remained active to the last days of his life, working on, among many other projects, the publication of his collected studies on medieval kingship, *Kaiser, Könige und Päpste*. In these volumes Schramm surveyed his entire life's work, added and corrected details, augmented the bibliography, and injected personal reminiscences and anecdotes that make the books a joy to read. He was able to edit five volumes (published in 1968–71) before his death on 12 November 1970. Posthumous volumes were planned but never materialized: no one could match the devoted collecting and personal editorial efforts of the author.

Schramm learned to read fast early in life and was able to assimilate enormous amounts of information. He organized this lifelong collection of data with a critic's eye and from it culled numerous references and images. Not only was his study overflowing with notes written on the backs of papers (perhaps a frugal habit from his burgher past or from the years of rationing), as well as photographs and sketches, but his students also often received such scribblings with bibliographical or other references, frequently on picture postcards sent from faraway countries by the avid traveler, with the inimitable brief "Greetings, P.E.S." at the end. Schramm was a great storyteller, and in lectures students often did not realize the deeper importance of an anecdote until the professor came to the point at the end. His house—Herzberger Landstrasse 66, high above the university city, surrounded by the villas of scholars whose names like his are recalled on marble plaques and by generations of students—was always open to his pupils and to many friends and visitors from Germany and abroad. In the mornings he liked to walk down the Nikolausberger Weg to the old building of the Historisches Seminar, accompanied by a student or an assistant, telling about his last night's readings and the ideas they brought to his mind. In a lecture given maybe an hour later, on "Selected Chapters of Medieval Intellectual History" (one of his favorite titles), the companion may have been amazed to hear a fully formulated ("ready-to-print") presentation of those newly conceived ideas.

Although published second among his books, Schramm's first major project was *Kaiser, Rom und Renovatio* (1929). It is still a classic on the interrelation of ancient and medieval concepts in the formulation of imperial ideas in Carolingian and Ottonian times, particularly around the year 1000. The book follows the evidence, demonstrating how idea and reality of ancient and Christian Rome exercised the minds of early-medieval thinkers and rulers. Schramm demonstrated that the young "dreamer" Otto III and his teacher Gerbert of Aurillac (later Pope Sylvester) were the most devoted adherents of a Christian "renewal" of Roman greatness rather than engineers of a "German empire," as many political historians have argued then and now. Schramm emphasized the Christian-universalist character of the "dream" of Otto and Sylvester, in stark contrast to the imperialist ideas of his times. His later articles on Poland and the year 1000 also underline the fact that the medieval "new Europe" that Otto III envisaged was different from the "new order" preached by German nationalists and later by the Nazis. Much has been written since about that great turning point in central European history, but Schramm's monograph with its rich collection of relevant texts and images has not become obsolete.

While completing *Kaiser, Rom und Renovatio* Schramm embarked on a field that was to define five decades of his scholarly life. As an omen for his future main interests the inspiration came from a picture: the illuminated double page of a gospel book in the Munich Staatsbibliothek, depicting Emperor Otto III presented with tributes and gifts (Cod. Lat. monac. 4453 fol. 23v, 24r). This magnificent image not only summarized the ideas inherent in Otto III's *renovatio* but pointed to a series of problems central to the understanding of medieval rulership. Inspired by the miniature, Schramm later wrote, "I felt that it is deeply classical but at the same time unmistakably medieval. It raised a series of questions in my mind." The search for answers led him to the study of book illumination, medieval art, Byzantine iconography and its impact on Latin culture, and more.

A lecture on the image of rulers in the early Middle Ages given in 1923 at the Warburg Library in Hamburg marked the inauguration of Schramm's iconological research. The choice of place was no coincidence, for the work done at the library and the writings of the circle of Aby Warburg, including Ernst Cassirer, Fritz Saxl, and Erwin Panofsky, were crucial for Schramm's initial orientation and scholarly development. However, he contested several of their notions on the "survival of antiquity," finding them too mechanical and negligent of the medieval millennium. He also found that the Warburg circle was lacking proper appreciation of the nonclassical (Germanic or Slavic) roots of the European Middle Ages. Schramm insisted that the coexistence and conflict of these diverse elements characterized medieval ideas and institutions; he never tired of rejecting the romanticized and nationalistic overestimation of Germanic constituents, as argued by many, especially in the Third Reich.

Schramm's first published book, *Die deutschen Kaiser und Könige in Bildern ihrer Zeit* (1928), was an annotated catalog of images of German kings and emperors on seals, coins, manuscripts, and other objects from 751 to 1152. In addition to presenting a critical list of images this study presaged several of Schramm's later conclusions about continuity and change and about the use of pictorial models and their transmission. One of his most important insights concerned the function of the images of rulers. Schramm abandoned as anachronistic the earlier approach that concerned itself with the likeness of the portrait and person. Most images of rulers were not made to commemorate the features of a king or emperor but were aimed at conveying essential traditional features that identified the ruler *qua* ruler. The person's dress, insignia, gestures, and position were what was emphasized. Schramm explored this "presentational" character of the iconography as evidence for the "idea of the state" not only in *Kai-*

ser und Könige but in additional studies on Carolingian and Ottonian portraiture as well.

These investigations drew Schramm's attention to the politically momentous "liturgical plays" in which the insignia of rulership were transferred to the new ruler. The coronation *ordines* (scripts and stage directions for these "constitutional spectacles" of the Middle Ages), give life to the emblems of rulership, augmenting them with political and theological allegory and symbolism. Mostly in opposition to the ecclesiastical historian Eduard Eichmann, and in harmony with Carl Erdmann, Schramm proceeded to edit, date, and categorize the early coronation orders of the West Frankish, Anglo-Saxon, and German kingdoms. Much of this work is still the basis for *ordines* studies, even though several datings and filiations suggested by Schramm have been refuted or corrected. This research led Schramm to the processes of intricate borrowing and returning and the multifarious interrelationships among European kingdoms in transferring forms and ideas and adapting them to local conditions, themes that became central in his later work.

Schramm envisioned a comparative survey of medieval kingship in the light of its symbology, to be composed together with pupils and colleagues. A sketch of the history of English coronation (1937) appeared first, somewhat hurriedly completed for the inauguration of King George VI, and secured Schramm a seat as spectator in Westminster Abbey. (It is ironic that this book was the only full-length work by Schramm translated into English from the German original.) The two volumes on the king of France, *Der König von Frankreich: Das Wesen der Monarchie vom 9. zum 16. Jahrhundert, ein Kapitel aus der Geschichte des abendländischen Staates* (1939), offer a better model of what can be gained by a historical and analytical study of this kind. Considering the political nature of such a study, it may be worth noting that Schramm published the book about the French monarchy, evincing appreciation for French political development, at a time of the Nazi attack on France and when other German medievalists published books on the Carolingian Treaty of Verdun with the purpose of legitimizing Hitler's aggression. In the Germany of the 1930s positive treatment of French subjects was the expression of opposition, admittedly mild, to Nazi Germanomania. Schramm's book begins by surveying West Frankish and French kingship, with a history of succession, election or approbation, and inauguration from Charles the Bald to Saint Louis. The change from elective to hereditary succession, and the assertion of the exclusive right of the archbishop of Reims to crown and anoint the king and of the monastery of Saint-Denis to keep the Holy Ampulla, are important points in this process. A survey of "royal myth" and "monarchical religion" under Louis IX is followed by a detailed study of the coronation ceremony and the symbology of rulership in its mature thirteenth-century form. What Schramm referred to as "coagulation" (*Verdichtung*) of the state from personal rule to abstract institution is demonstrated by the analysis of events and ideas surrounding the accession and consecration of the ruler. Schramm observed that the French monarchy, unlike the English, became the essence of the state, and the monarchic state, unlike the German-Roman empire, became identified with the nation.

This argument, one of the few syntheses formulated by Schramm, seems to be valid not only for the Western Frankish realm. Comparing the metamorphoses of medieval kingship with progress in science and technology, Schramm wrote (my translation):

> In regard to the state the process is entirely different. It does not develop from the simpler to the more sophisticated but changes from a still undefined condition to a well-circumscribed one, that is, to a stage where the forms are more filled out with content than before. The tribal empires of the migration period, held together by ties of kinship . . . become territorial realms in the Middle Ages. They are formed by men who do not know each other any more . . . , and it is from these kingdoms that the modern nation-states "coagulate," not in a straight, linear process but through considerable detours and backslides that can still be recognized in the diversity of European states. The farther back we look in time the less the word "state" can be appropriately applied, as it is inevitably defined by anachronistic notions. . . . To write the history of the medieval state is to show how kingship changed from an honor with certain rights and duties to an institution that surpasses the individual. This institution is abstract enough to be transferred, at the demise of the father, to the son. Its justification derives from faith, law, history, and a concept of world order. Having reached this point, it will become apparent that there is something that is common to ruler and people, in which the king is only a carrier of certain defined functions: and that is the state [Schramm (1939), 1: 1–2].

Although Schramm completed no study of this magnitude for other European countries, a number of articles on the Spanish kingdoms and a few of the sixty-odd doctoral dissertations supervised by him mark the road toward the planned great survey. However, he did assemble a monumental collection of evidence for such an enterprise, the three volumes on insignia and rulership symbology titled *Herrschaftszeichen und Staatssymbolik* (1954–56). Schramm called this work, published in the Schriften series of the Monumenta Germaniae Historica, a foundation for a *corpus regalitatis medii aevi*. Having investigated the different functions of objects associated with the rulers and other persons in authority (judges, prelates, officers), Schramm suggested a refined classification of "signs" (*Zeichen*). Those actually worn or carried by a ruler as visible emblems of his invisible office he termed *Herrschaftszeichen*. As the medieval king "stood for" the authority that can be called "the state," so the insignia "stood for" him. These insignia of rulership became the subjects of Schramm's major medievalist studies after World War II, when he attempted a truly panEuropean survey. The three *Herrschaftszeichen* volumes constitute the centerpiece. Their fifty constituent studies, including the contributions of nine collaborators coordinated by the editor with extensive indexes, form a veritable handbook of insignia. Two "vertical" studies introduce the work: the first, "From the Roman Emperor's *trabea triumphalis* Through the Byzantine *lorum* to the *stola* of Western Rulers: An Example of the Changes in Form and Meaning Through the Centuries and Through Their Transfer from One Country to Another," and the second, "The Spiritual and Secular Miter, with Digressions on the Papal Tiara." The rest of the sections are chronologically and topically organized. Covering the period from prehistory through the late sixteenth century, they treat golden bows, rings, swords, lances, scepters, crowns, and thrones, as well as royal iconography on coins and seals, diplomatic evidence for royal presentation, and the use of crowns, crown wearing, and coronation in lands from Scotland to Sicily, from Byzantium to the Scandinavian north and Poland in the east. If one adds the notes and sketches now published in the collected works, with papers on Russia, southeast Europe, and Spain, one can see what Schramm conceived of as medieval European unity.

Herrschaftszeichen und Staatssymbolik was augmented by additional special studies. In cooperation with Josef Deér and Olle Källström Schramm published in 1955 a study of the insignia of Frederick II of Hohenstaufen. Dedicated to Ernst H. Kantorowicz, it adds a valuable dimension to Kantorowicz's biography of the emperor, the "wonder of the world." Schramm often claimed that with the help of insignia the historian can penetrate to a medieval ruler's personal perception of his estate and office. The insignia of Frederick do indeed lead us near to the man: we know that the Byzantine-style closed crown, the *kamelaukion*, found in the grave of Constanza, Frederick's first wife, was placed by the bereaved king into the sarcophagus with his own hands. Schramm proved that a crown presently in Stockholm was bequeathed by Frederick to the reliquary of his remote relative Saint Elizabeth of Thuringia, whose *elevatio* he attended barefooted, in a penitent's robes.

A short study published in 1957 (in reality raw material gathered for further investigation of the uses of insignia) offers textual evidence on insignia presented to churches and princes, sold, mortgaged, or otherwise alienated. With some sketches on the wearing of crowns this study was to show the different functions of the insignia beyond their "signifying" character. In 1958 a special volume, *Sphaira-Globus-Reichsapfel*, was devoted to a single symbol and insignia, the orb. The subtitle is "Wanderings and Metamorphoses of an Insigne from Caesar to Elizabeth II." Schramm intended this richly illustrated though motley collection—it includes everything spherical connected with rulership—as a commentary on his old controversy with the Warburg school: the survival of antiquity. Hardly any object fitting the proposed framework, from antique globes to the Atomium at the 1958 Brussels Expo escaped his attention; but the completeness is not matched by the traditional thoroughness. The work triggered a discussion about the transformation of a late-antique and Byzantine symbol ("iconographic reality") into an actual object included in western rulers' set of insignia—a *Herrschaftszeichen* proper. Probably Josef Deér was right when he challenged Schramm's view about a western "misunderstanding" of a Byzantine abstraction (Deér [1961]: 291ff.). Whatever the case may be, the debate clarified a number of theoretical and methodological issues.

One of Schramm's last medieval works, prepared in collaboration with an art historian, is an impressive volume that widened the scope of the corpus he was about to assemble. The *Denkmale der deutschen Könige und Kaiser* (1962) contains a splendidly illustrated catalog of several hundred objects connected with German rulers from the early Middle Ages to the time of Frederick II. *Denkmale* would be poorly translated by "monuments." Yet with the use of this antiquated word Schramm intended to convey the notion of souvenirs, antiquities, and memorials at the same time. An introduction stakes out the wide range of objects. The proposed survey includes not only the "things" connected with royal presentation proper—that is, insignia in the widest sense—but everything that was in any way connected with the ruler. Since many of these were not as durable as valuable jewels or precious manuscripts, the collection amounts to an "imaginary museum." In his introductory study Schramm reconstructs what constituted the "hoard" (*Hort*) of a ruler in the Middle Ages. Many of these objects did not play immediate roles in such obvious political acts as a coronation or a festive court assembly, but Schramm implied that nothing that was connected with the ruler can be regarded as irrelevant to the "public presentation" of rulership and the state. Displayed at festive occasions or in daily business, bequeathed to churches or laypeople, given away in dowries or included in the show of gifts received from subjects or foreign rulers—all of these objects played a role in royal symbology.

In retrospect, one might say that the *Denkmale* volume answered the questions raised by the Otto miniature. The program set out by Schramm fifty years before has been well-nigh fulfilled at least for the medieval empire and, partially, for the major countries of Europe. Schramm wrote about his program (my translation):

> While in the times of Georg von Below it could be disputed whether there existed a "state" in the Middle Ages at all, our attention is focused rather on the essential differences between the medieval and the modern state. Medieval kingdoms were "less of a state" to the degree that they contained "primitive" components; but, rooted as the medieval state was in religious tradition, with its ruler surrounded by a genuine aura of holiness surpassing even the theatrical glamour of the Baroque, it included elements modern states lack [Schramm (1954), 1: 1].

Most of the "things"—objects, images, texts—and "show" actions of kings and emperor were inspected and analyzed; a symbology of the medieval state was outlined. The problems raised in the discussions of late nineteenth-century constitutional historians like Georg von Below were not wholly solved by this work alone, but many of the characteristics that distinguish the medieval from the modern state became clearer to our eyes. The insignia and their public display, if understood in the context of their medieval significance, can show the elements added to the personal rule of the tribal era, making it "more of a state." The interaction between secular and spiritual concepts, the admixture of religious notions and "political" ones, are well illustrated in the imagery of rulership.

Schramm explored three major avenues in his attempt to reconstruct the form and meaning of medieval royal symbology: the investigation of existing objects or pictures and descriptions of them; the evaluation of written evidence about the usage and significance of "signs"; and a critical survey of the images of rulers as information about their insignia.

Schramm delineated the methods for the analysis of these pieces of evidence in his introduction to a dissertation by Berend Schwineköper, "The Gauntlet in Law, Administration, Custom and Folklore" (1938). These methods of analysis may be regarded as his methodological testament to future historians. First, the evidence has to be ordered and distinguished clearly according to its origin. In the field of symbology, however, it is often overlooked that the words of an imaginative poet, of a monk secluded from the world, and of a legally minded and schooled author of the royal entourage have to be weighed differently. As the use and interpretation of signs and symbols never became standardized, typical practice or accepted understanding must be, as far as possible, distinguished from the unique exception or individual fancy.

Pieces of evidence from different times and places are to be kept apart. This second requirement may sound self-evident, but the temptation of all-round comparison has induced many historians to disregard it. Schramm was careful to point out the limitations of ethnographic comparison, for which he cited the work of James G. Frazer and what we may now call the methods of social anthropology. Though he acknowledged the contribution of the author of *The Golden Bough* in having suggested unthought-of connections across centuries and continents, Schramm felt that historians should now trace the dissimilar, the singular, that which belonged to a certain society in a defined period of time.

Permanence and continuity must be considered simultaneously with change and transformation. This was the gist of Schramm's polemic against the Warburg school. By looking simultaneously at continuity and change Schramm never ceased to emphasize that medieval people were not only heirs and transmitters but also creators, who in the spirit of what they inherited produced new symbols, transformed and reinterpreted old ones, disjoined them and rearranged them in new forms to suit new content. It is in this context that Schramm's endeavor to take account of the Byzantine sphere in our understanding of the Latin Middle Ages has to be understood. In the world of symbology and of insignia Byzantium stood as a pole of stability and continuity. When Schramm began his studies of medieval symbology, most European medievalists regarded the Orthodox East as a field of study in itself, with little relevance to the history of the West. The ongoing debates between Schramm and Deér, and other Byzantinists, as well as the cooperation with Byzantine scholars like André Grabar, were new features and opened the eyes of many a continental scholar to the Byzantine roots of much western medieval symbology and iconography.

Schramm taught that the idioms of the symbolic language of the Middle Ages constitute a complex unity: visible signs, insignia, symbols, symbolic gestures and "as if" presentations (e.g., when dukes acted at the king's table "as if" they were his household servants; in general when actions or objects stand for others, usually in the sense of *pars pro toto* or simple for complicated). In "as if" presentations metaphor and allegory are the main genres of the symbological "sign system" of the Middle Ages. Like insignia they must be considered in their full complexity. Schramm did not try to answer the question of why the Middle Ages were so enchanted by the allegorical, analogical, metaphorical view. As with many other ontological problems he simply presented the evidence for its numerous manifestations. Yet summarizing his findings, he pointed to the "unique ability of medieval men to dress the invisible mysteries in a visible garment and to spy out the hidden invisible meaning in the visible object" (Schramm [1968–71], 4/2: 671).

Schramm demanded careful use of terminology. Warburg's insistence on the use of appropriate terms made him aware of the need for categories, the establishment of which itself constituted a step toward analysis. He was almost obsessed by the program of making terms into *Greifwerkzeuge*, tools to "apprehend." He tried to replace the word "source" (*Quelle*) by "testimony" or "evidence" (*Zeugnis*), arguing that the former stemmed from an unjustified retrospection by the modern researcher. He also wished to ban that "misleading metaphor," influence, from the historian's vocabulary. Though he may not have succeeded in all these endeavors, Schramm enriched the inventory of technical terms in his field of study, symbology, by several "apprehending tools," distinguishing precisely among signs, ensigns, symbols, attributes, and so on. Schramm's terminology has a heuristic advantage. Whether an object (e.g., an orb) depicted in the hand of the emperor is a "symbol"—that is, a pictorial abbreviation for an abstract content—or an actual sign or insigne, which the ruler displayed in real life, makes a difference.

Schramm's contribution to scholarship is above all his work on the images and symbols of rulership. The methodological elaboration of iconography as source and evidence for political notions secures him a place among the innovators in medieval scholarship. Pictures of historical personalities and remnants of imperial garments were certainly studied by earlier historians. They were, however, seen as mere illustrations of statements derived from textual evidence. Schramm gave the testimony of signs, symbols, and images, correctly analyzed, equal standing with other sources of information.

There is in Schramm's oeuvre more raw material, or rather "half-manufactured product," than "processed goods." Schramm was not the only German historian after World War II who shied away from writing an all-inclusive history of an institution, country, or epoch. The lessons learned from grand syntheses based on the philosophies of the past hundred years counseled modesty. Yet along the road of collecting the evidence a formidable frame of methodological propositions was erected. Schramm realized, though he did not state it in so many words, that the answers to his questions were to be found by systematic and exhaustive survey of the evidence. Many studies on medieval kingship and the state drew conclusions from selected samples; but this is possible only if a preconceived frame is to be filled out with examples. Schramm's undertaking took into account the fact that differences between medieval and modern states lay in the minutiae. He attempted to survey all the available data, their descriptions, and the interpretations given to them. His works often have the character of virtual museums in attempting complete coverage. They resemble warehouses of building materials, well-sorted and organized, cleaned from accretions, ready to be used for a monumental construction of a history of medieval kingship. They could be mistaken for an antiquarian's collection were they not accompanied by such a scrupulous methodological commentary, which in itself constitutes an important stage of the building. Still the modern reader cannot overlook a certain one-sidedness in Schramm's medieval studies. He was interested almost exclusively in the rulers, rarely glancing even at their entourage and their aristocratic or clerical helpers. He justified this position once by stating (my translation):

> In my medieval studies I was concerned with the rulers, because there was much to say about them. The task was to penetrate the historical curtain woven of wars, treaties, power struggles, and so on in order to elucidate how nomadic hordes became in the one sense nations, in another states. The study of signs of rulership, symbology, and "presentation" of the state promised to answer this question. The common people or, more correctly, the ruled did not attract me because they left too few records and because they did not constitute a factor in moving history ahead or, for that matter, in any other direction. In modern times, however, I was interested in the ruled people, since it was they who by their economic activity were able to shatter the old social pyramid and made it possible for the emphasis of world history to shift decidedly [Personal communication, 1970].

The books on Hamburg and Hanseatic history and those on contemporary issues demonstrate that Schramm took this difference between medieval and modern subjects seriously.

In a unique combination of *Geistesgeschichte* and the thorough critical methods for which German medievalists are famous, Schramm cleared a path to the past that had until his work been virtually untrodden. His pioneering study of the medieval state introduced entirely new approaches to "political history," reviving a field that in his time had appeared near its demise.

SELECTED BIBLIOGRAPHY

Publications on contemporary history have been omitted. For a complete bibliography to 1963, see Ritter.

Works

BOOKS AND ARTICLES

"Die Briefe Kaiser Ottos III. und Gerberts von Reims aus dem Jahre 997." *Archiv für Urkundenforschung* 9 (1924): 87–122.

"Das Herrscherbild in der Kunst des frühen Mittelalters." *Vorträge der Bibliothek Warburg 1922–23* 2 (1924): 145–239.

Die deutschen Kaiser und Könige in Bildern ihrer Zeit: 1. Teil, bis zur Mitte des 12. Jahrhunderts (751–1152). Leipzig: Teubner, 1928.

Kaiser, Rom und Renovatio: Studien zur Geschichte des romanischen Erneuerungsgedankens vom Ende des karolingischen Reiches bis zum Investiturstreit. 2 vols. Leipzig: Teubner, 1929.

"Studien zu frühmittelalterlichen Aufzeichnungen über Staat und Verfassung." *Zeitschrift der Savigny-Stiftung für Rechtsgeschichte* 49, Germanistische Abteilung (1929): 167–232.

"Die Ordines der mittelalterlichen Kaiserkrönung: Ein Beitrag zur Geschichte des Kaisertums." *Archiv für Urkundenforschung* 11 (1930): 285–390.

Geschichte des englischen Königtums im Lichte der Krönung. Weimar: Böhlaus, 1937. Translated as *A History of the English Coronation* by L.G. Wickham Legg. Oxford: Clarendon, 1937.

"Die Erforschung der mittelalterlichen Symbole—Wege und Methoden." Preface to *Der Handschuh im Recht, Ämterwesen, Brauch und Volksglauben*, by B. Schwineköper. Berlin: Juncker and Dünnhaupt, 1938.

Der König von Frankreich: Das Wesen der Monarchie vom 9. zum 16. Jahrhundert, ein Kapitel aus der Geschichte des abendländischen Staates. 2 vols. Weimar: Böhlau, 1939.

Hamburg, Deutschland und die Welt: Leistung und Grenzen hanseatischen Bürgertums in der Zeit zwischen Napoleon I. und Bismarck: Ein Kapitel deutscher Geschichte. Munich: Callwey, 1943.

"Sacerdotium und Regnum im Austausch ihrer Vorrechte." *Studi gregoriani* 2 (1947): 403–57.

"The Meaning of the Name of Schramm." *Schramm Family Society News* 7 (1948): 137–39.

"Die Anerkennung Karls des Grossen als Kaiser: Ein Kapitel aus der Geschichte der mittelalterlichen 'Staatssymbolik.'" *Historische Zeitschrift* 172 (1951): 449–515.

"Der König von Navarra (1035–1512)." *Zeitschrift der Savigny-Stiftung für Rechtsgeschichte* 68, Germanistische Abteilung (1951): 110–210.

Herrschaftszeichen und Staatssymbolik: Beiträge zu ihrer Geschichte vom dritten bis zum sechzehnten Jahrhundert. 3 vols. Monumenta Germaniae Historica Schriften, vol. 3, parts 1–3. Stuttgart: Hiersemann, 1954–56.

Kaiser Friedrichs II. Herrschaftszeichen: Mit Beiträgen von Josef Deér und Olle Källström. Göttingen: Vandenhoeck and Ruprecht, 1955.

"Herrschaftszeichen: verschenkt, verkauft, verpfändet. Belege aus dem Mittelalter." *Nachrichten der Akademie der Wissenschaften in Göttingen, Philologisch-historische Klasse* 1 (1957): 161–226.

Sphaira-Globus-Reichsapfel: Wanderung und Wandlung eines Herrschaftszeichens von Caesar bis Elisabeth II: Ein Beitrag zum "Nachleben" der Antike. Stuttgart: Hiersemann, 1958.

Las insignias de la realeza en la edad media española. Trad. y prologo de Luis Vasquez de Parga. Madrid: Instituto de Estudios Politicos, 1960.

Polen in der Geschichte Europas. Bonn: Bundeszentrale, 1961.

Ed. with Florentine Mütherich. *Denkmale der deutschen Könige und Kaiser.* 2nd ed. Munich: Prestel, 1962–78.

"Versuch einer Rekonstruktion des Hortes und sonstigen beweglichen Herrscherbesitzes." In *Denkmale der deutschen Könige und Kaiser,* edited by Florentine Mütherich and Percy Ernst Schramm, pp. 16–152. Munich: Prestel, 1962–78.

Neun Generationen. Dreihundert Jahre deutscher "Kulturgeschichte" im Lichte der Schicksale einer Hamburger Bürgerfamilie (1648–1948). 2 vols. Göttingen: Vandenhoek and Ruprecht, 1963–64.

"Il simbolismo dello stato nella storia del medievo." In *La storia del diritto nel quadro delle scienze storiche. Atti del 1 Congresso internazionale della Societa italiana di storia del diritto,* edited by B. Pardisi, pp. 247–67. Florence: Olschki, 1966.

Kaiser, Könige und Päpste: Gesammelte Aufsätze zur Geschichte des Mittelalters. 4 vols. in 5. Stuttgart: Hiersemann, 1968–71.

LETTERS AND PAPERS

Schramm's manuscripts, papers, and letters, including his unpublished memoirs, are deposited in the Staatsarchiv Hamburg.

Sources

Bak, J.M. "Medieval Symbology of the State: Percy E. Schramm's Contribution." *Viator* 4 (1973): 33–63.

———. "Introduction: Coronation Studies—Past, Present and Future." In *Coronations: Medieval and Early Modern Monarchic Ritual,* edited by J.M. Bak, pp. 1–15. Berkeley: University of California Press, 1989.

Becker, H., H.-J. Dahms, and C. Wegeler, eds. *Die Universität Göttingen unter dem Nationalsozialismus: Das verdrängte Kapitel ihrer 250 jährigen Geschichte,* pp. 99 f., 256 ff. Munich: Saur, 1987.

Boyce, Gray C. "Percy E. Schramm." *American Historical Review* 76 (1971): 961–62.

Brandt, A. von. "Percy Ernst Schramm (1894–1970)." *Hansische Geschichtsblätter* 89 (1971): 1–14.

Cantor, Norman. *Inventing the Middle Ages: The Lives, Works and Ideas of the Great Medievalists of the Twentieth Century,* pp. 79–117. New York: Morrow, 1991.

Deér, J. "Byzanz und die Herrschaftszeichen des Abendlandes." *Byzantinische Zeitschrift* 50 (1957): 405–36.

———. "Der Globus des spätrömischen und des byzantinischen Kaisers: Symbol oder Insigne?" *Byzantinische Zeitschrift* 54 (1961): 53–85.

Detwiler, D.S. "Percy Ernst Schramm, 1894–1970." *Central European History* 4 (1971): 90–93.

Elze, R. "Percy Ernst Schramm." *Deutsches Archiv für Erforschung des Mittelalters* 27 (1971): 655–57.

Grabar, A. "L'archéologie des insignes medievaux du pouvoir." *Journal des savants* (1956): 5–19, 77–92.

Grolle, J. *Der Hamburger Percy Ernst Schramm—ein Historiker auf der Suche nach der Wirklichkeit.* Hamburg: Verein für hamburgische Geschichte, 1989.

Heimpel, H. "Königtum, Wandel der Welt, Bürgertum: Nachruf auf P.E. Schramm." *Historische Zeitschrift* 214 (1972): 96–108.

Johnsen, A.O. "Percy Ernst Schramm: Kaiser, Könige und Päpste." *Mediaeval Scandinavia* 6 (1973): 198–205.

Kamp, N. "Percy Ernst Schramm und die Mittelalterforschung." In *Geschichtswissenschaft in Göttingen*, edited by Hartmut Boockmann and Hermann Wellenreuther, pp. 344–63. Göttingen: Vandenhoeck and Ruprecht, 1987.

LeGoff, Jacques. "Is Politics Still the Backbone of History?" *Daedalus: Journal of the American Academy of Arts and Sciences* 100 (1971): 1–19.

Ritter, A. "Veröffentlichungen von Professor Dr. Percy Ernst Schramm [to 1963]." In *Festschrift Percy Ernst Schramm zu seinem siebzigsten Geburtstag von Schülern und Freunden zugeeignet*, 2 vols., edited by Claus-Peter Classen and Peter Scheibert, vol. 2, pp. 291–321. Wiesbaden: Steiner, 1964.

Sturm, V. "Eine Deutsche in einer 'gefährlichen' Stadt: Ehrengard Schramm und Kalavrita, das griechische Oradour. Ehrung zum Geburtstag." *Frankfurter Allgemeine Zeitung* (4 October 1975).

ERNST H. KANTOROWICZ

(1895–1963)

Robert E. Lerner

When Ernst Kantorowicz was asked to fill out a sales promotion form for *The King's Two Bodies* in 1957, he put down under "places lived": "Munich, Berlin, Heidelberg, Frankfurt, Rome, Brussels, Berkeley, Princeton," and under "travels": "too many to be recorded here: all of Western and Central Europe, Turkey, Greece, etc." Had there been a space for "military campaigns," he might have provided: "Verdun, Russia, Turkey, Posen, Berlin, and Munich (last three paramilitary)"; and had there been another for "controversies waged," he might have provided: "Mythical View" controversy (1929–30), Frankfurt Jewish Professor controversy (1933–34), Berkeley Loyalty Oath controversy (1949–50). Given the peripaties of such a career, one wonders at the perseverance that enabled him to produce some of the most carefully researched, original, and influential work in medieval history of the twentieth century.

Ernst Kantorowicz was born in 1895 to a Jewish liqueur-manufacturing family of great wealth in Posen (now Poznań) in imperial Germany. His parents, Joseph and Clara (née Hepner), saw to it that he learned English as a child from a governess, but apparently no Hebrew and surely no Yiddish. (He picked up a handful of Polish words from domestics and always pronounced his family name the Polish way—Kantor-ó-vitch.) Attending a Humanistic Gymnasium in Posen, he performed poorly and graduated with the lowest possible passing grades in all his academic subjects, history included. Groomed for a career in the family firm, he served a business apprenticeship in Hamburg from the spring of 1913 until the outbreak of war the following summer.

Like most young German men, Jews as well as Gentiles, Kantorowicz volunteered for military service in early August 1914. By September he was fighting in an artillery regiment on the western front. In June 1915 he received the Iron Cross, second class, for service in Lorraine. In June 1916 he was engaged in the first episode of gas warfare, and a month later he was wounded by a grenade fragment at Verdun, lying thereafter in a field hospital for two weeks. Once recovered, he was sent to the Russian front, and then, for a little over a year, he was attached to Turkish troops assigned to oversee the "Berlin to Baghdad" rail line in Anatolia and Syria. For his service with the Sultan he received an "Iron Crescent" to wear next to his Iron Cross. An extended furlough in the spring of 1918 allowed him to matriculate at the University of Berlin for a semester, whereupon he returned to the western front to serve in a decoding detachment. At the time of the armistice he was once more in Berlin, now for special language training.

The armistice was to offer no farewell to arms, for Kantorowicz hardly had been demobilized before he became a paramilitarist, fighting Poles and "Reds." Although formally enrolled at the University of Berlin from November 1918 until the end of January 1919, he rushed to Posen sometime around the new year to defend family property unsuccessfully against rebellious Poles, and then he fought briefly against the far-left Spartacists (followers of Karl Liebknecht and Rosa Luxemburg) in Berlin. In February 1919 he matriculated at Munich, but, as coincidence would have it, this was just in time to join a new paramilitary campaign, the *Freikorps* repression of the Munich "soviet republic" in early May 1919. Kantorowicz later stated that his motivation for fighting the "Reds" was that they were keeping him from going on with his studies: they were "turning out the lights on him," so he reached for his gun to make sure the lights would go back on. Be that as it may, Kantorowicz never denied that in the postwar period he was a right-wing nationalist.

Having fought in four armed engagements in a single year, the young swashbuckler finally became a real civilian when conditions around him became more stable. In the fall of 1919 he moved from Munich to Heidelberg to complete his studies. He received his doctoral degree in June 1921 but remained enrolled for a semester thereafter. Given his later career, one might have thought that Kantorowicz concentrated in medieval history during his university years, but this was by no means the case, for in both Munich and Heidelberg he enrolled in the faculty of "political economy." In Heidelberg he chose as his special subjects "history of economics, geography, and Arabic philology," and his dissertation, supervised by the political economist Eberhard Gothein, was on Islamic artisanal corporations. Kantorowicz almost certainly never took any university courses in western medieval history.

Why then did he begin working on a medieval subject, a biography of the Hohenstaufen emperor Frederick II? The answer lies in the personal influence exerted by Stefan George, Germany's most celebrated poet in the years following World War I. George had become dedicated to shaping the lives of a circle of brilliant young male disciples toward the long-term goal of making them the nucleus of a revived and "purified" nation. George, whose model in this regard was Socrates, chose his disciples for their wit, good breeding, and awe for his own person. Once admitted into the George circle, they were expected to address the poet as "Master" and to refer to him in the third person. They were expected to know his poetry by heart, to admire the same authors he did (Plato, Dante, Shakespeare, Goethe, Hölderlin), and to dislike what he disliked (naturalism, modern theater, music). Late-hour sessions were Platonic symposia in which "the Master" discoursed on literary, philosophical, and historical issues. Ultimately the disciples were expected to enunciate George's ideals as eloquently and forcefully as possible to all of Germany.

George's ideals were elitist, pagan, and authoritarian—in a word, Nietzschean; George referred to Nietzsche as "savior." Admitted into the George circle soon after his arrival in Heidelberg, the young Kantorowicz sought a way to express these ideals once he had completed his studies and found it in a biography of Frederick II. He was wealthy enough not to worry about having to make a living. Not only had the Hohenstaufen been recommended by Nietzsche as "the great Free-Spirit, the genius among the German emperors," and "the first European after my own taste," but George had apostrophized him as "the greatest of the Fredericks, the true desire of his people." Kantorowicz began to gather data about Frederick II in 1922, and in less than five years his 632–page biography was finished. It was published in 1927 on Stefan George's recommendation by a firm devoted to bringing out the works of George and his disciples.

Kantorowicz's *Frederick II* was an immediate success, one of the most widely discussed history books appearing in Germany in the interwar years. Lacking documentary apparatus, and devoted to the action-filled reign of one of the most fascinating of rulers, the book clearly reached out to a nonspecialist reading public. Kantorowicz's style, moreover, made the book even more attractive. The style was poetic, oracular, and emotive—full of luxuriant scene painting, ironic juxtaposition, and stirring incident. Here, for example, is the description of the execution of young Conradin: "The Frenchman ordered the death sentence to be carried out in his presence before the pressing crowd that had never yet seen a royal beheading. But as the head of the last Staufen king rolled to the ground, an eagle, so it was said, swept down from the skies, skimmed its right wing in Conradin's blood, and, stained with the blood of the saint, swept, swift as an arrow, up into the ether."

What really assured *Frederick II* a wide readership, however, was its message. An example can be seen in the lines immediately following the ones just quoted: "'How can the Germans,' sang a Venetian troubadour, 'how can they bear to live when they know of this end? They have lost their best and harvested shame! If they don't take revenge soon they will be completely dishonored!' But the Germans . . . did not think of revenge. . . . They have neither cleansed the blood-stained eagle, nor have they let the Sicilian Vespers be followed by a German Vespers." In light of subsequent events it must be emphasized that the "German Vespers" Kantorowicz would have welcomed was nationalist but not racist. Although George and his circle assumed the existence of identifiable national traits (perhaps the most notorious line in *Frederick II* is its reference to "loyalty, possible since the beginning of time only among Germans"), they did not insist on any one nation having a monopoly of worthy characteristics. Kantorowicz's chosen hero was thus a dynastic hybrid, half-German, half-Norman, who wished to bring to Germany gifts from the Mediterranean world, such as classical learning and Roman law, and in whose reign "the splendor of imperial glory glowed with a southern light in the palaces on Neckar and Rhine." Kantorowicz's *Frederick II* nonetheless was surely a manifesto for the restoration of Germany's lost greatness by a renewal of its national pride and a rallying around a coming charismatic leader. Such a manifesto apparently was uplifting to many German readers in the last days of the Weimar Republic.

The scholarly reception of *Frederick II* will be treated later. It need only be said here that the popular success of *Frederick II* earned the author an honorary professorate at the University of Frankfurt in 1930. Meanwhile he had been working on a volume of documentation to accompany the biography, promised since 1927; its appearance in 1931 removed any doubts about his scholarly credentials. When the full professor for medieval history at Frankfurt, Fedor Schneider, died in 1932, Kantorowicz was chosen to succeed him. The well-paid appointment seemed to come at just the right moment: Kantorowicz had lost most of his family fortune in 1931 owing to embezzlement by one of the directors (not a family member) of the Kantorowicz firm. He held his full professorship for one semester. The Nazi seizure of power was to show that the moment was not so ideal after all.

A law of April 1933 forced all Jewish professors to take immediate retirement, except those who had fought for the Fatherland during the world war or in ensuing actions against Spartacists and "Separatists." Although the "front-fighter clause" exempted Kantorowicz on more than one count from having to stop teaching, he requested a leave of absence for the summer semester of 1933 as an expression of protest against racial measures and on the grounds of unwillingness to be placed in a position whereby the expression of nationalistic views might look like opportunism. Although he' had been far to the right in his politics, he had never looked favorably on the Nazis. Changing tactics in the fall, he returned to his post and delivered a courageous opening lecture in November 1933 in which he opposed the values of a "hidden Germany," already a theme of *Frederick II,* to those of the current regime. But after student boycotts he recognized the hopelessness of trying to persevere. For two more semesters he again resorted to "leaves of absence," and when he was faced with having to sign an oath of loyalty to Hitler in August 1934, he refused and negotiated his retirement. Formally "professor emeritus," he received a pension from the German government, which continued to be paid until the end of 1941.

From 1934 until 1939 Kantorowicz's future was uncertain. During the first half of 1934 he occupied an unpaid position at New College, Oxford. Then he worked as a private scholar with headquarters in Berlin. Kantorowicz's research in the years 1935–38 took him for various lengths of time to Brussels, Paris, and several places in Italy and England. Until the Nazi annexation of Austria in March 1938 he had nurtured hopes that he might continue to live in Germany and publish his scholarly works in Austria, but by the summer of 1938 he was energetically seeking to emigrate. Although difficulties in gaining a new passport delayed his departure, in December 1938 he managed to leave for England; after two months in Oxford he traveled to the United States. (His mother, who stayed in Germany, died in Theresienstadt.) In the spring and summer of 1939 Kantorowicz lived in New York City. In the fall he took up a position at the University of California, Berkeley.

Although he was to stay at Berkeley for eleven years, at first it must have seemed to him that he was no more secure professionally there than he had been in Europe. An opening in medieval history had been created at Berkeley by the retirement in 1939 of James Westfall Thompson. Nonetheless, for budgetary reasons, Kantorowicz received a skein of one-year appointments from 1939 until 1945; often he did not know until the last minute whether he was going to be rehired. Only in 1945 was he granted a full professorship with tenure, and only then did it seem as if his life finally would be calm. Undergraduates flocked to his lectures, a coterie of top-flight graduate students attended his seminars, and he flourished in the cosmopolitan society of Berkeley faculty friends.

New clouds enveloped him, however, when in 1949 the Regents of the University of California demanded that all faculty members swear that they did not believe in overthrowing the United States government and were not Communists. Kantorowicz, who had resigned his professorship in Frankfurt rather than swear loyalty to Hitler, immediately became a vociferous opponent of the California loyalty oath. He wrote the president of the University of California in October 1949:

> My political record will stand the test of every investigation. I have twice volunteered to fight actively, with rifle and gun, the left-wing radicals in Germany; but I know that by joining the white battalions I have prepared, if indirectly and against my intention, the road leading to National-Socialism and its rise to power. I shall be ready at any moment to produce sworn evidence before the Federal Bureau of Investigation, which has admitted me to citizenship during the war. But my respect for the University of California and its tasks is such that I cannot allow myself to believe that the base field of political inquisition, which paralyzes scholarly production, should be within the range of its activities.

After meetings and skirmishes that lasted for more than a year Kantorowicz was among thirty-one last-ditch "nonsigners" who were dismissed, in most cases being stripped of tenure, by a vote of the Regents on 25 August 1950. A collective lawsuit to which he was party resulted in an order for reinstatement in April 1951, but meanwhile he had left Berkeley for good. During the academic year 1950–51 he held the position of visiting scholar at the Dumbarton Oaks research institute, and from 1951 until his death he was professor in the School for Historical Studies at the Institute for Advanced Study in Princeton. A passage from the statement supporting his nomination for the latter post, written by institute faculty members Harold Cherniss and Erwin Panofsky, begs to be quoted: "Besides [his] professional ability . . . Ernst Kantorowicz recommends himself to us by the quality of his mind, easier to sense than to define, which enlivens whatever it touches." Kantorowicz's years in Princeton were calm and fruitful, although his health began to decline toward the late 1950s. He died of an aneurysm in September 1963.

In reviewing Kantorowicz's historiography it is convenient to begin with the "Mythical View" controversy surrounding *Frederick II*; the issues it raised offer insights both into that book and into his subsequent scholarly work. Lacking documentation, the volume did not seem addressed to scholars, but scholars gradually came to recognize that it was worthy of their attention. With or without footnotes it was evidently based on exhaustive research. Yet once they started looking at it, they could also see that its author was laying down some bold challenges to reigning historiographical positivism.

These challenges became the subject of a scathing attack on *Frederick II* by Albert Brackmann, then one of Germany's most prominent medievalists. In "The Emperor Frederick II in 'Mythical View,'" a paper delivered to the Prussian Academy of Sciences in 1929 and then printed in the *Historische Zeitschrift*, Brackmann identified three characteristics of Kantorowicz's work he deemed threatening to the integrity of serious scholarship. One was Kantorowicz's blatant ideological bias. Whereas the member of the George circle apparently wrote in order to advance preconceived notions, Brackmann insisted that valid history could not be written "either as a George disciple, or as a Catholic, Protestant, or Marxist, but only as a truth-seeking human being." Brackmann's second criticism concerned Kantorowicz's heavy reliance on what might be called "nonpositivistic" sources. Hitherto German academic historians, and medievalists in particular, had been expected to rely on the most objective sources available, but Kantorowicz began his account almost perversely by adducing poetry, continued it with frequent reference to manifesto and rumor, and ended it by citing prophecy.

Third, Brackmann criticized Kantorowicz's penchant for drawing symbolic meaning out of ceremonies. Choosing a particular case, he argued that Kantorowicz had twisted and exaggerated the significance of Frederick II's self-crowning in Jerusalem; Kantorowicz had interpreted this event as a manifestation of Frederick's ambitions for world rule, but Brackmann maintained that it had no such connotations and was nothing other than a defensive response to political exigencies. As Brackmann saw it, all of Kantorowicz's failings were interrelated, for had he not been driven by preconceptions, and had he relied as strictly as possible on the most objective sources, such distortions would not have occurred. The senior historian insisted that especially in the case of Frederick II it was necessary to cleanse "the true picture" from its "overpainting with contemporary colors"; Kantorowicz, however, full of *imagination créatrice*, was drawing on myths to create myths.

The controversial young author responded combatively in two rejoinders of 1930, a general one presenting his views on the writing of history, given as an address to the annual German Historians' Conference, and a specific response to Brackmann published in the *Historische Zeitschrift*. In the first Kantorowicz proclaimed bias as a virtue. Not only did he advance the customary subjectivist point that it is impossible to write history without opinions, but he flourished with pride the standard of the "George disciple," who writes with a passionate commitment to "the dogma of the worthy future and honor of the nation." Kantorowicz was equally unrepentant in his *Historische Zeitschrift* piece. Here he insisted that the search for historical truth could not be limited to reconstructing events (*Tatsachen*) but had to include a search for the "thought-colors" (*Denkfarben*) of the past. Hence it had to draw on "chronistic (subjective)" as well as "diplomatic (objective)" source material and to employ *imagination créatrice* as a means of warding off *réalisme destructeur*.

Neither side won the "Mythical View" controversy. If there was any consensus, it voted with Brackmann that tendentiousness ought to be eschewed, that Kantorowicz sometimes oversimplified or exaggerated, and that he was insufficiently scrupulous in labeling myths as myths. Nevertheless, many younger scholars appreciated Kantorowicz's defense of subjective sources and the legitimacy of seeking "thought-colors." Felix Gilbert, who was studying history in Berlin in 1930, recalls that he and others like him admired Kantorowicz's book for "overcoming the rigidification that had set in in medieval history" and for "reveal[ing] the ideas and values that motivated the rulers of the Middle Ages." Kantorowicz was not the only scholar pursuing such methods and goals at the time, only the most controversial. In his rejoinder to Brackmann he cited Percy Ernst Schramm's *Kaiser, Rom und Renovatio* (1929) as a work that demonstrated the meaning of "pictures and symbols." If one recognizes that not only Schramm but other young German historians of Kantorowicz's generation, such as Carl Erdmann and Herbert Grundmann, were demonstrating the values of "nonpositivistic sources" around 1930, it may be that this contingent won the "Mythical View" controversy in the largest sense.

Kantorowicz's statements of 1930 can serve as points of reference for addressing a central question regarding his subsequent work—whether after the Nazi seizure of power his historical writing underwent a dramatic mutation caused by repentance for his earlier nationalistic tendentiousness. The argument for mutation is dramatically illustrated by comparing some major traits of his first and last books. *Frederick II* is a rousing narrative about a German emperor, published without documentation and replete with ideological judgments; *The King's Two Bodies* (1957) is an obtrusively learned study, addressed to elucidating a peculiarity of English law and lacking apparent ideological agenda. Granted such a contrast, how else can one explain it than by a spectacular change of heart caused by repentance for having contributed to the rise of Nazism and a consequent retreat into esoteric superspecialization?

Parts of the mutation-repentance thesis stand up to scrutiny. Kantorowicz abandoned his nationalism and admiration for authoritarianism at least from the time he began a new career in the United States. From then on his writings contain scattered critical references to "Fascist devotions," "nationalistic ravings," "weird dogmas," and "idols of modern political religions." As these expressions show, his change of views was accompanied by a new tone of distancing irony. Determined himself to avoid "ravings," he altered his style; its magniloquent and bardic qualities became lapidary and aloof. Even Kantorowicz's lavish displays of technical erudition had a rhetorical aspect: apparently he now meant to subvert "devotions," "dogmas," and "idols" by dissecting them clinically. Nevertheless, he by no means intended to write history primarily on the basis of ideological partisanship, for expressions of political views in his postemigration publications are present only incidentally or obliquely. In the preface to *The King's Two Bodies* Kantorowicz virtually repudiated his position of 1930 about the virtues of bias by insisting that "the fascination emanating as usual from the historical material itself prevailed over any desire of practical or moral application."

All this granted, greater continuities exist in Kantorowicz's historiographical career than are often recognized. In the first place, certain contrasts may be more apparent than real. Although *Frederick II* had initially appeared without footnotes, the author announced in 1927 that he intended to supply them; that this took him four years might be attributed to "positivistic" earnestness about getting them right. In addition, he was showing signs before 1933 of becoming more of a professional historian and less of a *littérateur*. His acceptance of an honorary professorship in Frankfurt in 1930 was one such sign, and his inclusion of ten supererogatory scholarly appendixes in the companion volume for *Frederick II* another. Correspondence of 1932 with Percy Schramm shows that Kantorowicz still wished to write "truly political" history but that he was simultaneously exchanging scholarly information with academic medievalists like Schramm and Friedrich Baethgen. A full professor, from 1932, he inevitably would have published thickly documented works, and the fact that once the Nazis took power in 1933 none came out until 1937 was obviously no fault of his own.

Another way of recognizing continuities is to observe that the points Kantorowicz made about sources and "thought-colors" in 1930 continued to guide his work for the rest of his life. Although confusion arises from the publication date of 1946, his second book, *Laudes Regiae*, followed immediately in composition upon the companion volume for *Frederick II*. Kantorowicz began writing parts of *Laudes Regiae* in 1934, and a complete version was ready for publication in German in 1936, but then "conditions made publication impossible." Five years later Kantorowicz submitted an

English version to the University of California Press, but then came another five-year delay before the book saw the light of day. Once this chronology is cleared up, it is easier to see how much *Laudes Regiae* picks up where *Frederick II* leaves off. The connection is most directly evident in the first chapter, a general introduction, which, the author said in the preface, "started from an investigation on the legend of the Sicilian gold *bullae* of Frederick II."

Kantorowicz clearly wrote *Laudes Regiae* to exemplify the worth of "subjective" sources and the value of studying ceremonies. The sources he now adduced were liturgical formularies, hitherto underutilized by historians. In addition he was fortunate in gaining the collaboration of a musicologist, Manfred Bukofzer, who showed how musical evidence could help the historian. Kantorowicz noted drily in his preface that "it is really no longer possible for the mediaeval historian to . . . deal cheerfully with the history of mediaeval thought and culture without ever opening a missal." Then he set out to prove this. By studying liturgical acclamations he showed how Anglo-Irish saints' litanies became fused in the eighth century with late-antique Roman acclamation formulas in Frankish Gaul to strengthen the new pontifical kingship of the Carolingians; how the "Gallo-Frankish" *laudes* were superseded during the reign of Louis the Pious by a "Franco-Roman" form that gave greater prominence to pope than to emperor; and how *laudes* sung for all bishops were transformed, probably during the twelfth century, into "imperialized" papal *laudes* that celebrated the pope alone as highest ruler. Kantorowicz demonstrated in *Laudes Regiae* how "seemingly insignificant changes" in liturgical texts reflected changes of the greatest magnitude in "theocratic concepts of secular and spiritual rulership."

Kantorowicz's thirty-some articles (he selected his favorites for reprinting in the posthumous *Selected Studies*) deserve more attention than can be given them here. Several were devoted to high-medieval thought and education (he once had planned to bring out a collection of studies "following in some way the traces of the late Ch. H. Haskins"), but most were about theories, slogans, and ceremonies of rulership. These draw on a wide range of sources, both written and pictorial—not just oracles, odes, and oaths, but coins, carvings, and cartoons. As in *Laudes Regiae* Kantorowicz delighted in these articles in revealing (perhaps the better word is intimating, since he never wished to be unsubtle) the larger implications of seemingly insignificant changes, as well as in startling the reader by pointing to unsuspected concatenations of influences. Above all he concentrated on surprises and ironies inherent in the influence of pagan usages on Christian ones and in the medieval and early-modern ricocheting of influences between spiritual and secular realms.

Much that has been said about *Laudes Regiae* and the articles can be said of Kantorowicz's masterpiece, *The King's Two Bodies*. Here too the author drew on a wide range of sources, written and visual. Almost as in symmetry to the innovative use of liturgy in *Laudes Regiae*, he drew innovatively in *The King's Two Bodies* on legal evidence—law manuals, casebooks, legal maxims—and beyond that on the iconography of manuscript illuminations and funerary monuments, and he lavished two entire chapters on the imagery and ideas of major works of literature. (Shakespeare and Dante, the subjects of those chapters, were favorites of Kantorowicz from George-circle days.) *The King's Two Bodies* proposes to lay out the historical background of the legal fiction of the "two-bodied king" ("body mortal" and "body politic") formulated by Tudor jurists. It posits chronologically successive models of "Christ-Centered Kingship," "Law-Centered Kingship," and "Polity-Centered Kingship," and then attempts to show how "Polity-Centered Kingship," enthroned in England and France by 1300, acquired a conception of the polity as a "corporation" in England alone that became the basis for the Tudor doctrine of "the King's Two Bodies." Throughout Kantorowicz's long, dense, often heavily theoretical, and sometimes seemingly digressive account, one finds his usual alertness to Christian borrowings from paganism and transferences between spiritual and secular, as well as his relish for noticing the larger implications of apparently negligible details.

Whether *The King's Two Bodies* has a thesis is debatable. The author himself may not have thought so: his prefatory statement indicates that he was merely exposing "transformations, implications, and radiations." In the publicity form for *The King's Two Bodies* he left blank the space asking for "the author's own version of the thesis of his book." Yet if *The King's Two Bodies* perhaps lacks a governing thesis, it certainly develops several important central ideas (not to mention many fascinating individual observations), such as the succession of medieval models of kingship, differences in the ideological underpinnings of the western nation-states and other European polities, and differences between France and England. It also concludes convincingly with the proposition that the Tudor doctrine of "the King's Two Bodies" descends from Christian theological constructs rather than pagan legal ideas.

The most frequently voiced criticisms of *The King's Two Bodies* are that Kantorowicz seems indifferent to the material contexts in which his ideas were generated and that he seldom tells of their practical consequences. Beryl

Smalley complained that the book offered "a diet of jam without bread" because it lavished attention on ideas and metaphors without "measur[ing] their distance from the facts of life." Yet without denying the "theory for theory's sake" quality of the book, Kantorowicz surely believed that "fiction is a figure of the truth" (the motto, in Latin, appears as a heading for one of his subsections), and thus that "fictions" inevitably have bearing on the conduct of life. He had no desire to dwell on relationships between his fictions and mundane existence, but, with particular reference to the fiction of "the King's Two Bodies," he did propose in one crucial passage that this helped the English to challenge, and even behead their mortal king "without . . . doing irreparable harm to the King's body politic." When Kantorowicz notes in this context with uncharacteristic earnestness that "there were very great and serious advantages in the English doctrine of the King's Two Bodies," we may be licensed to conclude not only that he thought ideas really did make a difference but that his greatest book was offered to some degree as an act of homage to Anglo-American constitutionalism.

It would take a separate essay to treat satisfactorily the long-term influence and present standing of Kantorowicz's large body of work. *Frederick II* has stood the test of time least well. Subsequent biographies of Frederick by T. Van Cleve and D. Abulafia have purposely distanced themselves from Kantorowicz's "mythicizing" of the Hohenstaufen ruler, and these are more likely to be used today. Yet Kantorowicz's work of 1927 made enduring contributions to scholarship in highlighting the sacral characteristics of Frederick II's rule, as well as in other specifics, such as Frederick's patronage of learning. One should not trade in one's Kantorowicz when acquiring either of the two newer biographies.

Laudes Regiae is more enduring, for it remains unchallenged as the single work in English, and perhaps in any language, that best displays the importance of liturgy for the understanding of medieval history. The articles in *Selected Studies* not only accomplish many separate research triumphs and feats of sleuthing but reveal enduringly the value of a wide range of "subjective" sources in helping to recreate the "thought-colors" of the medieval past. Had Kantorowicz written nothing but *Laudes Regiae* and the articles, his position among the most erudite, imaginative, and influential of twentieth-century medieval historians would be secure. Yet that still leaves his masterpiece, *The King's Two Bodies*, which, having always been appreciated by specialists, has come into vogue in the last ten or fifteen years as one of the most widely discussed books throughout international academia. It appeared in Spanish in 1985, in French and Italian in 1989, and in German in 1990. One of the causes for this vogue must be that the book reflects a new international interest in "the rites of power." Another cause may be the growing awareness—as Cherniss and Panofsky knew long ago—that Kantorowicz's intellect "enlivens whatever it touches."

SELECTED BIBLIOGRAPHY

For a complete listing of Kantorowicz's publications see *Selected Studies*, xi-xiv.

Works

BOOKS

Kaiser Friedrich der Zweite. Berlin: Bondi, 1927. Translated as *Frederick the Second* by E.O. Lorimer. London: Constable, 1931.

Kaiser Friedrich der Zweite, Ergänzungsband. Berlin: Bondi, 1931.

Laudes Regiae: A Study in Liturgical Acclamations and Mediaeval Ruler Worship. Berkeley: University of California Press, 1946.

The Fundamental Issue: Documents and Marginal Notes on the University of California Loyalty Oath. Berkeley: Privately printed, 1950.

The King's Two Bodies: A Study in Mediaeval Political Theology. Princeton, N.J.: Princeton University Press, 1957.

Selected Studies. Locust Valley, N.Y.: Augustin, 1965.

LETTERS AND PAPERS

The main collection of Kantorowicz's papers is held by the Leo Baeck Institute in New York City. Many letters from Kantorowicz to Stefan George as well as letters pertaining to the publication of Kantorowicz's biography of Frederick II are in the Stefan-George-Archiv, Stuttgart. Other letters by Kantorowicz (or original materials pertaining to his career) are in numerous public or private collections in Germany and the United States.

Sources

Abulafia, David. "Kantorowicz and Frederick II." *History* 62 (1977): 193–210.

Baethgen, Friedrich. "Ernst Kantorowicz." *Deutsches Archiv für Erforschung des Mittelalters* 21 (1965): 1–17.

Boureau, Alain. "Introduzione." In *I due corpi del Re* by Ernst H. Kantorowicz, pp. xiii-xxviii. Turin: Einaudi, 1989.

Elze, Reinhard. "Die Herrscherlaudes im Mittelalter." *Zeitschrift der Savigny-Stiftung für Rechtsgeschichte, kanonische Abteilung* 40 (1954): 201–23.

Fleckenstein, Josef. "Ernst Kantorowicz zum Gedächtnis." *Frankfurter Universitätsreden* 34 (1964): 11–27.

Giesey, Ralph E. "Ernst H. Kantorowicz: Scholarly Triumphs and Academic Travails in Weimar Germany and the United States." *Yearbook of the Leo Baeck Institute* 30 (1985): 191–202.

———. "Les deux corps du roi." In his *Cérémonial et puissance souveraine: France, XVe-XVIIe siècles*, pp. 9–19. Paris: Colin, 1987.

———. "Deux modèles du pouvoir selon Ernst Kantorowicz: entretien avec Ralph Giesey." *Préfaces* 10 (1988): 113–20.

Grünewald, Eckhart. *Ernst Kantorowicz und Stefan George: Beiträge zur Biographie des Historikers bis zum Jahre 1938 und zu seinem Jugendwerk "Kaiser Friedrich der Zweite."* Wiesbaden: Steiner, 1982.

Lerner, Robert E. "Ernst Kantorowicz and Theodor E. Mommsen." In *An Interrupted Past: German-Speaking Refugee Historians in the United States after 1933,* edited by Hartmut Lehmann and James J. Sheehan, pp. 188–205. New York: Cambridge University Press, 1991.

Malkiel, Yakov. "Ernst H. Kantorowicz." In *On Four Modern Humanists: Hofmannsthal, Gundolf, Curtius, Kantorowicz*, edited by Arthur R. Evans, Jr., pp. 146–219. Princeton, N.J.: Princeton University Press, 1970.

Salin, Edgar. "Ernst Kantorowicz, 1895–1963." N.p.: Privately printed, 1963.

Wolf, Gunther, ed. *Stupor Mundi: Zur Geschichte Friedrichs II. von Hohenstaufen.* Darmstadt: Wissenschaftliche Buchgesellschaft, 1966. (Contains the Brackmann-Kantorowicz exchange from the "Mythical View" controversy and three detailed early reviews of *Frederick II.*)

Salo Wittmayer Baron

(1895–1989)

Norman Roth

Salo Baron, the foremost twentieth-century historian of Jewish culture, was born in Tarnow, Galicia in 1895. His remarkable range of knowledge covered Jewish history from the most ancient period to modern America, yet much of his most important work was devoted to medieval subjects. While other scholars may be more "expert" in a narrow segment of medieval Jewish history, Baron was undoubtedly the master of the overall subject.

Baron received his doctorate in history from the University of Vienna in 1917. He earned further doctorates at Vienna in political science (1922) and jurisprudence (1923), while concurrently completing the arduous studies necessary for a rabbinical degree from the prestigious Jewish Theological Seminary of Vienna in 1920. This thorough training, coupled with a phenomenal mastery of languages, was to prove invaluable in the task that he ultimately set for himself: nothing less than writing a complete history of the Jews from the biblical period to the modern. That task was never to be completed, at least in his monumental *Social and Religious History of the Jews*, which remained unfinished at his death in 1989. However, numerous other books and articles have dealt with aspects of modern Jewish history, making contributions that range from the merely significant to the pioneering.

While Baron had already written several articles, primarily in Hebrew, and some important book reviews (for example, of works by his predecessors in Jewish history, Heinrich Graetz and Simon Dubnov), it was in 1928 that his first major article appeared, interestingly in English, and it is significant that it was on a medieval theme. In "Ghetto and Emancipation" he criticized the prevalent notion that the emancipation had brought a glorious new age for the Jews, freeing them from the "nightmare" of the (for Jews) protracted Middle Ages, during which they shared no "equal rights." Baron pointed out that no one had "equal rights" in the Middle Ages and that in fact Jews were not the subject of special discrimination. One paragraph noted a major area where Jews indeed had a superior right to that of most in the medieval period: they could move freely from one place to another.

Here too was an important statement on the *servi camera* question ("serfs," as usually translated, somewhat unjustly, "of the royal chamber"), in which Baron again pointed out that Jews were not serfs of local masters but serfs in the sense of public law. They "belonged" to the king in the same way that modern citizens "belong" to the state, and the medieval Jews had certain privileges no longer enjoyed in the modern state. Many of these observations, challenged by scholars who could not tolerate revision of what Baron was to call the "lachrymose conception of Jewish history," were later forgotten or revised to a great extent by Baron himself. They nevertheless remain as valid as when he first wrote them.

Likewise accurate was his remark that the "ghetto" (in any case not a medieval but a Renaissance creation) had its origin in the Jews' desire to have their own exclusive areas of residence in many medieval European towns. This worked therefore as much to the benefit of the Jews as to their detriment. Indeed the "emancipation" of modern Jews exacted a terrible price: the creation of a (false) notion of the Jewish "religion," stripped of all nationalist claims, leading ultimately to assimilation.

Although Baron was actively engaged in communal work, both on behalf of various Jewish communities and in general as a member of the commission on minority rights of the League of Nations, he concurrently continued to write essays and book reviews. By 1937 he had already published in three volumes his first version of *Social and Religious History of the Jews*, and in 1939 he founded, and edited until his death, the important journal *Jewish Social Studies*. The same year he became president of what was to be the Conference on Jewish Social Studies, a post he held for many years.

It was during this period that he turned his attention to Maimonides, a natural consequence of the Octocentennial (1935), for which he edited a volume of essays, including his own on "The Economic Views of Maimonides" in his *Essays on Maimonides* (1941). More significant was his major essay (over a hundred printed pages) on "The Historical Outlook of Maimonides" (reprinted in *History and Jewish Historians*), a thorough examination of the historical theory and treatment of Jewish and pagan history of the foremost Jewish philosopher and legal codifier. Baron's essay analyzes in detail Maimonides's approach to these subjects, not just in his great code of Jewish law but throughout his writings. He concludes by pointing out that Maimonides's historical outlook was to a large extent a product of his time and typical of that held by medieval Jews. The essay was to have an impact on many Jewish chroniclers and writers.

Remarkable as is this essay, it is largely the notes (nearly as long as the essay) that demonstrate Baron's erudition and command of a wide variety of sources. Many important observations are buried in these notes, some of which could have saved later scholars embarrassment and difficulty had they bothered to read them. Baron's correct assumption, for instance, that both the letter in which Maimonides criticized the French rabbis and his "ethical testament" were forgeries has gone largely unnoticed; these texts continue to be published and translated as genuine.

A few years later, in 1941, Baron turned his attention to another important medieval figure, Judah ha-Levy, renowned poet of Spain and author of the polemical work (hardly "philosophical," as it is often called) known as the *Khuzari*. Baron's article "Yehudah Halevi: An Answer to an Historical Challenge" is less noteworthy than his essay on Maimonides; yet it also contains information of importance and is perhaps the chief contribution in English on the subject, despite some errors of interpretation.

In 1942 Baron published his three-volume "trial run" of what was to become his magnum opus, this time with the title *The Jewish Community: Its History and Structure to the American Revolution*. The same year produced another major essay, "The Jewish Factor in Medieval Civilization," his presidential address to the American Academy for Jewish Research. While some of the introductory remarks in that address, and especially in the notes, are better left unread today, the body of the essay is again an important contribution that surveys several factors in medieval Jewish civilization. The section on "biological" factors, such as questions of racial anti-Semitism, is less satisfactory, perhaps having been influenced by events of the time in Europe. His discussion of the "economic" factors of Jewish life, however, and particularly of the "cultural contributions" of Jews remains worthwhile reading. It is remarkable that Baron's call for updating the pioneering work of the nineteenth-century scholar Moritz Steinschneider on Jewish contributions to medieval science, "by the more significant qualitative evaluation" of each contributor, remains largely ignored.

In the same essay, less strikingly revisionist but still in line with what he had written in the Maimonides essay, and with his by then well-known views on the "lachrymose conception of Jewish history," are his remarks on how the Jewish group as a whole was considered legally under the aspect of a corporate body in medieval society. These are suggestive ideas that have never been pursued but that may hold the key to the situation of medieval

Jews. Similarly Baron rejected the outdated theories of Jews as "aliens," without denying that the Middle Ages often saw the Jew as "permanent stranger." (One wonders why he titled one of his most important chapters on medieval Jews "Aliens.") Baron could not have been expected to distance himself entirely from his own upbringing and the influences of a traditional Jewish education. His statement in the essay (never repudiated in later writing) that "the Church" demanded "full control over Jewry because Jewish subjection was merely the effect of the Jewish repudiation of Christ" ("Jewish Factor": 38) is simply wrong.

Another frequently recognized shortcoming of Baron's theoretical framework was his obsession with nationalism as the major cause of intolerance. An article published in 1929, "Nationalism and Intolerance," was marred by errors of fact and perception, which were to become all too apparent with the events of World War II; yet the author could still state, in a later presidential address (1941), that none of the criticism had shaken his conviction in the "validity" of the theory. It is perhaps no surprise to find attempts in *Social and Religious History* to postulate a "nationalism" in medieval Europe as early as the thirteenth century in a manner with which few if any general medievalists could agree.

On the other hand Baron's interest in nationalism, no doubt prompted by his own work on behalf of minority national rights in the League of Nations and by his continuing efforts on behalf of the world Jewish community, led him to write studies not only on nationalism in the modern period but on the important revolutions that swept Europe in 1848. Not as well known even to Jewish historians as they ought to be, these important works dealt with a topic hitherto hardly researched at all. These studies culminated in his broader book *Modern Nationalism and Religion* (1947), a classic sociological-historical investigation that in actuality has little or nothing to do with Jewish civilization.

By 1952 Baron was able to issue a completely revised version of what was to become the first volume of *Social and Religious History of the Jews*. In 1957 the first of the volumes on the medieval period (Volume 3), the central part of the total *History*, was published. In the end at least eight volumes (out of eighteen) were given over to the Middle Ages, as well as portions of subsequent volumes that dealt with the Renaissance. Volume 3 begins with the Jews in the Byzantine Empire, Italy, Visigothic Spain, Persia, and the pre-Islamic Arabian peninsula. It continues with chapters on "Mohammed and the Caliphate," the Jew as "Protected Minority" in the Muslim world, and a less satisfactory one on eastern Europe (essentially the Khazars and their conversion to Judaism). There are some errors, particularly in the earlier chapters, and some information on Jews in the Muslim world that must be corrected in light of later research by David Corcos and Abraham Halkin, particularly on the Almohad era. Nevertheless, this important volume was the first modern attempt at a synthetic overview of the medieval period, bringing together the results of hundreds of articles and books in various languages. For the Muslim period it remains far superior to such efforts as S.D. Goitein's *Jews and Arabs* or Bernard Lewis's *The Jews of Islam* (1984); both authors could have profited from a careful reading of Baron's volume.

Volume 4 of the *History, Meeting of the East and West*, is perhaps the one most likely to be of interest to medievalists. It focuses on Christian Europe in the High Middle Ages (ca. 800 to 1200). The chapter on "Western Christendom," actually on the church and the Jews, is valuable for its bibliographical expertise. Early in his career Baron had complained that generalists in medieval history tend to ignore Jewish subjects altogether in their research and writing (this is still generally true). His discussion in the footnotes of such topics as canon law and even "Conciliarism" (although technically the latter had nothing to do with Jews) reveals on the contrary a comprehensive awareness of all pertinent bibliography on these issues, whereas many historians to this day are not even aware of the existence of Baron's work.

There are, however, again some striking errors in the volume, such as the puzzling claim that the famous "Constitutio pro judaeis" (*Sicut judaeis*) issued by every pope from Gregory I on through the Middle Ages was aimed only at "Roman Jewry," i.e., Jews in Italy. This is incorrect and was contradicted as long ago as the pioneering study of Solomon Katz on Gregory I and the Jews and subsequently in the work of Solomon Grayzel and others. Minor errors include the statement that the "catalog" of the Muslim library of Córdoba in the tenth century lists 400,000 volumes, when in fact there was, and is, no catalog; this claim has long been known to be legend. Legend too is the famous story of the "Jewish mistress" of King Alfonso VIII of Castile. In addition, while it is true that some of the early Carolingian privileges to individual Jews bore certain aspects similar to vassalage and "feudal concepts," they were not these; nor did they imply any kind of religious vassalage, much less use "Christological terms." Nevertheless, Baron's bibliographical knowledge once again was astounding. He remains the only Jewish historian who, although not a specialist on Spain, not only was able to read Spanish but knew a surprising proportion of the relevant Spanish sources and secondary literature.

The chapter on the Crusades begins with a classic sentence, "In many ways 1096 marked a turning point in Jewish history," that reinforces what most Jewish scholars have long believed to be true of the First Crusade. This claim, which sparked much research, is no longer recognized as fact. Robert Chazan's *European Jewry and the First Crusade* (1987) lays to rest this myth along with numerous others concerning the Crusade. Baron errs also when he states that Christians espoused a "millenarian" theory that viewed the year 1000 as a cataclysmic event (disproved by Charles Homer Haskins and Norman Cohn). Nevertheless, overall this chapter remains an important analysis not only of the Crusades and the Jews but of such anti-Jewish persecutions as the famous Spires and Blois incidents, replete with detailed footnotes that analyze the sources and secondary literature. Two seminal studies of these topics by Robert Chazan have been important direct results.

The chapter on "Economic Transformations" is without question the most important in Volume 4 of the *History*. Valuable information is to be found, again, not only in the text but even more in the comprehensive notes, which need to be read carefully both for the bibliographical references and for material not included in the text itself. This chapter details Jewish activity in commerce, agriculture, trades and crafts, and the professions primarily in Christian Europe and to some extent in the Muslim world. (This chapter was written before Goitein's generally thorough and accurate study of these topics in the Mediterranean world—chiefly Egypt.) The chapter's minor shortcomings have to do with the Jewish role in slavery, a subject that needs a fresh treatment.

Volume 5, *Religious Controls and Dissension*, is of more specific Jewish interest. For example, the chapter on "Communal Controls" concerns such topics as the internal Jewish community and rabbinical authority. Nevertheless, it is important for even non-Jewish specialists who want some insight into the workings of the medieval Jewish community, a topic with wider implications for Jewish-Christian relations. The crucial chapter on "Polemics and Religious Controversies" remains the only systematic overview of these subjects in English.

Like almost all Jewish writers on the subject of Jewish-Christian debate in the Middle Ages, Baron focused on Christian polemic and hardly touched on the equally harsh anti-Christian statements in Jewish polemical and other writing. To some extent this deficiency is now remedied by David Berger's edition and translation of an important postmedieval Jewish polemical work, with notes that take full account of many of the medieval sources (*The Jewish-Christian Debate in the High Middle Ages*, 1979). Far more has been written on the Christian side of the issue; but precisely because the sources are Hebrew the time has surely come for a detailed analysis of Jewish anti-Christian polemic. Volume 5 concludes with a thorough treatment of "Messianism and Sectarian Trends" in the Jewish community and the "Karaite Schism," the story of an interesting antirabbinical heretical sect.

Volumes 6, 7, and 8 likewise focus almost exclusively on topics of concern to the medieval Jewish community with only occasional reference to the broader non-Jewish community. Volume 6 deals with Jewish legal interpretation, codification and commentary, homiletical and chronological literature, and biblical interpretation. Volume 7, *Hebrew Language and Letters*, is most in need of revision and reinterpretation in light of current scholarship; yet until such a survey is published Baron's work provides an important overview of the subject. The volume deals not only with the revival of the Hebrew language (Roth [1983]: 63–84), but with Jewish liturgical and religious customs, Hebrew poetry and literature; it concludes with an interesting chapter on Jewish magic and mysticism. Volume 8, *Philosophy and Science*, explores the important and problematic controversy between "faith and reason" in the Jewish sources and then provides considerable information on Jewish contributions to science, mathematics, and medicine. The volume gives a firm foundation to the subsequent research of scholars like Bernard Goldstein in the United States and others in Israel. Much new information coming to light in Spain is particularly important.

Volumes 13, 14, and 15 focus on the late-medieval period and the early Renaissance, with much attention given to the Iberian Peninsula, the "Marrano" (or, more correctly, *converso*) problem, the cultural and scientific accomplishments of Spanish Jews, the Inquisition, and the Expulsion. There is considerable overlap here, both with what has already been stated in previous volumes and in time periods, so that the discussion of "Marranos," for example, stretches far beyond the medieval period.

The text of *A Social and Religious History of the Jews*, remarkably lucid and easy to read, serves a wide variety of audiences. The informed layperson will benefit from this work, likely to be the last attempt by one author to tell the whole story of Jewish civilization in detail. Were a reader to choose only one work on Jewish civilization to be read in a lifetime, this would be it. The footnotes alone are an invaluable mine of information. There is no telling how many dissertations, articles, and books have had their origin in these notes, nor how many more useful studies could be produced if Jewish scholars in particular would utilize them more than they have in the past. The work has a fairly comprehensive index (not prepared by the author and hence with some oversights), if only for the first eight volumes, but includes no bibliography, an unfortunate omission in that many of the references in footnotes are given in abridged form or with enigmatic personal abbreviations. (Puzzled readers may wish to know, for example, that the frequently used SRIHP, stands for the Hebrew journal *Yediyot ha-makhon le-heqer ha-shirah ha-ʿivrit*!) Baron's death ended any possibility of the *History* being completed, though perhaps some of Baron's students will be prevailed upon to produce the much-needed bibliography and the list of abbreviations and to index the remaining volumes.

Baron's *History* supersedes the work of Heinrich Graetz and of Simon Dubnov, who were both more or less successful in their attempts to write a history of a people. Graetz is of interest today only for some sources uncovered in his footnotes; and while Dubnov's work is still useful, especially for eastern Europe, it suffers from some serious problems. (The English translation, which claims to be from the original Russian but is actually from a Yiddish translation, is uniformly inaccurate.) It is almost certain that no single historian will ever again attempt what Baron undertook, much less carry it to completion.

A Social and Religious History of the Jews was an ambitious undertaking in the tradition of nineteenth-century European Jewish scholarship: it was no less than an attempt to detail the entire history of a people. To an extent the attempt failed, not because of its occasional errors (inevitable in such a vast work) but because it was never completed. One cannot but regret the time and energy Baron devoted to such topics as American and Russian Jewish history (*The Russian Jew Under Tsars and Soviets*, 1967; 2nd revised and enlarged ed., 1976). Yet Baron's *History*, which has been translated into numerous languages (French, Spanish, Hebrew, and others), in its totality is the single most important twentieth-century contribution to the study of medieval Jewish civilization. It is likely to remain the starting point for research and the most important general source to consult on topics of medieval Jewish interest.

Baron's contributions to the medieval history of the Jews did not end, however, with the publication of *A Social and Religious History of the Jews*. *Ancient and Medieval Jewish History: Essays* (1972) incorporated important earlier writings, some translated from other languages, with such new essays as "Some Medieval Jewish Attitudes to the Muslim State." Most important for non-Jewish specialists are the essays in Part 3 on medieval Europe, including "The Jewish Factor in Medieval Civilization," "Medieval Jewish Nationalism and Jewish Serfdom," and—of primary importance—an English translation from Hebrew of his "'Plenitude of Apostolic Powers' and 'Medieval Jewish Serfdom,'" both of which deal with the controversial issue of *servi camera* and the status of the Jew. Of a more general nature, and interesting as an example of what has come to be called "medievalism," is the essay "Medieval Heritage and Modern Realities in Protestant-Jewish Relations," reprinted from *Diogenes* (1968).

Baron had many distinguished students. Given the virtually nonexistent state of Jewish studies when he began teaching at Columbia University, relatively few of those students were able to go on to academic careers in Jewish history, but those who did had distinguished careers. Those of us who were never privileged to be his students in actuality may still consider ourselves his students in an intellectual sense, for it is no exaggeration to say that he played the leading role in the emergence of Jewish studies in American universities and colleges. His late wife, whose untimely death was the tragic event in his career, correctly stated that Baron "through his teaching and writings opened new horizons for the understanding of Jewish history." Jeannette Meisel Baron was herself an eminent scholar, a distinguished sociologist as well as a historian of American Jewish life.

Salo Baron was proverbially generous with his time and resources. After his retirement from active teaching, he opened his home to students and scholars and often assisted others in their research. His last public address was at the University of Wisconsin, where in 1983 he was honored with the prestigious Hilldale Lectureship. His stirring and memorable speech, "Is America Ready for Ethnic Minority Rights?" was followed the next day by a request to speak to the undergraduate students in the Jewish history course. For over an hour he held a packed room of students spellbound with reminiscences ranging from Heinrich Graetz to his own work with the League of Nations, and with comments on Jewish history and current world problems. Baron was the last product of an age and a culture that no longer exist. He was an eminent historian and one of the last of the gentleman-scholars.

Selected Bibliography

This bibliography includes only those works relevant to medieval subjects.

Works

Books and Articles

"Graetzens Geschichtsschreibung." *Monatsschrift für Geschichte und Wissenschaft des Judentums* 62 (1918): 5–15.

"Ghetto and Emancipation: Shall We Revise the Traditional View?" *Menorah Journal* 14 (1928): 515–26.

"Nationalism and Intolerance." *Menorah Journal* 16 (1929): 405–15; 17: 148–58.

"The Historical Outlook of Maimonides." *Proceedings of the American Academy for Jewish Research* 6 (1935): 5–113. Reprinted in his *History and Jewish Historians*.

A Social and Religious History of the Jews. 3 vols. New York: Columbia University Press, 1937.

Ed. *Essays on Maimonides: An Octocentennial Volume*. New York: Columbia University Press, 1941.

"Yehudah Halevi: An Answer to an Historical Challenge." *Jewish Social Studies* 3 (1941): 243–72. Reprinted in his *Ancient and Medieval Jewish History*.

"Rashi and the Community of Troyes." In *Rashi Anniversary Volume*, edited by Alexander Marx, pp. 47–71. New York: American Academy for Jewish Research, 1941. Reprinted in his *Ancient and Medieval Jewish History*.

"The Jewish Factor in Medieval Civilization." *Proceedings of the American Academy for Jewish Research* 12 (1942): 1–48. Reprinted in his *Ancient and Medieval Jewish History*.

The Jewish Community: Its History and Structure to the American Revolution. 3 vols. Philadelphia: Jewish Publication Society of America, 1942.

"Saadia's Communal Activities." In *Saadia Anniversary Volume*, edited by Boaz Cohen, pp. 9–74. New York: American Academy for Jewish Research, 1943. Reprinted in his *Ancient and Medieval Jewish History*.

Modern Nationalism and Religion. New York: Harper, 1947.

A Social and Religious History of the Jews. 18 vols. New York: Columbia University Press, 1952–83.

Ed. with others. *Great Ages and Ideas of the Jewish People*. New York: Random House, 1956.

"Moses Maimonides." In *Great Jewish Personalities in Ancient and Medieval Times*, edited by Simon Novek, pp. 204–30. New York: Farrar, Straus and Cuhady, 1959.

"'Plentitude of Apostolic Powers' and 'Medieval Jewish Serfdom'." (In Hebrew.) In *Sefer yovel le-Yishaq Baer*, edited by S. Ettinger et al., pp. 102–24. Jerusalem: Central Press, 1960. Translated in his *Ancient and Medieval Jewish History*.

"Medieval Nationalism and Jewish Serfdom." In *Studies and Essays in Honor of Abraham A. Neuman*, edited by Meir Ben-Horin, Bernard D. Weinryb, and Solomon Zeitlin, pp. 17–48. Leiden: Brill, 1962. Reprinted in his *Ancient and Medieval Jewish History*.

"Some Recent Literature on the History of the Jews in the Pre-Emancipation Era (1300–1800)." *Cahiers d'histoire mondiale* 8 (1962): 137–71.

History and Jewish Historians: Essays and Addresses. Edited by Arthur Hertzberg and Leon A. Feldman. Philadelphia: Jewish Publication Society of America, 1964.

The Russian Jew Under Tsars and Soviets. 1967. 2nd ed. rev. and enlarged. New York: Macmillan, 1976.

"Medieval Heritage and Modern Realities in Protestant-Jewish Relations." *Diogenes* 61 (1968): 32–51. Revised and annotated in his *Ancient and Medieval Jewish History*.

Ancient and Medieval Jewish History: Essays. Edited by Leon A. Feldman. New Brunswick, N.J.: Rutgers University Press, 1972.

Sources

Baron, Jeanette M. "Bibliography." In *Salo Wittmayer Baron Jubilee Volume: On the Occasion of His Eightieth Birthday*, edited by Saul Lieberman, vol.1, pp. 1–37. Jerusalem: American Academy for Jewish Research, 1974.

Berger, David. *The Jewish-Christian Debate in the High Middle Ages*. Philadelphia: Jewish Publication Society of America, 1979.

Blau, Joseph L. "The Historic Quest." In *Essays on Jewish Life and Thought: Presented in Honor of Salo Wittmayer Baron*, edited by Joseph L. Blau et al., pp. vii-xi. New York: Columbia University Press, 1959.

Chazan, Robert. "The Blois Incident of 1171: A Study in Jewish Intercommunal Organization." *Proceedings of the American Academy for Jewish Research* 36 (1968): 13–31.

————. "A Twelfth-Century Communal History of Spires Jewry." *Revue des études juives* 128 (1969): 253–57.

————. *European Jewry and the First Crusade*. Berkeley: University of California Press, 1987.

Dubnov, Semen Markovich. *Weltgeschichte des jüdischen Volkes, von seinen Uranfängen bis zur Gegenwart*. Translated from the Russian by A. Steinberg. 10 vols. Berlin: Jüdischer Verlag, 1925–29.

————. *History of the Jews*. Translated from the Russian by Moshe Spiegel. 5 vols. South Brunswick, N.J.: Yoseloff, 1967–73.

Goitein, S.D. *Jews and Arabs: Their Contacts Through the Ages*. New York: Schochen, 1955.

Graetz, Heinrich. *Geschichte der Juden von ältesten Zeiten bis auf die Gegenwart*. 11 vols. Leipzig: Leiner, 1863–1902.

Lewis, Bernard. *The Jews of Islam*. London: Routledge and Kegan Paul; Princeton: Princeton University Press, 1984.

Roth, Norman. "Jewish Reactions to the ʿArabiyya and the Renaissance of Hebrew in Spain." *Journal of Semitic Studies* 28 (1983): 63–84.

————. "Polemic in Hebrew Religious Poetry of Medieval Spain." *Journal of Semitic Studies* 34 (1989): 153–77.

DOROTHY WHITELOCK

(1901–1982)

Henry Loyn

Dorothy Whitelock, eminent Anglo-Saxonist of social and literary history, was born in Leeds on 11 November 1901 and died in a Cambridge nursing home on 14 August 1982. The youngest of six children, she was brought up in a Yorkshire family and remained devoted all her life to the shire, its traditions, and its forthrightness. Her father, Edward, died when she was only two, and there followed a period of financial worry. Her mother, Emmeline, coped magnificently, and the children were able to take full advantage of the educational opportunities offered at that time in the public sector. Though frail, Whitelock showed academic ability from an early age. She followed the golden road open in the early twentieth century to all bright children from stable and supportive families and received a good grounding in the humanities at the local grammar school. Leeds High School was in fact outstanding, fit to be compared with the top civic schools at Birmingham, Bristol, or Manchester. Whitelock proved an excellent pupil and was offered a place at Newnham College, Cambridge, at the age of eighteen. It is a measure of her family's support that, although money was tight, there was no question of her not taking up her place. Sensibly she was encouraged to delay a year, which she spent profitably studying at the local University of Leeds, an institution already making a reputation for itself as a strong center for early English language and literature. She was therefore a little more mature academically than many of her fellow first-year undergraduates when she went to Cambridge in October 1921 to read the relatively new Section B of the English Tripos under the direction of H.M. Chadwick.

The Cambridge of the early 1920s was still in a state of turmoil after World War I, struggling to get back to normal, mourning the loss of the golden generations, slowly absorbing the curious amalgam of war survivors and schoolboys and girls. The women's colleges, Girton and Newnham, were less affected directly, but their position was insecure and regarded with suspicion by the more narrow-minded members of the academic community, who, proud of their male domination, were exclusive and clannish. Fortunately such men were not in a majority, and the female undergraduates, mostly from middle-class homes, were on the whole taught well and were received by most university tutors, male and female, on an equal footing with the men. Even so it comes still as a shock to realize that scholars of the caliber of Whitelock were not received as full members of their university until 1948, after the trauma of World War II. But the teaching was the principal matter of importance, not the technicalities of degree-awarding and status, and in this respect Whitelock was fortunate. Chadwick quickly recognized her ability. She read the difficult course that he had himself designed, a formidable mixture of Anglo-Saxon and Old Norse and a good leaven of archaeology and wider historical study. Her contemporaries knew how good she was, and no one was surprised when she achieved a First. The rest of the Tripos seems to have been something of an anticlimax, but she did well enough, and late in life her own memories singled out her tutor, Joan Bennett, and the lectures of G.G. Coulton, Stanley Bennett, and I.A. Richards. Chadwick's vision of what could be done in the field of Anglo-Saxon studies seized the imagination of this serious-minded young Yorkshire student and, reinforced by awareness of what such men as Cyril Fox were doing in archaeology, helped to shape the patterns of thought that were to prove so productive later in her career.

Success as an undergraduate was the first essential step. With Chadwick's support she then spent six full-time and hard-working years as a research student, financed by a college studentship at Newnham (1924–26), a Cambridge University studentship at the University of Uppsala (1927–29), and the prestigious Allen studentship at Cambridge (1929–30). The visible product of these years was the important *Anglo-Saxon Wills* (1930), a substantial contribution toward the realization of the Chadwickian dream. The invisible products were equally important, among them knowledge of modern diplomatic technique, a mastery of Old Norse, and confidence in handling the other Scandinavian languages, notably Swedish.

In one respect the years were aberrant. Whitelock hated travel, and indeed her whole career and life were bound up in her native Yorkshire and her two universities, Cambridge and Oxford, with regular descents on London for learned-society business and later for British Academy affairs. She enjoyed her two years in Sweden, but never went abroad again. The many invitations, notably from Scandinavia and the United States, were always politely refused on the grounds of busyness or health or both. Her health was in fact basically good. She suffered from occasional migraines and other minor ailments but was throughout her career and for a decade and more after retirement capable of long sustained periods of hard work. The heart of the matter in relation to travel was that she hated to be away from her routine, her own books, her favorite libraries, and her own circle of relations and close friends. She could lecture well, but did not enjoy lecturing as such. Her own austere comment was that one should never lecture unless one had something original to say. Her sense of duty led her to take on some examining at other universities, but she did so reluctantly. Her favored means of communication were through the well-tried one-to-one tutorial methods of Cambridge and Oxford and through her writing. Though not wealthy, for much of her life after the age of thirty she enjoyed enough comfort to provide the background for an academic career that helped to shape the direction of the disciplines of English and history. Immobility was one of the conditions of her success; later in her career she looked with horror upon the jet-set professor.

Academic posts in the late 1920s were few, but Whitelock was an obvious candidate, and in 1930 she was appointed as a teacher in the English School at St. Hilda's College, Oxford. St. Hilda's was small and poor, with only a hundred or so students and six tutorial fellows. Whitelock was in the early years without tenure, and not until 1936 was she admitted to a formal tutorship, with a full fellowship coming to her in 1937. She served St. Hilda's for twenty-seven years (1930–57), acting as vice-principal for six years. She was especially delighted when the college elected her to an honorary fellowship. For all that period her main routine tasks were connected with the instruction of undergraduates in the language side of the English School: Anglo-Saxon, Old Norse, and a certain amount of Middle English and general philology.

Whitelock's Oxford years were not uniformly happy, though she made many good and permanent friends there. She suffered a disappointment when on J.R.R. Tolkien's translation to the Merton Chair of English Language and Literature in 1945 she failed to succeed him as Rawlinson and Bosworth professor, in spite of strong support from Sir Frank Stenton and Kenneth Sisam. C.L. Wrenn proved the successful candidate. In 1957, on the retirement of Bruce Dickins, the corresponding chair in Cambridge fell vacant, and to general acclaim Whitelock was elected to the senior Anglo-Saxon post in her old university and to a fellowship in Newnham, her own former college. It was a perfect choice. She inherited the Chadwick tradition but with a reserve of Yorkshire common sense that enabled her to see how Chadwick's inspiration could best be served in the second half of the twentieth century. She was no lover of committees, but she knew how to use them and quickly showed herself to be an excellent administrator, concentrating on essentials with a minimum of fuss. She built up a splendid department, helped greatly by the fine scholar Peter Hunter Blair, then at the height of his powers as an interpreter of Bede and Northumbrian history, and by two younger scholars, both of whom she appointed and both of whom in turn succeeded her in the Cambridge chair, Peter Clemoes in Anglo-Saxon and Raymond Page in Scandinavian studies. Relationships with Nora Chadwick, Chadwick's widow and herself a formidable Celtic scholar, were sometimes strained, principally on the grounds that she placed too much emphasis on the Celtic contribution; but with the appointment of Kathleen Hughes Celtic studies also were brought fully into the team effort. Hughes became one of Whitelock's closest friends, one whose skills as an interpreter of Irish history and as a teacher she admired. Hughes's illness and early death in 1977 proved a lasting grief. In the mid-1960s this group of creative scholars under Whitelock's quiet leadership proved as fine a training ground for undergraduates interested in the language and history of Britain and Ireland in the early Middle Ages as was to be found anywhere in the world. Her final administrative triumph was to bring the Anglo-Saxon Tripos back into its natural home, the English School, away from archaeology and anthropology, an enclave into which Chadwick had guided it when the Cambridge English School was itself in disarray.

Academic and national recognition came during the later phases of Whitelock's career. She proceeded to the degree of D.Litt. at Cambridge in 1950, was elected a fellow of the British Academy in 1956, and was appointed CBE in the birthday honors list of 1964. She retired from her chair in 1969 and received the accolades of friends and fellow scholars in a Festschrift edited by Clemoes and Hughes. She continued to be active in the scholarly world, virtually up to her illness late in 1980. Sir Frank Stenton, her great mentor and guide in her later years, died in 1967, and she succeeded to two of his key offices as chairman of the Sylloge Committee of the British Academy (1967–78) and president of the English Place-Name Society (1967–79). Unmarried and used to college life for almost all her mature years, she might have found retirement traumatic, but fortunately her widowed sister, Phyllis Priestly, was free to set up house with her and the two sisters made what turned out to be a happy home for themselves in a small modern house in Cambridge.

The bare bones of the career set out above give the impression of a sound and successful academic life, and such an impression is true. What distinguishes Dorothy Whitelock from the ordinary run of good scholars is the quantity and quality of her published work. There was no early breakthrough. She was clever but also thorough and took time and patience to master the necessary techniques, and above all languages, before she set pen to paper. Her *Anglo-Saxon Wills* (1930) is typical in this respect. The product of six years of hard labor, it provided a reliable text and translation of a corpus of documentation essential for understanding the workings of late Anglo-Saxon society. The strength of its footnotes further ensured its value deep into succeeding generations. They also show that, unselfconsciously, and more by native instinct, Dorothy Whitelock was already moving into the mainstream of advanced medieval social history, exemplified by the work of Eileen Power in England and Marc Bloch in France (with neither of whom she had any significant personal contact, though Bloch commented favorably on her book in an early number of the *Annales d'histoire économique et sociale*). She was probing deep through the evidence of the wills into the realities of the social order, the transmission of land, laws of inheritance concerning property as well as land, and kindred ties and obligations.

The following years were a semifallow period for publication, a fact explicable by a heavy teaching routine seriously conducted and by the strains and obligations of the war. Whitelock produced a fine edition of Wulfstan's *Sermo Lupi ad Anglos* in 1939, which won her a Leverhulme Fellowship (though the war precluded her taking it up). Articles in the *English Historical Review* (1941 and 1948) and the *Transactions of the Royal Historical Society* (1942) established her as one of the leading authorities on Wulfstan and gave to historians as well as to language students an intelligible picture of the career of this outstanding figure, statesman and archbishop, homilist and drafter of laws for Ethelred and Cnut. During these years she played an active part in learned societies with an increasing historical bent. She became president of the Viking Society for Northern Research (1940–41) and editor of the *Saga-Book*, to which she contributed a perceptive article of permanent value on the conversion of the eastern Danelaw to Christianity. Elected fellow of the Royal Historical Society in 1930, she served on its council 1945–48. In 1945 she became a fellow of the Society of Antiquaries. This was all worthy scholarly activity, and she was respected in the scholarly world. Sir Frank and Lady Stenton had become firm friends in the 1930s and were to have massive influence on her approach to Anglo-Saxon studies. Sir Goronwy Edwards, through his editorship of the *English Historical Review,* became and remained an influential adviser. But had she died at the age of fifty, Whitelock would have been remembered as a scholar of promise with some original contributions to her credit on wills, on Wulfstan, and on the conversion of the Danes in the eastern Danelaw, and no more.

The books she produced in the brief period 1951–55 lifted Dorothy Whitelock into the world class. They applied to both sides of her disciplines and interests, the literary and historical, with the emphasis increasingly and heavily on the historical side. Much of her teaching had been directed to Anglo-Saxon poetry, and she had already contributed a penetrating analysis of "The Seafarer," in which she placed the poem in the context of Christian attitudes to penitential exile. The duality of her intellectual interests had come together in a general paper on "Anglo-Saxon Poetry and the Historian," an exercise in the judicious use of literary evidence. In 1951 she published *The Audience of Beowulf*, an important statement based on three lectures given at the University of London, arguing for a probable late eighth-, early ninth-century origin for the poem. This was followed by the influential volume in the Pelican History of England, which she called *The Beginnings of English Society* (1951); a facsimile volume in the Early English Texts in Facsimile series on the *Peterborough Chronicle* (1954); and finally in 1955 the first volume of *English Historical Documents* (to 1042), over a thousand pages of ripe scholarship, including not only a mass of reliable translation from Latin and Anglo-Saxon but shrewd comments on diplomatics connected with the manuscript sources and excellent bibliographies. This masterpiece opened up serious teaching of the Anglo-Saxon period to scholars throughout the world.

The result of all this professional activity, together with the move to Cambridge in 1957, confirmed what had become increasingly obvious: this teacher of Old English in an English faculty had developed into one of the most significant historians of her generation. When Whitelock talked to the local press at Cambridge about her appointment, she described herself as an "Anglo-Saxon historian" and welcomed her election for the prospect it opened to her for further work in the historical field. This was borne out by her publications during the tenure of the chair: her inaugural lecture (published in 1958) on *Changing Currents in Anglo-Saxon Studies*, her revision of Stevenson's edition of *Asser's Life of Alfred* (1959) and her subsequent defense of Asser's authenticity (1968), her work on the *Anglo-Saxon Chronicle* (1961), her introduction to E.O. Blake's edition of the *Liber Eliensis* for the Camden Society (1962), a series of articles in Festschriften, and, most important of all, her contribution to the magnificent edition of *The Will of Aethelgifu* for the Roxburghe Club (1968). At the same time her reputation as a literary historian deepened. Her literary output was far from neglected, and she published in 1967 a revised edition of Sweet's *Anglo-Saxon Reader* that remains in use in many university departments. King Alfred's work was a key element in her thinking, and the Gollancz memorial lecture for the British Academy on the "Old English Bede" (1962) and her general statement on the prose of Alfred's reign in *Continuations and Beginnings*, edited by E.G. Stanley (1966), laid down the basic canon of orthodoxy for Alfred's literary achievements.

In retirement Whitelock remained an active writer, working on the records of the great abbeys of eastern England, Ely and Bury St. Edmund, and advancing three formidable projects, two of which she brought to a successful conclusion. In 1979 she brought out a revision of her *English Historical Documents*, unaltered in main structure but enriched and updated in bibliography and minor emendments. The following year, before her final illness, she read the proofs of her contribution (the whole period before 1066) to the vastly important *Councils and Synods*, which she edited with Christopher Brooke and Martin Brett. Her third project, the one that ironically was closest to her intellectual interests, was not so successful. She had long planned a full-scale biography of King Alfred, but although she left a draft of the book with copious notes, it has not proved possible to mold it into publishable form. Even so the achievements of her eighth decade were impressive, especially when put side by side with her continuing activity on behalf of learned societies, such as the English Place-Name Society and the British Academy. In concentrating as we have in this section on the cold facts of Whitelock's published work we should not forget how throughout her long career she had been a tower of strength in Anglo-Saxon studies, encouraging and criticizing the work of younger scholars, reading manuscripts and generously offering material from her own vast store of knowledge that has helped to save from error or to deepen the arguments in the published studies of many grateful authors.

Whitelock's reputation rests on the strength and wide-ranging influence of her published work. *English Historical Documents* opened up the early-medieval period of British history to those with no Anglo-Saxon and little Latin. Elsewhere she struck out time and time again at the central themes; and we turn to her for authoritative statements on the *Chronicle*, *Beowulf*, the work of Wulfstan, the achievements of King Alfred, the social content of laws, charters, and wills. Her introduction to the edition of *The Will of Aethelgifu* (1968) is an illustration of her best work, but all her contributions are informed by a scrupulous regard for evidence carefully sifted and a sense of what might be called Yorkshire realism. She never forgot that she was dealing with the writings and actions of human beings and always applied the right questions to the evidence and facts that she had disentangled, often from amorphous material. She distrusted, sometimes excessively, intuitive scholars and actively disliked those who allowed themselves to be led on by preconceived ideas in the face of evidence. Some of her severity over the Asser controversy is to be explained in terms of this basic distrust.

In Whitelock's younger days, the 1920s and 1930s, both Old English language and literature and Anglo-Saxon history were in a curious in-between state. Old English was taught and examined as a compulsory part of a degree course in English in virtually all British universities. Justified on linguistic and historical grounds, the study of Old English was for many, probably most, undergraduates, a hideous chore, designed by grammarians anxious that the English discipline should not be regarded by their classical colleagues as too much of a soft option. At the theoretical level Old English studies did not fit well with developing literary criticism. Teachers of Old English were themselves divided in their approach. Some, like H.M. Chadwick, brought it heavily into contact with archaeology, history, and anthropology. Others developed it as an instrument natural to sophisticated schools of Germanic philology. All paid lip service to the strength of its poetry and the precocity of its prose without truly finding a proper intellectual home for it. Not even W.P. Ker, the most influential figure in the preceding generation, had been altogether happy over its part in European chronology. What was lacking was a sense of true historical perspective. Dorothy Whitelock realized this at an early stage in her career, and her finest and subtlest achievement, obvious from her early work on wills in 1930 and then constant throughout her professional life, was to fix the language and literature firmly in an intelligible context of both English and western European development.

To help establish Old English as an intellectual discipline in its proper historical setting was not easy. For Anglo-Saxon history itself was in an unsatisfactory state in the 1920s and 1930s. The general attitude was determined by the political historians, and among them the dominant note was that struck by the dismissive nineteenth-century belief that there was little to Anglo-Saxon history save the record of the battles of kites and crows. One had to go back as far as J.M. Kemble in the 1840s to find a strong voice capable of expressing the richness of the Anglo-Saxon scene with its complex interweaving of literary, archaeological, and numismatic evidence. But, stimulated by the genius of Frederic W. Maitland and the industry of Paul Vinogradoff and John Horace Round, some scholars were aware of the potential value of the social approach to pre-Norman history, and prominent among them was Frank M. Stenton (1880–1967).

It was a great good fortune that Whitelock in her Oxford period was able to cement a permanent friendship with Frank and Doris Stenton at their

Reading home and academic center. Stenton was a mature scholar, a fellow of the British Academy since 1926, with an international reputation for his Domesday Book studies, his knowledge of the medieval structures of the Danelaw, and his mastery of place-name and charter evidence. He was one of the leading feudal historians in the country, but his interests in the period before 1066 were sharpened when he was entrusted with the difficult task of writing the volume on *Anglo-Saxon England (c. 500–1087)* for the Oxford History of England. Whitelock was in touch throughout the formative period of the work and rightly recognized it as one of the greatest history books of the century when it appeared in 1943; she used to refer to her own book in the Pelican history as "complementary" to Stenton's work. She underestimated herself. Stenton had brought Anglo-Saxon history into the mainstream of the historical discipline almost singlehandedly, but he lacked Whitelock's linguistic expertise. While respecting his judgment, she was also able to add insights and observations based on her own profound knowledge of the language and literature.

Behind the scenes Stenton and Whitelock were a formidable combination. She consulted him regularly on historical matters; he referred linguistic problems to her. With none of the abstract theorizing characteristic of the *Annales* school in France, they together reached a conception of history that respected the totality of evidence from the past, archaeological, numismatic, and linguistic. As the younger scholar Whitelock was able to move things farther than Stenton could. Both of them recognized the importance of numismatics: the close connection they established after the war with Christopher Blunt (1904–87) and the impetuous Michael Dolley (1926–83) ensured a fruitful generation of scholarship. Notable likewise is their support of Anglo-Saxon archaeology as a discipline. It had been in an indeterminate state, but their close friendship with J.N.L. Myers (1902–89) and firm support for the newly founded Society for Medieval Archaeology of which Whitelock was vice-president for the first six years of its existence (1957–63), indicated more than a token awareness of the advances, in fact and in potential, being made in that newly vitalized discipline. Stenton died in 1967, and it was Whitelock who with Doris Stenton saw to it that a volume of his essays was produced posthumously and that the third and standard edition of his *Anglo-Saxon England* was brought out successfully in 1971. No one could have been better equipped for the task. Stenton and Whitelock were the two central figures who seemed to make Anglo-Saxon studies respectable in the vibrant modern historical world.

For this reason, and for her central position in the discipline of Old English, Dorothy Whitelock was among those few to have helped mold two major fields of study. The work of Dorothy Whitelock will long serve as a sure guide to the development of Anglo-Saxon society and to the validity of evidence from sources as disparate as *Beowulf* and Anglo-Saxon wills, Asser and the homilies, and the laws of Wulfstan. It is in her combination of linguistic and historical expertise that her contribution is unique. She has left work of enduring use and value to succeeding generations.

SELECTED BIBLIOGRAPHY

A more detailed bibliography up to 1970, including a host of learned reviews and obituary notices for such scholars as Sir Frank Stenton and Florence Harmer, appears in Clemoes and Hughes, 1–4.

Works

BOOKS AND ARTICLES

Ed. and trans. *Anglo-Saxon Wills*. Cambridge: Cambridge University Press, 1930.

"A Note on Wulfstan the Homilist." *English Historical Review* 52 (1937): 460–65.

Ed. *Sermo Lupi ad Anglos*, by Wulfstan. London: Methuen, 1939.

"Wulfstan and the So-called Laws of Edward and Guthrum." *English Historical Review* 56 (1941): 1–21.

"The Conversion of the Eastern Danelaw." *Saga-Book of the Viking Society* 12 (1941): 159–76.

"Archbishop Wulfstan, Homilist and Statesman." *Transactions of the Royal Historical Society*, 4th ser., 24 (1942): 25–45.

"Wulfstan and the Laws of Cnut." *English Historical Review* 63 (1948): 433–52.

"Anglo-Saxon Poetry and the Historian." *Transactions of the Royal Historical Society*, 4th ser., 31 (1949): 75–94.

"The Interpretation of the Seafarer." In *The Early Cultures of North-West Europe: H.M. Chadwick Memorial Studies*, edited by Cyril Fox and Bruce Dickins, pp. 259–72. Cambridge: Cambridge University Press, 1950.

The Audience of Beowulf. Oxford: Clarendon, 1951.

The Beginnings of English Society. Harmondsworth: Penguin, 1952.

Ed. *The Peterborough Chronicle*. Early English Manuscripts in Facsimile, 4. Copenhagen: Rosenkilde and Bagger, 1954.

Ed. *English Historical Documents. I: c. 500–1042*. London: Eyre and Spottiswoode, 1955. 2nd rev. ed., 1979.

Changing Currents in Anglo-Saxon Studies: An Inaugural Lecture. Cambridge: Cambridge University Press, 1958.

"The Dealings of the Kings of England with Northumbria in the Tenth and Eleventh Centuries." In *The Anglo-Saxons: Studies in Some Aspects of Their History and Culture Presented to Bruce Dickins*, edited by Peter Clemoes, pp. 70–88. London: Bowes and Bowes, 1959.

"Recent Work on Asser's Life of Alfred." In *Asser's Life of King Alfred*, edited by W.H. Stevenson, pp. cxxxii–cliii. Rev. ed. Oxford: Clarendon, 1959.

Ed. and trans. with S. Tucker and D.C. Douglas. *The Anglo-Saxon Chronicle: A Revised Translation*. London: Eyre and Spottiswoode, 1961.

"The Old English Bede." Sir Israel Gollancz Memorial Lecture. *Proceedings of the British Academy* 48 (1962): 57–90.

Foreword to *Liber Eliensis*. Edited by E.O. Blake, pp. ix–xviii. London: Offices of the Royal Historical Society, 1962.

"Wulfstan at York." In *Franciplegius: Medieval and Linguistic Studies in Honor of Francis Peabody Magoun, Jr.*, edited by J.B. Bessinger, Jr. and R.P. Creed, pp.

214–31. New York: New York University Press, 1965.

"The Anglo-Saxon Achievement." In *The Norman Conquest: Its Setting and Impact: A Book Commemorating the Ninth Centenary of the Battle of Hastings*, edited by C.T. Chevallier, pp. 13–43. London: Eyre and Spottiswoode, 1966.

"The Prose of Alfred's Reign." In *Continuations and Beginnings: Studies in Old English Literature*, edited by E.G. Stanley, pp. 67–103. London: Nelson, 1966.

Ed. *Sweet's Anglo-Saxon Reader: In Prose and Verse*. 15th ed. London: Oxford University Press, 1967.

The Genuine Asser. 1967 Stenton Lecture. Reading: University of Reading, 1968.

Trans. and examined (with contributions from Neil Ker and Lord Rennell). *The Will of Aethelgifu: A Tenth Century Anglo-Saxon Manuscript*. Oxford: Oxford University Press for the Roxburghe Club, 1968.

"Wulfstan Cantor and Anglo-Saxon Law." In *Nordica et Anglica: Studies in Honor of Stefán Einarsson*, edited by Alan H. Orrick, pp. 83–92. The Hague: Mouton, 1968.

"William of Malmesbury and the Works of King Alfred." In *Medieval Literature and Civilization: Studies in Memory of G.N. Garmonsway*, edited by D.A. Pearsall and R.A. Waldron, pp. 78–93. London: Athlone, 1968.

"Fact and Fiction in the Legend of St. Edmund." *Proceedings of the Suffolk Institute of Archaeology* 31 (1969): 217–33.

"The Authorship of the Account of King Edgar's Establishment of Monasteries." In *Philological Essays: Studies in Old and Middle English Language and Literature in Honour of Herbert Dean Meritt*, edited by J.L. Rosier, pp. 125–36. The Hague: Mouton, 1970.

"The Pre-Viking Age Church in East Anglia." *Anglo-Saxon England* 1 (1972): 1–22.

"The Appointment of Dunstan as Archbishop of Canterbury." In *Otium et Negotium: Studies in Onomatology and Library Science Presented to Olaf von Feilitzen*, edited by Folke Sandgren, pp. 232–67. Stockholm: Nordstedt and Soner, 1973.

"The List of Chapter-Headings in the Old English Bede." In *Old English Studies in Honour of John C. Pope*, edited by R.B. Burlin and E.B. Irving, Jr., pp. 263–84. Toronto: University of Toronto Press, 1974.

Some Anglo-Saxon Bishops of London. Chambers Memorial Lecture. London: Lewis, 1975.

"Bede and His Teachers and Friends." In *Famulus Christi: Essays in Commemoration of the Thirteenth Centenary of the Birth of the Venerable Bede*, edited by Gerald Bonner, pp. 19–39. London: Society for Promoting Christian Knowledge, 1976.

"Some Charters in the Name of King Alfred." In *Saints, Scholars and Heroes: Studies in Medieval Culture in Honour of Charles W. Jones*, 2 vols., edited by Margot King and W.M. Stevens, vol. 1, pp. 77–98. Collegeville, Minn.: Hill Monastic Manuscript Library, Saint John's Abbey and University, 1979.

From Bede to Alfred: Studies in Early Anglo-Saxon Literature and History. London: Variorum Reprints, 1980.

History, Law and Literature in 10th–11th Century England. London: Variorum Reprints, 1981.

Ed. with M. Brett and C.N.L. Brooke. *Councils and Synods: With Other Documents Relating to the English Church, 1: A.D. 871–1204*. Oxford: Clarendon, 1981.

LETTERS AND PAPERS

Whitelock's letters and papers are housed at Trinity College, Cambridge, under the custodianship of Dr. Simon D. Keynes, Reader in Anglo-Saxon history.

Sources

Clemoes, Peter, and Kathleen Hughes. *England Before the Conquest: Studies in Primary Sources Presented to Dorothy Whitelock.* Cambridge: Cambridge University Press, 1971.

George Ostrogorsky

(1902–1976)

Bariša Krekić

George Ostrogorsky, eminent twentieth-century Byzantinist and socioeconomic historian, was born on 19 January 1902, in St. Petersburg, Russia, and died on 24 October 1976 in Belgrade, Yugoslavia. The son of Alexandra Konstantinovna Leman and Alexander Yakovlievitch Ostrogorsky, himself an educator, the young Ostrogorsky attended the classical gymnasium, where he learned Greek. Completing his studies, Ostrogorsky left his native city with his family after the Bolshevik revolution and ended up in Germany, where he eventually became a student of philosophy and sociology at the prestigious University of Heidelberg (1921). It was there that this man who always felt a great affinity for Russian literature first came in contact with and developed an interest in Byzantine studies.

In Germany Ostrogorsky had among his teachers Karl Jaspers, Alfred Weber, Ludwig Curtius, and others, but it was Percy Ernst Schramm who introduced him to Byzantium. Upon graduation from Heidelberg Ostrogorsky spent two years in Paris studying Byzantine history with Charles Diehl, Gabriel Millet, and Germaine Rouillard. He obtained his doctorate in 1927 from Heidelberg; his dissertation instantly gained him recognition in scholarly circles. In 1928 he became a *Dozent* (assistant professor) for Byzantine history at the University of Breslau (Wrocław). His publications established him, in spite of his youth, as a prominent European Byzantinist, and when the University of Belgrade was looking for a professor of Byzantine history in 1933, Ostrogorsky was the obvious choice. He remained in Belgrade until his death, forty-three years later.

It was in Belgrade that Ostrogorsky wrote the masterly works that established his reputation. In 1946 Ostrogorsky became a corresponding, and in 1948 a full, member of the Serbian Academy of Sciences and Arts. In subsequent years he became a member of numerous other Yugoslav and foreign academies and scholarly societies (Yugoslav Academy of Sciences and

Arts in Zagreb, Medieval Academy of America, Académie des Inscriptions in Paris, Austrian Academy in Vienna) and was granted doctorates *honoris causa* from Oxford University, the Sorbonne, the University of Strasbourg, and other institutions, as well as a number of Yugoslav and foreign decorations, medals, and awards, among them the German order "Pour le Mérite" in Arts and Sciences.

A great scholar and teacher, Ostrogorsky was also a tireless organizer of scholarly work. As founder and first director (1948–76) of the Byzantine Institute of the Serbian Academy of Sciences and Arts, he gathered a small group of students and young scholars and guided them with wisdom, patience, and tact, creating what later became known as the "Belgrade Byzantine School." With his calm, unpretentious authority, his modesty, warmth, and tact, Ostrogorsky enjoyed spontaneous devotion and deep respect from his students and collaborators. He was a teacher and a friend, always ready to help, in scholarship and in daily life, a man from whom one learned not only the secrets of Byzantine history but also the wisdom of coping with contemporary life's problems.

He was married twice. His first wife, Irene, with whom he had a daughter, Olga, died in 1948. He later married Fanula Papazoglu, a professor of ancient history at the University of Belgrade, with whom he had a daughter and a son. In his private life Ostrogorsky, a quiet and refined man, enjoyed books and the company of friends. In his later years he was especially proud of the progress his students had made, among them the late Franjo Barišić and Ivanka Nikolajević, Jadran Ferluga, Božidar Ferjančić, Ljubomir Maksimović, Mirjana Živojinović, and Bariša Krekić, and of the success of the Byzantine Institute and its publications, to which he dedicated much time and energy until the last days of his life.

Ostrogorsky's scholarly activity spans fifty years, from 1926 until his death in 1976. His early articles dealt with the Byzantine taxation system and Byzantine art. His first published article ("Vizantijskij podatnoj ustav") treated the former subject, as did his doctoral dissertation, *Die ländliche Steuergemeinde des byzantinischen Reiches im X. Jahrhundert*, published in 1927, which immediately became a landmark in Byzantine economic and social history. It was reviewed positively by some of the most prominent scholars of the time, such as H. Grégoire, E. Stein, and A. Andreades, which indicates its importance and impact. By comparing the Byzantine Farmer's Law (late seventh or early eighth century) and a treatise on taxation (most probably from the first half of the tenth century), Ostrogorsky analyzed the evolution of the position of the Byzantine peasant in that period. Although both sources mentioned the existence of free peasants—mostly Slavs, in

Ostrogorsky's opinion—and of peasant communities, the later text shows that the peasant communities in the tenth century had undergone a process of visible social differentiation, with richer members of the community holding separate properties. Collective payment of taxes by the peasant community to the state persisted, while the social and economic diversification was transforming the peasant community from a free institution into a fiscal one.

Ostrogorsky's other interest, Byzantine art, found its early expression in *Studien zur Geschichte des byzantinischen Bilderstreites* (1929). Like his work on taxation this book also found an immediate and favorable reception in scholarly circles; among its reviewers were such luminaries as F. Dölger, F. Dvornik, and V. Grumel. With care and patience, Ostrogorsky had studied the iconophile texts, treaties, and speeches to uncover and reconstruct as much as possible the ideas, views, and attitudes of the iconoclasts. The quality and results of his analysis assured Ostrogorsky's work an honorable place among studies of Byzantine art and mentality. Between 1927 and 1939 Ostrogorsky published articles on Byzantine iconoclasm and art, the most significant being "Les débuts de la Querelle des Images" (1930); "Otnoshenie cerkvi i gosudarstva v Vizantii" (1931); and "Rom und Byzanz im Kampfe um die Bilderverehrung" (1933).

Both socioeconomic history and art history continued to attract Ostrogorsky's attention throughout his life, the former becoming a major focus of his research. From the late 1920s to the early 1940s he dedicated articles to problems of Byzantine society and economy, especially the life of the peasantry (e.g., "Die wirtschaftlichen und sozialen Entwicklungsgrundlagen des byzantinischen Reiches" [1929], "Löhne und Preise in Byzanz" [1932], "Agrarian Conditions in the Byzantine Empire in the Middle Ages" [1941]). He also published valuable studies on early Byzantine sources ("Die Chronologie des Theophanes im VII. und VIII. Jahrhundert" [1930], "Slavyanskij perevod hroniki Simeona Logofeta" [1932]) and wrote a series of important articles analyzing the hierarchical order and structures in Byzantium and related countries ("Das Mitkaisertum im mittelalterlichen Byzanz" [1930], "Die Krönungsordnungen des Zeremonienbuches" [1932], "Avtokrator i samodržac" [1935], "Die byzantinische Staatenhierarchie" [1936]). After his arrival in Belgrade in 1933 Ostrogorsky became more directly interested in the relations between Byzantium and the southern Slavs, an interest that resulted in yet another group of significant articles in the 1930s ("Iz čega i kako je postala Vizantija" [1934], "Historische Entwicklung der Balkanhalbinsel im Zeitalter der byzantinischen Vorherrschaft" [1936], "Pismo Dimitrija Homatijana Sv.Savi" [1939]). Finally, he never forgot his Russian roots, and in his work he paid attention to problems of the Russian past ("Das Projekt einer Rangtabelle aus der Zeit des Caren Fedor Alekseevič" [1933], "Vladimir Svyatoi i Vizantiya" [1939]; "L'expédition du Prince Oleg contre Constantinople en 907" [1939]).

In some of his articles published in the 1930s Ostrogorsky began to develop his ideas on the emperor Heraclius's reforms in the first half of the seventh century and their role in the development of Byzantine society, administrative structure, and military establishment. These views found their fullest expression in Ostrogorsky's major work, *Geschichte des byzantinischen Staates*, published in 1940. Although it appeared while World War II was raging, the book found an immediate, powerful, and positive response throughout the scholarly community. Elegantly written, reviewed by scores of leading scholars in the most prestigious journals, Ostrogorsky's work confirmed its author's rank among a handful of leading Byzantinists in the world, all of them much older than he was at the time.

After World War II Ostrogorsky's *Geschichte* was reedited three times in German (1952, 1963, 1965; at the time of his death he was preparing a new edition) and translated into Serbo-Croatian (1947, 1959, 1970), French (1956), English (1956, 1957, 1968, 1969), Slovenian (1961), Polish (1967, 1968), and Italian (1968). The standard Byzantine history in universities throughout the world and the main reference work for scholars, Ostrogorsky's *Geschichte* achieved this status for its originality of ideas, cogent reasoning, and clarity of presentation; its depth and meticulousness of source analysis and thorough knowledge of the bibliography; and its breadth of synthesis. Having established the three basic elements that, according to him, created the uniqueness of Byzantium—"Roman political concepts, Greek culture, and the Christian faith"—Ostrogorsky, in "Die Perioden der byzantinischen Geschichte," divided Byzantine history into eight periods: the Early Byzantine State (324–610); the Struggle for Existence and the Revival of the Byzantine State (610–711); the Age of the Iconoclast Crisis (711–843); the Golden Age (843–1025); Government of the Civil Aristocracy (1025–81); the Rule of the Military Aristocracy (1081–1204); Latin Rule and the Restoration of Byzantium (1204–82); and the Decline and Fall of Byzantium (1282–1453).

It was in the second chapter of his *Geschichte* that Ostrogorsky formulated his views of Heraclius's reforms and their role in Byzantine history. In Ostrogorsky's opinion Heraclius, while preparing for the war against Persia, undertook a radical reform of the provincial organization by creating in Asia Minor the first of the new military-administrative units, the *themes*. The head of each *theme*, its *strategos*, exercised both civilian and military authority in his area. From Asia Minor the *themes* spread gradually into the

European portion of the empire and became the mainstay of its strength in subsequent centuries. Inside each *theme* troops were settled and grants of land made to soldiers (*stratiotika ktemata*), on condition of hereditary military service. According to Ostrogorsky, these soldier-farmers, *stratiotai*, became the main military force of the Byzantine Empire and helped to save it first from the Persians and later from other enemies. The soldier-farmers constituted a vigorous new component of the Byzantine society and state and had a deep and positive influence on their development. Ostrogorsky's thesis was not unanimously accepted. It provoked a lively debate (e.g., with Paul Lemerle, J. Karayannopoulous, J. Haldon, and others) that is still going on. Ostrogorsky himself remained faithful to these ideas to the end of his life and restated them in several of his works.

Another part of Ostrogorsky's *Geschichte* deserves mention, the two last chapters (7 and 8), in which he deals with the fate of Byzantium after 1204. This is a period that earlier Byzantinists had tended to slight in the belief that after the collapse of Constantinople in 1204 the remaining years of the empire were just a slow agony leading to its inevitable demise. But Ostrogorsky showed that the Byzantine Empire in Asia Minor—the Nicaean Empire—had become a healthy and viable state and that after the restoration of Byzantium in Constantinople in 1261 the empire remained vigorous, under the skillful leadership of Michael VIII Palaeologos. It was only after his death in 1282 that the decline set in, caused in part by internal exhaustion, weakness, and divisions, and in part by foreign threats, especially, after the mid-fourteenth century, by the overwhelming Ottoman pressure.

After World War II, alongside his work as a professor at the University of Belgrade and his new duties as director of the Byzantine Institute of the Serbian Academy of Sciences and Arts (founded in 1948) and as editor of Volumes 1–17 of its *Zbornik radova* (1952–76), Ostrogorsky continued his own research and publishing. His interest in Byzantine society, especially landholdings and peasantry, was undiminished, as witnessed by numerous articles on those topics, published between 1947 and 1973. The most important work in this area is his book on the *pronoia*, a type of temporary landholding, in Byzantium and the south Slavic lands, *Pronija: Prilog istoriji feudalizma u Vizantiji i južnoslovenskim zemljama* (1951), in which he focused his attention on late Byzantine history and on the feudal elements in Byzantine society. Ostrogorsky put the emergence of the *pronoia* in the period of Alexius Comnenus (1081–1118), who wanted to base the empire's military strength on new resources. With the disappearance of the *stratiotika ktemata* in the early eleventh century, the feudal component had become the mainstay of the Byzantine military, and the *pronoia* developed as an outgrowth of that change. In the Palaeologan period the *pronoia* underwent modifications (especially sporadic transformation from temporary into hereditary landholding) and spread into south Slavic lands. From his studies of the peasantry and the *pronoia* Ostrogorsky concluded, contrary to the opinion of some other historians, that Byzantine feudalism had taken shape before the Fourth Crusade and that the impact of the crusaders on the development of Byzantine society was not as decisive as had been frequently thought.

In the post-World War II period Ostrogorsky remained involved in research on Byzantine-south Slavic relations. He was the editor of the multivolume *Byzantine Sources for the History of the Peoples of Yugoslavia* (sole editor of Volumes 1 and 2, co-editor with Franjo Barišić of Volumes 3 and 4) and published a number of articles on those subjects: "Une ambassade serbe auprès de l'empereur Basile II" (1949); "Dušan i njegova vlastela u borbi sa Vizantijom" (1951); "Byzantium and the South Slavs" (1963); and "Autour d'un prostagma de Jean VIII Paléologue" (1967). His highest achievement in this field is *Serska oblast posle Dušanove smrti* (1965), in which he argues that after 1355 in the disintegrating Serbian empire, Serres became the center of a state in which first the Serbian emperor Dušan's widow, Helen, and then Despot Jovan Uglješa Mrnjavčević held power until 1371. Located in the area of the Serbian empire that was closest to Byzantium, its lay and ecclesiastical organization followed most closely the Byzantine model; the state of Serres also encompassed within its borders the important monastic establishment of Mount Athos. Perhaps most significant, however, was the disturbing reality that Serres was closest of all Serbian lands to the area of Ottoman invasion and was among the first to feel the impact of the Ottoman expansion. The ruler of Serres, Jovan Uglješa, together with his brother, the Serbian king Vukašin Mrnjavčević, led the first Serbian army that confronted the Ottomans in a major battle, on the River Maritsa in 1371. The Serbian defeat opened wide the gates of southeastern Europe to the Ottomans, who never stopped until they reached Vienna in the sixteenth century. From detailed, accurate, and systematic study of sparse and little-known documents, Ostrogorsky mined important new information and outlined a lively, innovative, and comprehensive picture of internal and international affairs of this important region in a crucial period of its history, a period that fatefully affected all southern Slavs.

Although focusing mainly on Byzantine socioeconomic history and Byzantine-south Slavic relations in his most productive post-World War II period, Ostrogorsky remained interested in other aspects of the Byzantine past that had been part of his earlier research. This is especially evident in his persistent interest in the organization of the *themes*, in the Byzantine hierarchical order, and in Russia and its relations with Byzantium. Likewise, Ostrogorsky continued to be open to new ideas and topics, as witnessed by his articles on Byzantine society and cities in the early period and on the Moravian Mission. In 1969–70 Ostrogorsky had a rare tribute paid to his work, when the major publishing house in Belgrade, Prosveta, published his *Collected Works* in six volumes, including all his books and most of his articles, all of them translated into Serbo-Croatian (*Sabrana dela Georgija Ostrogorskog*). Although he continued to publish until 1973, his *Collected Works* are an immense source of knowledge and information and remain the principal place for the study of Ostrogorsky's methodology and of his approach to Byzantine history and to historical research in general.

A product of the classical German historical school, George Ostrogorsky was also much more than that. He brought to his research an unswerving love of Russian culture and a high regard for the achievements of Russian Byzantinists. Having spent most of his life in Yugoslavia, he acquired a permanent attachment to that area, which had long been under Byzantine domination and had preserved strong Byzantine cultural influences. At the same time he was a cosmopolitan. He participated in many congresses, conferences, and symposia and lectured throughout Europe. He visited the United States twice, in 1957 and in 1969, spending most of his time at Dumbarton Oaks, in Washington, D.C., but also lecturing at American universities. Fluent in many languages, he had no trouble adjusting to different milieus and communicating with people. Early in his life Ostrogorsky established ties with distinguished scholars all over the world. He maintained those links and kept up with contemporary trends and innovations in historical research and writing, while himself exercising a powerful influence on modern historiography. He generously opened many doors for his students and collaborators, enabling them to take advantage of institutions and scholars the world over and to be included in the international scholarly community.

Ostrogorsky's work was characterized by meticulous and penetrating analysis of sources. It is amazing to see the amount of information that he was able to extract from archival and narrative sources, and the scope of conclusions that he was able to draw from those texts. Yet he never went beyond the limits of careful scholarship, never "forcing" sources to yield information or conclusions that were not there. A second characteristic of Ostrogorsky's work was the originality of his ideas, especially ideas concerning Byzantine society: peasants and their position, administrative structure and hierarchical order, relations between Byzantium and the southern Slavs, and the chronological sequence of Byzantine history. Ostrogorsky formulated his ideas after long and painstaking meditation, but once having formulated them he remained convinced of their correctness and, gentle as he was, defended his positions with persistence and determination.

The third—possibly the most important—characteristic of Ostrogorsky's work was his ability to view history from a broad perspective, to grasp the long-term historical processes and evaluate them as part of a wide-ranging whole rather than as fragments of single historical developments. His work has had an enormous influence on Byzantine scholarship and medieval studies in general, remaining fundamental for the study of Byzantine and medieval south Slavic history. The fact that controversies surrounding some of his ideas and some portions of his *oeuvre* are still going on almost twenty years after his death is perhaps the best tribute to his greatness and to his lasting impact on historiography.

Selected Bibliography
For complete bibliographies of Ostrogorsky's works see Krekić and Radojčić; and Krekić, Radojčić, and Djurić.

Works

Books and Articles
"Vizantijskij podatnoj ustav" [The Byzantine Taxation System]. *Recueil Kondakov* (1926): 109–24.
"Die ländliche Steuergemeinde des byzantinischen Reiches im X. Jahrhundert." *Vierteljahrschrift für Sozial- und Wirtschaftsgeschichte* (hereafter *VSWG*) 20 (1927): 1–108. New ed. Amsterdam: Hakkert, 1969.
Studien zur Geschichte des byzantinischen Bilderstreites. Breslau: Marcus, 1929. New ed. Amsterdam: Hakkert, 1964.
"Die wirtschaftlichen und sozialen Entwicklungsgrundlagen des byzantinischen Reiches." *VSWG* 22 (1929): 129–43.
"Über die vermeintliche Reformtätigkeit der Isaurier." *Byzantinische Zeitschrift* (hereafter *BZ*) 30 (1930): 394–400.
"Die Chronologie des Theophanes im VII. und VIII. Jahrhundert." *Byzantinisch-Neugriechische Jahrbücher* 7 (1930): 1–56.
"Les débuts de la Querelle des Images." *Mélanges Charles Diehl: Études sur l'histoire et sur l'art de Byzance* 1 (1930): 235–55.
"Das Mitkaisertum im mittelalterlichen Byzanz." In *Doppelprinzipat und Reichsteilung im Imperium Romanum*, edited by E. Kornemann, pp. 166–78. Leipzig: Teubner, 1930.
"Otnoshenie cerkvi i gosudarstva v Vizantii" [The Relationship of the Church and State in Byzantium]. *Seminarium Kondakovianum* (hereafter *SK*) 4 (1931): 119–34.
"Das Steuersystem im byzantinischen Altertum und Mittelalter." *Byzantion* (hereafter *Byz.*) 6 (1931): 229–40.
"Die Krönungsordnungen des Zeremonienbuches." *Byz.* 7 (1932): 185–233.
"Slavyanskij perevod hroniki Simeona Logofeta" [The Slavic Translation of the Chronicle of Symeon Logothetes]. *SK* 5 (1932): 17–37.
"Löhne und Preise in Byzanz." *BZ* 32 (1932): 293–333.
"Rom und Byzanz im Kampfe um die Bilderverehrung." *SK* 6 (1933): 73–87.

"Das Projekt einer Rangtabelle aus der Zeit des Caren Fedor Alekseevič." *Jahrbücher für Kultur und Geschichte der Slaven* 9 (1933): 86–138.

"Iz čega i kako je postala Vizantija?" [From What and How Did Byzantium Originate?]. *Srpski književni glasnik* (1934): 508–14.

"Avtokrator i samodržac" [Autocrat and Absolutist]. *Glas Srpske kraljevske akademije* 164 (1935): 97–187.

"Zum Stratordienst des Herrschers in der byzantinisch-slavischen Welt." *SK* 7 (1935): 187–204.

"Historische Entwicklung der Balkanhalbinsel im Zeitalter der byzantinischen Vorherrschaft." *Revue internationale des études balkaniques* 4 (1936): 389–97.

"Die byzantinische Staatenhierarchie." *SK* 8 (1936): 41–61.

"Vozvyshenie roda Angelov" [The Rise of the Angelos Family]. *Sbornik Russkogo Arheologicheskogo Obshestva v Yugoslavii* (1936): 111–29.

"Autokrator Johannes II und Basileus Alexios." *Annales de l'Institut Kondakov* 10 (1938): 179–83.

"Pismo Dimitrija Homatijana Sv.Savi" [The Letter of Demetrius Chomatianus to Saint Sava]. *Svetosavski Zbornik* 2 (1939): 89–113.

"Vladimir Svyatoi i Vizantiya" [Saint Vladimir and Byzantium]. In *Vladimirskij Sbornik*, pp. 31–40. Belgrade, 1939.

"L'expédition du Prince Oleg contre Constantinople en 907." *Annales de l'Institut Kondakov* 11 (1939): 47–62.

Geschichte des byzantinischen Staates. Munich: Beck, 1940. Translated as *Istorija Vizantije.* Belgrade: Prosveta, 1947, 1970; as *Histoire de l'état byzantin.* Paris: Payot, 1956; as *History of the Byzantine State* by Joan Hussey. Oxford: Blackwell, 1956; rev. ed., Brunswick, N.J.: Rutgers University Press, 1969; as *Zgodovina Bizanca.* Ljubljana: Državna založba Slovenije, 1961; as *Dzieje Bizancjum.* Warsaw: Państwowe Wydawnietwo Naukowe, 1967; and as *Storia dell'Impero Bizantino.* Torino: Einaudi, 1968.

"Die Perioden der byzantinischen Geschichte." *Historische Zeitschrift* 163 (1941): 229–54.

"Agrarian Conditions in the Byzantine Empire in the Middle Ages." In *Cambridge Economic History of Europe*, edited by J.H. Claphem and Eileen Power, vol. 1, pp. 194–223, 579–83. Cambridge: Cambridge University Press, 1941.

"The Peasant's Pre-emption Right: An Abortive Reform of the Macedonian Emperors." *Papers Presented to N.H. Baynes. Journal of Roman Studies* 37 (1947): 117–26.

"Vizantijskie piscovye knigi" [Byzantine Cadastral Books]. *Byzantinoslavica* 9 (1948): 203–306.

"Serbskoe posol'stvo k imperatoru Vasiliyu II" [The Serbian Embassy to the Emperor Basil II]. *Glas Srpske akademije nauka* 193 (1949): 15–29.

"Elevteri: Prilog istoriji seljaštva u Vizantiji" [Eleutheri. Contribution to the History of the Peasantry in Byzantium]. *Zbornik Filozofskog fakulteta Univerziteta u Beogradu* 1 (1949): 45–62.

"Le grand domaine dans l'empire byzantin." *Recueils de la Société Jean Bodin* 4 (1949): 35–50.

"Une ambassade serbe auprès de l'empereur Basile II." *Byz.* 19 (1949): 187–94.

Pronija: Prilog istoriji feudalizma u Vizantiji i južnoslovenskim zemljama [Pronoia: Contribution to the History of Feudalism in Byzantium and in South Slavic Lands]. Belgrade: Naučna Knjiga, 1951. Translated as *Pour l'histoire de la féodalité byzantine.* Brussels: Institut de Philologie et d'Histoire Orientales et Slaves, 1954.

"Urum-Despotes: Die Anfänge der Despoteswürde in Byzanz." *Festschrift für F. Dölger. BZ* 44 (1951): 448–60.

"Dušan i njegova vlastela u borbi sa Vizantijom" [Dušan and His Nobility in the

Struggle with Byzantium]. *Zbornik u čast šeste stogodišnjice Zakonika cara Dušana* 1 (1951): 79–86. Translated as "Étienne Dušan et la noblesse serbe dans la lutte contre Byzance." *Byz.* 22 (1952–53): 151–59.

"Postanak tema Helada i Peloponez" [The Creation of the Themes of Hellas and Peloponnesus]. *Zbornik radova Vizantološkog instituta* (hereafter *ZRVI*) 1 (1952): 64–77.

"Taktikon Uspenskog i Taktikon Beneševića: O vremenu njihovog postanka" [The Uspenski Taktikon and the Beneševič Taktikon: On the Time of Their Origins]. *ZRVI* 2 (1953): 39–59.

"Sur la date de la composition du Livre des Thèmes et sur l'époque de la constitution des premiers thèmes d'Asie Mineure." *Byz.* 23 (1953): 31–66.

"O vizantiskim državnim seljacima i vojnicima-dve povelje iz doba Jovana Cimiska [On Byzantine State Peasants and Soldiers]. *Glas Srpske akademije* 214 (1954): 23–46.

Quelques problèmes d'histoire de la paysannerie byzantine. Brussels: Éditions de Byzantion, 1956.

"Staat und Gesellschaft der frühbyzantinischen Zeit." *Historia mundi* 4 (1956): 556–69.

"The Byzantine Emperor and the Hierarchical World Order." *Slavonic and East European Review* 35 (1956): 1–14.

"Byzance, état tributaire de l'empire turc." *ZRVI* 5 (1958): 49–58.

"Das byzantinische Kaiserreich in seiner inneren Struktur." *Historia mundi* 6 (1958): 445–73.

"Pour l'histoire de l'immunité à Byzance." *Mélanges Rodolphe Guilland. Byz.* 28 (1958): 165–254.

"Byzantium in the Seventh Century." *Dumbarton Oaks Papers* 13 (1959): 1–21.

"Byzantine Cities in the Early Middle Ages." *Dumbarton Oaks Papers* 13 (1959): 47–66.

"L'Exarchat de Ravenne et l'origine des thèmes byzantins." In *Corsi di cultura sull'arte ravennate e bizantina*, fasc. 1, pp. 99–110. Ravenna: Longo, 1960.

"Radolivo, selo svetogorskog manastira Ivirona" [Radolivo, Village of the Monastery Iviron on Mount Athos]. *ZRVI* 7 (1961): 67–84.

"La commune rurale byzantine: loi agraire—traité fiscal—cadastre de Thèbes." *Byz.* 32 (1962): 139–66.

"Byzantium and the South Slavs." *Slavonic and East European Review* 42 (1963): 1–14.

"Alexios Raul, Grossdomestikos von Serbien." In *Festschrift für Percy Ernst Schramm*, edited by Peter Classen and Peter Scheibert, pp. 340–52. Wiesbaden: Steiner, 1964.

Serska oblast posle Dušanove smrti [The Region of Serres After Dušan's Death]. Belgrade: Naučno Delo, 1965.

"La prise de Serrès par les Turcs." *Mémorial Henri Grégoire. Byz.* 35 (1965): 302–19.

"The Byzantine Background of the Moravian Mission." *Dumbarton Oaks Papers* 19 (1965): 1–18.

"The Palaeologi." In vol. 4, part 1 of *The Cambridge Medieval History*, pp. 331–87 and 897–908. 2nd ed. Cambridge: Cambridge University Press, 1966.

"Agrarian Conditions of the Byzantine Empire in the Middle Ages." In vol. 1 of *The Cambridge Economic History of Europe*, edited by M.M. Postan, pp. 205–34 and 774–79. 2nd. ed. Cambridge: Cambridge University Press, 1966.

"Autour d'un prostagma de Jean VIII Paléologue." *ZRVI* 10 (1967): 63–85.

"Problèmes des relations byzantino-serbes au XIVe siècle." In *Proceedings of the 13th International Congress of Byzantine Studies*, pp. 41–55. London: Oxford University Press, 1967.

"Vizantiya i kievskaya knyaginya Ol'ga" [Byzantium and the Kievan Princess Olga].

In vol. 2 of *To Honor Roman Jakobson*, pp. 1458–1473. The Hague: Mouton, 1967.

"Prostagme srpskih vladara" [The Prostagmas of the Serbian Rulers]. *Prilozi za književnost, jezik, istoriju i folklor* 34 (1968): 245–57.

"Das Chrysobull des Despoten Johannes Orsini für das Kloster von Lykusada." *ZRVI* 11 (1968): 205–13.

Sabrana dela Georgija Ostrogorskog [Collected Works of George Ostrogorsky]. Edited by Živorad Stojković. 6 vols. Belgrade: Prosveta, 1969–70.

"Die Pronoia unter den Komnenen." *ZRVI* 12 (1970): 41–54.

"Observations on the Aristocracy in Byzantium." *Dumbarton Oaks Papers* 25 (1971): 1–32.

"Komitisa i svetogorski manastiri" [Komitisa and the Monasteries of Mount Athos]. *ZRVI* 13 (1971): 221–56.

"Drei Praktika weltlicher Grundbesitzer aus der ersten Hälfte des 14. Jahrhunderts." *ZRVI* 14/15 (1973): 81–101.

LETTERS AND PAPERS

Ostrogorsky's letters and papers are housed at his home in Belgrade; his library is in the Byzantine Institute of the Serbian Academy of Sciences and Arts in Belgrade.

Sources

Barišić, Franjo. "Ostrogorski, Georgije." In *Enciklopedija Jugoslavije*, vol. 6, pp. 396–97. Zagreb: Izd. Leksikografskog zavoda FNRJ, 1965.

———. "Akademik Georgije Ostrogorski kao organizator naučnih istraživanja." *ZRVI* 18 (1978): 281–85.

Ćirković, Sima. "Akademik Georgije Ostrogorski u jugoslovenskoj istoriografiji." *ZRVI* 18 (1978): 278–81.

Dinić, Mihailo. "Povodom pedesetogodišnjice Georgija Ostrogorskog." *ZRVI* 1 (1952): 275.

Ferjančić, Božidar. "Akademik Georgije Ostrogorski u svetskoj vizantologiji." *ZRVI* 18 (1978): 269–74.

———. "Georgije Ostrogorski, 1902–1976." In *Glas Srpske akademije nauka i umetnosti* 372, Odelenje istorijskih nauka 8 (1993): 57–95.

Krekić, B. and B. Radojčić. "Bibliographie de Georges Ostrogorsky." *ZRVI* 8:1 (1963): vii–xviii [*Mélanges G. Ostrogorsky*].

Krekić, B., B. Radojčić, and I. Djurić. "Bibliografija radova akademika Georgija Ostrogorskog." *Zbor. Fil. fak.* 12:1 (1974): 1–14 [*Spomenica Georgija Ostrogorskog*].

Nikolajević, Ivanka. "Istraživanja Georgija Ostrogorskog o principima vizantijske umetnosti." *ZRVI* 18 (1978): 275–77.

Ševčenko, Ihor, Ernst Kitzinger, and William Huse Dunham, Jr. "George Ostrogorsky." *Speculum* 52 (1977): 774–76.

BERYL SMALLEY

(1905–1984)

Henrietta Leyser

Beryl Smalley, pioneer of the study of the Bible in the Middle Ages, was born on 3 June 1905 at Cheadle in Derbyshire, her parents' first child. There were to be three more children, a break during World War I, and then another two, but it was Beryl, the firstborn, who remained all her life a source of astonishment to her parents. Her father, Edgar, a successful Manchester businessman, dealt in cotton, but his chief passion was horses. (Smalley's youngest brother, Richard, would later become the Grand National's starter.) Her mother, Lilian (née Bowman), to whom she remained devoted until her death at the age of ninety-one, Beryl could sometimes shock—she turned up in Derbyshire in the 1930s in a most outrageous hat from Paris, a pillbox creation no less—but more often Beryl simply perplexed her. There really was, she would say, no need for Beryl to work so hard; it was quite unnecessary (and not what was expected) to go to Oxford. Dances, parties, and marriage were the plan. Smalley, never for an instant stuffy, took to both the dances and the parties, but marriage was not part of her horizon. Her family, their marriages, children, and grandchildren, were close to her all her life. As the oldest child she had her own share of parenting early on. She would take the younger ones for walks, write poetry for them, read to them, even, when scarlet fever made school impossible, teach them. The young Smalleys had a nurse but no governess; Beryl had everything in hand. Years later she would attribute her powers of concentration to those nursery years. She grew accustomed to doing her own homework surrounded by clamorous siblings, keeping them satisfied and in order by regular helpings of "yes" and "no." As an established scholar in Oxford, she would punctuate her reading in the Bodleian by these habitual negative and affirmative utterances, much to the astonishment of others in the library.

At thirteen Smalley was sent away to Cheltenham Ladies' College. Cheltenham was, and in some ways still is, an austere, high-minded school.

Discipline was rigorous; early-morning runs regardless of the weather; parade-ground-type inspections of clothing and appearance. But founded as it was by Miss Dorothea Beale, a pioneer of women's education and the founder also of St. Hilda's, Oxford, where Smalley would later go, it was a school committed to academic excellence. Smalley was soon spotted to be a pupil of exceptional promise, and she was not allowed to forget it. The expectations were relentless. In 1923, her last year, Smalley was awarded a scholarship to read history at St. Hilda's, but she paid a heavy price for the honor. Smalley's toughness had another side, an inner nervosity. Very few who knew her ever saw this, though they may have guessed at it, but her family always recognized the oncoming of crisis times when she would need to be allowed to collapse and to be succored. Today Smalley's condition would be described as anorexic, but back then it was not generally looked for in English society.

In 1924 the role of succorer fell to an aunt, who took Smalley to Rome for some months for a change of air and scenery. Rome supplied both, and something more. It laid the foundation for Smalley's conversion five years later to Catholicism. What it did for her anorexia it is more difficult and possibly unnecessary to know. All her life Smalley smoked heavily and ate little—she could be a most frustrating dinner guest, although sometimes culinary temptation was possible (with stewed red cabbage, for instance). Not that she was in any sense an ascetic. Her youngest sister, Suzanne, remembers well how Smalley, now at Oxford, came to visit her while she was still at school in Cheltenham and the look of horror on the housemistress's face at the full extent of the older sister's glamour, red nails included. As a tutor her elegance was legendary; her pupils felt quite dowdy in her presence. Her colleagues called her Queen Nefertiti, and even in her seventies she could be found asking for "what they are wearing now." It would be wrong to suggest that Smalley was frail. Suzanne remembers how easily her sister could outwalk her, how intrepid she was as a traveler, and friends testify to her zest for impromptu river swims.

As an undergraduate (1924–27) Smalley is an elusive figure: she made a fleeting but unforgettable appearance as the archangel Gabriel in a freshers' Nativity play; she earned distinction in her first public examination (History Previous) and exemption from the notorious "divvers" (religious studies); she went to a galaxy of tutors around the university, but none supplanted Agnes Leys, St. Hilda's medievalist, in her affection. Smalley's great disappointment was getting a second-class degree in her finals, and it was Agnes Leys who stood by her at that critical time. Why Smalley failed has remained a puzzle: some attribute it to her inability to master one of the compulsory texts for the political-science paper or to her distaste for the Stubbsian syllabus, with its heavy bias toward English constitutional and political history. Yet it was this syllabus, virtually unaltered, that she herself would come to teach for twenty-five years with unstinting dedication on succeeding Agnes Leys at St. Hilda's in 1944. If it dismayed her as an undergraduate, this was not something she betrayed later to her pupils.

Smalley's training at Oxford laid the foundation for her later precision as a teacher. There was never a whisper of subversion of the Oxford syllabus in her tutorials, and those who persevered got their rewards. But to talk about Saint Bernard with Smalley was exhilarating in a way that 1066 had never been. Her tutorials were never sober or dull, but they were both awe-inspiring and serious: no smoking (a sacrifice on Smalley's part, whatever it may have meant to her pupils), no backsliding, and you wore your gown. What mattered was scholarship and discipline.

The direction of Smalley's lifework was fixed in her final undergraduate year (for much of what follows see Richard Southern's memoir). She had attended F. M. Powicke's Ford Lectures on Stephen Langton, and Agnes Leys saw to it that they met each other. At the time Powicke (later described by Smalley as "that leaper over academic walls" [Smalley (1973), 12]) was beginning to be interested in the vast amount of Langton's work dating from his Paris days that remained unpublished and unstudied. He founded "a little group of students" to carry the discussion further (Southern [1986], 456). Smalley became one of the group, and in her first year after finals she served as his research student. Powicke, professor then at Manchester, was based close to Smalley's own home; she could in effect commute between Manchester and Buxton, where her family then lived. Her father was not sympathetic to this prolongation of her academic work; it may have come as a relief that the search for manuscripts took her not only to Cambridge and London but also in early 1929 to Paris.

Smalley's task as allotted by Powicke was the sorting out of Langton's commentaries on the Bible. The work was both pioneering and taxing; it demanded perseverance and exactitude. The manuscript tradition was confused and much of the content dreary. In Paris Smalley was helped and guided by Monsignor Georges Lacombe, a scholar whose subject was the commentaries of Langton's contemporary Prepositinus. In the work they published together in 1931 Smalley gives an impression of both the labors and the occasional rewards of their enterprise:

> A very large proportion of Langton's work is composed of extracts
> from the Gloss, Biblical quotations, allegorical and moral excursions

which recall the worst type of twelfth century sermon. It is often necessary to read through many folios of such material before arriving at an interesting *questio* or one of Langton's incomparably pithy *dicta* [Southern (1986), 457].

Reading these folios trained Smalley in manuscript scholarship, but she also found in Paris a new academic home. Subsequently her work would be published as often in French as in English journals. It was in Paris also that she began her friendship with Marie-Thérèse D'Alverny, an outstanding medievalist who like Smalley often found the world reluctant to give female scholars their due.

Her doctorate completed, Smalley got a job in 1931 lecturing at Royal Holloway College, London. She turned her scholarly attention to investigating the nature of the Gloss, so often used by Langton. The Gloss was assumed to be the work of the ninth-century German monk Walafrid Strabo; Smalley argued that it was in origin a product of the late eleventh and early twelfth centuries, masterminded at Laon under the aegis of Anselm. The complete story of the Gloss, known by the early thirteenth century as the *Glossa Ordinaria*, may have eluded her—indeed it has yet to be told—but it was Smalley, in Richard Southern's words, who "laid the foundations and indicated the lines of inquiry for the future [and who] made the origins and a large part of the process clear for the first time" (Southern [1985], 7).

In 1935 Smalley became research fellow at Girton College, Cambridge, although she had not been Girton's first choice. She had published four articles (in addition to her work with Georges Lacombe), but her work was so unusual as to be considered eccentric. In her years at Cambridge Smalley had to validate once and for all the importance of her chosen field for all medieval scholars. It was at Cambridge that *The Study of the Bible in the Middle Ages* took shape. It was conceived, in Smalley's words, as "a history of the origins and development of biblical scholarship . . . through the Middle Ages up to c.1300" (Smalley [1983], vii). The hero of the book came to be Andrew of Saint Victor (d. c. 1150). Medieval schoolmen had traditionally favored symbolic exegesis; Andrew's achievement was to begin a reevaluation of the literal meanings of the text:

No western commentator before him had set out to give a purely literal interpretation of the Old Testament, though many had attempted a purely spiritual one. There was general uncertainty as to the content of the letter. There were no rules for defining it, just as there were no rules for establishing one's text. Andrew would have to define how much the literal interpretation included for himself [*ibid.,* 169].

In his quandaries Andrew turned to the Jews. It seemed a reasonable assumption that literalism and Jewish exegesis would go hand in hand—and he was right, though this had been so only since the late eleventh century. In her pursuit of Andrew and his methods Smalley herself would need to "go to school with the Jews" (*ibid.,* 156). As Richard Southern has pointed out, it was for Smalley a considerable solace, in the late 1930s, to be in the position of needing the help of Jewish scholars. Andrew's appeal to them had been made in comparable circumstances: his lifetime too had coincided with the rise of anti-Semitism in Europe.

There are perhaps further reasons why Andrew's approach may have appealed to Smalley, especially when set beside her response to Joachim of Fiore (the apocalyptic prophet and abbot). She never made any attempt to be "objective" about her characters. Writing about her commentators in the preface to *The Gospels in the Schools,* she defends her position:

> The historian who studies characters has to establish some sort of contact with them. He has to come clean about his subjective impressions of them as persons. Many commentaries originated in lecture courses. Sitting in on a lecture cannot but make him admire or like, criticise or dislike the lecturer as such [Smalley (1985), ix].

Joachim was one of those she intensely disliked. In the third edition of *The Study of the Bible* there is a note of repentance, but it is halfhearted. Joachim and Joachism were no longer "an attack of senile dementia in the spiritual exposition"; the spiritual exposition "in its old age" had, she conceded, "produced a thriving child." But, she continued, "it was not one that I would care to adopt" (Smalley [1983], xiii).

Smalley was passionately idealistic, but as the author of *The Study of the Bible* she had already rejected visions of any age to come, such as Joachim favored. Her concerns had become more immediate and pragmatic. Asked once by her sister what her Marxism meant to her, she replied, "I met my charwoman in the High Street and I carried her baby." Those who knew Smalley can imagine the relish with which she would have said this, a remark as meaningful on one level as it is absurd on another.

It was also at Cambridge and during the writing of *The Study of the Bible* that Smalley had to reconcile her Catholicism with Marxism. Although there is some discrepancy in the memories of her undergraduate contemporaries as to her position in the General Strike of 1926, there can be no doubt that for the best part of her adult life (and most probably for all of it) Smalley was a staunch left-winger. Her conversion to Catholicism in no way represented a lurch to the right. On the contrary her religious inspiration was derived from the radicals of the church, the Dominicans. Initially her work on the *The Study of the Bible* dovetailed nicely with her newfound faith. Both represented a departure from the Protestant traditions of Cheltenham, St. Hilda's, and Bishop Stubbs. Rome and Paris had offered horizons undreamed of in Derbyshire and only hinted at in the sheltered atmosphere Oxford provided for women in the 1920s. But the traumas of the 1930s demanded that all allegiances be reexamined. Were they adequate for the herculean task of combating Nazi aggression in Europe? For some, especially after Munich, the Catholic church became the ark where they could find shelter. Not so for Smalley. It was not so much that she renounced her faith; it simply faded away. The horrors of the here and now seemed to her to require an earthly savior. She turned toward Russia.

Smalley's communism was by no means uncommon in her day, though after the war it never ceased to amaze some of her colleagues at St. Hilda's. She entertained frequently at high table; a murmured question would go round—were the guests "h" or "c," historians or communists? Perhaps they were both. But the Hungarian rising of 1956 would change all that; its brutal suppression made it impossible for Smalley to support communism any longer. The lack of a creed, of a basis for social justice, whether religious or secular, she found as impoverishing as it was unavoidable.

The Study of the Bible was published in 1941. The middle of the war was a bad time for reviews; those that appeared were not enthusiastic. English scholarship was still insular—continental interest in medieval learning had barely crossed the Channel—and the book soon went out of print. There was no new edition until 1952. With no permanent job Smalley returned to Oxford to work as a temporary assistant in the Department of Western Manuscripts in the Bodleian. Congenial as this job may have been, it was still a cause of relief and joy to her to be appointed in 1944 the successor to Agnes Leys at St. Hilda's, where she remained until her retirement in 1969. From 1957 to 1969 Smalley was also vice-principal of St. Hilda's, an exacting office but one she filled, according to her colleague and fellow historian Menna Prestwich, with a typical blend of irony and conscientiousness. Asked about her duties, she is said to have replied "one attends to the seating for guest nights and conferences and sends flowers for illness—and of course for funerals" (Prestwich, 11).

If Smalley was an enigma to her parents, so she was also to many of her colleagues and pupils. There were countless paradoxes. She was utterly loyal to her college and yet had no firm friends within it; she was a dedicated teacher, yet the center of her scholarly interests was far removed from nearly everything she taught; she had a heart of gold and could be relied on to give generously of herself to those in any kind of distress, yet it is her acerbic remarks that are the more often remembered. A pupil, for example, returning some work she had been lent, told Smalley she had found it so enthralling she had read it late into the night; the compliment was quickly crushed: "my work is not for bedside reading." She was an ardent socialist who looked as if she had stepped straight out of the pages of *Vogue*. To attempt to fathom such paradoxes would be foolhardy indeed, yet it is worth remembering that even Smalley's singularities had their contexts; it is perhaps her refusal to accommodate herself smoothly to them that gave both her scholarship and her personality their cutting edge and integrity. Her school, her church, her party, her university, have each on occasion drowned lesser mortals in their waters. Smalley, not one to make flamboyant gestures from the bank, would dive gracefully in and then swim against the current.

In 1944, when Smalley became a tutor at St. Hilda's, the study of medieval manuscripts in England was still regarded as primarily "of antiquarian curiosity, interesting but hardly 'serious.'" M.R. James, best remembered by the general public for his ghost stories, had indeed inspired Eton pupils with a passion for manuscripts, among them Neil Ker and Roger Mynors. (As undergraduates neither had read history.) As scholars at Oxford these two, with Richard Hunt, Christopher Cheney, William Pantin, Richard Southern, and Smalley, would come to "dominate medieval studies in Britain." The above quotations and the prosopography come from Richard and Mary Rouse's edition of the *Registrum anglie de libris doctorum et auctorem veterum*, itself a long-awaited offspring (1991, xxi, xxvi, xxvii). It was within this loose circle that what the Rouses call a move away from "politico-institutional history" first took shape. Smalley's contribution to this development was considerable.

Smalley saw her own work as clustering around three main books, *The Study of the Bible* (1941, 1952, 1983), *English Friars and Antiquity in the Early Fourteenth Century* (1960), and *The Becket Conflict and the Schools* (1973). (She seems to have discounted somewhat a more "popular" book, *Historians in the Middle Ages* (1974), written for students and "the general reader," well-loved though it is for its wit, lucidity, and idiosyncratic choice of historians.) Her two collections of essays, *Studies in Medieval Thought and Learning from Abelard to Wyclif* (1981) and *The Gospels in the Schools, c. 1100–c. 1280* (1985), were both intended to supplement the main books. Smalley, typically, is her own best critic. In the third edition of *The Study of the Bible* she refers to her original text as "a period piece." It is in fact a tribute to the work she herself either undertook or generated that it would have required on her own reckoning two volumes rather than one to bring it up to date. *The Gospels in the Schools* presents her major corrective; *The Study of the Bible* had given "only passing glances" to the New Testament.

The Gospels in the Schools, published posthumously, shows both the strengths and the self-imposed limitations of Smalley's work. Her concern and her primary contribution was to offer a methodology for scholarly inquiry. When Smalley started her research, the importance of both the Old and the New Testaments for an understanding of the Middle Ages had in no way been recognized. In her own lifetime all that was written on biblical models of kingship, on the search for the *vita apostolica*, on the revival of preaching and the spread among the laity of Franciscan-inspired piety bears witness to the growing realization of the Bible's many and crucial roles. And yet Smalley herself was curiously content to remain, as it were, at ground level. In the foreword to *The Gospels* she writes that before discussing any commentator one must always ask "who, when, and where?"; next one must trace sources; finally one can choose further questions; what these are "are his own business" (Smalley [1985], vii). The reader is not, in short, presented with any imperative understanding, any all-encompassing vision. What matters is the situating of the text for the reader.

Smalley's very questions—"who, when, where"—come straight from the pages of early-medieval exegesis, "persona, locus, tempus." It is as if she not only read but also internalized the outlook of her commentators. The words of Hugh of Saint Victor throw light on Smalley's methodology:

> It is not without value to call to mind what we see happen in the construction of buildings, when first the foundation is laid, then the structure is raised upon it, and finally, when the work is all finished, the house is decorated by the laying on of colour.

> So too, in fact, must it be in your instruction. First you learn history and diligently commit to memory the truth of the deeds that have been performed, reviewing from beginning to end what has been done, where it has been done, and by whom it has been done. For these are the four things which are especially to be sought for in history—the person, the business done, the time and the place. . . . Do not look

down upon these least things. The man who looks down on such smallest things slips little by little. . . . I know there are certain fellows who want to play the philosopher right away. . . . The knowledge of these fellows is like that of an ass. . . . The man who moves along step by step is the one who moves along best [*Didascalion*, book 6, chs. ii-iii, Minnis and Scott, 74].

Smalley would have been in no doubt that in her work on the Bible she was indeed far from "decorating the house"; she explicitly saw herself as offering "guide-lines to future research."

But what of *English Friars and Antiquity*; what of *The Becket Conflict*? There is indeed much more a sense here of finished buildings, possibly because both books are presented as studies in lost causes. In *The Becket Conflict and the Schools*, subtitled *A Study of Intellectuals in Politics in the Twelfth Century* (and delivered in Oxford as the Ford Lectures), we are given an illuminating picture of Becket's circle, a nuanced interpretation of the interplay of principle and self-interest, of personality and theory. But once the drama is over and the blood is off the walls, the protagonists become bored; the quarrel now seems "stale and tiresome." Similarly in *The Friars*; beguiled we may be—as were Smalley's friars (and the example is chosen at random) by tales of Virgil the wizard who "built a palace of clotted air, which reflected absolutely everything in the world" (231)—we still finally have to be brought down to earth. The friars' love of classics is an episode unto itself; the classicizing movement in England does not and could not have turned into humanism. To expect otherwise would be to behave like children planting orange pips, who watch the pips sprout and then are disappointed that they don't turn into fruit. The simile takes us back to the likeness between Smalley and her commentators. Her audience is never allowed to nod off. Her prose is crisp and compelling, and she is as capable as any thirteenth-century friar of introducing exempla to make her point: the "attitude to space" among the English public who heard her friars is illustrated by a snippet of conversation overheard in a Derbyshire bus, retold in broad dialect. The concreteness of such comparisons (a quality Smalley herself affectionately ascribes to the work of the Provençal friar Armand de Bezier) keeps us wide awake and in touch with everyday reality. For historians this is essential—for historians must be level-headed. They should not expect too much from their characters; on the other hand they do not have to show much patience with those in their cast who themselves let grandiose ideas get the better of them. We have seen this already in the case of Joachim of Fiore; another example would be John Wyclif, reprimanded for his refusal to accept Thomas Aquinas's "down-to-earth" solution to the problem of scriptural tenses; his belief that he can change the world leads him to end his life as "a mere bore, inventing fresh insults in default of new ideas" (Smalley [1981], 415).

We can still hear Smalley's voice in the work of her pupils and colleagues. *The Bible in the Medieval World*, written in her honor but published, alas, only as a memorial volume, presents a sampler of the work of a whole generation of medievalists, deeply influenced by Smalley, for whom the Bible has become a scholarly primer. Whereas once, as Richard Southern found in Paris in the early 1930s, it was possible to study all the vicissitudes of the reign of Charles the Bald without for one moment considering the Old Testament imagery of his kingship, now biblical imagery is recognized as "a central influence in the conduct of business and in the concept of established government" (Southern [1985], 16). The new "Israelites of the West" were indeed a people of the book; we accept now that if we are to begin to understand how they thought and acted we must start by looking at their uses of the Bible. This is Smalley's legacy. But she left more besides, explicit pointers to further research—"the comforting thought," as she wrote in her posthumously published *The Gospels in the Schools*, "is that one person's end may mark another's beginning" (vii). There is indeed still much to be done. For example, Smalley's discovery of Wyclif's lost biblical lectures (a discovery published with a characteristic lack of ostentation in *The Bodleian Library Record*) has even now not been fully absorbed. But what is already clear is how Beryl Smalley's exemplary scholarship, her unremitting journeys through "nettles and thickets" (Smalley [1973], 16), "through unknown, pathless ways" (Smalley [1983], 357), has made it impossible ever again to marginalize either the Bible or its exegetes. As medievalists we know now to ask at every juncture how the Bible was being read; how schoolmen were interpreting its texts.

In his recent *The Medieval Theory of Authorship* A.J. Minnis pays tribute to Smalley in words she would surely have cherished as an epitaph: she has become a "primary efficient cause" (Minnis, xviii), an "efficient cause" being, in Aristotelian terms, "the moving force which brought something from potentiality into actual being" (Minnis, 28). There had indeed been a time in Smalley's career, in the 1930s, when she alone had believed in the potential of her work. It is a measure of her achievement that by the time of her death, on 6 April 1984, it had become impossible to imagine a Middle Ages without the study of its Bible.

SELECTED BIBLIOGRAPHY
Thanks are due to Beryl Smalley's family, friends, and pupils, who generously
shared their memories with me.

Works

BOOKS AND ARTICLES

With Georges Lacombe. "Studies on the Commentaries of Cardinal Stephen Langton."
Archives d'histoire doctrinale et littéraire du moyen âge 5 (1930): 5–266.
———. "The Lombard's Commentary on Isaias and Other Fragments." *New Scho-
lasticism* 5 (1931): 123–62.
"Stephen Langton and the Four Senses of Scripture." *Speculum* 6 (1931): 60–76.
"*Exempla* in the Commentaries of Stephen Langton." *Bulletin of the John Rylands
Library* 17 (1933): 121–29.
"Master Ivo of Chartres." *English Historical Review* 50 (1935): 680–86.
"Gilbertus Universalis, Bishop of London (1128–1134) and the Problem of the 'Glossa
Ordinaria.'" *Recherches de théologie ancienne et médiévale* (hereafter *RTAM*)
7 (1935): 235–62.
"La *Glossa Ordinaria.*" *RTAM* 9 (1937): 365–400.
"Andrew of St. Victor, Abbot of Wigmore: A Twelfth Century Hebraist." *RTAM* 10
(1938): 358–73.
"A Collection of Paris Lectures of the Later Twelfth Century in the MS *Pembroke
College, Cambridge 7.*" *Cambridge Historical Journal* 6 (1938): 103–13.
"The School of Andrew of St. Victor." *RTAM* 11 (1939): 145–67.
*Hebrew Scholarship Among Christians in XIIIth Century England As Illustrated by
Some Hebrew-Latin Psalters*. London: Shapiro, Vallentine, 1939.
The Study of the Bible in the Middle Ages. Oxford: Clarendon, 1941. 2nd ed.,
Blackwell, 1952. 3rd ed., 1983.
With Hermann Kantorowicz. "An English Theologian's View of Roman Law: Pepo,
Irnerius, Ralph Niger." *Mediaeval and Renaissance Studies* 1 (1943): 237–52.
With S. Kuttner. "The 'Glossa Ordinaria' to the Gregorian Decretals." *English His-
torical Review* 60 (1945): 97–105.
"Two Biblical Commentaries of Simon of Hinton." *RTAM* 13 (1946): 57–85.
"A Commentary on Isaias by Guerric of St. Quentin O.P." *Studi e testi* 122 (1946):
383–87.
"Some More Exegetical Works of Simon of Hinton." *RTAM* 15 (1948): 97–106.
"Robert Bacon and the Early Dominican School at Oxford." *Transactions of the Royal
Historical Society*, 4th ser., 30 (1948): 1–19.
"The *Quaestiones* of Simon of Hinton." In *Studies in Medieval History Presented to
Frederick Maurice Powicke*, edited by R.W. Hunt, W.A. Pantin, and R.W.
Southern, pp. 209–22. Oxford: Clarendon, 1948.
"William of Middleton and Guibert of Nogent." *RTAM* 16 (1949): 289–91.
"Some Thirteenth Century Commentaries on the Sapiential Books." *Dominican Studies*
2 (1949): 318–55.
"Some Thirteenth Century Commentaries on the Sapiential Books." *Dominican Studies*
3 (1950): 41–77, 236–74.
"A Commentary on the Hebraica by Herbert of Bosham." *RTAM* 18 (1951): 29–65.
"John Wyclif's *Postilla Super Totam Bibliam.*" *Bodleian Library Record* 4 (1952/53):
186–205.
"Thomas Waleys O.P." *Archivum Fratrum Praedicatorum* 24 (1954): 50–107.
"Gerard of Bologna and Henry of Ghent." *RTAM* 22 (1955): 125–29.
"The Biblical Scholar." In *Robert Grosseteste: Scholar and Bishop*, edited by D.A.
Callus, pp. 70–97. Oxford: Clarendon, 1955.
"Robert Holcot O.P." *Archivum Fratrum Praedicatorum* 26 (1955): 5–97.

"John Ridewall's Commentary on *De Civitate Dei.*" *Medium Ævum* 25 (1957): 140–53.

"Flaccianus, *De Visionibus Sibyllae.*" In *Mélanges offerts a Étienne Gilson, de l'Academie Française,* pp. 547–62. Toronto: Pontifical Institute of Mediaeval Studies; Paris: Vrin, 1959.

English Friars and Antiquity in the Early Fourteenth Century. Oxford: Blackwell, 1960.

"Problems of Exegesis in the Fourteenth Century." In *Antike und Orient im Mittelalter.* Vol. 1 of *Miscellanea Medievalia: Veröffentlichungen des Thomas-Instituts an der Universität Köln,* edited by Paul Wilpert, pp. 266–77. Berlin: De Gruyter, 1962.

"The Bible in the Middle Ages." In *The Church's Use of the Bible Past and Present,* edited by D.E. Nineham, pp. 57–71. London: Society for the Promotion of Christian Knowledge, 1963.

"Wyclif's *Postilla* on the Old Testament and His *Principium.*" In *Oxford Studies Presented to Daniel Callus,* pp. 253–96. Oxford: Clarendon, 1964.

Ed. and Intro. *Trends in Medieval Political Thought.* Oxford: Blackwell, 1965.

"Sallust in the Middle Ages." In *Classical Influences on European Culture* A.D. 500–1500, edited by R.R. Bolgar, pp. 165–75. Cambridge: Cambridge University Press, 1971.

The Becket Conflict and the Schools: A Study of Intellectuals in Politics in the Twelfth Century. Oxford: Blackwell, 1973.

Historians in the Middle Ages. London: Thames and Hudson, 1974.

Studies in Medieval Thought and Learning from Abelard to Wyclif. London: Hambledon, 1981.

The Gospels in the Schools, c. 1100–c. 1280. London: Hambledon, 1985.

Sources

Minnis, A.J. *The Medieval Theory of Authorship: Scholastic Literary Attitudes in the Later Middle Ages.* 2nd ed. Aldershot: Wildwood House, 1988.

Minnis, A.J., A.B. Scott, with the assistance of David Wallace, eds. *Medieval Literary Theory and Criticism c. 1100–c. 1375: The Commentary-Tradition.* Oxford: Clarendon, 1988.

Prestwich, Menna. "Beryl Smalley." *St. Hilda's College Record,* 1984.

Rouse, Richard, and Mary Rouse, eds. *Registrum Anglie de Libris Doctorum et Auctorum Veterum.* London: British Library, 1991.

Southern, R.W. "Beryl Smalley and the Place of the Bible in Medieval Studies, 1927–84." In *The Bible in the Medieval World: Essays in Memory of Beryl Smalley,* edited by Katherine Walsh and Diana Wood, pp. 1–16. Oxford: Blackwell, 1985.

———. "Beryl Smalley, 1905–1984." *Proceedings of the British Academy* 72 (1986): 455–71.

Walsh, Katherine, and Diana Wood, eds. *The Bible in the Medieval World: Essays in Memory of Beryl Smalley.* Oxford: Blackwell, 1985.

GUSTAVE E. VON GRUNEBAUM

(1909–1972)

Franz Rosenthal

Gustave von Grunebaum, humanist and eminent Islamicist, was born in Vienna on 1 September 1909 and died in Los Angeles on 27 February 1972. These dates tell us much about von Grunebaum's development as a human being and scholar. A student of Islam, he started out in a great scholarly tradition and gave it new directions. His father, Egon Ritter von Grünebaum, as well as his paternal grandfather, whose first name was passed on to him, was prominent in the Austrian railway system; his mother, Edith Weissel, also had strong roots in Austria. He was thus born into a family firmly established in the Austrian social and intellectual life that flourished in the nineteenth century until the upheavals caused by World War I.

Educated in his own country, von Grunebaum obtained his D.Phil. in oriental studies from the University of Vienna in 1931 at a young age and took a simultaneous library degree as something to fall back on if the uncertainties of an academic career in his chosen field proved overpowering. After a few years as a postgraduate in Berlin, he settled in Vienna to avid reading and publishing. The humanism and cosmopolitanism of Vienna, with its openness to foreign languages and cultures, its appreciation of the good life and graciousness in human intercourse, and above all its free-flowing intellectualism, took firm hold in von Grunebaum. In fact all the dominant themes and ideas manifested in his later scholarship began germinating in his Viennese period. Throughout his career he saw to it that his English publications also appeared in German translation. Speaking at a memorial celebration in 1972 held at the Near Eastern Center of UCLA, which von Grunebaum had founded and which was named for him after his death, his American friend Lynn T. White, Jr., remarked that all his life "Gustave remained incredibly Viennese." It was no doubt due to his early upbringing that a prominent younger Arabist, R. Sellheim, could remember him as "never excited, mild mannered and fair, amiable and full of humor—a humanist of high culture" (private communication).

After the Nazi Anschluss in March 1938 von Grunebaum might have easily passed the test of "Aryan" heritage, but he felt that there was no place for him among the barbarians and their hatred of all that was good and noble in European culture. He accepted an invitation from the Asia Institute in New York, which under the leadership of its founder, Arthur Upham Pope (1881–1969), provided a refuge for displaced European orientalists when such a refuge was needed most. After five years he was offered a position as assistant professor of Arabic at the University of Chicago, where, quickly moving up to the rank of professor, he remained until 1957.

World War II stimulated a remarkable growth of Near Eastern studies in the United States. The University of California at Berkeley had for many years been practically the only place on the West Coast where such studies were cultivated. Now the university's campus at Los Angeles (UCLA) was expanding together with the city. The search for someone to build a prestigious program in Islamic studies led to von Grunebaum, whose scholarship was matched by energy and organizational ability. From the beginning at UCLA he ceaselessly planned and guided scholarly conferences in this country and abroad, particularly in France and Germany, where he made Frankfurt am Main the center of his activities just six years after the end of the war. He foresaw the potential of such conferences and similar cooperative efforts for the production of publications that added to the store of knowledge. With equal zest he participated in scholarly meetings all over the Muslim world and closely observed the rapid transformation that was taking place in collective attitudes toward the West and its orientalists as well as toward its own civilization, all the while publishing the results of his own research. His death from stomach cancer in 1972 took him away at the height of his career. At UCLA the biennial conferences named by him after the great Italian humanist and orientalist Giorgio Levi Della Vida (1886–1967), which he established in 1967 "in order to give recognition to an outstanding scholar whose work has significantly and lastingly advanced the study of Islamic civilization," continue to keep his memory alive. He also did not exclude Europe from his activities. At the Artemis Verlag in Zurich he founded Die Bibliothek des Morgenlandes, a series devoted to Islamic subjects, of which about fifteen have appeared to date.

Von Grunebaum's career progressed smoothly. There were no serious impediments, only a steady advance in professional experience and competence. His twenties, the decade of his postdoctoral years, were spent in comparatively unencumbered study in Vienna, where he was given the opportunity, so helpful for a growing scholar, to widen his horizon by reviewing a great variety of books for the *Wiener Zeitschrift für die Kunde des Morgenlandes*, the professional organ of Austrian orientalists. His early thirties in New York were a period mainly of research in the New York Public Library, then the richest repository of Near Eastern publications in the United States. His acclimatization to American life proceeded rapidly under tolerable if restricted conditions. (I remember our sharing copies of the *New York Times* to save a nickel, when during vacations I also worked in the Oriental Reading Room of the library.) Soon he was ready to construct his new model of Islamic studies.

When speaking about "Islamic studies" and the "Middle Ages" conceived principally as a period in European history, one must understand how these two concepts mesh. Periodizations of history are arbitrary notch marks in a flowing continuum. Some of them are whimsical exercises and soon forgotten; others linger on, waiting to be replaced; a few gain wide acceptance and long-lasting currency. The "Middle Ages" as a period in western civilization has proved its heuristic worth, though its use has not escaped criticism. The concept, however, is without intrinsic meaning for Islam; if it occurs occasionally in modern Muslim usage, it is as a calque from western terminology. The far-flung regions under Muslim control underwent constant development and vast changes over time, yet there was no break that would place one distinctive stretch of time in the middle between what was before and what happened thereafter. *Medieval Islam* was nevertheless a most fortunate choice for the title of von Grunebaum's seminal work published in 1946 and subtitled *A Study in Cultural Orientation*. As well as one word can, "medieval" expresses to the westerner looking at Islam the twin ideas (1) that for the longest time Muslim civilization as a spiritual and material configuration has run parallel to what in the West is called the Middle Ages, and (2) that therefore the two can legitimately be compared for mutual illumination on major issues, apart from the many connections that extend in both directions but mainly from East to West via Spain and Italy.

"Medieval" as applied to Islam also at least hints at the fact that when the West started in earnest to develop away from its Middle Ages, it was getting ready, if ever so slowly, to penetrate the resistant surface of Islam. With the spread of the Ottoman Empire and its conquest of Egypt in 1517, contacts between the West and the world of Islam became more visible, and with Napoleon's invasion of Egypt western influence on Islam expanded everywhere and became so obvious that it is possible, and indeed has become customary, to speak from then on about "medieval Islam" before and "modern Islam" thereafter. A word of caution is necessary, however: objections in the contemporary Muslim world to past western political dominance have been joined by objections to perceived western influence in the cultural sphere. Total rejection and even vehement denial of western cultural values are expressed ever more emphatically. It remains to be seen how deeply western spirituality, which von Grunebaum stressed as much more important for cultural comparison than the "materialism" supposedly characteristic of the West, has taken root in the Muslim world and where the process of cultural leveling will eventually lead. The voices of protest were less strident when von Grunebaum was active than they have become during the last few decades. But the constant intrusion of contemporary concerns of this sort combined with the unbroken continuity of Muslim civilization makes it almost inescapable for the Muslim medievalist to have a foot in the modern world of Islam and to busy himself with the lessons to be drawn from it for a remote past that is felt to be very much alive.

These factors sharpened von Grunebaum's insight into the presuppositions and cognitional possibilities of cross-civilizational research. The application of this approach to the study of medieval Islam is at the core of his work. He was convinced that trying to understand another civilization involves full immersion in and total dedication to one's own. Westerners looking at Islam must first know and have a feeling for western civilization, how it originated, how it developed, and what makes it work. Only then can they make a valid contribution. Their views of Islam will often be in open conflict with things as seen from inside Islam. There is no objective criterion for one generally acceptable truth. Certain technical approaches, facts, figures, or methods of analysis may inspire confidence, but the observer's angle of vision cannot be ignored. Since all historical interpretation contains a political component regardless of the historian's intentions, once a potential bearing upon perceived present-day political reality is discerned, or merely suspected, insights seemingly uncontroversial run the risk of touching a sensitive political nerve. Islam's cultural continuity gives its past much more present-day relevancy than is normally the case in western history. Matters seemingly remote and abstract can excite fierce polemic because a more or less tenuous connection is made with political concerns of today. Vicious attacks, at times of a personal nature, can be made even on medieval Islamicists, for allegedly being motivated in their work by conspiratorial evil designs or at the very least misled by prejudice. It takes courage to face the threat of such attacks. Von Grunebaum possessed such courage. Neither contentious nor willfully undiplomatic, he insisted that scholars state their views unequivocally. This he did at all times, never swerving from his conviction that his outsider's look at Islam was determined by his roots in western civilization, whether or not such a position was branded "Eurocentric."

A less embattled factor in the study of medieval Islam is the early proximity of two other great civilizations, the Persian-Sassanian and the Hellenistic-Byzantine. Noteworthy elements in Muslim cultural development have to be checked and rechecked for their possible connection with either or both. This fact constitutes a challenge to cross-cultural investigation. It requires Islamicists to have wide, often recondite knowledge, as well as the sensitivity to balance possibilities and coincidences so as not to underestimate or distort what was fundamentally new in and specific to Muslim civilization. Von Grunebaum possessed these attributes and knew how to use them. He resisted, however, the temptation to take the further step of speculating at any length about the relationship of Islam to the ancient civilizations of Asia, although he was well aware of their potential as points of origin for influence. His growing curiosity about the more recent stages of Muslim civilization led him to study the vast Muslim areas of south and southeast Asia as well as sub-Saharan Africa, whose marginality illustrated the great variety that exists within the unity of Muslim civilization.

Von Grunebaum's understanding of civilization, wherever it had evolved, drew much of its strength from ideas that pervaded the atmosphere of the country of his birth. It is informed by the psychological concept of the "self." The term reoccurs in his publications in many places and in many composite nouns that linguistically are more at home in German than in English but flow quite naturally in his English style. The "know thyself" of Greek philosophy, with its long and fertile history in both western and Muslim thought, was extended to encompass larger units of society and held indispensable for the shapes they took and the degrees of perfection they achieved. Self-cognition and self-understanding are of the essence to a civilization's vitality. Scholars of civilization must evaluate the levels of self-cognition in their own cultures and in the cultures they are studying and then compare them. For von Grunebaum the pull toward civilizational self-cognition has always been strong in the West, most markedly so in recent times. In the Muslim orbit, as he saw it, the pull was weaker and unevenly distributed, not necessarily a handicap in medieval Islam but a source of constant misunderstanding during the centuries of western ascendancy. His conclusion was that Islam has as yet to consolidate its "self-image." If true when he wrote, however, the proposition may have since become questionable.

Regardless of their broader views, western Islamicists have the obligation to make available concrete data of Muslim civilization to westerners in order to enrich their knowledge and provide for a more securely based understanding of it. Von Grunebaum always kept this obligation in mind, and not all his publications are concerned with pressing his general approach, even if it always looms in the background.

What mattered to von Grunebaum was cultural history rather than the political history prevalent in Muslim historiography itself and in the western scholarship dealing with Muslim history. A factual look at a four-teenth-century Arabic world history was a natural exercise for the young student. His mature judgment is reflected in an excellent overview of medieval Muslim history published in the *Propyläen-Weltgeschichte* (von Grunebaum [1963], 5: 23–179); he wrote and edited the sequence *Die islamischen Reiche nach dem Fall von Konstantinopel* in *Fischer Weltgeschichte* (1971). Yet for him only the intellectual facets of Islam, including the pervasive religious determinants provided the clue to Islam's meaning in world history.

It was fortunate that young von Grunebaum's attention was drawn in Vienna to Arabic poetry. (Muslim scholars were proud of their poetical efforts, and he too later published some of his own early verses and plays.) Poetry was the principal intellectual and artistic medium of expression for pre-Islamic Arabs. For us it constitutes almost the only means of access to the mind, and indeed the civilization, of the ancient Arabs. Islam brought profound changes, and its vast literature opened up many other channels of information. Still, poetry, in Arabic and all the other languages spoken by Muslims, continued to play a preeminent role. Von Grunebaum's first book dealt with this poetry in a manner foreshadowing the literary criticism that has since become so prominent in Arabic studies. *Die Wirklichkeitweite der früharabischen Dichtung: Eine literaturwissenschaftliche Untersuchung* [*The Extent of Realism in Early Arabic Poetry: An Essay in Literary Criticism*] makes copious use of translated passages but significantly aims at the sort of generalizations that would provide outlines for a picture of Muslim civilization measured by self-expression and self-understanding. Nature in early Arabic poetry, von Grunebaum finds, is deprived of artistic autonomy (another "self" composite of great power) and with its many nuances serves to prove that the world of sense perception is only a tool for human formation (von Grunebaum [1937], 186: "Bei aller Vielfalt bleibt die Sinnenwelt Apparat der Menschengestaltung").

In von Grunebaum's analysis the relationship of male and female, which puts its mark on every civilization, finds meaningful expression in ancient Arabic poetry. While this poetry offers a pseudoindividualistic characterization for men, it does not even attempt to do the same for women. As is the case with nature, artistic autonomy is not considered appropriate for women (*ibid.*, 47). And while stylistic formality tends to deprive human experience of its rightful place (*ibid.*, 106: "unausweichliche Strenge des Stilgesetzes . . . völlige Entrechtung des Erlebnisgehaltes"), the imagined reality of poetry includes both physically and psychologically rounded human forms making statements about their actual being that follow necessarily from their essential being (*ibid.*, 49: "so bringt der imaginäre Raum der dichterischen Wirklichkeit auch menschliche Gebilde, die, gleichmässig psychisch wie physisch geglückt, ihre Daseinsäusserungen zwangsläufig aus der Fülle ihres Soseins abgeleitet erhalten"). The courage—occasionally becoming foolhardiness—that is needed to make a stab at seeing the whole announces itself in this early work. The frequent aphoristic formulations are striking if at times forced. The ideas in some ways reflect those current among earlier scholars, but their sum total presages a new program for Islamic studies.

Von Grunebaum participated in the necessary yeoman work of collecting the fragments of some poets. He soon found himself attracted to the sophisticated Arabic literary criticism focusing on poetry that came into being in the ninth century and then enjoyed steady refinement throughout the Muslim Middle Ages. A short technical book published in 1950, *A Tenth-Century Document of Arabic Literary Theory and Criticism*, stimulated work that has assumed growing proportions in the intervening years but is still far from exhausting its subject. For von Grunebaum it was one of the keys to the aims and means of Arabic literature in general and "proves a dependable guide toward the origin of [the critic's] attitudes and ideas, be they genuinely Arab or inherited from other cultural traditions" (vii). The inheritance from another cultural tradition to be sensed in Arabic imaginative literature in both poetry and prose was exemplified by that famous collection of tales known to us as the *Arabian Nights*, soon to be elaborated in the chapter "Creative Borrowing; Greece in the *Arabian Nights*" in his *Medieval Islam*.

Reading thoroughly in the universe of medieval Muslim texts, *Medieval Islam* (1946) isolates and then recombines telling aspects of religious, social, political, and intellectual life so as to represent a colorful mosaic of Muslim self-understanding and the organization of the Islamic world. Trying to capture the "mood" and flavor of the Muslim Middle Ages, it throws into relief the similarities and differences with the non-Muslim world, while never forgetting that from the Middle Ages to the present the Christian world devoted more attention to Islam than it received from it (von Grunebaum [1946], 42). Always factual and informative, von Grunebaum contributed new interpretations to topics that had long occupied Islamicists, but the larger vision is his own. The underlying value system is consciously that of western civilization. "The muddled waters of cultural relativism," as von Grunebaum phrased it in a letter to Francesco Gabrieli dated 12 June 1959, were not for him. When he spotted faults, he mentioned them, just as he was always ready to give Islam's accomplishments their full due; but he never succumbed to the illusion cherished by some orientalists that it might be possible for them to understand a nonwestern civilization from the inside or take an outsider's attitude toward the West.

The same vision guided von Grunebaum in his occupation with modern Islam. Unlike his work on the Middle Ages, here peremptory statements tend to overwhelm the unwary reader. An extreme example occurs in a favorable review of Albert Hourani's *Arabic Thought in the Liberal Age*, where von Grunebaum speaks of the "demonic-bewitched traits of development" in modern Islam that in his opinion had escaped the author: the self-destructiveness that at least partially attaches to the spiritual change in the Arab East, the pursuit of *ignes fatui* from one to the other, from being to talk and from talk to being, the shadow concepts that hinder any new self-fixation but still exert fetishistic hypnosis, the impatience that robs the active statesman of the framework of theory prior to action, the constant lagging behind historical developments of ideas that is the fault of intellectual indifference, as is the remoteness from the true centers of modern history (von Grunebaum [1965–66], 379; my translation from the original German). The imaginative mind's love of words and concepts mingles here with the scholar's groping for insightful precision. We realize that it takes an alert and knowledgeable reader to appreciate von Grunebaum's ideas and the cognitive limitations inherent in all historical generalizations. As he himself intimated frequently, he was well aware of those limitations.

Yet he went still farther, venturing into the limitless realm of psychology in his effort to probe deeply into Muslim civilization. One of his major attempts in this direction, cut short by his death, was a comprehensive history of the human imagination that was to deal with the "visionary elements in clinical and trance material and in religion, literature, and intellectual history, sociology, and language," according to an outline preserved in his papers and kindly made available to me by his widow, Giselle von Grunebaum. The work was planned as a continuation and expansion of a symposium organized by him and Roger Caillois in 1962 that had led to the publication of *The Dream and Human Societies* (1966). It was no doubt due to early Viennese influences that he saw in the study of dreams the opportunity for a "signal increase in the scope of the cultural sciences" (von Grunebaum and Caillois, 3) in the twentieth century. Here, more openly than anywhere else in his work, he welcomed psychology, anthropology, and sociology as suitable means for a renewal and growth of Islamic scholarship. Unfailingly he hit upon the fundamental distinction between the dream lore of old and the modern occupation with dreams. Whereas in antiquity and in the Middle Ages the dream was "an instrument for cognition of outside reality," in the modern West it serves as "an instrument for introspection and [collective] self-recognition" (*ibid.*, 21). The topic of dreams was part of von Grunebaum's larger vision of the meaning of culture and the meaningful comparison of civilizations as constituting the apex of the large pyramid of Islamic studies in all their variety. But in his own contribution to the volume he again showed his reliance upon the indispensable solid base, the knowledge of sources, texts, and philologically well-founded interpretations.

Von Grunebaum enriched Islamic studies by his philological discipline and skillful use of literary sources. Even on the elementary level his work makes the old and the new appear in a different light and passes the crucial test of bearing constant rereading. He made the most of his privileged position at the confluence of nineteenth-century tradition and twentieth-century progress. Driven by his unshakable conviction of what cross-civilizational research should be like and how it should be executed, he tested its validity on the civilization of Islam. He did not shy away from calling upon the new disciplines that had gained prominence during his lifetime. He took judicious account of the tremendous expansion of scholarship. The current ease of travel requires a neverending discourse with living traditions, inasmuch as such discourse is useful for understanding the past. The shrinking of distances has opened new organizational possibilities for worldwide collaboration. Von Grunebaum showed how these opportunities can be exploited for scholarship. Seeing that research on modern studies has and will continue to have the edge over medieval studies in the number of participants and public support, he made the resources available for modern Near Eastern work do for medieval research—a legitimate procedure given the nature of Muslim civilization. The lessons he taught are not easily adopted by those of a less universal mind, but his example is there to be followed if it cannot be duplicated.

Von Grunebaum attempted to show what wrestling with the elusive essence of a civilization demands from someone who is not a part of that civilization. His insights are in danger of being obscured by the rapid growth of Near Eastern as well as all humanistic scholarship, which is leading to an increasing clamor for seeing one's civilization only from within and doing away with western standards. Useful as such an approach may be for momentary political gain, it carries within itself the seeds of destruction for irreplaceable values and for a unique edifice of learning, one that no doubt has architectural faults but is as a whole solid and unique in human history. In viewing Islam from its heights von Grunebaum succeeded in redefining the meaning of the Middle Ages in the historical sweep of Muslim civilization.

SELECTED BIBLIOGRAPHY

Thanks are due to Giselle von Grunebaum, Wolf Leslau, and Rudolf Sellheim for the information they provided. A full bibliography of von Grunebaum's publications appears in von Grunebaum (1969), 427–43, and in Tikku, 219–48.

Works

BOOKS

Die Wirklichkeitweite der früharabischen Dichtung: Eine literaturwissenschaftliche Untersuchung. Vienna: Selbstverlag des Orientalischen Institutes der Universität, 1937.

Medieval Islam: A Study in Cultural Orientation. Chicago: University of Chicago Press, 1946. Translated as *Der Islam im Mittelalter.* Zurich: Artemis, 1963.

A Tenth-Century Document of Arabic Literary Theory and Criticism. Chicago: University of Chicago Press, 1950.

Muhammadan Festivals. New York: Schuman, 1951.

Islam: Essays in the Nature and Growth of a Cultural Tradition. Menasha, Wisc.: American Anthropological Association, 1955.

Kritik und Dichtkunst: Studien zur arabischen Literaturgeschichte. Wiesbaden: Harrassowitz, 1955.

Modern Islam: The Search for Cultural Identity. Berkeley: University of California Press, 1962.

"Der Islam: Seine Expansion im Nahen und Mittleren Osten, Afrika, und Spanien." In *Islam: Die Entstehung Europas, Propyläen-Weltgeschichte,* vol. 5, edited by Golo Mann, Alfred Heuss, and August Nitschke, pp. 23–179. Berlin: Propyläen-Verlag bei Ullstein, 1963.

A Review of *Arabic Thought in the Liberal Age* by Albert Hourani. *Oriens* 18–19 (1965–66): 377–79.

With Roger Caillois. *The Dream and Human Societies.* Berkeley: University of California Press, 1966.

Studien zum Kulturbild und Selbstverständnis des Islams. Zurich: Artemis, 1969.

Die islamischen Reiche nach dem Fall von Konstantinopel. In *Fischer Weltgeschichte.* Vol. 14: *Der Islam,* edited by G.E. von Grunebaum. Frankfurt: Fischer, 1971.

Themes in Medieval Arabic Literature. Edited by Dunning S. Wilson. London: Variorum Reprints, 1981.

Sources

Anawati, G.C. "La civilization musulmane dans l'oeuvre du Professeur von Grunebaum." *Mélanges de l'Institut Dominicain d'Études Orientales du Caire* 10 (1970): 37–82.

Arkoun, Mohammad. "L'Islam moderne vu par le Professeur G.E. von Grunebaum." *Arabica* 11 (1964): 113–23.

Banani, Amin. "G.E. von Grunebaum: Toward Relating Islamic Studies to Universal Cultural History." *International Journal of Middle East Studies* 6 (1975): 140–47.

Laroui, Abdallah. "For a Methodology of Islamic Studies: Islam Seen by G. von Grunebaum." *Diogenes* 83 (1973): 12–39.

Tikku, G.L., ed. *Islam and Its Cultural Divergence: Studies in Honor of G.E. von Grunebaum*. Urbana: University of Illinois Press, 1971.

Waines, David. "Cultural Anthropology and Islam: The Contribution of G.E. von Grunebaum." *Review of Middle East Studies* 2 (1976): 113–23.

White, Lynn T., Jr. An Address in *G.E. von Grunebaum 1909–1972: In Memoriam*. Los Angeles: Near Eastern Center, University of California, 1972.

INDEX